P9-CRE-346

iMovie '09 & iDVD

THE MISSING MANUAL

David Pogue and Aaron Miller

POGUE PRESS™
O'REILLY®

Beijing · Cambridge · Farnham · Köln · Sebastopol · Taipei · Tokyo

iMovie '09 & iDVD: The Missing Manual

by David Pogue and Aaron Miller

Copyright © 2009 David Pogue. All rights reserved.
Printed in Canada.

Published by O'Reilly Media, Inc., 1005 Gravenstein Highway North, Sebastopol, CA 95472.

O'Reilly books may be purchased for educational, business, or sales promotional use. Online editions are also available for most titles (*safari.oreilly.com*). For more information, contact our corporate/institutional sales department: (800) 998-9938 or *corporate@oreilly.com*.

Printing History:

April 2009:   First Edition.

Nutshell Handbook, the Nutshell Handbook logo, the O'Reilly logo, and "The book that should have been in the box" are registered trademarks of O'Reilly Media, Inc. *iMovie '09 & iDVD: The Missing Manual*, The Missing Manual logo, Pogue Press, and the Pogue Press logo are trademarks of O'Reilly Media, Inc.

Many of the designations used by manufacturers and sellers to distinguish their products are claimed as trademarks. Where those designations appear in this book, and O'Reilly Media, Inc. was aware of a trademark claim, the designations have been printed in caps or initial caps.

While every precaution has been taken in the preparation of this book, the publisher and authors assume no responsibility for errors or omissions, or for damages resulting from the use of the information contained herein.

 This book uses Otabind,™ a durable and flexible lay-flat binding.

ISBN: 978-0-596-80141-0
[TI]   [7/09]

Table of Contents

The Missing Credits

About the Authors

 **David Pogue** (original author, editor) is the weekly tech columnist for the *New York Times*, an Emmy-winning correspondent for *CBS News Sunday Morning*, weekly CNBC contributor, and the creator of the Missing Manual series. He's the author or co-author of 50 books, including 24 in this series and six in the *"For Dummies"* line (including *Macs*, *Magic*, *Opera*, and *Classical Music*). In his other life, David is a former Broadway show conductor, a piano player, and a magician. He lives in Connecticut with his wife and three awesome children.

Links to his columns and weekly videos await at *www.davidpogue.com*. He welcomes feedback about his books by email at *david@pogueman.com*.

 Aaron Miller (author, '09 update) is a part-time lawyer and part-time professor, and runs a software company serving nonprofit organizations. In all of his spare time, he authors the blog Unlocking iMovie (*http://www.unlockingimovie.com*), his own little way of trying to make the Mac world a better place. If he's not at his computer, he's probably playing Ultimate Frisbee or "tickle monster" with his kids. Email: *ilifer08@gmail.com*.

About the Creative Team

Peter Meyers (project manager) is the managing editor of O'Reilly Media's Missing Manual series. He lives with his wife, daughter, and cats in New York City. Email: *meyers@oreilly.com*.

Dawn Frausto (wrangler of copy editors and indexers) is assistant editor for the Missing Manual series. When not working, she plays soccer, beads, and causes trouble. Email: *dawn@oreilly.com*.

Nellie McKesson (production editor) lives in Brighton, Mass., where she makes t-shirts for her friends and plays music with her band Dr. & Mrs. Van Der Trampp (*http://myspace.com/drmrsvandertrampp*). Email: *nellie@oreilly.com*.

Michele Filshie (copy editor), previously an O'Reilly employee, now works as a freelance copy editor from her home in Sebastopol (*www.linkedin.com/pub/7/a0/0*).

Nancy Reinhardt (copy editor) is a freelance copy editor living in the Midwest, who enjoys swimming, biking, and history. She is surrounded by electrical engineers and yet she is "…still fairly certain that given a cape, a wand, and nice tiara, she could save the world" (to quote Leigh Standley). Email: *reinhardt8@comcast.net*.

Alison O'Byrne (copy editor) is a freelance editor from Dublin, Ireland. Alison has provided editorial services for corporate and government clients at home and internationally for over six years. Email: *alison@alhaus.com*. Web: *www.alhaus.com*.

Ron Strauss (indexer) is a full-time freelance indexer specializing in IT. When not working, he moonlights as a concert violist and alternative medicine health consultant. Email: *rstrauss@mchsi.com*.

Acknowledgments

The Missing Manual series is a joint venture between Pogue Press (the dream team introduced on these pages) and O'Reilly Media (a dream publishing partner). I'm indebted, as always, to Tim O'Reilly, Laurie Petrycki, Peter Meyers, and the rest of the gang.

The book in your hands is an updated version of *iMovie '08 & iDVD: The Missing Manual*, so it represents a lot of effort from that earlier book's production staff. That includes copy editor Teresa Noelle Roberts, photographer Tim Geaney, layout designer Phil Simpson, iDVD guru Erica Sadun, and graphics goddess Lesa Snider King.

Helpful writings by Karl Petersen and Tim Franklin, prepared for earlier editions, live on in this one. Sohaila Abdulali, Kate Briggs, Stephanie English, Sada Preisch, and Ellen Keyne Seebacher shared proofreading duties on that edition. Thanks to Randy Ubillos, the creator of iMovie '09; David Rogelberg, my agent; and especially to Aaron Miller, who cheerfully undertook the challenge of updating this book to reflect the changes in iMovie '09 without making it sound like two different authors were at work. He did a seamless, witty, professional job.

Above all, thanks to Jennifer, Kelly, Tia, and Jeffrey, whose patience and sacrifices make these books—and everything else—possible.

—David Pogue

Many thanks to David Pogue for the great opportunity and for the masterful editing (even if keeping up with his writing prowess felt like chasing an Olympic sprinter). Thanks as well to Peter Meyers for expertly guiding me through the publication details and deadlines, and to the O'Reilly professionals behind the scenes who make it all work.

Thanks to Peter Miller for great advice, and to all the friends and family members whose smiling faces appear throughout the book.

Many thanks to those at Apple: Randy Ubillos, Dion Scoppettuolo, Paul Towner, Kirk Paulsen, and the entire iMovie team, whose abilities turn our home movies into treasures. Warmest thanks, in particular, to Randy for kindly and patiently answering questions, even during his vacation.

Finally, my deepest gratitude to Katie, Luke, Sam, Thomas, and the soon-to-arrive Mystery Boy #4 for love, support, and antics that make great home movies.

—Aaron Miller

The Missing Manual Series

Missing Manuals are witty, superbly written guides to computer products that don't come with printed manuals (which is just about all of them). Each book features a handcrafted index; cross-references to specific pages (not just chapters); and RepKover, a detached-spine binding that lets the book lie perfectly flat without the assistance of weights or cinder blocks.

Recent and upcoming titles include:

Access 2007: The Missing Manual by Matthew MacDonald

AppleScript: The Missing Manual by Adam Goldstein

AppleWorks 6: The Missing Manual by Jim Elferdink and David Reynolds

CSS: The Missing Manual by David Sawyer McFarland

Creating a Web Site: The Missing Manual, Second Edition by Matthew MacDonald

David Pogue's Digital Photography: The Missing Manual by David Pogue

Dreamweaver 8: The Missing Manual by David Sawyer McFarland

Dreamweaver CS3: The Missing Manual by David Sawyer McFarland

Dreamweaver CS4: The Missing Manual by David Sawyer McFarland

eBay: The Missing Manual by Nancy Conner

Excel 2003: The Missing Manual by Matthew MacDonald

Excel 2007: The Missing Manual by Matthew MacDonald

Facebook: The Missing Manual by E.A. Vander Veer

FileMaker Pro 9: The Missing Manual by Geoff Coffey and Susan Prosser

FileMaker Pro 10: The Missing Manual by Geoff Coffey and Susan Prosser

Flash 8: The Missing Manual by E.A. Vander Veer

Flash CS3: The Missing Manual by E.A. Vander Veer and Chris Grover

Flash CS4: The Missing Manual by Chris Grover with E.A. Vander Veer

FrontPage 2003: The Missing Manual by Jessica Mantaro

Google Apps: The Missing Manual by Nancy Conner

Google SketchUp: The Missing Manual by Chris Grover

The Internet: The Missing Manual by David Pogue and J.D. Biersdorfer

iMovie 6 & iDVD: The Missing Manual by David Pogue

iMovie '08 & iDVD: The Missing Manual by David Pogue

iPhone: The Missing Manual, Second Edition by David Pogue

iPhoto '08: The Missing Manual by David Pogue

Introduction

iMovie is video-editing software. It grabs a copy of the raw footage from your digital camcorder or still camera. Then it lets you edit this video easily, quickly, and creatively.

That's a big deal, because over the years, home movies have developed a bad name. You know what it's like watching other people's camcorder footage. You're captive on some neighbor's couch after dessert to witness 60 excruciating, unedited minutes of a trip to Mexico, or 25 too many minutes of the baby wearing the spaghetti bowl.

Deep down, most people realize that the viewing experience could be improved if the video were edited down to just the good parts. But until iMovie came along, editing camcorder footage on the computer required several thousand dollars' worth of digitizing cards, extremely complicated editing software, and the highest-horsepower computer equipment available. Unless there was a paycheck involved, editing footage under those circumstances just wasn't worth it.

Then along came iMovie, the world's least expensive version of what the Hollywood pros call *nonlinear* editing software. The "nonlinear" part is that no tape is involved while you're editing. There's no rewinding or fast-forwarding; you jump instantly to any piece of footage as you put your movie together.

The world of video is exploding. People are giving each other DVDs instead of greeting cards. People are watching each other via video on their Web sites. People are quitting their daily-grind jobs to become videographers for hire, making money filming weddings and creating living video scrapbooks. Video, in other words, is fast becoming a new standard document format for the new century.

If you have iMovie and a camcorder, you'll be ready.

The Difficult Birth of iMovie '08 and '09

Within six months of its release in October 1999, iMovie had become, in the words of beaming iMovie papa (and Apple CEO) Steve Jobs, "the most popular video editing software in the world."

Apple only fanned the flames when it released iMovie 2 in July 2000 (for $50), iMovie 3 in January 2003 (for free), and then—as part of the iLife software suite—iMovie 4, iMovie HD, and iMovie 6 in successive Januaries.

Then, in August 2007, Apple dropped a bombshell. Or, rather, it dropped iMovie.

The company's new consumer video editing program, called iMovie '08, was, in fact, not iMovie at all. It was a totally different program, using all-new code and a different design, and built by different people. It was conceived, according to Steve Jobs, by Randy Ubillos, an Apple programmer who wanted to edit down his vacation footage—but found the old iMovie too slow and complicated. So the guy sat down and wrote his own little program, focused primarily on editing speed above all. Steve loved it, and decided that it would replace the old iMovie.

Many people were stunned by Apple's move—and I, your humble author, was among them. In my *New York Times* email column, I wrote about just how different iMovie '08 was from its predecessors:

> iMovie '08 has been totally misnamed. It's not iMovie at all. It's designed for an utterly different task.
>
> The new iMovie, for example, is probably the only video editing program on the market with no timeline—no horizontal, scrolling strip that displays your clips laid end to end, with their lengths representing their durations. You have no indication of how many minutes into your movie you are.
>
> The new iMovie also gets a D for audio editing. You can't manually adjust audio levels during a scene (for example, to make the music quieter when someone is speaking). All the old audio effects are gone, too. No pitch changing, high-pass and low-pass filters, or reverb.
>
> The new iMovie doesn't accept plug-ins, either. You can't add chapter markers for use in iDVD, which is supposed to be integrated with iMovie. Bookmarks are gone. Themes are gone. You can no longer export only part of a movie. And you can't export a movie back to tape—only to the Internet or to a file.
>
> All visual effects are gone—even basic options like slow motion, reverse motion, and fast motion. Incredibly, the new iMovie can't even convert older iMovie projects. All you can import is the clips themselves. None of your transitions, titles, credits, music, or special effects are preserved.
>
> On top of all that, this more limited iMovie has steep horsepower requirements that rule out most computers older than about two years old.

Pretty harsh, I know. But listen, I was an absolute whiz at iMovie 6. I knew it like the back of my mouse. And it looked to me like Apple was junking that mature, powerful program for what amounted to a video slideshow program.

Fortunately, many of those "doesn't haves" were restored in iMovie '09. Furthermore, iMovie '09 comes with so many useful features of its own, it's far more difficult to resist.

It's far more modern than the old iMovie, for example. It's equally adept at importing video from the new tapeless camcorders (DVD, hard drive, or memory-card models)—and from digital still cameras—as it is at importing from tape. And it's all hooked up to the Web, so that a single command can post your masterpiece on YouTube.

Then there are the cool features that the old iMovie could only dream about. The image-stabilizing, color-correction, and frame-cropping tools are unprecedented in a consumer program. You can really, truly delete unwanted pieces of your clips, thus reclaiming hard drive space. (iMovie '08, on the other hand, preserves an entire 20-minute clip on your hard drive even if you've used only 3 seconds of it.)

iMovie '09 creates titles, crossfades, and color adjustments instantly. There's no "rendering" time, as there was in the old iMovie. So you gain an exhilarating freedom to play, to fiddle with the timing and placement of things.

So, no, iMovie '09 is not a descendant of the old iMovies. It's a different program, with a different focus and a different audience. But it's here to stay, and it has charms of its own.

iDVD

As you may have noticed, this iMovie book comes with a free bonus book: *iDVD '09: The Missing Manual*, which constitutes Chapters 16 through 18. iDVD can preserve your movies on home-recorded DVDs that look and behave amazingly close to the commercial DVDs you rent from Netflix or Blockbuster.

iDVD '09 isn't what you'd call a huge update from the previous version; in fact, it's *identical* to the previous version. Be grateful that Apple even kept it alive, considering how strongly it feels that the DVD is a dead technology.

iMovie: What's It Good For?

If you're reading this book, you probably already have some ideas about what you could do if you could make professional-looking video. Here are a few possibilities that may not have occurred to you. All are natural projects for iMovie:

- **Home movies.** Plain old home movies—casual documentaries of your life, your kids' lives, your school life, your trips—are the single most popular creation of camcorder owners. Using the suggestions in the following chapters, you can improve the quality of your footage. And using iMovie, you can delete all but the best scenes (and edit out those humiliating parts where you walked for 20 minutes with the camcorder accidentally filming the ground bouncing beneath it).

This, too, is where iMovie's Internet smarts come into play. Instead of burning and shipping a DVD of your home movies, you can shoot the finished product up to a Web page or YouTube, where your lucky, lucky family and friends can enjoy them.

- **Web movies.** But why limit your aspirations to people you know? This is the YouTube Era, dude. If you've got something funny or interesting on "film," why not share it with the Internet population at large? In iMovie, YouTube is only one menu command away—and that's just the beginning. New film festivals, Web sites, and magazines are springing up everywhere, all dedicated to independent makers of *short* movies.

- **Business videos.** It's very easy to post video on the Internet or burn it onto a cheap, recordable CD or DVD, as described in Part 3. As a result, you should consider video a useful tool in whatever you do. If you're a real estate agent, blow away your rivals (and save your clients time) by showing movies, not still photos, of the properties you represent. If you're an executive, quit boring your comrades with stupefying PowerPoint slides and make your point with video instead.

- **Video photo albums.** A video photo album can be much more exciting, accessible, and engaging than a paper one. Start by filming or scanning your photos. Assemble them into a sequence, add some crossfades, titles, and music. The result is a much more interesting display than a book of motionless images, thanks in part to iMovie's Ken Burns effect (page 238). This emerging video form is becoming very popular—videographers are charging a lot of money to create such "living photo albums" for their clients.

- **Just-for-fun projects.** Never again can anyone over the age of eight complain that there's "nothing to do." Set them loose with a camcorder and the instruction to make a fake rock video, commercial, or documentary.

- **Training films.** If there's a better use for video than providing how-to instruction, you'd be hard-pressed to name it. Make a video for new employees to show them the ropes. Make a video that accompanies your product to give a humanizing touch to your company and help the customer make the most of her purchase. Make a DVD that teaches newcomers how to play the banjo, grow a garden, kick a football, use a computer program—and then market it.

- **Interviews.** You're lucky enough to live in an age where you can manipulate video just as easily as you do words in a word processor. Capitalize on this fact. Create family histories. Film relatives who still remember the War, the Birth, the Immigration. Or create a time-capsule, time-lapse film: Ask your kid or your parent the same four questions every year on his birthday (such as, "What's your greatest worry right now?" or "If you had one wish…?" or "Where do you want to be in five years?"). Then, after five or 10 or 20 years, splice together the answers for an enlightening fast-forward through a human life.

- **Broadcast segments.** Want a taste of the real world? Call your cable TV company about its public-access channels. (As required by law, every cable company offers a channel or two for ordinary citizens to use for their own programming.) Find out the time and format restraints, and then make a documentary, short film, or other piece for actual broadcast. Advertise the airing to everyone you know. It's a small-time start, but it's real broadcasting.

- **Analyze performances.** There's no better way to improve your golf swing, tennis form, musical performance, or public speaking style than to study footage of yourself. If you're a teacher, camp counselor, or coach, film your students, campers, or players so that they can benefit from self-analysis, too.

- **Turn photos into video.** Technically, you don't need a camcorder at all to use iMovie; it's equally adept at importing and presenting still photos from a scanner or digital camera. In fact, iMovie's Ken Burns effect brings still photos to life, gently zooming into them, fading from shot to shot, panning across them, and so on, making this software the world's best slideshow creator.

A Camcorder Crash Course

For years, when you said "camcorder," it was understood that you meant "*tape camcorder.*" And, to be sure, the least expensive and most popular camcorder type today (by a hair) records onto tape: MiniDV cassettes.

The popularity of digital tape camcorders is crashing, however. Their sales have been declining 10 to 15 percent a year.

As you can imagine, these numbers are causing some consternation at the headquarters of Sony, Canon, and other camcorder makers. What's going on? Don't people want to preserve memories of their lives anymore?

As best they can tell, the problem is the cassettes themselves. They're too hard to find in the drawer when the neighbors want to see the highlights of your latest vacation, and they take too long to rewind and fast-forward.

What the world wants, the camcorder manufacturers have decided, is *random access:* the ability to jump directly to any scene without having to wait. In theory, a tapeless camcorder also saves you time when transferring the video to your computer for editing, because you don't have to play the video from the camcorder in real time. The video files are stored on a memory card, hard drive, or DVD as regular computer files, which you should be able to simply drag and drop onto your Mac's hard drive. (In practice, it doesn't quite work out that way—see page 38—but you get the idea.)

That's why the industry has been flooding the stores with tapeless camcorders: cameras that record onto memory cards, onto hard drives, or onto little DVDs—anything but tape.

The Downsides of Tapeless

Unfortunately, most tapeless camcorders can't match the incredible video quality of MiniDV tape camcorders. In order to store a reasonable amount of video on that tiny memory card, hard drive, or DVD, the camera must *compress* it to an alarming degree, using less information to describe each frame of video. Video recorded onto MiniDV tapes, on the other hand, is essentially uncompressed. What you see on playback is what the camera recorded.

Remember, too, that each kind of tapeless camcorder has its own kinds of storage limitations:

- **DVD camcorders.** The miniature blank DVDs used by DVD camcorders generally hold only 20 minutes of video apiece—only 15 minutes in high definition. (Some models can record onto the newer double-sided discs, which roughly doubles the recording time.) And you can't play the resulting disc in a regular DVD player unless you first "finalize" it, a sort of software shrink-wrapping process that can take 10 or 15 minutes inside the camcorder. In fact, you can't play the resulting DVDs in a *Mac* at all. Macs expect full-size DVDs; these miniature, 8-centimeter discs can literally trash your drive.

- **Hard-drive camcorders** can record several hours of video (say, five hours at best quality) before running out of space—but at that point, you're dead in the water. Your camcorder is useless until it has a date with your computer, so you can dump the video off the camcorder to empty its hard drive.

- **Memory-card camcorders** might be able to store, for example, one hour of video on a four-gigabyte memory card. And you can carry a couple of extras around in case of emergency. But memory cards are far too expensive for long-term storage. In other words, nobody but Donald Trump can afford to buy a new memory card for every vacation, holiday, and wedding. Everybody else empties out the camcorder onto the computer every time the memory card gets full.

NOTE The new world of tapeless camcorders is filled with exceptions, footnotes, and caveats. Apple has noted a few of the quirks here–*http://support.apple.com/kb/HT3290*–but the best advice is to use Google before you buy any camcorder to ensure its compatibility with iMovie. (Search for *Sony SR7 imovie 09*, for example.)

High Definition

A growing number of camcorders film in gorgeous, widescreen, ultrasharp *high definition*. The video looks absolutely incredible when viewed on an HDTV set. Your own life looks like it was filmed by a Hollywood movie crew.

If you're shopping for a camcorder now, you should seriously consider going to high-def right now. High-definition camcorders are available in both tape and tapeless models. The really cool thing about the tape models, in fact, is that they record onto ordinary MiniDV cassettes, exactly the same ones used by regular tape camcorders. The signal recorded on these tapes is different, of course—it's in a format called HDV—but you still gain the convenience and economy of those ordinary drugstore tapes (Figure I-1).

You may as well start filming your life in high definition now, because in a few years, standard definition will look as quaint as daguerreotype photographs.

Figure I-1:
High-def camcorders like the Canon HV30 record onto ordinary MiniDV tapes. The image quality, however, is anything but ordinary.

AVCHD, MPEG-2, and Other Such Jargon

Tapeless camcorder stores video as ordinary computer files—on a DVD, hard drive, or memory card—that you can copy to your Mac and edit in iMovie. But what are those files? Every computer document is some format, whether JPEG (the usual format for photos) or TXT (text files). What format are these video files?

Some digital camcorders, especially old ones, record in formats called MPEG-1, MPEG-2, and MPEG-4. (The abbreviation stands for Motion Picture Experts Group, the association of geeks who dream up these standards.) iMovie '09 recognizes and imports MPEG-2—usually. Unfortunately, there are multiple flavors of MPEG-2, and iMovie doesn't recognize all of them.

iMovie can also work with the movies created by most digital still cameras, like .mov, .avi and MPEG-4 files. Here again, though, your mileage may vary.

TIP It's worth repeating: If you're tempted to buy a certain camcorder, but you're not sure if iMovie works with it, Google it.

The good news is that iMovie also recognizes *AVCHD*, which is the most popular file format for high-definition tapeless camcorders. (It stands for Advanced Video Coding/High Definition, and yes, it's an annoying acronym. Do they really think they're going to make video editing more attractive by dreaming up names like this?)

Anyway, AVCHD is a high-def format concocted by Sony and Panasonic in 2006, and is now available on camcorders from Sony, Panasonic, Canon, Samsung, and others. This format offers roughly the same video quality as MPEG-2 or MPEG-4, but takes up even less space on your camcorder's memory card, miniDVD, or hard drive.

As it turns out, AVCHD is the same as H.264, which is the video format as Blu-ray high-definition DVD discs (and also the format of videos from the iTunes Store). That's a handy feature for people who own both an AVCHD camcorder that records onto miniature DVDs and a Blu-ray DVD player (or Playstation 3), because you can pop the DVD right out of the camcorder and into the Blu-ray player to play on your TV.

That's the good news. The bad news is that AVCHD still takes up a lot of space; a DVD camcorder of this type holds only 15 minutes of best-quality video per disc. (On the newer double-sided discs and camcorders that accept them, you get 27 minutes.)

The bigger bummer is that AVCHD doesn't take kindly to being edited. When you import AVCHD video to iMovie, for example, your Mac first converts it to another format that can be edited (page 38), which takes a very long time. In fact, one hour's worth of video takes over two hours to convert, which neatly erases the importing-time advantage that your tapeless camcorder would have had over a MiniDV tape camcorder.

Camcorder Features: Which Are Worthwhile?

So how do you know which camcorder to buy? Here's a rundown of the most frequently advertised camcorder features, along with a frank assessment of their value to the quality-obsessed iMovie fan.

FireWire connector

FireWire is Apple's term for the tiny, compact connector on the side of most MiniDV tape camcorders—and most Macs. When you attach a FireWire cable, this jack connects the camera to your Mac. Other companies have different names for this connector—you may see it called IEEE-1394, i.Link, DV In/Out, or DV Terminal.

On tapeless camcorders, FireWire jacks are usually missing altogether. That's OK; you have other ways to get your video off the camcorder and onto the Mac, as described in Chapter 1.

NOTE Since Apple thinks that tape camcorders are dead, it thinks FireWire is dead, too. Some recent Mac models, like the MacBook and MacBook Air, don't have FireWire jacks at all, and you can expect their disappearance to continue.

Analog inputs

This single feature may be important enough to determine your camcorder choice by itself. Analog inputs are connectors on the camcorder (Figure I-2) into which you can connect older, pre-DV equipment, such as your VCR, your old 8mm camcorder, and so on.

Unfortunately, this is one of those features that the camcorder makers have been quietly eliminating in an effort to shave costs. That's too bad, because there's no easier, less expensive method of transferring older footage into your digital camcorder—or directly into iMovie.

This technique is described in more detail in Chapter 4. For now, note only that the only other method of transferring pre-DV footage into digital format is to buy a $200 converter box.

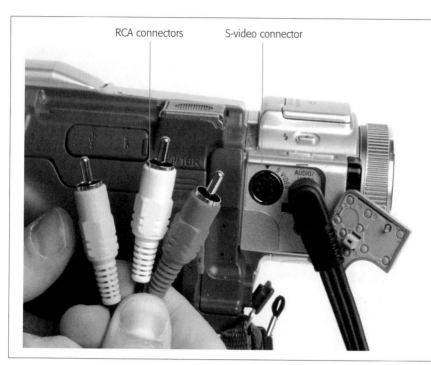

RCA connectors   S-video connector

Figure I-2:
Certain tape camcorders offer inputs for older, analog video. (Actually, what you'll probably get is a special cable with RCA connectors on one end and a miniplug on the camcorder end, like the one shown here. Don't lose this cable! You also need it to play your camcorder footage on TV.) A few older models offer an S-video connector too, for much higher quality.

Three chips (CCDs)

Professional camcorders offer three individual image sensors, one for each color component of a video picture: red, green, and blue. These camcorders are advertised as having three chips or CCDs (*charge-coupled devices*—electronic plates, covered with thousands of individual light sensors, that convert light rays into a digital signal). The result is even more spectacular picture quality, resolution, and color rendition than the less-expensive, one-CCD cameras.

Unfortunately, three-chip camcorders tend to be more expensive than one-chip cams—but they deliver much better color.

Not all three-chip models are big and pricey. Panasonic, in particular, has developed a line of three-chip camcorders that aren't much larger or more expensive than one-chip models. Note, however, that they usually contain three very *small* CCDs, so the quality improvement is visible primarily in bright, outdoor scenes.

Image stabilizer

Certain film techniques scream "Amateur!" to audiences. One of them is the instability of handheld filming. In a nutshell, professional video is shot using a camera on a tripod (Woody Allen's "handheld" period notwithstanding). Most home camcorder footage, in contrast, is shot from the palm of your hand.

A stabilizing feature (which may have a marketing name, such as Sony's Steady-Shot) takes a half step toward solving that problem. As shown in Figure I-3, this feature neatly eliminates the tiny, jittery moves present in handheld video. (It can't do anything about bigger jerks and bumps, which are especially difficult to avoid when you're zoomed in.) It also uses up your battery faster.

This kind of anti-shake feature comes in two forms:

- **Electronic or digital stabilization** is what you get on cheaper camcorders. Its workings are described in Figure I-3.

- **Optical stabilization** is much preferable. This mechanism involves two transparent plates separated by a special optical fluid. As the camera shakes, these plates create a prism effect that keeps handheld shots clearer and steadier than electronic (digital) stabilizers. The images are clearer because optical stabilizers don't have to crop out part of the picture as a buffer, unlike the stabilizers illustrated in Figure I-3.

  NOTE What could possibly be better than image stabilization on your camcorder? Image stabilization in your editing software. iMovie '09's amazing stabilizing feature is described on page 154.

Manual controls

Better camcorders let you turn off the automatic focus, automatic exposure control, automatic white balance, and even automatic sound level. This feature can be useful in certain situations, like when you want to change focus between two objects in the same shot (known to the pros as a focus-pull). If you've decided to pay extra for this feature, look for a model that lets you focus manually by turning a ring around the lens, which is much easier than using sliders.

Figure I-3:
Digital stabilization features work by "taking in" more image than you actually see in the viewfinder. Because the camcorder has some buffer, its computer can compensate for small bumps and jitters by keeping an "eye" on prominent features of the image. On less-expensive camcorders, unfortunately, this buffer zone means that your camcorder is absorbing less video information, to the detriment of picture quality.

Optical zoom

When you read the specs for a camcorder—or read the logos painted on its body—you frequently encounter numbers like "12X/300X ZOOM!" The number before the slash tells you how many times the camera can magnify a distant image, much like a telescope. That number measures the *optical* zoom, which is the actual amount that the lenses themselves can zoom in. Such zooming, of course, is useful when you want to film something that's far away. (As for the number *after* the slash, see page 15.)

You should know, however, that the more you've zoomed in, the shakier your footage is likely to be, since every microscopic wobble is magnified by, say, 12 times. You also have to be much more careful about focusing. When you're zoomed out all the way, everything is in focus—things near you, and things far away. But when you're zoomed in, very near and very far objects go out of focus. Put into photographic terms, the more you zoom in, the shorter the *depth of field* (the range of distance from the camera that can be kept in focus simultaneously).

Finally, remember that magnifying the picture doesn't magnify the sound. If you're relying on the built-in microphone of your camcorder, always get as close as you can to the subject, both for the sound and for the wobble.

> **TIP** Professional video and film work includes very little zooming, unlike most amateur video work. The best zooming is subtle zooming, such as when you very slowly "move toward" the face of somebody you're interviewing.
>
> For this reason, when shopping for camcorders, test the zooming if at all possible. Find out if the camcorder has *variable-speed* zooming, where the zooming speed increases as you press the Zoom button harder. Some camcorders offer only two different speeds—fast and faster—but that's still better than having no control at all. (Variable-speed zooming isn't something mentioned in the standard camcorder literature; you generally have to try the camcorder in the store to find out how it does.)

Minutes-remaining readout

Fortunately, the problems exhibited by camcorder batteries of old—such as the "memory effect"—are a thing of the past. (When you halfway depleted a pre-digital camcorder battery's charge several times in a row, the battery would adopt that halfway-empty point as its new *completely* empty point, effectively halving its capacity.) Today's lithium-ion battery technology eliminates that problem.

Some camcorders—mostly from Sony, JVC, and Canon—even display, in minutes, how much juice the battery has remaining. A glance at the viewfinder or the LCD screen tells you how many minutes of recording or playback you've got left— a worthy feature.

> **TIP** The number of minutes' recording time advertised for camcorder batteries is *continuous* recording time–that is, the time you'll get if you turn the camcorder on, press Record, and go out to lunch. If you stop and start the camera to capture shorter scenes, as almost everyone does, you'll get much less than the advertised amount of time out of each battery charge.

Built-in light

Insufficient lighting is one of the leading causes of "amateuritis," a telltale form of poor video quality that lets viewers know that the footage is homemade. In the best—and most expensive—of all possible worlds, you'd get your scene correctly lit before filming, or you'd attach a light to the "shoe" (light connector) on top of the camera. Those few cameras that have such a shoe, or even have a built-in light, give you a distinct advantage in filming accurate colors.

Scene modes

Many camcorders come with a number of canned focus/shutter speed/aperture settings for different indoor and outdoor environments: Sports Lesson, Beach and Snow, Twilight, and so on. They're a useful compromise between the all-automatic operation of less expensive models and the all-manual operation of professional cameras.

Remote control

Some camcorders come with a pocket-sized remote control. It serves two purposes. First, its Record and Stop buttons give you a means of recording *yourself,* with or without other people in the shot. Second, when you're playing back footage with the camcorder connected to your TV or VCR, the remote lets you control the playback without needing to have the camcorder on your lap. You may be surprised at how useful the remote can be.

FlexiZone or Push Focus

All camcorders offer automatic focus. Most work by focusing on the image in the center of your frame as you line up the shot.

That's fine if the subject of your shot is in the center of the frame. But if it's off-center, you have no choice but to turn off the autofocus feature and use the manual-focus ring. (Using the camcorder isn't like using a still camera, where you can point the camera directly at the subject for focusing purposes, and then—before taking the shot—shift the angle so that the subject is no longer in the center. Camcorders continually refocus, so pointing the camera slightly away from your subject makes you lose the off-center focus you've established.)

Some Canon, Sony, and Sharp camcorders let you point to a specific spot in the frame that you want to serve as the focus point, even if it's not the center of the picture. (This feature is called FlexiZone on the Canon models, or Push Focus on high-end Sony models. On Sony cams with touch-screen LCD panels, it's especially easy to indicate which spot in the frame should get the focus.) If the model you're eyeing has this feature, it's worth having.

Night-vision mode

Most Sony camcorders offer a mode called NightShot that works like night-vision goggles. In this mode, you can actually film (and see, as you watch the LCD screen) in total darkness. The infrared transmitter on the front of the camcorder measures the heat given off by various objects in its path, letting you capture an eerie, greenish night scene. Rent *The Silence of the Lambs* for an idea of how creepy night-vision filming can be. Or watch any episode of *Survivor*.

The transmitter's range is only about 15 feet or so. Still, you may be surprised how often it comes in handy: on campouts, during sleepovers, on nighttime nature walks, and so on.

Still photos

All modern camcorders can take still photos. The camcorder freezes one frame of what it's seeing, and records it either on the tape (for, say, a 7-second stretch) or as a regular JPEG photo file on a memory card.

The photo quality, unfortunately, is pretty terrible. The resolution may be OK (some camcorders offer two- or even three-megapixel resolution), but the quality isn't anywhere near what you'd get using a dedicated digital still camera. It turns out that the lenses and circuitry that best serve video are all wrong for stills.

If the camcorder you're considering offers this feature, fine. But it may be redundant for the iMovie owner. iMovie can grab one-megapixel still frames from *any* captured video, as described in Chapter 10.

Progressive-scan CCDs

This special kind of image sensor is primarily useful for capturing still images. It ensures that the entire image is grabbed, not just one set of alternating, interlaced scan lines (the usual video signal). If you plan to catch still frames from your camcorder, a progressive-scan CCD will spare you some of the jagged lines that may appear. However, if your primary goal is to make movies, this expensive feature isn't worth paying for, especially since you can buy a digital *still* camera with much greater resolution for about the same added cost.

Useless Features

Here are some features you'll see in camcorder advertising that you should ignore completely (and definitely not pay extra for).

Title generator

Some camcorders let you superimpose *titles* (that is, lettering) on your video as you film. In your case, dear iMovie owner, a title-generating feature is useless. Your Mac can add gorgeous, smooth-edged type, with a selection of sizes, fonts, colors, and even scrolling animations, to your finished movies, with far more precision and power than the blocky text available to your camcorder. (Chapter 8 shows you how.)

> **TIP** A title generator on the camcorder is actually *worse* than useless, because it permanently stamps your original footage with something you may wish you could amend later. In fact, as a general rule, you should avoid using (or paying for) *any* of the in-camera editing features described in this chapter—title generator, fader, special effects—because you can do this kind of editing much more effectively in iMovie. Not only are they redundant, but they commit you to an editing choice in advance, thus limiting how you can use your footage.

Special effects

Most DV camcorders offer a selection of six or seven cheesy-looking special effects. They can make your footage look solarized, or digitized, or otherwise processed (see Figure I-4).

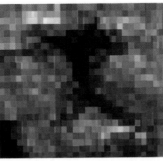

Figure I-4:
Using the stock collection of special effects built into your camcorder, you can create special, hallucinogenic visuals. The question is: why?

Avoid using these effects. iMovie has its own special-effects options. And it gives you far greater control over when they start, when they end, and how intensely they affect the video.

In fact, unless you're shooting a documentary about nuclear explosions or bad drug episodes, consider avoiding these effects altogether.

Date/time stamp

Every camcorder offers the ability to stamp the date and time directly onto the footage. As you've no doubt seen (on *America's Funniest Home Videos* or *America's Scariest Cop Chases*), the result is a blocky, typographically hideous stamp that permanently mars the footage. Few things take the romance out of a wedding video, or are more distracting in spectacular weather footage, than a huge **20 SEP 09 12:34 PM** stamped in the corner.

Nor do you have to worry that you'll one day forget when you filmed some event. As it turns out, digital camcorders automatically and invisibly date- and time-stamp *all* footage. You'll be able to see this information when you connect the camcorder to your Mac; then you can choose whether or not to add it to the finished footage (and with much more control over the timing, location, and typography of the stamp).

Digital zoom

Much as camera owners mistakenly jockey for superiority by comparing the mega-pixel rating of their cameras (more megapixels don't necessarily make sharper pictures), camcorder makers seem to think that what consumers want most in a camcorder is a powerful digital zoom. Your camcorder's packaging may "boast" zoom ratings of "50X," "100X," or "500X!"

When a camcorder uses its *digital* zoom—the number after the slash on the cam-corder box—it simply enlarges the individual dots that compose its image. Yes, the image gets bigger, but it doesn't get any *sharper*. As the dots get larger, the image gets chunkier, coarser, and less recognizable, until it ends up looking like the blocky areas you see superimposed over criminals' faces to conceal their identity on *Cops*. After your digital zoom feature has blown up the picture by 3X, the image falls to pieces. Greater digital zoom is not something worth paying extra for.

The Long-Term Storage Problem

No matter which kind of camcorder you choose, you have more to think about than just features and prices; you have the future to consider. Every kind of cam-corder presents serious challenges if you hope to preserve your video for future generations.

- **DVD camcorders.** Nobody has yet figured out how long those home-burned DVDs actually last. They don't last essentially forever, as Hollywood DVDs do. In Hollywood, they *stamp* DVDs, pressing a pattern into the plastic. Home DVD burners, though, record a pattern in a layer of organic dye on the bottom of the disc—a dye that can take between several *months* and several *decades* to break down.

• **Memory-card and hard-drive camcorders.** Once the card or drive is full, you're finished shooting for the day. The camcorder is worthless until you offload the video to a computer, thereby freeing up space to continue shooting.

But what then? Are you going to burn hour after hour of captured video onto DVDs? Not only is that practically a full-time job, but then you're stuck with those homemade DVDs and their questionable lifespan.

You could, of course, just keep the video on hard drives, even though that's a very expensive and bulky solution. Here again, though, you have to wonder: Will the hard drive you buy today still be functioning 50 years from now?

• **Tape camcorders.** Digital tapes may deteriorate over a decade or two, just as traditional tapes do.

The solution to all of these problems, of course, is simple vigilance. Every 10 or so years, you'll have to copy your masterworks onto newer tapes, discs, hard drives, or whatever the latest storage format happens to be.

About This Book

Don't let the rumors fool you. iMovie and iDVD may be simple, but they're not simplistic. Unfortunately, many of the best techniques aren't covered in the only "manual" you get with iLife—its electronic help screens.

This book is designed to serve as the iMovie/iDVD manual, as the book that should have been in the box. It explores each iMovie feature in depth, offers illustrated catalogs of the various title and transition effects, offers shortcuts and workarounds, and unearths features that the online help doesn't even mention.

> **NOTE** The camcorder and iMovie produce video of stunning visual and audio quality, giving you the *technical* tools to produce amazing videos. But most people don't have much experience with the *artistic* side of shooting—lighting, sound, and composition—or even how to use the dozens of buttons packed onto the modern camcorder. If you visit this book's "Missing CD" at *www.missingmanuals.com*, you'll find a bonus appendix in PDF form: three chapters designed to give you the basics of lighting, composition, and camera technique.

About the Outline

iMovie '09 & iDVD: The Missing Manual is divided into three parts, each containing several chapters:

• Part 1, *Editing in iMovie*, is the heart of the book. It leads you through transferring your footage into iMovie, editing your clips, placing them into a timeline, adding crossfades and titles, working with your soundtracks, and more.

• Part 2, *Finding Your Audience*, helps you take the cinematic masterpiece on your screen to the world. iMovie excels at exporting your work to the Web, to YouTube, to an iPod or iPhone, to an Apple TV, to a QuickTime file on your hard drive, or to iDVD for burning (your best bet for maintaining the visual quality of the original). This part of the book offers step-by-step instructions for each of these methods, and also shows you how you can use QuickTime Player Pro to supplement the editing tools in iMovie.

- Part 3, *iDVD '09*, is just what you'd expect: a bonus volume dedicated to the world's easiest-to-use DVD design and burning software. It goes way, way beyond the basics, as you'll see.

At the end of the book, four appendixes await:

- Appendix A provides a menu-by-menu explanation of iMovie menu commands.

- Appendix B is a comprehensive troubleshooting handbook.

- Appendix C is a master cheat sheet of iMovie's keyboard shortcuts.

- Appendix D is a visual reference to all of the little symbols, stripes, badges, and color-coded doodads that, sooner or later, will clutter up your iMovie window and leave you bewildered. Turn to this two-page cheat sheet in times of panic.

About → These → Arrows

Throughout this book, and throughout the Missing Manual series, you'll find sentences like this one: "Open your Home → Library → Preferences folder." That's shorthand for a much longer instruction that directs you to open three nested folders in sequence, like this: "In the Finder, choose Go → Home. In your Home folder, you'll find a folder called Library. Open that. Inside the Library window is a folder called Preferences. Double-click to open it, too."

Similarly, this kind of arrow shorthand helps to simplify the business of choosing commands in menus, as shown in Figure I-5.

Figure I-5:
In this book, arrow notations help to simplify folder and menu instructions. For example, "Choose → Dock → Position on Left" is a more compact way of saying, "From the menu, choose Dock; from the submenu that then appears, choose Position on Left," as shown here.

Technical Notes for PAL People

If you live in the Americas, Japan, or any of 30 other countries, your camcorder, VCR, and TV record and play back a video signal in a format that's known as *NTSC*. Even if you've never heard the term, every camcorder, VCR, TV, and TV station in your country uses this same signal. (The following discussion doesn't apply to high-definition video, which is the same across continents.)

What it stands for is National Television Standards Committee, the gang who designed this format. What it *means* is incompatibility with the second most popular format, which is called PAL (Phase Alternating Line, for the curious). In Europe, Africa, the Middle East, Australia, and China (among other places), everyone's equipment uses the PAL format. You can't play an American tape on a standard VCR in Sweden—unless you're happy with black-and-white, sometimes jittery playback.

> **TIP** France, the former Soviet Union countries, and a few others use a third format, known as SECAM. iMovie doesn't work with SECAM gear. To find out what kind of gear your country uses, visit a Web site like *www.vidpro.org/standards.htm*.

Fortunately, iMovie converses fluently with both NTSC and PAL camcorders. When you launch the program, it automatically studies the camcorder you've attached and determines its format.

However, most of the discussions in this book use NTSC terminology. If you're a friend of PAL, use the following information to translate this book's discussions.

The Tech Specs of NTSC

Whether you're aware of it or not, using the NTSC standard-definition format means that the picture you see is characterized like this:

- **30 frames per second.** A *frame* is one individual picture. Flashed before your eyes at this speed, the still images blend into what you perceive as smooth motion.

- **575 scan lines.** The electron gun in a TV tube paints the screen with this number of fine horizontal lines.

- **The DV picture measures 720 × 480 pixels.** This figure refers to the number of screen dots, or *pixels*, that compose one frame of image in the *DV* (digital video) version of the NTSC format.

The Tech Specs of PAL

When iMovie detects a PAL camcorder (or when you inform it that you're using one), it makes the necessary adjustments automatically, including:

- **25 frames per second.** Video fans claim that the lower frame rate creates more flicker than the NTSC standard. On the other hand, this frame rate is very close to the frame rate of Hollywood films (24 frames per second). As a result, many independent filmmakers find PAL a better choice when shooting movies they intend to convert to film.

- **625 scan lines.** That's 20 percent sharper and more detailed than NTSC. The difference is especially visible on large-screen TVs.

- **The DV picture measures 720 × 576 pixels.** This information may affect you as you read Chapter 12 and prepare still images for use with iMovie.

About MissingManuals.com

At *www.missingmanuals.com*, you'll find news, articles, and updates to the books in this series.

But if you click the name of this book and then the Errata link, you'll find a unique resource: a list of corrections and updates that have been made in successive printings of this book. You can mark important corrections right into your own copy of the book, if you like.

In fact, the same page offers an invitation for you to submit such corrections and updates yourself. In an effort to keep the book as up to date and accurate as possible, each time we print more copies of this book, we'll make any confirmed corrections you've suggested. Thanks in advance for reporting any glitches you find!

In the meantime, we'd love to hear your suggestions for new books in the Missing Manual line. There's a place for that on the Web site, too, as well as a place to sign up for free email notification of new titles in the series.

The Very Basics

You'll find very little jargon or nerd terminology in this book. You will, however, encounter a few terms and concepts that you'll see frequently in your Macintosh life. They include:

- **Menus.** The *menus* are the words in the lightly striped bar at the top of your screen. You can either click one of these words to open a pull-down menu of commands (and then click again on a command), or click and *hold* the button as you drag down the menu to the desired command (and release the button to activate the command). Either method works fine.

    NOTE   Apple has officially changed what it calls the little menu that pops up when you Control-click (or right-click) something on the screen. It's still a *contextual* menu, in that the menu choices depend on the context of what you click—but it's now called a *shortcut* menu. That term not only matches what it's called in Windows, but it's slightly more descriptive of its function. Shortcut menu is the term you'll find in this book.

- **Clicking.** This book offers three kinds of instructions that require you to use the mouse or trackpad attached to your Mac. To *click* means to point the arrow cursor at something onscreen and then—without moving the cursor at all—press and release the clicker button on the mouse (or laptop trackpad). To *double-click*, of course, means to click twice in rapid succession, again without moving the cursor at all. And to *drag* means to move the cursor while keeping the button continuously pressed.

  When you're told to ⌘-*click* something, you click while pressing the ⌘ key (next to the Space bar). Such related procedures as *Shift-clicking, Option-clicking,* and *Control-clicking* work the same way—just click while pressing the corresponding key on the bottom row of your keyboard.

  NOTE   On Windows PCs, the mouse has two buttons. The left one is for clicking normally; the right one produces a tiny shortcut menu of useful commands. (See the previous Note.) But new Macs come with Apple's Mighty Mouse, a mouse that looks like it has only one button but can actually detect which side of its rounded front you're pressing. If you've turned on the feature in System Preferences, you, too, can right-click things on the screen.

  That's why, all through this book, you'll see the phrase, "Control-click the photo (or right-click it)." That's telling you that Control-clicking will do the job—but if you've got a two-button mouse or you've turned on the two-button feature of the Mighty Mouse, right-clicking might be more efficient.

- **Keyboard shortcuts.** Every time you take your hand off the keyboard to move the mouse, you lose time and potentially disrupt your creative flow. That's why many experienced Mac fans use keystroke combinations instead of menu commands wherever possible. ⌘-P opens the Print dialog box, for example, and ⌘-M minimizes the current window to the Dock.

  When you see a shortcut like ⌘-Q (which closes the current program), it's telling you to hold down the ⌘ key, and, while it's down, type the letter Q, and then release both keys.

If you've mastered this much information, you have all the technical background you need to enjoy *iMovie '09 & iDVD: The Missing Manual.*

—David Pogue

Safari® Books Online

 When you see a Safari® Books Online icon on the cover of your favorite technology book, that means the book is available online through the O'Reilly Network Safari Bookshelf.

Safari offers a solution that's better than e-Books. It's a virtual library that lets you easily search thousands of top tech books, cut and paste code samples, download chapters, and find quick answers when you need the most accurate, current information. Try it free at *http://my.safaribooksonline.com/?portal=oreilly*.

Part One:
Editing in iMovie

1

Importing Video

Let's say you've filmed something. You've captured some video on your camcorder, digital camera, or Flip, or maybe you've just assembled some videos on your hard drive. Now it's time for the heart of this book: editing your footage on the Mac using iMovie. This chapter introduces you to iMovie and its importing window, which can slurp in video from tape camcorders, tapeless camcorders, and old iMovie projects. It can also record video live, in real time, from a camcorder or an iSight video camera.

iMovie: The Application

So far in your moviemaking adventures you've probably thought about nothing but *hardware*—the equipment. In the end, however, the iMovie story is about *software*, both the footage as it exists on your Mac and the iMovie program itself.

iMovie on a New Mac

If you bought a new Mac since February 2009, iMovie '09 is probably already on your hard drive. Open the Macintosh HD icon → Applications folder. Inside is the star-shaped icon for iMovie itself. Its icon is probably in your Dock, too.

iMovie for an Existing Mac

If your Mac didn't come with iMovie '09, you can buy it as part of the $80 iLife '09 software suite. That's one DVD containing the latest versions of GarageBand, iMovie, iPhoto, iWeb, and iDVD. (It's available from Apple's Web site, Apple stores, or popular Mac mail-order sites like *www.macmall.com* and *www.macwarehouse.com*.)

Apple says that iMovie requires a Mac (running Mac OS X version 10.5.6 or later) in one of these categories:

- Any Mac with an Intel processor (MacBook, MacBook Pro, Mac Pro, recent iMacs). An Intel-based Mac is required if you want to work with *AVCHD* video (page 7).

- A Power Mac G5 with dual 2.0-gigahertz chips or faster.

- An iMac G5 whose chip runs at 1.9 gigahertz or faster.

Apple also recommends a machine with at least 1 gigabyte of memory—and *requires* it if you want to work with high-def video. It goes without saying, of course, that the more memory you have, the bigger your screen, and the faster your processor, the happier you and iMovie will be. This program is *seriously* hungry for horsepower.

If you've bought iLife, now run its installer and choose which programs you want.

> **TIP**   Consider installing GarageBand even if you're not a musician. You may use it to assist iMovie with things like editing sound.

When the installer is finished, you'll find an icon called iMovie in your Applications folder and in your Dock.

> **TIP**   If you've got iMovie '08 already on your Mac, the '09 version replaces it. If you have iMovie HD (also known as iMovie 6), though, the installer thoughtfully preserves it. You'll find a folder called "iMovie (previous version)" in your Applications folder, ready to run when necessary. To find out why Apple left the old version on your hard drive, read page 256.

".0.1" Updates

Like any software company, Apple occasionally releases new versions of iMovie: version 8.1, version 8.2, and so on (or even 8.1.1, then 8.1.2, etc.). Each free upgrade adds better reliability to the program. They're well worth installing for any program, but they're especially important for iMovie; Apple does more than squash bugs with these updates, they often add features to iMovie that you'll want to use.

You don't have to look far to find these updates. One day you'll be online and the Mac's Software Update dialog box will appear, letting you know that a new version is available and offering to install it for you. You can also download the updates from within iMovie by choosing iMovie → Check for Updates.

When the updater finishes, your original copy of iMovie '09 has morphed into the newer version of the program. (One way to find out what version of iMovie you have is to open the program and then choose iMovie → About iMovie.)

This book assumes that you have at least iMovie 8.0.3.

Getting into iMovie

After you've installed iMovie, open it by double-clicking its icon in the Applications folder, or by single-clicking its star-shaped icon in the Dock.

Now, just in case it had somehow slipped your attention that iMovie is a totally new program, a special starter screen appears to let you know (Figure 1-1).

Figure 1-1:
This window welcomes you to the new concepts of iMovie. The most significant element of this billboard is the Video Tutorials button, which takes you online to see some videos that go over iMovie's basic features. Click OK to close the welcome screen and get down to work.

When you click Close, you arrive at the main iMovie screen. Figure 1-2 is a cheat sheet for iMovie's various screen elements, but don't spend time memorizing their functions now; the rest of this book covers each of these tools in context and in depth:

- **Project Library.** If you're used to the old iMovie, the new iMovie's way of doing things may come as a shock. You create new movie projects the same way as always, by choosing File → New Project (or pressing ⌘-N). But now, after you type a name for the new movie, you're not asked where you want to save it. Instead, iMovie just adds its name to this Project Library list, alongside all of your projects, past and present. More on projects in the next chapter.

- **Project storyboard.** You'll spend most of your editing time up here. Here's where you see your movie represented as filmstrips—short sequences of representative frames from each clip. Parallel colored strips indicate blocks of sound that play simultaneously.

- **Viewer.** You watch your footage in this window.

- **Toolbar.** Here's where you'll find most of iMovie's onscreen controls.

- **Event Library.** In the new iMovie scheme, *all* your raw footage is available to *all* your movie projects at all times. The Event Library lists all the video you've ever imported into iMovie '09, on all your hard drives. It's organized by *event*— wedding, vacation, graduation, and so on. You can read much more about Events on page 59; for now, it's enough to know that your Events are listed here, organized into folders by year.

- **Event browser.** This area stores the raw, unedited *clips*—"filmstrips" of footage, individual shots—that you'll rearrange into a masterpiece of modern storytelling. Exactly what you see here changes; it shows the contents of the Event whose name you click in the Event Library.

- **Playhead.** The Playhead is like the little handle of a normal scroll bar. It shows exactly where you are in the footage.

If you've just opened iMovie, it probably looks pretty barren at the moment. But you'll fix that.

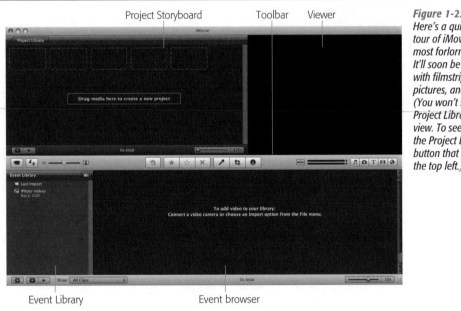

Project Storyboard   Toolbar   Viewer

Event Library   Event browser

Figure 1-2:
Here's a quick grand tour of iMovie at its most forlorn-looking. It'll soon be seething with filmstrips, clips, pictures, and sound. (You won't see the Project Library in this view. To see it, just click the Project Library button that appears at the top left.)

Importing from a Tape Camcorder

If you have a MiniDV tape camcorder, high-def or not, transferring your recordings to the Mac for editing is straightforward. All you have to do is connect your two machines—the camcorder and the Mac—with a cable.

It's called a *FireWire* cable, and it looks like the one in Figure 1-3. The big end of the cable goes into the FireWire jack on the front, side, or back of your Mac; it's marked by a radioactive-looking ⚛ symbol.

> **TIP** Unfortunately, not all Mac models have FireWire jacks anymore, or they use a newer version called FireWire 800. If your Mac has a FireWire 800 jack, you can find a cable that works with your camera. The MacBook Air and the regular aluminum MacBook, though, lack *any* FireWire jack. If you have MiniDV tapes full of recorded video, you're out of luck: There's no adapter box or converter that can connect your camcorder's FireWire jack to a Mac that doesn't have this jack. Your best bet is to borrow a Mac model that has a FireWire jack, dump all of your tapes into it, and then sell your old camcorder.

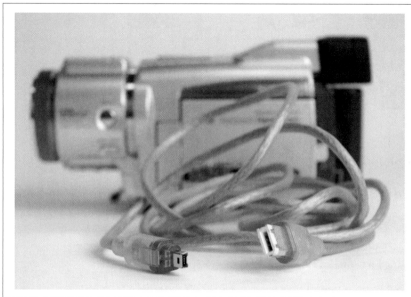

Figure 1-3:
Plug the larger end of the FireWire cable—the six-pin end, as Apple calls it—into the corresponding jack on the Mac. The tiny end may look almost square, but it fits in only one particular way, thanks to a little indentation on one side. Be gentle with it.

On the other end is a much smaller, squarish plug (the four-pin connector). Plug this tiny end into the FireWire connector on your camcorder, which, depending on the brand, may be labeled "FireWire," "i.Link," or "IEEE 1394." It's almost always hidden behind a plastic or rubber door or flap on the camcorder.

This single *FireWire* cable communicates both sound and video from the camcorder to the Mac. Once it's connected, proceed like this:

1. **Turn on the camcorder. Switch it into Play mode (Figure 1-4).**

   The camcorder's playback mode may be labeled Play, VCR, VTR, or just ▶.

   At this point, iMovie's big blue Import window is supposed to open automatically. If it doesn't, run through the troubleshooting checks described on page 421.

Figure 1-4:
Your camcorder's Play
Mode should be a fairly
prominent knob or menu
setting. If you can't find it,
check the manual.

TIP   You'll probably want to open the camcorder's LCD screen, which also turns on its speaker. Otherwise, you'll have no way to hear the audio as you play back the tape.

2. **Specify what you want to import.**

If you want to import the whole tape, make sure the Automatic/Manual switch (lower left) is on Automatic, and then click Import. This is a convenient option, since you can walk away and do other things while iMovie works. The "Save to" dialog box appears (Figure 1-5); skip to step 3.

If you want to import only some of what's on the tape, set the Automatic/Manual switch to Manual. At this point, the window sprouts a set of playback control buttons (Figure 1-6). You can actually use the ◄◄, ►►, ■, and ► buttons on the screen to control the camcorder.

TIP   You have to keep the mouse button down on the ◄◄ and ►► buttons continuously to make them work. If you use these buttons while the video is playing, you scan through the video; if you click Stop (■) first, these buttons zoom much faster through the tape, but of course you can't see where you are until you hit ► again.

What you're doing now, of course, is scanning your tape to find the sections that you want to include in your edited movie. When you find a shot that's worth bringing onto the Mac, click the Import button at the lower-right corner of the window. The "Save to" dialog box appears (Figure 1-5); read on.

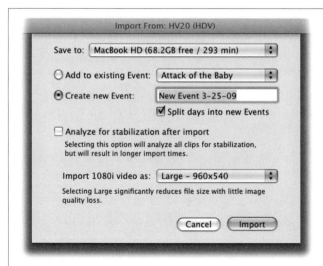

Figure 1-5:
This dialog box wants to know: Where do you want to save the incoming clips (which hard drive)? What Event do they belong to? Do you want iMovie to stabilize your jerky camera work (page 154)? And how big do you really need hard drive footage to be?

Figure 1-6:
There are no keyboard shortcuts for these buttons. Use your mouse to operate the camcorder by remote control, or just use the playback controls on the camcorder itself.

3. **Indicate where you want to save the imported video clips.**

Most people, most of the time, save incoming video onto the main Mac hard drive. But true iMovie addicts wind up buying additional hard drives to hold their movies. That's why the "Save to" pop-up menu appears here—so that you can choose a different hard drive to hold your video.

4. **Specify an Event.**

The pair of choices shown in Figure 1-5 let you answer these questions: Were the scenes you're about to import filmed at a new Event? Or should they more properly be filed along with scenes you've already imported as part of an existing Event?

Answering this question, of course, requires that you know what Apple means by an Event. See the box on page 34.

NOTE   What you see in the "Add to existing Event" pop-up menu depends on which hard drive you've selected. That's because iMovie only "knows about" the Events on the currently selected hard drive.

5. **Turn on "Analyze for stabilization after import", if you've got the time.**

The built-in footage stabilizer is one of iMovie's most important and most effective new features. It converts unsteady video into footage that looks as though the camera was on a tripod.

The downside of this miraculous option is that your Mac requires a long period of thoughtful analysis before it can do this stabilizing. It literally studies the first frame of video, compares each pixel to what's on the second frame, and so on. And that takes a long time—hours, in some cases.

Fortunately, you can always apply the stabilization feature to individual parts of the movie, which saves huge amounts of time. In other words, the only reason to turn on "Analyze for stabilization after import" at this stage is because you intend to let the Mac crunch away for half a day (or night) after the importing is complete.

6. **If you have a high-definition camcorder, choose either "Large – 960 × 540" or "Full – 1920 × 1080".**

This final option appears only when you're importing video from a high-definition camcorder, one that captures video in the so-called 1080i format. (That term refers to the fact that it reproduces a scene using 1,080 fine horizontal lines, which is very sharp indeed. Actually, the "i" means that you see two sets of 540 lines, odds and evens, interlaced with each other, flashed alternately on the screen.)

iMovie is offering you the chance to import a quarter-scale version of that gigantic video canvas, for the purposes of saving hard drive space. For assistance in making the Large vs. Full decision, see the box on page 32.

7. **Click Import.**

If you chose the Automatic option, iMovie now rewinds the tape to the beginning, then commands the camcorder to begin playback. As it plays, iMovie captures the video and stores it on your Mac. You can interrupt the process by clicking

Stop, if necessary; at this point, iMovie displays a little congratulations message, revealing how many minutes' worth of video you imported. You can click
OK and then import some more, if you like, starting from step 2.

Or you can walk away while iMovie works. You can even surf the Web, crunch
some numbers, organize your pictures in iPhoto, or whatever you like. Since
iMovie is a Mac OS X program, your Mac doesn't have to devote every atom of its
energy to capturing video. It continues to give priority to capturing video, so your
other programs may act a little drugged. But you can get meaningful work or
reading done while you're dumping your footage into iMovie in the background.

If you let the Automatic importing proceed without interruption, iMovie auto-
rewinds the tape when it reaches the end.

If you chose the Manual setting, you can use playback controls to operate the
tape, shuttling through it to find the parts you want; use the Import button
(and its alter ego, the Stop button) to capture only the good parts.

TIP   When you come to a scene you want to bring into iMovie, capture 3 to 5 seconds of footage before and after the interesting part. Later, when you're editing, that extra leading and trailing
video (called *trim handles* by the pros) will give you the flexibility to choose exactly the right
moment for the scene to begin and end. Furthermore, you need extra footage at the beginnings
and ends of your clips if you want to use crossfades or similar transitions between them.

Unfortunately, the process isn't the speedy joyride it was in the previous version of iMovie, where you could just tap the space bar (or click Import) every
time you wanted to start or stop importing during playback.

In iMovie '09, each time you click Stop, iMovie locks you out for a minute or
two while it displays the "Generating Thumbnails" message. That's iMovie's
way of saying, "I'm processing this video and making some live, 'skimmable'
filmstrips" (which are described on page 68).

Once that message disappears, you can use the playback controls to find the
next bit of video that's worth importing—but you'll have to fill out the box
shown in Figure 1-5 all over again, every time.

These frequent "Generating Thumbnails" and "Save to" interruptions are, for
many people, a pretty strong argument for avoiding the Manual settings. The
Automatic setting winds up saving you a lot of time—and doesn't cost you any
extra disk space. (See the box on page 36.)

8. **When you and iMovie are both finished, click Done.**

The Import window goes away. You return to the iMovie screen, where you can
click the name of the Event you specified in step 4 to see the newly imported
clips within it. Proceed to Chapter 2.

UP TO SPEED

Large vs. Full

High-def is great and all. Truly it is. It's mind-blowingly sharp, clear, and colorful. One frame of a true high-def 1080i picture is made up of 1,920 by 1,080 pixels. (Compare that with the pathetic dimensions of standard TV: 640 by 480 pixels.)

But high-def video also takes up a ridiculous amount of hard drive space: 40 *gigabytes per hour*. (Standard-resolution DV video takes up less than a third that much space.)

If your 160-gig hard drive is already half full with programs, photos, music, and other software, then you've got room for only 120 minutes of high-def video. And depending on how trigger-happy you are as a videographer (and how cute your kids are), that's not very much at all.

Apple is pointing out here, though, that 1080i video is actually overkill for most of the things people do with their home movies. It's much too big for a standard DVD, for example, whose picture is only 640 by 480 pixels. It's way too big to watch from a Web page. That size image may even be too big to fit on your monitor (an Apple 20-inch screen has a maximum resolution of 1,680 by 1,050 pixels—too small for a full 1080i movie).

So Apple is offering you the opportunity to import your video at a *scaled-down* size: 960 by 540 pixels. If you do the math, you'll realize that that's actually only *one-quarter* the area of the original high-def picture (half in each dimension), which makes Apple's name for this—"Large"—a little suspicious.

Still, importing your high-def video at the Large (quarter-size) setting means that each hour of video takes up only 13 gigabytes per hour instead of 40. You'll also get smoother playback on slower Macs. And for most end-result showcases—like the Web, a DVD, or computer-screen playback—the resolution is still sensational. It's unlikely that you'd see any difference between the Large and the Full settings.

There *are* times when the Full setting is appropriate, however. You'd want that setting when you plan to export your edited version to Final Cut Pro (Apple's professional video editing program); when you intend to broadcast it on TV or use it in an actual, professional movie; or when you hope to burn it to a *high-definition* DVD someday (when such burners become available on the Mac).

Furthermore, as you weigh this decision, just remember one thing: You're making this choice forever. Hard drives will get bigger and cheaper. High-def DVDs will eventually become commonplace. Computer horsepower will someday double or quadruple. If you're working with precious, important video that you expect to be watched for decades to come, it might be worth keeping the full resolution just in case.

Note: Check your camcorder's manual. Not all camcorders advertised as "1080i high-def" do, in fact, record at the full 1,920 by 1,080 pixels. And if yours *doesn't*, there's very little downside to using the "Large" option here.

Automatic Scene Detection

You'll notice a handy iMovie feature when the importing is all over: It automatically creates an individual filmstrip (clip) for each scene you shot. An hour's worth of tape doesn't wind up as a single, mega-chunk of video—instead, you wind up with 30 or 40 individual clips, just the way you shot them.

What iMovie is actually doing is studying the *date and time stamp* that digital camcorders record into every frame of video. When iMovie detects a break in time, it assumes that you stopped recording, if only for a moment, and therefore that the next piece of footage should be considered a new shot. It turns each new shot into a new clip.

In general, this feature doesn't work if you haven't set your camcorder's clock. Automatic scene detection also doesn't work if you're playing from a nondigital tape using one of the techniques described on page 44.

Importing from Tapeless Camcorders

The beauty of tapeless camcorders is that, because they store video as computer files on a hard drive, on a DVD, or in memory, you don't have to wait for them to play into your Mac in real time. Instead, the importing process takes only as much time as iMovie needs to copy those files onto your Mac's hard drive. (At least in theory; read on.)

> **NOTE**   If your camcorder records onto miniature DVDs, see page 39 for some additional notes.

Once you're ready to transfer some video from your camcorder, here's what to do:

1. **Connect the camcorder's USB cable to your Mac.**

   Most tapeless camcorders connect to the Mac using a USB cable, which comes right in the box. It connects to any of the Mac's skinny rectangular USB jacks, as shown in Figure 1-7. (If you have one of those tiny, very popular Flip camcorders, plug in its pop-out USB jack instead.)

Figure 1-7:
Tapeless camcorders generally come with a USB cable. The little end plugs into the camcorder (you may have to open some tiny plastic doors on the camera to find the jack). The big end plugs into any of your Mac's USB jacks.

UP TO SPEED

The Definition of an Event

In iMovie terms, an Event is an organizational tool, like a label or a filing folder.

Sometimes, what constitutes an Event is obvious. A wedding, a graduation, a birthday party, and a ski trip would all be considered individual Events. You'd want all of the video scenes for somebody's wedding filed under a single heading, even if they were filmed over the course of a whole wedding weekend.

Sometimes, though, "Event" is a little nebulous. What if you film little scenes of your new baby every other day for a couple of months? Would they all be one Event called "August"? Or would you have a lot of little Events like "Overturned spaghetti bowl" and "First steps"?

Or what if you take a 10-day cruise, featuring a stop every other day in a different port of call? Would the Event be "Mediterranean Cruise"? Or would you create individual Events for "Naples," "Monaco," and "Tunisia"?

The answer is, of course, "That's up to you." And that's why the options in Figure 1-5 appear at this point. If you want to create a new Event, type a name for it into the "Create new Event" box. But if you're importing more footage into an Event category you've already created, click "Add to existing Event," and then choose which Event from the pop-up menu.

Note: If you opt to create a new Event, you're also offered a checkbox called "Split days into new Events." If this option is turned on, then each day's worth of shooting becomes an Event all its own, even if it was all shot on the same vacation or wedding weekend. iMovie automatically adds day numbers to the Event names, like "Wedding – Day 1" and "Wedding – Day 2."

NOTE If you're using an original Flip or Flip Ultra camera, you need to install the 3vix codec software that comes with your camera. When your Flip is connected, find its icon on your desktop. Double-click it to open a window containing the "Flip Video for Mac" installer software. Double-click the installer icon to get the necessary codec (page 292). Once you've done that, iMovie can talk to your Flip camera without a problem.

2. **Turn on the camcorder. Switch it into PC mode.**

   The wording might vary, but every tapeless camcorder has a mode for making PC or Mac connections (Figure 1-8).

   At this point, iMovie should open automatically, if it wasn't open already. If everything is going well, a message appears at the top of the screen that says, "Generating thumbnails." Then, after a minute, you see the Importing screen depicted in Figure 1-9.

   If iMovie *doesn't* open, or if the Importing screen doesn't appear, then choose File → Import From Camera, or run through the troubleshooting steps described on page 421.

Figure 1-8:
*Every camcorder has a
switch or command that
lets you connect it to a PC
(or, in this case, a Mac).
Most tapeless
camcorders have a
dedicated position on the
main mode dial for this
purpose, like this one.*

Figure 1-9:
*You can select individual
scenes for importing
without rewinding or
fast-forwarding. You can
also preview the
recorded scenes before
you bother importing
them to the Mac. If your
intention is to bring in
most of the clips, just turn
off the checkboxes that
you don't want. If you
want to import less than
half of them, though,
click Uncheck All, and
then turn the checkboxes
back on for the shots that
you do want.*

FREQUENTLY ASKED QUESTION

Reclaiming Disk Space

I'm worried about using the Automatic importing option. It seems like overkill if it brings in a whole hour of video, and I wind up using only 10 minutes of it.

Yes, it's true that imported digital video eats up 13 gigabytes of disk space per hour of footage. (And that's standard-definition video. High-definition video eats up 40 gigs, at least if you choose the Full option described on page 32.)

The good news: As you work on your project, you can always delete the pieces you're not using—and reclaim the disk space they were using.

Details appear on page 109, but the point is this iMovie '09 feature is a big improvement over the previous iMovie version, where deleting part of a clip did not, in fact, reclaim any disk space. (iMovie 6 hung onto the *entire* clip, behind the scenes, just in case you ever changed your mind about which piece you were using in your movie.)

You're about to experience one huge payoff of using a tapeless camcorder: instant access to individual scenes on the camcorder. That means, first of all, that you don't have to rewind or fast-forward to find a certain shot. Furthermore, as you can see in Figure 1-9, iMovie lets you import only the shots you want, leaving the duds behind. That feature alone can represent a huge time savings over the old "import the whole tape" method.

TIP   If your camcorder stores its video on memory cards—SD cards, for example—then you have another option at this juncture. You could remove the card from the camcorder and insert it into a *card reader* that's attached to your Mac. (Card readers are super cheap—under $10. They're like tiny disk drives that attach to your Mac's USB jack.) The advantage of the card-reader method is that you don't use up the camcorder's battery power while you're transferring your video.

3. **Inspect the shots on the camcorder to see what's worth importing.**

   To play a shot, click its thumbnail and then click the ▶ button. Click the ◀ or ▶| buttons to skip to the previous or next shot on the camcorder (or just click the thumbnails on the screen in front of you).

4. **Specify which shots you want to import.**

   If you want to import everything on the camcorder, click Import All; then skip to step 5.

   If you want to import only some of the shots, move the Automatic/Manual switch in the lower-left corner of the Import window to Manual. Now you'll see little checkboxes appear on the shot thumbnails. All of them start out with checkmarks, meaning that iMovie intends to import all of them. See Figure 1-9 for tips on selecting the scenes you want. Once the correct shots have checkmarks, click Import Checked.

   At this point, the top of the window sprouts a little sheet of options (see Figure 1-10).

5. **Indicate where you want to save the transferred video clips.**

Most people save the incoming clips onto the main Mac hard drive. But if you've bought additional hard drives to hold your movies, you can use the "Save to" pop-up menu to choose a different hard drive to hold your video.

6. **Specify an Event.**

The pair of choices shown in Figure 1-10 lets you answer these questions: Were the scenes you're about to import filmed at a new Event? Or should they more properly be filed along with scenes you've already imported as part of an existing Event? See the box on page 34 for the definition of an Event—and suggestions on what to choose here.

7. **If you have a high-def camcorder, choose either "Large – 960 × 540" or "Full – 1920 × 1080".**

You may not see the final option shown in Figure 1-10. It appears only when you're importing video from a high-definition camcorder, one that captures video in the so-called 1080i format. See the box on page 32 for a discussion of this option and advice on what to choose.

8. **Turn on "Analyze for stabilization after import", if you've got the time.**

The built-in footage stabilizer is one of iMovie's most important, and most effective, new features. It converts unsteady video into footage that looks as though the camera was on a tripod—but this "analysis" can take hours. See step 5 on page 30 for help in making this decision.

Figure 1-10:
This dialog box looks just like the one that appears when you import from tape. Once again, it wants to know: Where do you want to save the incoming clips (which hard drive)? What Event do they belong to? And how big do you really need the hard drive footage to be?

9. **Click Import.**

   Now iMovie swings into action. It begins slurping in the video from the camcorder's hard drive, DVD, or memory card. As it works, a progress counter ticks off the remaining shots left to import (Figure 1-11).

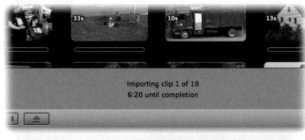

Figure 1-11:
Top: The counter here not only tells you how much longer you have to wait in "minutes: seconds" format, but also shows you how many video shots remain to be imported.

Bottom: When it's all over, the word "Imported" appears on each thumbnail. That's a handy reminder when you've only opted to import some of the clips.

Considering that fact that a tapeless camcorder is supposed to spare you the real-time importing process of a tape, you may be surprised at how much time the importing takes. AVCHD footage, in particular (page 8), takes a long time because iMovie has to convert it into an editable format; depending on the speed of your computer, you may wind up waiting 2.5 minutes for each minute of video. An hour's worth of video, in other words, can take two and a half hours to import. You've been warned.

But never mind that; once the job is done, a message appears to congratulate you. It lets you know how many minutes and seconds of video you've imported, total, and how many clips (Figure 1-12).

Figure 1-12:
Hey, you did it! You successfully imported some video from the camcorder to the Mac. You can now turn off the camcorder and put it away.

UP TO SPEED

Camera Archives: The Quick-Camcorder-Dump Trick

One big problem with tapeless camcorders is that, well, they're tapeless. If you're on a four-day trip to Disneyworld and the camcorder fills up after one day, you're finished. You can't exactly duck into a drugstore and buy a new hard drive. Until you empty out your camcorder onto your Mac (or start deleting stuff from the camcorder), you're dead in the water.

You could, of course, travel with a laptop, and empty out your camcorder into iMovie at the end of each day. The problem there is that if it's a high-def camcorder, iMovie will automatically convert the footage into its Apple Intermediate format (described in the box on page 43). And the problem there is that this conversion takes forever—and eats up a lot more space on the hard drive than the original files from the camcorder do.

There's a cool, completely under-hyped new feature in iMovie '09 that rather neatly solves these problems. It's called the Camera Archive, and it's designed to let you empty out the camera onto the Mac's hard drive in one simple step. There's no format conversion, no choices to make, no weeding out the bad clips; it just empties the camcorder in a hurry. You can open up the dumped footage in iMovie later, when you have more time and disk space.

To use this feature, begin following steps 1-2 on page 33. But when the Import window appears, click the Archive All button at the bottom of the window. iMovie asks you to choose a folder location (your Desktop is a good bet) and folder name (iMovie proposes the camcorder name and today's date)—and then gets right to work sucking in all the contents from the camcorder. When it's all over, you'll find a folder called Samsung 08-22-09 (or whatever), filled with video files in the camcorder's original format, like AVCHD. Nothing, at this point, has been imported into iMovie itself.

(Actually, the archive folder probably has other folders within it, containing still photos, audio files, and whatever else was on the camcorder. Great way to grab everything off the camcorder.)

Later, when you're back from Disneyworld and have more time, you can open up iMovie and choose File → Import → Camera Archive. Click the archive folder and then click Import. iMovie opens up its standard Import window, exactly as though the camcorder is connected (which is pretty freaky). Proceed to import the video files into iMovie from step 3, exactly as described on page 37.

10. Click OK.

The congratulations message goes away.

11. Click ▲ to eject the camcorder, and then click Done.

The Import screen goes away. You arrive at the main iMovie screen, where your new video appears in the Events list at the left side of the screen. Page 59 describes this structure in more detail.

You can now turn off the camcorder to save battery power, if you like.

Importing from DVD Camcorders

In general, DVD camcorders are a mess. They're fussy, they take a long time to "initialize" and "finalize" a blank DVD, each disc doesn't hold very much footage, the recorded discs may not have a very long lifespan in your closet, and the miniature DVDs can actually damage your Mac.

If that's what you've got, though, the routine for importing video from a DVD camcorder—at this writing, the most popular format on the market—is exactly the same as it is for other tapeless camcorders. The instructions begin on page 33.

There are, however, a few caveats:

- iMovie can't import video from DVD camcorders that use the AVCHD video format (page 7). Unfortunately, that pretty much rules out all the *high-definition* DVD camcorders.

- Thanks to the hostility of the engineers who dreamed up the recordable DVD camcorder disc, most DVD camcorders offer multiple recording *formats*, with such cheerful names as DVD-Video and DVD-VR. Each has tradeoffs: One plays back in more DVD players, another lets you erase scenes before committing the DVD to plastic, and so on.

The thing is, you have to choose which format you want *when you put the blank DVD into the camcorder.* That's when the screen offers you the choice of formats. The key here is to choose the DVD-Video format, sometimes called Standard. If you choose VR or DVD-VR instead, iMovie won't be able to import your recorded video. (When you connect the camcorder, it thinks that you've just inserted a DVD, rather than thinking that you've attached a disk full of video.)

Recording Live from a Camcorder or iSight Camera

iMovie is also happy to capture video straight from a tape camera, sending whatever it "sees" directly into iMovie, live. You can perform this stunt in either of two ways:

- **Using an iSight camera.** All recent Mac laptops and iMacs have this tiny Apple video camera built right in, just above the screen (Figure 1-13).

- **Using a camcorder.** Alternatively, you can connect a MiniDV camcorder to your Mac and use it as a glorified eyeball. (This doesn't work with tapeless and USB camcorders, and doesn't work if your Mac lacks a FireWire jack [page 27].)

    NOTE You can even use an ordinary Webcam, as long as it has a FireWire connector. Not many do.

Here are the steps:

1. **If you're using a camcorder, set its mode switch to Camera or Record (rather than VCR or Play, as you would if you were importing something you'd already recorded).**

    If you're using an iSight or a FireWire Webcam, you can skip this step.

2. **Choose File → "Import from Camera" (⌘-I), or click the camcorder-shaped button at the left side of the screen.**

    Either way, the Import window opens. If everything's going your way, you'll see a live video image from your camera.

**Recording Live from a
Camcorder or iSight
Camera**

Figure 1-13:
*This tiny lens, in the top of every Mac laptop
and iMac, records live video with surprisingly
good quality.*

Video Chat with Linda, Jesse, and Margot

NOTE   If you have *more than one* camera connected—a camcorder connected to a Mac with an iSight, for example—choose the camera you want to use from the Import From pop-up menu (at the lower-left corner of the Import window).

3. **Click Capture.**

   Now the usual "Save to" dialog box appears, just as shown in Figure 1-5.

4. **From the "Save to" pop-up menu, choose a hard drive's name.**

   You're specifying where you want the imported video to be saved.

5. **Specify an Event.**

   The pair of choices shown in Figure 1-5 lets you answer these questions: Were the scenes you're about to import filmed at a new Event? Or should they more properly be filed along with scenes you've already imported as part of an existing Event? See the box on page 34 for details on this choice.

6. **Click OK.**

   iMovie begins to import the live video image.

7. **To end the recording, click Stop.**

   iMovie enters its usual "Generating Thumbnails" state of catatonia for a few minutes.

   To record some more, repeat all this from step 2.

8. **When you're finished recording, click Done.**

Your video recording appears in the Event you specified, ready for editing.

Importing Old iMovie Projects

Most software companies, most of the time, stick with certain time-honored traditions concerning software upgrades. One of them happens to be compatibility: If you release BeeKeeper Pro 7, it goes without saying that it can open files created by BeeKeeper Pro 6.

iMovie '08 and '09, though, are not actually updated versions of iMovie 6 (also known as iMovie HD); they're versions 1.0 and 2.0 of a completely different program, written from scratch. Their ability to import older iMovie projects is extremely limited.

To bring in an older iMovie project, choose File → Import → iMovie HD Project. The dialog box shown in Figure 1-14 appears. Here, you should make two decisions before choosing the old iMovie project you want to open:

- **Where you want to save the imported, converted project.** The "Save to" pop-up menu lists your hard drives and shows you how much space is available on each one.

- **How you want iMovie to handle high-definition video projects.** See page 32 for details on making a choice here.

Figure 1-14:
In this dialog box, you specify what, where, and how you want to open an older iMovie project.

Apple Intermediate Codec

iMovie can *edit* lots more formats than the old iMovie could, including MPEG-2 SD (from memory-card camcorders), MPEG-4, iSight video (Photo JPEG), H.264, and DV.

But if you import the two high-definition camcorder formats, HDV (high-def tape camcorders) and AVCHD (high-def tapeless), it must first convert them to AIC.

A-I-what?

AIC stands for Apple Intermediate Codec. The conversion from high-def into AIC is what takes so bloomin' long when you try to import AVCHD clips.

There's a good reason for this: HDV and AVCHD were never intended for editing. They were intended to store a lot of video quality in very little space on camcorders. So when you import them to the Mac, you're dealing with gigantic, unwieldy files that would make your processor wheeze and gasp.

Enter AIC. The AIC format retains all the quality of the original video, but is much faster to edit, play, copy, paste, and so on.

When Apple calls this converter "intermediate," it's not kidding; the video remains in this format only while you're editing. When you finally do something with the finished movie, it's usually converted *back* into another format, like the H.264 format for YouTube or the MobileMe Web Gallery (Chapter 13).

All of this explains, by the way, why you can't drag movies into the main iMovie window to import them. You have to drag them into an *Event* or use the File → Import → Movies command. Both of those mechanisms convert incoming movies into the AIC format (and create filmstrip thumbnails for them) to prepare them for editing.

Once you've made those choices, navigate to the iMovie project you want to import, and double-click its name or icon.

iMovie '09 springs into action, importing the video clips (making a new copy of them) and generating the filmstrip thumbnails that you'll work with as you edit. This process can take a good long time.

When it's all over, whatever clips you had placed into the iMovie timeline appear in the Project (storyboard) area, in the correct sequence, correctly trimmed. Leftover clips (the ones that were left unused on the Clips pane of the old project) are brought in, too. They show up in the Event that contains your project, just in case you want to add them to the project later.

On the other hand, iMovie brings in only a few basic elements of the original iMovie project. To be precise:

- **You get only the clips.** iMovie '09 ignores all effects, titles, and credits. (Ouch.)

- **You lose all audio work you've done.** iMovie '09 ignores everything in the old iMovie's two audio tracks, including music, narration, sound effects, or the audio "paste-over" cutaways.

- **You lose all special transitions.** If you used any transition effects in your older iMovie project, iMovie '09 replaces them all with generic crossfade dissolves.

If you really, truly want to go to all this trouble, you can now start over again, repairing and reconstructing the movie, restoring the elements that got lost during the import process. You might find the effort worthwhile if you want to use some of the iMovie '09 tools that aren't available in the old iMovie, like video cropping, stabilization, rotation, or one-click exporting to YouTube.

Otherwise, though, you might want to consider leaving your old iMovie projects just as they are. As Chapter 11 makes clear, the old iMovie version is still perfectly usable and freely available to you, so it might make more sense to leave it in its original format.

Dragging Video In from the Finder

iMovie can import movies directly from your hard drive, too—no camcorder needed. Position the iMovie window so that you can see the movie files in the Finder, and then drag their icons directly onto an Event in the Event list.

Alternatively, use the File → Import → Movies command to find and select the movies you want to import. You'll be asked at that point which Event you want to contain the imported flicks.

Either way, you wind up with your digital movie files installed in an Event and ready to edit.

Importing Footage from Old Analog Tapes

We live in a transitional period. Millions of the world's existing camcorders and VCRs require VHS, VHS-C, or 8mm cassettes—that is, analog tapes instead of digital.

These days, people are buying only digital camcorders. But in the meantime, how are you supposed to import and edit the footage you shot before the digital era? Fortunately, this is fairly easy to do if you have the right equipment. You can take any of these four approaches, listed roughly in order of preference.

> **NOTE** When you use any of these approaches, iMovie won't be able to chop up the video into individual scene clips automatically, as it does for digital video. That's because old analog camcorders didn't stamp every frame of every shot with an invisible time code, so iMovie doesn't know when you stopped the camcorder.

Approach 1: Use a Camcorder with Pass-Through Conversion

If you're in the market for a new digital camcorder, here's a great idea: Buy a Sony or Canon MiniDV tape camcorder that has analog-to-digital *pass-through conversion*. In other words, the camcorder itself acts as a converter that turns the signal from your old analog tapes into a digital one that you can edit in iMovie.

The footage never hits a tape. Instead, it simply plays from your older VCR or camcorder directly into your Mac. (Not all camcorders have this feature, so ask before you buy. And on some models, you have to use the camcorder's own menu system to enable the live pass-through. And this requires a Mac model that has a FireWire jack.)

If you've got a drawerful of older tapes, such a camcorder is by far the most elegant and economical route, especially if you're shopping for a new camcorder anyway.

Approach 2: Record onto Your DV Camcorder

Even if your newish digital camcorder doesn't offer *real-time* analog-to-digital conversion, it may have analog inputs that let you record your older material onto a MiniDV tape in your *new* camcorder. If so, your problem is solved:

1. **Unplug the FireWire cable from the DV camcorder.**

   Most camcorders' analog inputs switch off when a FireWire cable is hooked up.

2. **Connect RCA cables from the Audio Output and Video Output jacks on the side of your older camcorder or VCR. Connect the opposite ends to the analog inputs of your DV camcorder.**

   Put a blank tape into your DV camcorder.

   TIP   If both your old camcorder and your DV camcorder have *S-video* connectors (round, dime-sized jacks), use them instead. S-video connections offer higher quality than RCA connections. (Note that an S-video cable doesn't conduct sound, however. You still have to connect the red and white RCA cables to carry the left and right stereo sound channels.)

3. **Switch both camcorders into VTR or VCR mode.**

   You're about to make a copy of the older tape by playing it into the camcorder.

   By now, every fiber of your being may be screaming, "But analog copies make the quality deteriorate!" Relax. You're only making a single-generation copy. Actually, you're only making half an analog copy; it's being recorded digitally, so you lose only half as much quality as you would with a normal VCR-to-VCR duplicate. In other words, you probably won't be able to spot any picture deterioration. And you'll have the footage in digital format now forever, ready to make as many copies as you want with no further quality degradation.

4. **Press the Record button on the DV camcorder, and press Play on the older camcorder or VCR.**

   You can monitor your progress by watching the LCD screen of your camcorder. Remember that a DV cassette generally holds only 60 minutes of video, compared with 2 hours on many previous-format tapes. You may have to change DV cassettes halfway through the process.

When the transfer is finished, you can rewind the newly recorded DV cassette in the DV camcorder and then import it into iMovie exactly as described in this chapter.

Approach 3: Use a Media Converter

If your digital camcorder doesn't have analog inputs, you can buy an *analog-to-digital converter*—a box that sits between your Mac and your VCR or older camcorder (Figure 1-15). It's an unassuming half-pound gray box, about 3 by 5 inches. Its primary features include analog audio and video (and S-video) inputs, which accommodate your older video gear, and a FireWire jack, whose cable you can plug into your Mac.

Figure 1-15:
The Canopus ADVC-55 (http://canopus.com, about $210) requires no external power because it draws its juice from the Mac via FireWire cable. It also offers double sets of inputs and outputs, so you can keep your TV and VCR hooked up simultaneously. And it can handle both NTSC (North American) or PAL (European) video signals (see page 18).

You'll be very pleased with the video quality. And when it comes to converting older footage, the media-converter approach has a dramatic advantage over DV camcorders with analog inputs: You have to sit through the footage only once. As your old VCR or camcorder plays the tape through the converter, the Mac records it simultaneously. (Contrast with Approach 2, which requires you to play the footage *twice:* once to the DV camcorder, and then from there to the Mac.)

Unfortunately, you can't control these devices using iMovie's playback controls, as described earlier in this chapter. Instead, you have to transfer your footage manually by pressing Play on your VCR or old camcorder and then clicking Import on the iMovie screen. In that way, these converters aren't as convenient as an actual DV or Digital8 camcorder.

Approach 4: Use a Digital8 Camcorder

Sony's Digital8 family of camcorders accommodate 8mm, Hi-8, *and* Digital8 tapes, which are 8mm cassettes recorded digitally. (Low-end models may not offer this feature, however, so ask before you buy.) Just insert your old 8mm or Hi-8 cassettes into the camcorder and proceed as described in this chapter. iMovie never needs to know that the camcorder doesn't contain a DV cassette.

Actually, a Digital8 camcorder grants you even more flexibility than that. Most Digital8 camcorders also have *analog inputs,* which let you import footage from your VCR or other tape formats, as described in Approach 2.

The Lay of the Land

If you're coming to iMovie '09 from iMovie HD (also known as iMovie 6), you're likely to be a bit confused; the design of this program is completely different. If you're coming to iMovie '09 from any *other* video-editing program, you'll be equally baffled. And if you've never used a video-editing program at all, well, you'll probably have no clue what's going on.

Before you delve into the actual experience of chopping and rearranging your video into a finished masterwork, therefore, it's worth sampling this brief chapter on what, exactly, iMovie is up to. Here's where you'll learn what's where on the screen, how to tailor the setup to your work habits, and where iMovie actually stores your video.

The Concept of Movie Projects

A *project*, in iMovie lingo, is an edited movie. The reason you're learning iMovie in the first place is to create these projects.

In previous versions of iMovie, a project was an icon on your desktop. It was really a cleverly disguised folder, and inside, you'd find all the gigantic movie clips that you'd used in your movie. This was convenient in one way: You could move the whole thing to another computer or back it up easily, for example.

But in another way, it wasn't ideal. If you wanted to use a particular piece of video in more than one project, you'd have to duplicate it (by pasting it into the second project), which ate up a lot more hard drive space.

iMovie '09 operates on a totally different system. The idea here is that your Events list (lower left of the iMovie window) shows every piece of video on your entire Mac—even video on other hard drives. All of it is available to all your projects, all the time.

When you choose a video clip to use in a project, you're not moving it anywhere. You're just providing a *pointer* for the project, showing iMovie where to look for each piece of video you want it to play.

This new system has a number of implications:

• You can use the same video clips in dozens of different movie projects, without ever eating up more disk space. (See Figure 2-1.)

• You can create multiple versions of the same project—a long one and a short one, for example—without worrying about filling up your hard drive.

> **NOTE** Each project takes up disk space, but only an infinitesimal amount—about as much as a word processor document. It contains only a text list of *pointers* to bits of video on your hard drive.

• Backing up or moving a single project is no longer simply a matter of copying a file. Yes, there's a folder that contains your individual project files. (It's the Home → Movies → iMovie Projects folder.) But if you attempt to drag one of these project files to another disk, you'll have nothing, because you'll be leaving behind the raw video that it points to. (In iMovie '09, there is, however, a way to move or copy a project to another folder or disk, together with all the Event footage the project needs. Page 54 tells all.)

Figure 2-1:
An orange line across the bottom edge lets you know which chunks of a source clip you've used in your project. When you click a different project, you'll see the orange lines jump around. It's showing that you've used a different chunk of the same source clip in the second project.

When you're finished editing a project, you'll probably want to *send* it somewhere: to YouTube, to a DVD, to a QuickTime movie, or whatever. Only then does iMovie meld together the editing information stored in the project file with the video information stored in the clips and produce a single, sharable movie file.

The Project Library

iMovie '09 keeps a handy list of all the projects you're working on, called the Project Library (Figure 2-2). This list shows the names and previews of each project. It also displays the length and date of each project, plus a set of icons that indicate if your project has been shared to YouTube, MobileMe, iTunes, or the Media Browser. (All of these sharing options are covered in Chapters 12 and 13.)

To begin editing an existing project, in the top left corner of the iMovie window, double-click the project, or click the Edit Project arrow button. On the other hand, if you're already editing a project, you can go back to your Project Library list by clicking the Project Library arrow (in the same spot where the Edit Project arrow used to be).

Figure 2-2:
The Project Library shows your list of projects and project folders, along with a skimmable preview of your project and other useful information like the project date, length, and shared status.

Creating a Project

To create a new project, you have three choices:

- Choose File → New Project.
- Press ⌘-N.
- Click the + button beneath the Projects list.

In each case, the New Project sheet appears, as shown in Figure 2-3. Here's where you give the project a name, and choose an *aspect ratio* for it. See the explanation on page 56 for details on aspect ratios. You can also choose a theme and a transition for iMovie to automatically apply. (Themes are covered on page 127 and transitions on page 113.)

Duplicating a Project

It's often useful to create several versions of the same project. You could have a short and a long version, an R-rated and a PG-rated version, or several differently edited cuts so you can get feedback on which one works best.

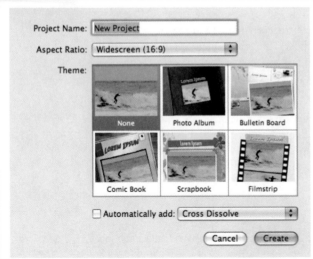

Figure 2-3:
Name your new project and specify the shape of the movie frame. You can also choose a project theme and automatic transitions. The project will appear in the list at lower left.

The beauty of iMovie '09 is that you can duplicate a project easily and simply, without filling up your hard drive with duplicated video files. Each version of the project calls upon the *same* underlying video files.

To duplicate a version, click its name, and then choose File → Duplicate Project. You'll see the new project appear in the Project Library, complete with a temporary name. (If the original was called "Baby Spaghetti on Head," the new one is called "Baby Spaghetti on Head 1.") Feel free to rename the project using the method described next.

You can now get to work editing the new version independently of the original.

Renaming a Project

To give a project a new name, double-click the old name. The renaming rectangle opens so you can type a new title.

Project Folders

It's great to have every project you've ever done right at your fingertips at all times. But when your projects start to pile up, and the list gets unwieldy, you can create virtual folders to organize them—for example, a 2009 Movies folder, a 2010 Movies folder, and so on.

Just click in the Project list and then choose File → New Folder. iMovie creates a new folder icon in the list, much the way iPhoto creates albums or iTunes creates playlists. Conveniently enough, you'll see these folders any time you use the Media Browser (page 279) to incorporate your iMovie work into iDVD, Keynote, and so on.

You can rename a folder by double-clicking it, or delete it (*and* everything inside it, as described next) by choosing File → "Move Folder to Trash" (⌘-Delete).

Deleting a Project

To get rid of a project, click its name, and then choose File → "Move Project to Trash", or just press ⌘-Delete.

POWER USERS' CLINIC

Behind the Scenes at iMovie '09

In this chapter, you'll read about some sneaky ways to go behind iMovie's back. For example, if you delete a project or an Event by accident, you can rescue it by opening your Mac's Trash and manually restoring the files to their rightful place.

That's because, in the end, iMovie '09 is nothing more than a glorified front end for the files that actually sit on your hard drive. And knowing the relationship between what you see in iMovie and what you find in the Finder can be extremely useful.

It turns out that every project, Event, and camcorder clip that you see in iMovie corresponds to an icon in the Finder. Want to see them?

Then open your Home folder (in the Finder, choose Go → Home), and then double-click the Movies folder. (Alternatively, click Movies in the sidebar at the left side of *any* Finder window.)

Here they are, the two special folders created by iMovie '09. One, called iMovie Projects, contains the icons for every project you've made in iMovie '09.

The other, called iMovie Events, contains individual folders for each import job you've done—one for each bunch of video you've imported. And inside *those* folders are the actual QuickTime video clips that you imported that day.

Every time you open iMovie '09, what you see in the Project Library and the Event Library is nothing more than a mirror of what's in the Finder, in those two iMovie folders within the Movies folder. (OK, you also see the videos you keep in iPhoto, but that's another story.)

In general, you shouldn't ever need to muck around in these Finder folders but there's no rule against doing so. If you rename, delete, or add to these files, you'll see those changes reflected in iMovie's lists the next time you open the program. Of course, this also means that if you delete or rename something in the iMovie Events folder, it will "break" any projects that incorporate that Event footage. (If you make a mistake, you can fix it by putting the folders or files back where they belong.)

(To get to a folder from within iMovie, you can Control-click or right-click any filmstrip and, from the shortcut menu, choose Reveal in Finder. You'll go right to the corresponding QuickTime clip.)

Keep your knowledge of this one-to-one correspondence tucked away for the day when you delete a project or an Event by accident. You'll be grateful that you know how to restore them by putting them back manually (see Figure 2-4).

Behind the scenes, iMovie moves the selected project to the *Macintosh* Trash. (To prove it to yourself, click the Trash icon on your Dock and open the iMovie Temporary Items folder.)

It may have disappeared from iMovie, but it's not *completely* gone until you return to your desktop, choose Finder → Empty Trash, and click OK.

Undeleting a Project

On the other hand, what if you delete a project and then change your mind? Or you delete the wrong one by accident?

As long as you haven't yet emptied the Macintosh Trash, you can get that project back. Figure 2-4 shows the procedure.

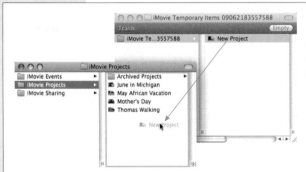

Figure 2-4:
Behind the scenes, every iMovie project is represented by an icon in your Home → Movies → iMovie Projects folder (front window). To rescue a project you've deleted by accident, open the Trash (click its Dock icon), open the iMovie Temporary Items folder, and then drag the project's icon from the Trash back into the iMovie Projects folder. The next time you open iMovie, you'll find the project right back in the Projects list, ready to go.

Moving a Project

Thanks to a new feature in iMovie '09, you can copy an entire project to another hard drive. This option comes in handy if, for example, you want to move a project to an external drive for editing on another computer. Because iMovie automatically lists all your hard drives in the Project Library, moving a project is just a matter of dragging the project to that drive's icon in the Project Library list.

At that point, iMovie shows a dialog box, pictured in Figure 2-5. If you choose "Copy project", iMovie makes a copy of the project—basically, just the pointers that describe the edits you've made—but *not* the Event footage that project uses. You'd use this method *only* if the other computer or hard drive already contains a copy of all the video you're working with.

In most cases, therefore, you'll want "Copy project and events" instead. This option ensures that you take everything the project needs to be editable elsewhere, including the raw video files from which it's made.

Figure 2-5:
If you move a project to another drive, iMovie lets you choose between moving just the project, or the project together with the Event footage it uses. Be sure to choose the latter if you're taking the project to edit on another computer.

Consolidating Project Media

Consolidating video is something like the opposite of moving a project; it keeps the project in place and moves the footage (and music) instead. Suppose, for example, that you're editing a project on your computer's internal hard drive, which incorporates raw video files from an external drive. This is no big deal as long as the external drive *stays* connected to your computer. But what if you're using a laptop, and you take it on a trip without that external hard drive? You won't be able to edit the project, unless you used the Consolidate command first, to copy all the necessary files to the laptop. (Nobody said this was going to be simple.)

iMovie knows this type of thing can happen and offers a convenient solution. Select the project in question by clicking its name in the Project Library. Then choose File → Consolidate Media. The dialog box shown in Figure 2-6 appears, giving you three options:

- **Copy the events.** This option copies *all* of the footage from *all* of the Events whose clips are used in the project, even clips you haven't used in your project. Use this option if you think you may want to incorporate other bits from those Events during an editing session later.

- **Copy the clips.** Unlike the first option, clicking this button copies *only* the video you've used in the project—just the pieces of just the clips—and not the surrounding Event footage. Use this option if you're finished editing the project, but still want to be able to export it at full quality. (Clearly, this option requires a lot less hard-drive space than "Copy the events".)

- **Move the events.** This option is the same as "Copy the events", except that it *deletes* the Events video from the old drive after moving it to the new one.

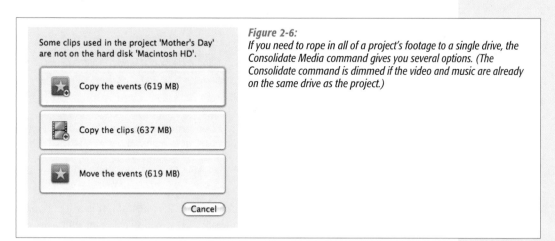

Figure 2-6:
If you need to rope in all of a project's footage to a single drive, the Consolidate Media command gives you several options. (The Consolidate command is dimmed if the video and music are already on the same drive as the project.)

All three of these options also copy any music files in the project to the new disk.

NOTE   Remember, choosing Consolidate Media moves footage to the drive where your project currently resides. If you want the footage *and* the project on another drive, move your project as described on page 54.

Aspect Ratios: The Missing Manual

Aspect ratio is an annoying geek term for *shape of the movie frame*. Having to learn about aspect ratios is an unfortunate requirement if you're going to master video editing.

A standard 1980 TV set's screen isn't the same shape as a movie screen. The TV is almost square but the movie is wide and short. They have different *aspect ratios* (see Figure 2-7).

Standard TV sets have a 4:3 aspect ratio. Those are the horizontal:vertical proportions. So if your screen is 4 feet wide, it's 3 feet high.

Figure 2-7:
iMovie offers you a choice of three aspect ratios: Standard (like a traditional TV), iPhone (which has a nonstandard screen shape), or Widescreen (like a high-def TV). You can always change your mind later.

High-def TV screens, on the other hand, are 16:9. If the width is 16 feet wide, then the height is 9 feet (and you have a heck of a big TV).

NOTE   Weirdly, 16:9 is *not* the standard aspect ratio for Hollywood movies! Those are usually 1.85:1 or 2.35:1. (Don't ask why movie aspect ratios always have 1 in the denominator. Nobody ever accused the video industry of being consistent.)

Believe it or not, those aren't even the only common aspect ratios. Consider the iPhone, which, of course, Apple hopes that *everybody* owns. Its screen is 3:2!

Every time you create a new project, iMovie asks you, "What aspect ratio would you like, O Master?"

If the result will play on a standard TV, choose "Standard (4:3)". If it will play on a high-def TV screen, choose "Widescreen (16:9)". If it will play on an iPhone, well, you can guess.

And if it will play on the Internet or as a QuickTime movie, the aspect ratio really makes no difference. Choose the one that best fits the original video shape.

Mismatched Aspect Ratios

One cool thing about iMovie '09 is that it can handle *multiple* aspect ratios in the same movie. You can mix and match source video that was filmed in different aspect ratios, within a single fixed-shape project.

How is this possible? Because whenever iMovie encounters source video that doesn't fit the frame, it does one of two things:

- Adds black letterbox bars above and below the picture (or on either side).

- Blows up the video large enough to fill the frame. In the process, of course, some of the picture gets chopped off at the top and bottom of the frame, or on the right and left sides.

Figure 2-8 shows both situations.

Figure 2-8:
Top: If you choose the Standard frame for your movie, then standard video fits fine but widescreen video, shown here, has to be either cropped or letterboxed.

Bottom: If you choose Widescreen for your movie, then standard 4:3 video, shown here, also has to be either cropped or letterboxed. (Actually, when the black bars are vertical, some people call them pillarbox bars.)

So those are iMovie's two solutions: letterbox bars, or cropping. But *you* have to tell iMovie which solution you prefer.

To do that, click the name of the project, and then choose File → Project Properties (⌘-J). In the Project Properties dialog box (Figure 2-9), first click the Stopwatch icon at the top labeled Timing. Then use the Initial Video Placement pop-up menu to choose either Crop (the misfitting video gets enlarged to fill the frame, even though you'll lose some at the edges), or "Fit in Frame" (you get letterbox bars). Click OK.

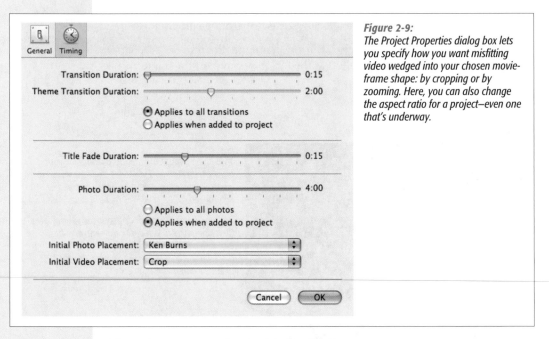

Figure 2-9:
The Project Properties dialog box lets you specify how you want misfitting video wedged into your chosen movie-frame shape: by cropping or by zooming. Here, you can also change the aspect ratio for a project—even one that's underway.

Changing Your Project's Aspect Ratio

Yes, iMovie asks you what aspect ratio you want when you first create a project. But you're not locked in. You can change your mind at any moment.

Suppose, for example, that you chose Widescreen when you created the project but later, after editing for a while, you realize that the vast majority of your footage is standard-definition video. In that case, you'll probably want to make the whole project Standard, to minimize the amount of time your audience spends staring at letterbox bars.

To change aspect ratios for a project that's already underway, click its name, and then choose File → Project Properties (⌘-J). On the Properties dialog box's General tab, choose a new aspect ratio from the Aspect Ratio pop-up menu at the top, and then click OK.

iMovie dutifully reformats the movie, adding *different* letterbox bars as necessary, or zooming mismatched videos *differently*.

All About Events

At the lower-left corner of the iMovie window, you see the Event library. It's supposed to be a massive repository of all the video on your entire computer, from all sources (Figure 2-10).

Figure 2-10:
When you click an Event name (left), iMovie shows you all the video clips that it contains (right).

It's organized like this:

- **Last Import.** Click this heading to view, in the clips area, all the video clips that you *most recently* imported from your camcorder. Often, this is precisely what you want.

- **iPhoto Videos.** Click this icon to see all the movie clips you've shot with your digital *still* camera (not your camcorder). In the Great iLife Master Plan, of course, it's not iMovie that handles photos and videos from still cameras—it's *iPhoto.* So here, iMovie is giving you handy, one-click access to all the videos that you've imported into iPhoto from your still camera.

- **2009, 2008, 2007...** These year headings organize your camcorder video collection into annual clumps. Click the flippy triangle to expand or collapse the year heading, so that you can see all the video batches within it.

What you actually see in one of these expanded lists is all the individual import jobs you performed during that year, each with whatever name you gave it. If you click one of these Event names, the right side of the window shows you all the video clips inside it.

Fine-Tuning the Events List

iMovie offers a slew of options designed to help you manage big video collections. (Some of these options make it clear that Apple expects all of us to have multiple two-terabyte hard drives in the very near future.)

- **Break it down by disk.** In the View menu, you'll find a command called Group Events By Disk. This command is made possible by iMovie's ability to see Events on multiple drives.

    So if you choose View → "Group Events by Disk", iMovie adds headings representing each of your hard drives, showing which video is stored on each. Clicking the hard-drive-icon button at the top of your Event list does the same thing as the menu command, and glows blue when you're viewing your Events by disk.

- **Break it out by month.** You can also make iMovie break down each year's worth of Events by *month*. Just choose View → "Group Events by Month". Now iMovie adds month subheadings within each year category: May, August, or whatever. (To save space, it adds headings only for the months when you actually shot video.)

- **Show days within Events.** Within an Event, or while viewing multiple Events at once, you may have footage that spans several days. To see when one day ends and another begins, choose View → "Show Separate Days in Events". iMovie inserts dated, gray bars before each day's worth of clips.

- **Reverse the sort order.** Ordinarily, iMovie lists your Events in reverse chronological order, from oldest to newest. If you choose View → "Most Recent Events at Top", then the sorting order is flipped. Newest video appears at the top.

- **Adjust the font size.** Out of the box, iMovie assumes that you have a lot of video to manage. If you don't, or if you have a nice big monitor (or aging eyes), you can ask iMovie to enlarge the type size for the Events and Projects lists. Choose iMovie → Preferences, click the Browser tab, and then turn on "Use large font for project and Event lists".

- **Add the dates.** Having your footage grouped by month is handy, but it can be even handier to see the exact *dates* of your filming. Once again, asking iMovie to display this information eats up screen space, but is very helpful if your Events list isn't already sprawling off the screen.

To make it so, choose iMovie → Preferences, and then turn on "Show date ranges in Event list". As shown in Figure 2-11, you now see little date ranges for your movies.

Changing the Date of an Event

It could happen. Maybe your camcorder didn't date-stamp your video properly. Maybe you've imported a bunch of analog VHS or Hi-8 videos, which show up as undated video clips. Or maybe you just need a serious alibi. Either way, you'll be happy to learn that you can manually change the date and time stamps on your video clips, and, therefore, the way that iMovie sorts them. (This works with any video imported into iMovie '09—even, for example, movies that you import from the hard drive or from iMovie 6.)

To make the change, select the Event clips needing a new date, and then right-click (or Control-click) them. In the shortcut menu, choose "Adjust Clip Date and Time".

iMovie shows you a dialog box with the old date and time, labeled From, and a chance to enter a new date and time, labeled To. The date setting follows the American convention of Month/Day/Year, while the time setting lets you set the new clip time down to the second. Clicking OK applies the needed date and time changes.

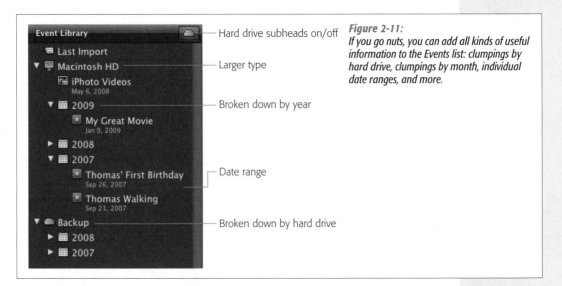

Figure 2-11:
If you go nuts, you can add all kinds of useful information to the Events list: clumpings by hard drive, clumpings by month, individual date ranges, and more.

Splitting Events

You'll often want to split one Event into two. After all, a MiniDV tape holds an hour of footage; a hard-drive camcorder holds five hours or more. On any given day, what you're importing to iMovie is probably made up of video you shot on different days. It will all wind up in one Event, unless you manually split it apart into different ones.

To split an Event, click its name in iMovie, and then proceed as shown in Figure 2-12.

Figure 2-12:
To split an Event, inspect the video clips within it by skimming and playing. When you find a clip that was obviously shot on a different day, as part of a different real-life event, click it. Then choose File → Split Event Before Selected Clip. iMovie places that clip, and all later ones, into a new Event. (The Event Browser is shown here, swapped to the top of the screen for clarity; see also Figure 2-13.)

Merging Events

You can combine Events, too. For example, if you import from your camcorder after each day at Disney World, you might want to combine it all into one Event at the end of the three-day vacation. To do that, see Figure 2-13.

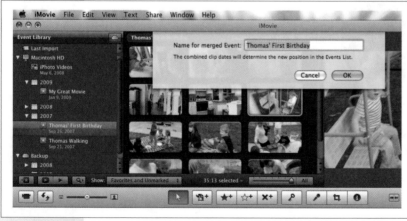

Figure 2-13:
To merge two Events, simply drag the name of one onto the name of another (top). iMovie asks what you want to name the newly merged Event; type a name, and then click OK. (Once again, the Event library is shown here swapped to the top of the screen.)

Renaming an Event

You rename an Event the same way you rename a project—double-click its existing name. The renaming rectangle appears, so you can edit or replace the name.

Deleting an Event

You delete Events the same way you delete projects: highlight an Event's name, and then press ⌘-Delete (or choose File → "Move Event to Trash").

iMovie gets rid of the Event and moves it to the Macintosh Trash. (You can even click the Trash icon on your Dock and *see* it inside the iMovie Temporary Items folder.)

Be careful, though. When you delete an Event, you're also deleting *all the video inside it!* All of those clips you so carefully imported are now sitting in the Trash, poised for extinction.

In a pinch, you can rescue them. Just open the Trash, open iMovie Temporary Items, and drag the Event's folder back into your Home → Movies → iMovie Events folder. The procedure is almost identical to what's depicted in Figure 2-4.

If you decide you're really finished with those clips, return to your desktop, choose Finder → Empty Trash, and then click OK. Now they're really, truly gone.

Four Ways to Remodel Your Workspace

iMovie '09 is refreshingly respectful of your screen real estate. It offers a bunch of different ways to maximize your working area without the hassle of buying a whole new monitor.

Hide the Projects or Events List

Once you're working on a movie, you don't need the list of projects staring you in the face. iMovie gets this. As soon as you open a project, iMovie hides the list of projects, giving you more space for the storyboard itself. (You can always bring the Projects list back by clicking the Project Library arrow in the top-left corner of your iMovie window.)

You can hide the Events list as well, and for the same reason: because when you're editing your Disney vacation video, you probably don't need to be staring at the list of other vacation footage. This time, choose Window → Hide Event Library, or click the Show/Hide Events List button (Figure 2-14). The list goes away, and the video-clip area expands.

To bring the Event list back, repeat the procedure. You can also use the Hide and Show commands in the Window menu to hide or show the Project Library and the Event Library.

> **TIP**   You can also make the *font* bigger in the Projects and Events lists (see page 60).

Make the Clips Smaller

In iMovie '09, your video clips are represented by *filmstrips*—multiframe horizontal strips whose lengths are proportional to the clip duration. You can read more about filmstrips in Chapter 3.

For now, it's enough to note that you can adjust the size of these filmstrips, both vertically and horizontally. Making them smaller gives you less information about what's in a clip, of course, but also makes more clips fit your screen.

See Figure 2-14 for instructions on making these adjustments.

> **NOTE** When you drag the filmstrip-length slider to its extreme-right position, every video clip is represented by *one* frame. The filmstrips' relative lengths are no longer represented; every clip has just one icon. This arrangement makes clips very easy to move around, resequence, and so on. It also makes iMovie more familiar, if you're used to working in previous versions of the program.

Adjust or Relocate the Viewer

The *Viewer*, in iMovie, is the playback window at the upper-right corner of the screen. If you have one monitor, it's always locked into the iMovie window. You can't drag it around freely, but you can change its size. If you have more than one monitor, you can use the secondary display to show the Viewer full screen.

To resize the Viewer, choose from the Window → Viewer submenu: either Small, Medium, or Large. Or better yet, learn the keyboard shortcuts for the sizes so you can flip between them while you work: ⌘-8, ⌘-9, and ⌘-0.

Thumbnail size   Filmstrip length (Projects)

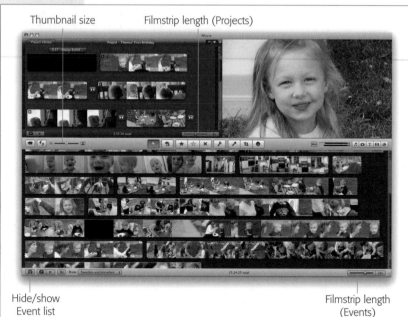

Hide/show
Event list

Filmstrip length
(Events)

Figure 2-14:
You can change the look of iMovie rather radically. You can hide the Event list (bottom left). To adjust the height of your filmstrips, drag the Thumbnail Size slider; it affects the filmstrips in both the Event browser and in the storyboard. To adjust the horizontal size of your filmstrips, drag the slider at the lower-right of the storyboard or Event Browser. At its far-left setting, each frame of a filmstrip represents a half-second of video. At its far-right setting, each clip is represented by a single frame.

The advantage of a large Viewer is, of course, that you get the best view of your movie as you work. The disadvantage is that a large Viewer eats up screen space. On smaller screens, it squishes down the Events area so much that you have to do more scrolling.

TIP For more gradations of size and control, you can resize the viewer by dragging the central, horizontal iMovie toolbar up or down. Use any blank spot as a handle.

If you're lucky enough to have a second monitor attached to your Mac, you can shove the Viewer out of the iMovie window altogether. Choose Window → "Viewer on Secondary Display". Now the preview fills the screen of your second monitor, giving you not only more editing room, but a much bigger Viewer as well. (Don't feel guilty if you buy a second monitor just for this feature. Many pro editors insist on having a second display to preview their edits.)

Swap the Two Clip Areas

When you first fire up iMovie, the storyboard area, where you actually build your movie, is fairly small. It's wedged in between the Project Library and the Viewer.

The source-clips area, on the other hand, gets far more space, because it doesn't have the Viewer to contend with.

As you work on your movie, therefore, you may want to *swap* these two areas. You may wish that the *storyboard* could be the one with room to run, especially in the later stages of editing.

In that case, choose Window → "Swap Events and Projects", or click the *Swap button* shown in Figure 2-15.

NOTE It probably goes without saying, but the first and most important step you can take to avoid having to use iMovie's scroll bars is to make the iMovie window itself as big as it can go! To do that, choose Window → Zoom, or click the little round, green Zoom button in the upper-left corner of the window.

Figure 2-15:
When you hit the Swap button, iMovie swaps the storyboard and Event Browser areas, complete with an animated "funneling" effect to make sure you understand how you've just flopped the iMovie layout upside-down. (For slow-motion fun, press the Shift key while you click the Swap button.)

Building the Movie

Whether you're working on your Mac or in a multimillion-dollar Hollywood professional studio, film editing boils down to three tiny tasks: selecting, trimming, and rearranging *clips*. Of course, that's like saying that there's nothing more to painting than mixing various amounts of red, yellow, and blue. The art of video editing lies in your decisions about which clips you select, how you trim them, and what *order* you put them in.

When you get right down to it, iMovie boils down to two big storage places for video clips. There's the *Event browser*, usually the bottom half of the screen, where all your raw, unedited video shots live. And there's the *storyboard*, usually the top half, which is where you assemble and edit your masterpiece.

At its simplest, then, iMovie editing is all about this three-step process:

1. **Review your video in the Event Browser and find the good parts.**

2. **Add those chunks to the storyboard, where iMovie plays them in one seamless pass, from left to right.**

3. **Add crossfades, titles (credits), music, and effects.**

This chapter is dedicated to showing you the mechanics of the first two tasks: selecting raw footage, and adding it to your movie. The following chapters cover the last step.

Phase 1: Review Your Clips (Skim + Play)

Video editing always starts out with a pile of raw, unedited footage. In iMovie's case, that's the bunch of clips in the Event Browser. Click an Event's name to see what video is inside.

Filmstrips

In iMovie '09, every imported camcorder shot is represented by a *filmstrip*—a horizontal bar whose length represents the duration of the clip. The filmstrip is made up of individual sample frames from the clip.

> **NOTE** If a filmstrip is too wide for the iMovie window, it wraps around to the next line. A ragged filmstrip edge tells you that it's been wrapped in this way. That ragged edge is the video version of a hyphen.

Each of these frames represents, for example, 5 seconds of actual video. So a 30-second video clip would appear as a filmstrip that's six frames long (Figure 3-1).

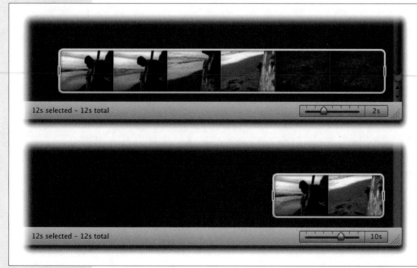

Figure 3-1:
Top: This filmstrip is 12 seconds long, so with the slider set to "2 seconds," each frame stands in for 2 seconds of video. That's why there are six frames.

Bottom: If you adjust the slider, you can change how many seconds of video each frame represents. Here, each frame represents a 10-second video chunk (or a part thereof), which is why there are now only two.

Using the slider at the lower-right corner of the window, you can adjust the relative lengths of the filmstrips in your Event Browser area. An identical slider appears beneath the project storyboard area, meaning that you can adjust the filmstrip lengths independently for these two clip display areas.

So what's the right setting for these sliders? That's totally up to you, but here are some suggestions:

- At the slider's extreme-right position, every video clip is represented by *one* frame. The filmstrips' relative lengths are no longer represented; every clip appears as an icon. This arrangement makes clips very easy to move around, resequence, and so on. It makes a very long movie fit on your screen without scrolling. It also makes iMovie a lot more familiar if you're used to working in previous versions of the program.

- At the slider's extreme-left position, each frame of the filmstrip represents a *half second* of video. At this position, you can actually make frame-by-frame edits; see the box on page 74.

- As you work, you can fiddle with the slider, zooming in and zooming out as necessary. When you need to tweak the precise starting point of a piece of audio, for example, you might want to zoom in (drag the slider to the left); when you want to get a good overview of a long movie, you might want to zoom out (drag the slider to the right).

Skimming

At this point, you're about to learn the two iMovie skills you'll use most of all: *skimming* and *playing*. Practice them, commit them to memory, make them automatic, and you'll absolutely fly through the editing process.

Skimming means moving your cursor across a filmstrip. Do not *drag*, which would mean pressing the mouse button. Just *point* with the mouse. Move the cursor across a filmstrip without clicking or dragging.

The *Playhead*—a vertical line, the height of the filmstrip—moves along with your cursor. And as you skim, the Viewer window shows the underlying video playing back at high speed—or medium speed, or slow speed, depending on your cursor speed. (You also see the same video playing within the filmstrip itself, beneath your cursor.)

> **TIP**   Skimming also plays the *sound* of whatever clip you're examining—fast or slow, forward or reverse. Usually, that's helpful. But if the audio is driving you crazy, you can shut it up. Click the Audio Skimming button, shown in Figure 3-2, so that it turns into a faded version of itself. Or choose View → Audio Skimming (⌘-K) so that the checkmark disappears. Repeat the process to turn audio skimming back on.

Skimming may take some getting used to, because it's such an unusual computer technique; it's probably the first time in history that moving the mouse without clicking has done *anything* besides, well, moving the cursor to a new spot. But it means that you can control not only the speed of the playback, but also the direction—forward or reverse—in real time, almost effortlessly.

UP TO SPEED

Secrets of the Filmstrip

When you stop and think about it, a filmstrip behaves just like a miniature QuickTime movie—and, in fact, that's precisely what it is.

You know how, after you import video, iMovie grinds to a halt and displays a message for several minutes that says, "Generating thumbnails"? What it's actually doing is creating a little tiny QuickTime movie, 190 by 60 pixels, for use as the filmstrip for that clip. When you skim by moving your pointer, all you're really doing is playing

back that QuickTime movie. You can even see these thumbnail movies. They're sitting right there in your Movies → iMovie Events → [Name of the event] → Movie Thumbnails folder. (Look, but don't touch. Leave these miniatures alone.)

iMovie's most impressive stunt, in other words, is the way it lets you work with these miniatures as a representation for the enormous, full-frame clips—and plays the big ones back on command.

Skimming works anywhere fine filmstrips are found—either in the Event Browser or in the project storyboard (Figure 3-2).

> **TIP**   You may sometimes wish that you could use the cursor as, well, a *cursor* instead of always making stuff play back. You may wish, for example, that you could freeze the frame as you skim—"Stay on this frame for just a sec"—while you go off to do something else with the cursor. You can. When you get to the spot you want to freeze, hold down the Control key. iMovie turns off skimming (leaves the same video frame on the screen) until you release the Control key.

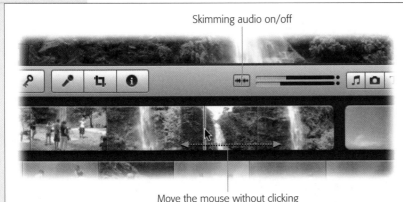

Skimming audio on/off

Move the mouse without clicking

Figure 3-2:
When you skim, you move the cursor across the face of a filmstrip without clicking. It's a fast, simple way to find out what's in a clip without having to sit through a full playback. Click the Audio button to turn off the audio scrubbing sound, which can be annoying.

Playback

Skimming is great for quickly getting the gist of what's in your captured clips. But unless you're some kind of quasi-mechanical cyborg, you'll find it very difficult to skim at exactly the right speed for *real-time* playback.

GEM IN THE ROUGH

Playhead Info

One nice thing about working with *digital* video is that every frame of every shot is, behind the scenes, date- and time-stamped. (This presumes, of course, that you set your camcorder's internal clock when you bought it!) Years later, you can return to some captured video and see when, exactly, you filmed it.

Ordinarily, iMovie hides this information, on the assumption that the screen is quite busy enough already. (Besides, you may already have asked it to show the dates of your imports right in the Events list, as described on page 60.)

To see the dates of your video, choose View → Playhead Info, or just press ⌘-Y. Now when you skim, a handy info balloon floats above your Playhead that says, for example, "Sunday, February 10, 2008, 4:35 PM." It also shows how many seconds into the clip your pointer is. If you're skimming within a *project* (an assembled video), the balloon also tells you the timecode (in minutes:seconds: frames) for that point in your project.

If iMovie has analyzed the video for stabilization (page 154), the balloon tells you that, too. It also tells you if the segment you're skimming is too shaky to stabilize. Press ⌘-Y again to hide the balloon.

Fortunately, iMovie can also play back clips all by itself, at the proper speed. To do that, use the space bar on your keyboard as the start/stop control. Hitting the space bar always begins playing video at the position of your cursor. And it always stops when you press the space bar again.

Once you've mastered that difficult technique, you're ready for the real gem: using skimming and playback *together*. It works like this: Point at a filmstrip with your mouse, skimming as you scan around, looking for the part you want to watch. When you get close to the right spot, tap the space bar. Playback begins from the precise position of your mouse.

Tap the space bar to stop playback, then move your mouse to another spot, and tap the space bar again. In this way, you can jump around, spot-inspecting your clips, or even *pieces* of your clips, without ever touching the mouse button—and without ever having to wait.

> **TIP** Actually, there are four other ways to play back a source clip or your movie in progress, complete with corresponding keyboard shortcuts. Page 84 has details on all four:
>
> • Play the selected chunk (/ key).
> • Play from the beginning (\ key).
> • Play the 2 or 6 seconds around your cursor ([or] key).
> • Play full screen (⌘-G).

Phase 2: Select the Good Bits

The reason you're reviewing the clips in the Event Browser, of course, is to find the good parts—the highlights, the pieces you want to include in your finished movie. Once you've selected a chunk, you can drag it into the storyboard to make it part of your movie.

GEM IN THE ROUGH

The Mighty Undo

As programs go, iMovie is a forgiving one. Its Edit → Undo (⌘-Z) command is an *unlimited* Undo command, meaning that you can retrace (undo) your steps, one at a time, working backward all the way back to the moment when you opened iMovie. (You can even unimport a clip from your camcorder!)

There's an Edit → Redo command, too (Shift-⌘-Z), so you can undo your undoing.

Selecting comes in handy for other purposes, too. As you'll read in the next chapter, you can designate part of a clip as either a Favorite (a snippet you know you'll want to come back to later) or as a Reject (a worthless shot). These steps, too, require that you first *select* the piece of clip that you want to flag.

Since selecting is such a critical step in iMovie moviemaking, Apple made sure you had all kinds of different ways to make a selection. The following pages review them one by one.

Select by Dragging

The first selection method is the one you'll probably use the most often: dragging. That is, slide the cursor across some footage while pressing the mouse button, just the way you'd select text in a word processor.

iMovie indicates which part of a clip you've selected by surrounding it with a yellow rectangle (Figure 3-3). The bottom edge of the iMovie window shows you how many seconds' worth of video you've highlighted, relative to the original clip. Once you've made a selection this way, you can adjust it; see page 75.

Figure 3-3:
You can highlight a piece of a clip by dragging across it. iMovie shows you what you've selected by enclosing it with a yellow boundary.

Select 4-Second Chunks

iMovie makes it easy to build your movie from video snippets that are all exactly the same length—4-second chunks, for example. The iMovie online help says, over and over again, that using chunks of the same duration throughout your movie creates "an evenly paced project."

Unless you're creating a music video of snowboarders, however, using all 4-second chunks also creates an artificially limiting project. Real-life events don't unfurl in consistent lengths. Still, having the ability to select tidy 4-second (or 2-second, or 10-second) chunks is occasionally handy—when you want to make the video match the chord changes in the background music, for example. To choose a 4-second chunk, just click a filmstrip in the Event Browser (without dragging). Your click marks the starting point; iMovie instantly selects the following four seconds of video.

> **TIP** You can change the factory setting, 4 seconds, to any length between 1 and 10 seconds. To do that, choose iMovie → Preferences, click the Browser tab, and drag the "Clicking in Event browser selects:" slider (Figure 3-4).

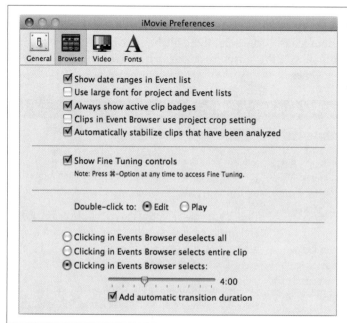

Figure 3-4:
What does a single click on a filmstrip in the Event Browser mean? That's up to you. Out of the box, it means "Select 4 seconds" (or whatever duration you choose using the slider). But you can have it mean, "Select the whole clip" if you prefer.

Selecting Entire Clips

In some cases, you may find that all of this dragging or 4-second-clicking business is just too much fussiness—that you really want to select *entire clips* from the Event Browser. Depending on the situation, you can select an entire clip in any of three ways:

- *Option-click* a filmstrip to highlight the whole thing.

- Click to select *part* of a clip, and then choose Edit → Select Entire Clip (⌘-A).

- Finally, if you *never* use that 4-second-clip selection feature, you can tell iMovie that one click on a filmstrip *always* selects the whole thing, even without the Option key. To do that, choose iMovie → Preferences, then click the Browser tab. Turn on "Clicking in Events Browser selects entire clip" (Figure 3-4) and then close the Preferences window.

NOTE These instructions apply only to selections in the Event Browser. When you click a clip in your *project storyboard*, you *always* select the entire clip.

Selecting Multiple Clips

It's often useful to be able to select *more* than one clip at a time. Imagine how much faster it can be to work with clips—delete them, drag them, cut and paste them, mark them as Favorites or Rejects, and apply keywords to them—all at once.

Clips in the storyboard now behave just like icons in the Finder. For example:

- **To highlight all the filmstrips.** Press ⌘-A (the equivalent of the Edit → Select All command).

- **To highlight random icons.** If you want to highlight, for example, only the first, third, and seventh clips in the storyboard, start by clicking icon No. 1. Then ⌘-click each of the others.

POWER USERS' CLINIC

Frame-Accurate Editing

If you're accustomed to a traditional timeline, like the kind found in iMovie HD, the storyboard in iMovie '09 could make editing feel fat-fingered. You might throw up your hands and decide that frame-precise editing is impossible. Happily, this isn't the case.

Modern digital video flashes about 30 pictures per second to create the illusion of motion. If you wanted to be able to edit down to a specific frame, then, you'd need to be able to zoom in close enough to see those 30 individual frames per second. It sure looks at first as though iMovie works in much larger chunks.

But you can indeed make those precise adjustments. First, zoom way in, using the "Frames per thumbnail"

slider at the lower-right corner of the window. In fact, if you drag this slider all the way to the left, each frame of the filmstrip represents a *half second* of video.

Then, if you drag the end of the yellow selection boundary carefully and slowly, you can actually feel it snap against *individual frames* of the recording—15 times for every filmstrip frame, in fact.

Let's see—each frame of your filmstrip represents half a second, and there are 15 snaps per frame. Sure enough, that's true frame-accurate editing. (The Shift-arrow key tip that appears on page 76 offers another method, one that doesn't require zooming in first.)

- **To remove a clip from the selection.** If you're highlighting a long string of icons and click one by mistake, you don't have to start over. Instead, just ⌘-click it again, so that the highlighting disappears. (If you do want to start over, you can deselect all selected clips by clicking any empty part of the window.)

  The ⌘ key trick is especially handy if you want to select *almost* all the icons in a window. Press ⌘-A to select everything in the storyboard, then ⌘-click any unwanted icons to deselect them.

- **To highlight consecutive clips.** Click the first clip you want to highlight, and then Shift-click the last one. All the clips in between are automatically selected, along with the two you clicked. (This one works in both the storyboard *and* the Event Browser.)

Adjusting a Selection

Once you've highlighted a portion of a filmstrip, you're not stuck with that yellow boundary just the way it is. You can adjust it within the filmstrip in any of four ways:

- Drag the vertical end handles of the yellow border to the right or left to select more or less of the clip.

- Shift-click another spot in the filmstrip. The nearest edge of the yellow border jumps to the location of your click, which makes the selection longer or shorter. Pressing Shift-arrow key (right or left) does the same thing.

- Drag the top or bottom edge of the yellow border to move the *entire* border, sliding it around without changing its length, on the filmstrip. This technique selects a new chunk of footage.

- Press the right or left arrow keys to slide the selection border right or left one frame at a time.

Figure 3-5 shows these techniques.

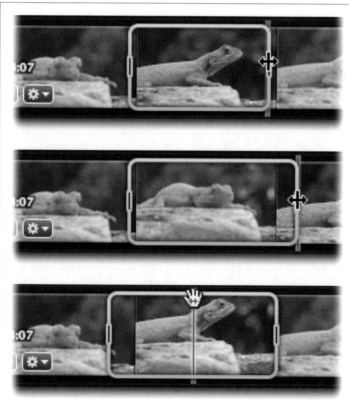

Figure 3-5:
Top: You can adjust the start or end points of a selection by dragging the side handles.

Middle: You can Shift-click to extend, or shrink, the right or left edge of the border. (iMovie adjusts whichever end of the border is closest to your Shift-click.)

Bottom: You can use the top or bottom edge of the yellow border as a handle to slide the entire selection area horizontally, without changing its duration. (You can also press the left or right arrow keys.)

TIP   These tips are great for making rough edits. For much finer control, get to know the new Precision Editor (page 96).

Playing a Selection

As you know, tapping the space bar always begins playing a video clip *at the position of the cursor*. But when you're making a selection, fiddling with that yellow border, that's not always what you want. In fact, it's probably *not* what you want.

A much more useful keystroke would be one that means, "Play what I've selected." And that's what the / key is for. (That's the slash next to the period key.) Tap it once to play whatever is selected; tap a second time to stop playback.

Deselecting

To *deselect* whatever's selected—that is, to take away the yellow border entirely—use any of these three techniques:

• Click anywhere in the dark gray background.

• Choose Edit → Select None.

• Press Shift-⌘-A.

Actually, there's another way, too, but it involves a little back story; see the box "The Arrow-Key Trick."

GEM IN THE ROUGH

The Arrow-Key Trick

By tapping the right or left arrow keys, you can "walk" through a clip frame by frame, as though you're watching the world's least interesting slideshow. You'll even hear "one frame" of the audio, if you've got the audio turned on.

Hold down these arrow keys steadily to make the frame-by frame parade go by faster—on a fast Mac, in fact, you get real-time playback when you hold down the arrow keys.

If you add the Shift key when you press the arrow, you make the nearest yellow selection border snap to your Playhead position. That's handy when you want to fine-tune a selection. You can slap the yellow border around a certain clip, walk with the arrow keys to see if there might be a better ending point, and—when you're about to land on just the right frame—press *Shift*-arrow. The closest vertical end of the yellow border snaps to the current frame.

In time, you can get extremely good at finding or selecting exact frames in a particular piece of footage by just mastering the arrow-key shortcuts. (These shortcuts work only when the clip isn't playing.)

Phase 3: Build the Storyboard

The project storyboard is the large work area that starts out at the top of the screen, as shown in Figure 3-6. The key to building a movie is moving your selected video bits from the Event Browser into this storyboard.

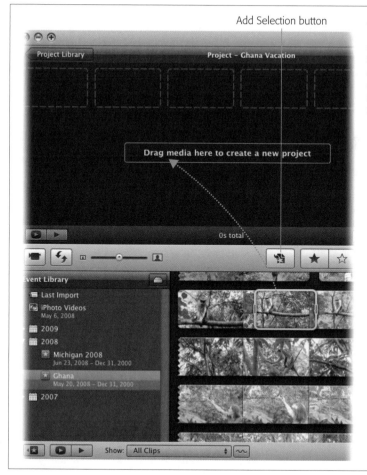

Add Selection button

Figure 3-6:
When the storyboard area is fresh and new, the message "Drag media here to create a new project" appears. (It means "drag movies here," of course.) But clicking the Add Selection button, or pressing the letter E, works just as well.

Adding to the End of the Storyboard

Most people, most of the time, build a movie by reviewing the raw footage from left to right—from beginning to end—and choosing bits, in sequence, to include in the edited masterpiece. In such cases, you'll want to add your selected clip or clips to the *end* of your storyboard.

iMovie offers two ways to do that. Select some video in the Event Browser, and then do one of these things:

- Press the letter E key.

- Click the Add Selection button (identified in Figure 3-6).

- If you have a Mac laptop with a multitouch trackpad (for example, a recent MacBook or MacBook Pro), swipe upward on your trackpad with three fingers.

In any case, you'll see the selected chunk(s) of video fly from the Event Browser to the *end* of your storyboard.

> **TIP** It's perfectly legal to add multiple clips to the storyboard at once; just Shift-click to select several filmstrips in the Event Browser first. But if you do so, iMovie scolds you: "You may achieve better results by individually adding only the best segments of your video." Yeah, yeah, we get it— less is more.

WORKAROUND WORKSHOP

When One Click Means "Deselect"

The way iMovie comes from the factory, *one click* on any clip in the Event Browser selects a piece of it. Four seconds of it, to be exact.

That's pretty unusual behavior, if you think about it. After all, one click in a word processor doesn't select four words; one click in Photoshop doesn't select four inches of a photo; and so on. In fact, what one click *usually* means in a creative program—word processor, Photoshop, and so on—is, "*Deselect* everything."

Apple's programmers must have had quite a discussion about this point: What should a single click in the Event Browser do? In the end, they went with the "4-second selection" thing, remaining true, as always, to the over-arching

goal of rapid movie assembly. But at least they've acknowledged the weirdness of that choice. And for anyone who's a little freaked out by the appearance of that 4-second yellow border every time they click, Apple has built in a way out.

Choose iMovie → Preferences. In the Browser tab, turn on "Clicking in Event browser deselects all". Then close the Preferences dialog box. From now on, one click anywhere in the Event Browser (except inside a yellow selection border) deselects everything. Of course, you can still select portions of clips (by dragging across them) or entire clips (by Option-clicking them); you just won't be surprised by the yellow border when you *don't* expect it.

To check the result, point to the storyboard (without clicking) just before the spot where the new video has landed, and then press the space bar.

Adding to the Middle

You don't *have* to add selected video to the end of the storyboard. You can also place it between two existing clips, smack in the middle of an existing clip, or even superimposed on a clip. These options are all part of a new feature in iMovie '09 called Advanced Drag and Drop. (You can read more about it on page 79.)

To add a chunk of footage between two clips, just drag the selected chunk (using anything inside the yellow border as a handle) right up into the storyboard. When iMovie shows you a green vertical line indicating where the clip will go, release the mouse (Figure 3-7 shows what this green line looks like). The chunk of video slips right in between the surrounding clips.

If you drop your chunk *on top* of a clip in your storyboard rather than between clips, iMovie displays the Drag and Drop menu. Its options include Insert, which splits the underlying clip into two pieces, and drops the chunk you added in between them.

Figure 3-7:
Once you've highlighted some video (bottom), you can drag it into position anywhere in the storyboard–in the gap between two existing clips, for example, or even right in the middle of an existing clip. In that case, iMovie splits the existing clip in half, and puts the new footage between the split pieces.

Advanced Insert Options

Suppose you're editing a project with some music, and you've worked hard to get the timing of the cuts to match up with the music. (Let's say you worked that hard because you haven't yet discovered the Beat Markers covered on page 207.) But as you're previewing your masterpiece, you realize that the clip of driving to the baseball game is just plain dull. You have something much more interesting to replace it with, but you know that unless your replacement is exactly the same length as the original shot, it will mess up the timing of your entire project.

iMovie offers three ways to replace a clip with a better one of the *exact same length*. If you haven't already done so, turn on the Advanced Tools (see the box on page 80). Select your replacement footage, drag it to your storyboard, and drop it onto the boring clip. In the Drag and Drop menu that appears, the following, confusingly named options appear:

POWER USERS' CLINIC

Show Advanced Tools

If your Drag and Drop menu gives you only four options, you're missing out on a bunch of iMovie '09's best features. Remember the Green Screen? Picture-in-Picture? These, and many other handy doodads become available only when you turn on Advanced Tools.

Evidently, iMovie's designer felt that revealing all of iMovie's goodies from the beginning would overwhelm the tremulous beginner and so he buried a lot of the good stuff. When you first run iMovie, a long list of buttons, commands, and features is hidden from you.

To make them appear, choose iMovie → Preferences. On the General tab, turn on Show Advanced Tools. Close the Preferences window.

You've just unleashed new iMovie capabilities all over the program; you'll read about them in the appropriate chapters of this book. Among them: iMovie now offers more than twice as many options when you drag footage or pictures on top of your project clips.

A cynic might complain that hiding half the features actually *creates* more confusion than it eliminates; in essence, there are two iMovies, and the novice may not realize that. But in any case, now you know how to turn those advanced features on or off.

- **Replace** replaces the entire underlying clip with the selection you're adding, no matter how long either one is. This option does *not* match lengths, and will alter your project's timing.

- **Replace from Start** resizes the incoming clip to match the length of the replaced clip—by adding, to the part you had selected, more footage to the *right*. It resizes the incoming clip by adding more footage to the end. (See Figure 3-8.)

So if the replaced clip is 8 seconds long, and you've selected only 4 seconds of the incoming clip, iMovie extends the incoming video by another 4 seconds (if there's unused footage available). Alternatively, if the incoming selection is *longer* than 8 seconds, iMovie *cuts* from the end of it to make it match the duration of the original clip.

NOTE   If the incoming clip isn't long enough to be extended in this way, iMovie warns you that the result will shorten your movie.

- **Replace from End** is a lot like Replace from Start, except that it resizes the incoming footage by extending your selection to the *left* (Figure 3-8, third from top). So if the clip being replaced is 8 seconds long, but the replacement selection is only 4 seconds long, iMovie extends your selection by including 4 seconds of footage toward the *beginning* of the selection. If the incoming video is longer than the original, on the other hand, the first part of it gets lopped off.

- **Replace at Playhead** is the same as the other "Replace from" options, but uses the start of your selected footage as a sort of anchor. iMovie deposits this anchor at the Playhead, and then extends or shortens the selection in both directions, as necessary, to fill the space formerly occupied by the replaced clip.

Original selection

Replace from Start

Footage added to end

Replace from End

Footage added to beginning

Replace at Playhead

Footage added to both ends

Figure 3-8:
You can replace clips in your project without having to select exactly the right amount of video from a clip in the Event Browser. In this example, you're replacing an 8-second project clip.

Top: You've selected only 4 seconds of video in the Event browser.

Second from Top: If you use Replace from Start, iMovie adds four more seconds of footage to the end of your clip, so that it will have the same length as the clip it replaced. (The little orange line shows what event footage has been added to your project.)

Third from top: If you use Replace from End, then instead of extending the selection by adding 4 seconds at the end of the clip, iMovie adds 4 seconds at the beginning of the clip.

Bottom: If you use Replace at Playhead, iMovie adds footage to the front and the end of the incoming clip. The amount of footage added to either end depends on where your Playhead was when you dropped the incoming clip.

TIP   If your resized footage doesn't display the moment just right, you can adjust it using the handy Clip Trimmer, covered on page 90.

The Orange Stripe

Each time you add some source video to your edited movie, iMovie slaps an orange stripe across the bottom of the original clip in the Event Browser. That's a reminder that you've *used* this segment in your project. As your work proceeds, you'll be able to tell, with a glance at your Event Browser, what proportion of the original video you've used in the finished opus.

Now, remember that all of your edited movies—your *projects*—draw upon the same well of source video on your computer. What's cool, therefore, is that iMovie memorizes the orange striping differently for every project. If you've used a different set of Little League footage in each of three projects, then you'll see the stripes jump around in the Event Browser as you click each project in turn.

> **TIP** An easy way to select a chunk of Event footage already used in your project is to double-click the orange stripe. iMovie automatically selects *just* the striped footage.

Don't Remember to Save

You don't have to save your work. iMovie '09 automatically saves as you go. (It doesn't even have a Save command.)

Phases 2–3 (Alternate): Paint-to-Insert

Having slogged this far into the chapter already, you might think that iMovie offers quite enough ways to drop footage into your movie. But believe it or not, there's yet another method.

This one makes throwing together a movie *crazy* fast. It turns your cursor into a sort of magic paintbrush. As you drag across filmstrips in the Event Browser, any segment that you "paint across" with your mouse instantly becomes part of your movie. You'll never see any yellow borders. It's not select-and-then-place; it's *selectandplace*. One step, not two.

First, you need to turn on the Advanced Tools (page 80). You may not notice at first, but there are now several additional buttons in the toolbar across the center of the iMovie window (Figure 3-9).

Here's how to set up this advanced technique:

1. **Make sure that no video is selected in iMovie.**

   If you have video somewhere, then some of the toolbar icons appear in washed-out light gray. In that case, try tapping the Esc key, and/or choose Edit → Select None. When nothing is selected, the toolbar tools are black and gray, ready to be used.

2. **Click the Edit tool, or press the letter E key.**

   The Edit tool, better described now as the Paint-to-Insert tool, is identified in Figure 3-9.

Figure 3-9:
In paint-to-insert mode, the second toolbar icon (to the right of the standard arrow cursor tool) is permanently selected. Now you can drag across bits of footage at high speed, each time adding it to the end of your storyboard.

All that is setup. Now you're ready to go to work.

From now on, forget everything you've read about (1) selecting a chunk of video and then (2) adding it to the storyboard. Instead, any time you drag the mouse across a filmstrip, iMovie adds it *instantly* to the end of the storyboard. If you know what you're doing, you can whip together a movie made of 15 shots with only 15 swipes of the mouse. This trick takes some getting used to. You have to train yourself to never touch the mouse button except when you're prepared to commit something to the finished movie.

You should still use the skim-and-play technique to identify the chunks you want to add; performed correctly, skimming and playing doesn't involve the mouse button at all. (Point and tap the space bar; point and tap the space bar.) When you've found a worthy chunk, *then* drag across it with the mouse button down. Or, faster still, Option-click a filmstrip to add the entire thing to the project.

If you add something by mistake, or if you undershoot or overshoot, remember iMovie's all-powerful Undo command. Hit ⌘-Z to rewind your last step and try again. To turn off paint-to-insert mode, press the letter E key (or click the Edit Tool icon) again. You're back in yellow-border mode.

Phase 4: Fine-Tune the Edit

Once you've got a rough cut of your storyboard, you may consider the Event Browser a lot less necessary. Your work focus will probably shift to the storyboard from here on out. Now, in other words, might be a good time to hide the Projects list and move the whole storyboard to the wider space at the *bottom* of the iMovie window, as described in the previous chapter.

The rest of this chapter explores a few of the ways you can fine-tune the movie in progress.

Storyboard Playback

You can use instant playback to spot-check your storyboard work in the Viewer window. Since you'll probably be doing a lot of this, iMovie offers multiple techniques:

- **Anyplace playback.** Point (without clicking) to any spot; press the space bar to begin playback. Press the space bar again to stop.

   TIP   As you near completion of your movie, you might want to make the Viewer bigger, so you see your work closer to full size. See page 64.

- **Selection playback.** Make a selection. (Either click a clip once to select the whole thing, or drag across it to choose just a part.) Then press the forward slash key (/, next to the period key) to play back *just that selection* from the beginning. Press / again to stop.

- **Two-second (or six-second) playback.** Here's a supremely handy feature: You can tap the [or] keys to play back the 3 or 6 seconds, respectively, immediately before and after the position of your cursor. It's sort of like a skim-and-play all at once.

   If some video is highlighted with the yellow boundary, then these keystrokes play back either the *first* second (or 3 seconds) of the selection, or the *last* second (or 3 seconds), depending on which is closer to your cursor.

   TIP   You can press these bracket keys even when your mouse button is down in the process of making a selection. That's a fantastic way to gauge whether you've selected exactly the right bit.

- **Whole-storyboard playback.** Press the backslash key (\, above the Return key) to play the *entire* storyboard from the beginning. Press \ again (or the space bar) to stop.

   NOTE   There are menu equivalents for all three of these commands in the View menu: Play, Play Selection, and "Play from Beginning". But it's far more efficient to use the keyboard shortcuts.

No matter how you started playback, you can always stop by clicking in the iMovie window or tapping the space bar.

Full-Screen Playback

You can make the Viewer window bigger to get a more detailed view of your video using the ⌘-8, ⌘-9, and ⌘-0 keystrokes; see page 64. But eventually, you'll want to treat yourself to iMovie's IMAX mode: *full-screen* playback. That's when all the controls and menus of iMovie itself disappear, and the video fills your entire monitor. Here again, iMovie offers different approaches:

- **Play from the pointer.** Point without clicking to any spot in the storyboard. Then press ⌘-G to begin *full-screen* playback of that selected video.

- **Play the entire storyboard.** Click the Full-screen Playback button (identified in Figure 3-10) to play your storyboard from the beginning. Choosing View → Play Full Screen does the same thing.

NOTE   In theory, ⌘-G is the keyboard equivalent for the View → Full Screen command. But they aren't, in fact, equivalent. ⌘-G is the *only way* to begin full-screen playback from a specific spot. If you choose View → Full Screen from the menu, iMovie begins playing the storyboard from the *beginning*. (It has to—since you moved your mouse to the menu, you're no longer pointing to a certain spot in the video!)

Figure 3-10:
Top: Click the Full Screen button to begin playback of your entire storyboard from the beginning.

Bottom: During full-screen playback, if you wiggle your mouse, you get the navigation filmstrip shown here at bottom. Click the filmstrip, then skim it or drag the mouse to jump to a new spot without exiting full-screen mode.

Once full-screen playback is underway, just moving your mouse produces the navigation strip shown in Figure 3-10. It starts out looking something like Cover Flow on the iPod or in iTunes, where all of your projects (if you were previewing a project) or your events (if you were previewing an event) appear as though they're flipping album covers. Here are the basics of how it works:

- Press the space bar to start and stop playback without exiting Full Screen mode. Or click the ▶ button at the left end of the navigation filmstrip.

- During playback, click another spot in the navigation filmstrip to jump there and pause.

- During playback, *double-click* another spot in the filmstrip to jump there *without* pausing.

- When you've paused playback, you can skim the navigation filmstrip (point without clicking) to explore the movie. Press the space bar to begin playback from any spot.

• Switch to a different event/project by either clicking one of the other filmstrips in the "cover flow," or by using the horizontal scrollbar underneath the clips.

You may have also noticed some other buttons on the left and right sides of the filmstrip. Their text labels don't appear unless you point to them without clicking, so here's a quick rundown of what they do:

• Switch between projects and events by clicking the ▣ button on the left of the filmstrip.

• Turn the Cover Flow (animated filmstrip-flipping) view on or off by clicking the ▫ button on the right of the filmstrip.

• The ▪ button hides and shows the navigator filmstrip after your mouse starts moving. If you let iMovie hide it, you have more room to preview your video.

When you're finished with full-screen playback, click the ⊗ button, or press the Esc key, to return to the iMovie window. (Or, if you wish that iMovie would exit Full Screen automatically after each playback, turn on that option by choosing iMovie → Preferences and visiting the General tab.)

> **NOTE** Usually, your camcorder's video has lower resolution than your Mac's screen. To fill your screen for playback, then, iMovie *stretches* the picture, which lowers its quality slightly. In a few other cases (for example, high-def video on a small laptop), the video may actually be too *big* for the screen. In that case, iMovie has to scrunch it *down* to fit.
>
> If you choose iMovie → Preferences and click the General tab, however, you can control all of this stretching and scrunching. The "Fullscreen playback size" pop-up menu lets you change the Entire Screen setting to Actual Size (the cleanest settings for video that's smaller than your screen), Half Size (best-looking if the video is bigger than the screen), or Double Size (good if you need to zoom in on low-rez footage from a still camera).

Rearranging Video

Unless your last name is Spielberg or Scorsese—and maybe even if it is—the first place you put a clip in the storyboard won't *always* be the best spot for it. Sooner or later, you'll wish you could move shots around in the film.

You can, if you know the secret.

1. **Select the part you want to move.**

   If it's an entire clip, simply click it in the storyboard. iMovie highlights the entire clip.

   If it's just part of a clip, drag to select the chunk you want. Fine-tune it with the arrow keys as described on page 76.

   > **TIP** At this point, consider adjusting the storyboard's zoom level (page 63) so you'll have finer control over where you're about to place the moved video.

2. **Drag the selection to its new location.**

Click carefully inside the outlined yellow-border area (shown in Figure 3-11) before you drag. When your cursor reaches the approximate destination, keep your finger on the mouse button, but move the cursor from side to side to find the precise target frame. Yes, you're actually skimming with the mouse button down, but don't let that confuse you.

You can drop the dragged clip in between two clips in the storyboard, but *not* right in the middle of a clip, as you can when adding footage from an Event. If you want to take one project clip and insert it in the middle of another project clip, just use the Copy or Cut commands discussed next.

Figure 3-11:
Rearranging scenes in the storyboard is a two step process. First, select what you want to move, whether it's a full clip or just part of one (top). Second, drag it where you want it to go, whether it's in between two clips or right in the middle of another clip (bottom).

Copying and Pasting Video

Dragging isn't the only way to move footage around in iMovie; the Copy, Cut, and Paste commands can feel more precise. These commands are also the *only* way to copy edited footage from one project to another.

> **NOTE** When you copy and paste clips, you're never duplicating files on your hard drive. So don't worry about eating up free space.

You already know how to indicate *what* you want to cut or copy; just use the selection techniques described on page 71.

Then use the Edit → Cut or Edit → Copy command (⌘-X or ⌘-C). Point where you want to paste the copied material (do not click), and then choose Edit → Paste (⌘-V). Presto! The cut or copied material appears at the position of your cursor, and shoves the rest of the movie to the right to make room.

POWER USERS' CLINIC

Comment Markers

As you're rearranging the furniture, you may find it useful to insert reminders about the different clips in your project. This can be especially handy if a lot of your clips look alike, such as footage of the video you shot of Grandpa sharing stories from the army. As useful as the little filmstrips are, they all look the same while you shuffle clips around.

To limit the potential confusion, iMovie offers you *comment markers*. These are little flags you can attach to a point in any project clip that let you type a brief note to yourself. They stay attached to the clip no matter where you move it, so you don't have to keep track of everything in your head.

Comment markers are considered an advanced feature, so you don't even see them until you've turned on Advanced Tools (page 80). Now when you go into your project, you see a tiny box in the top left corner of your storyboard. The box contains comment markers (brown,

as shown below) and chapter markers (orange with an arrow inside).

Just drag a comment marker from the little box onto any clip in your project. A text box becomes available inside the marker. Type in whatever words will help you remember; the comment marker stretches to show you as much of your note as it can.

To edit a comment marker, double-click it to open its text box. To move a comment marker to a new spot, just drag it there.

Shortening or Lengthening Clips

Almost nobody hits the camcorder's Record button at the precise instant when the action begins, or stops recording the instant the action stops. Life is just too unpredictable, not to mention animals, geysers, and children.

Most of the time, of course, you'll trim out the boring stuff in the Event Browser before you add it to the storyboard. Sometimes, though, you'll discover only *after* you've put the clips into the storyboard that the clip-shortening process isn't quite right. Maybe the shots are still *too* languorous, and should be shorter. Or the shots are *too* quick, and it's going to be hard for your audience to figure out what's going on.

In both cases, it would be nice to be able to lengthen or shorten a clip even after it's been placed in the storyboard.

> **NOTE**   "Lengthen a clip?" That's right. iMovie is a *nondestructive* editing program. No matter how much editing you do, iMovie never, ever changes the original imported video on your hard drive. For example, after you've shortened a clip by hacking a piece off the right end, you can later change your mind, even three Presidential administrations later. You can restore some or all of the missing footage, using the techniques described on these pages.

Fortunately, iMovie is crawling with ways to perform these adjustments, even after the clips are in the storyboard. They boil down to these approaches:

• Shorten a clip by selecting the part you want to *delete*.

• Shorten a clip by selecting the part you want to *keep*.

• Shorten, lengthen, or re-edit a clip in iMovie's Clip Trimmer window.

• Lengthen a clip by clicking iMovie's hidden Extend buttons.

> **NOTE** When you *shorten* a clip, all subsequent clips slide to the left to close up the gap. (That's called *ripple* editing.) On the other hand, when you lengthen a clip, exposing previously hidden footage, iMovie shoves all subsequent clips to the *right* to make room. Your movie, as a result, gets longer.

The following pages cover all four methods.

Select a Piece to Delete

Suppose a clip is running too long in your edited movie. Fortunately, having mastered the art of selecting a portion of a clip, as described earlier, you're ready to put it to work. You can shave off some footage from only one end of your clip, or even right from the middle. All you have to do is highlight the footage you want to delete, and then choose Edit → Cut (or press ⌘-X).

iMovie promptly trims away whatever was inside the yellow border. As a bonus, your invisible Clipboard now contains the snipped piece, which you're welcome to paste right back into the storyboard (at the position of your pointer) using the Edit → Paste command, in case you need it again.

> **TIP** You can also press the Delete key to get rid of the selected video. The difference is that the Delete key doesn't put the cut material onto the Clipboard, ready for pasting, as the Cut command does. On the other hand, the Delete/Clear command doesn't replace what's *already* on the Clipboard, unlike the Cut command.

If you're not prepared for it, the results can be startling. If you cut a chunk out of the middle of the clip, iMovie throws back at you the *two end pieces*—as two separate clips, side by side in the storyboard.

Select the Piece to Keep

If you want to trim some footage off *both* ends of a clip, it's quicker to highlight the part in the middle that you want to *keep*. That is, highlight the part you want, and then choose Edit → "Trim to Selection". (Or press ⌘-B. Why B stands for "trim to selection" is for you to figure out.) When you use this command, what used to be the selected part of the clip becomes, in effect, the *entire* clip. The clip is shorter now, as a tap on the space bar proves.

The Shortcut Menu

A lot of great commands appear in iMovie's shortcut menu. This menu appears wherever you right-click (or Control-click); it offers different options depending on where your cursor is at the time.

For example, if you're pointing to a partially selected project clip, the shortcut menu lets you delete that portion (Delete Selection), or delete everything *but* the selection ("Trim to Selection").

Some commands are available *only* via the shortcut menu. That's logical, since certain commands involve a reference to the Playhead, and so are useful only while skimming.

One such command is Trim to Playhead. Think of this command as iMovie's very own guillotine. Any time you choose this from the shortcut menu, the part of a clip *to the right* of your cursor gets the axe.

Similar Playhead-needy commands include Add Freeze Frame (page 242), "Add Still Frame to Project" (page 94), and a special version of Split Clip (page xx3). Put the shortcut menu to use, and you can have all kinds of hidden powers.

Play
Play Selection
Play from Beginning
Play full-screen
Cut
Copy
Delete Selection
Delete Entire Clip
Select Entire Clip
Trim to Selection
Split Clip
Detach Audio
Analyze for Stabilization
Add Comment Marker
Add Chapter Marker
Add Freeze Frame
Reveal in Event Browser
Reveal in Finder
Project Properties...

Use the Clip Trimmer

All right, the Delete and "Trim to Selection" commands—mirror images of each other—are both quick, efficient ways to *shorten* a clip in the storyboard. But what if you decide you've cropped out *too much*, and you want to restore some? Or what if you can't even grasp what you're looking at, and wish you could see the entire original clip?

That's what the Clip Trimmer is all about. You can open it in either of two ways:

- Point to a clip without clicking. Click the tiny gear icon that appears at its lower-left corner (Figure 3-12, top). Select Clip Trimmer from the list that appears.

- Click the clip in question and then choose Window → Clip Trimmer (⌘-R).

iMovie replaces the entire Event Library area with a new display, labeled Clip Trimmer. You can see it at bottom in Figure 3-12.

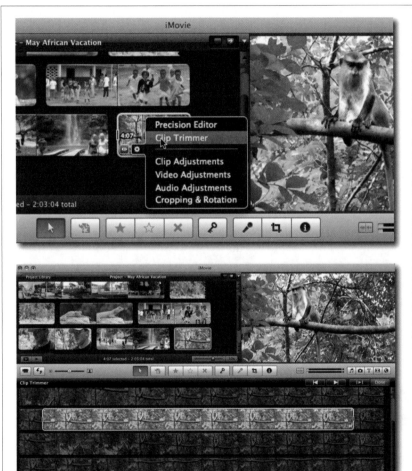

Figure 3-12:
Top: To open the Clip Trimmer, click the tiny gear button that appears when you point to a clip. (The number above it tells you how many seconds long the clip is at the moment.)

Bottom: In the Trim window, the yellow border shows which piece of the clip you're currently using in your movie. The darkened portions are the ones you've so far eliminated. Above the Trimmer window, the arrow between two lines plays your selection. The left and right arrows refocus the Clip Trimmer on the project clip that comes just before or after the current clip.

In essence, what you're seeing here is the full-length clip, just as it originally appeared in the Event Browser. The yellow border indicates which part you originally selected to include. You can use all the usual tricks to play back what's here, including skimming, hitting the space bar, or double-clicking. Or, in case you were just struck by a girder and have forgotten all of that, you can click the Play button that appears in the Trim window.

Your main business here is to readjust the selection border. Make it longer if you want to include more of the clip in your project, shorter if you want less. Or grab anywhere inside the yellow boundary and slide the entire thing horizontally to include an earlier or later portion (of the same duration). Page 75 details all the fun you can have with the yellow border.

> **TIP**   Press Option-left arrow or Option-right arrow to add one frame at a time to the video selection in the Trim window. (You're shifting either the beginning or the end of the yellow border, whichever is closest to your cursor.)

When you're finished with your reselection, click Done.

Fine-Tuning with the Extendo Buttons

The Trim window is a handy way to rechop a clip—especially if you want to *extend* the amount you're including in the project. But having to open a special editing window just to snap a few more frames onto a clip is a hassle.

Fortunately, there's another way to extend a cropped clip without having to bother with the Trim window: Use the Extendo buttons (what Apple calls the Fine Tuning buttons). To make them appear, you can use either the mouse or the keyboard:

- **Point to a clip** to make the tiny double-arrow icons appear in the corners (Figure 3-13) and then click one of them. (If you don't see the icons, they may have been turned off in Preferences.)

- **Point to either end of a clip**, and press ⌘-Option.

Extendo button

Figure 3-13:
Buttons appear in the corners of any storyboard clip that you've previously shortened from either end. Click one of these buttons to make the orange end-adjustment handles appear.

In either case, the ends of the selection border turn orange, and nearby filmstrips scoot away to make a little room. At this point, you can drag the orange handle to the left *or* right, either shortening the clip or (by revealing previously hidden footage) lengthening it by up to 1 second. As you drag the orange handle, numbers floating next to your cursor show you how long the clip will be and how many frames you're adding/subtracting.

To trim more than one second, you can either open the Trim window or just click and use the Extendo buttons again. And again. And again.

> **TIP** You can also *fine*-fine tune a clip's length with a secret keyboard shortcut. Press Option-left arrow or Option-right arrow. Each press makes the clip one frame shorter or longer. (You're changing either the beginning or the end of the clip, whichever is closest to your cursor.)

Splitting a Clip

The techniques described in the previous section work well when you want to remove some footage from a clip. Sometimes, however, it can be useful to split a clip *without* deleting footage in the process. For example, iMovie is capable of applying audio changes and video effects only to *entire clips*; if you want only *part* of your clip to get special treatment, you'll have to break that portion off into a standalone clip. Don't worry; it still looks like part of the bigger clip on playback.

> **TIP** If you were thinking of using Split Clip to insert something, maybe a picture, in the middle of a clip, save yourself the trouble and use the Advanced Drag and Drop feature discussed on page 79. For example, in a clip of a young snowboarder heading rapidly toward a ramp and then sailing into space, you could insert a quick shot of his parents' horrified faces faster with the Drag and Drop method.

Or you may just want to break off one piece of a clip to use somewhere else in the movie. The Split Clip command is exactly what you need in that case. Just make a selection in any storyboard filmstrip:

- **To chop the clip into two pieces**, select from the desired split point to the end (or beginning) of the clip.

- **To chop the clip into three pieces**, select whatever piece of it that you want to wind up as the *center* piece. The end pieces will wind up as separate clips.

Either way, you can use the Shift-arrow technique described on page 76 to find exactly the right spot. Then choose Edit → Split Clip. The results are shown in Figure 3-14.

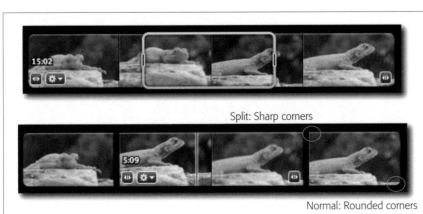

Split: Sharp corners

Normal: Rounded corners

Figure 3-14:
After you split a clip, you wind up with two or three pieces. (You can tell where these clips were split by examining the filmstrip corners; they're sharp rather than rounded.)

TIP If you change your mind immediately, you can always use the Undo command to take back that step. But if you split a clip and change your mind *much later*, after you've done a lot of other editing, iMovie can still accommodate you. Click either part of a split clip and choose Edit → Join Clip; iMovie plays marriage counselor and reunites it with its former soulmate, assuming that it's still adjacent. (If something else is now between them, get it out of the way so iMovie can do its job.)

GEM IN THE ROUGH

Split Clip at Playhead

If you grew up editing in previous versions of iMovie, you probably became accustomed to editing with the old Split Clip at Playhead command. To get at a good part in the middle of a clip, you'd cut off the front and back parts then delete them. These days, chiseling out the best parts of clips in this way is outdated, but the technique can still be useful for other things.

To split a project clip at the Playhead, skim to a split-worthy part and Control-click (or right-click) to bring up the shortcut menu. When you do this, iMovie selects the entire clip with its little yellow borders, but don't let that stop you. Choose Split Clip from the shortcut menu and—presto!—iMovie breaks the clip in two pieces right where your cursor was.

This trick works only with the shortcut menu, and *not* with Edit → Split Clip. It also doesn't work if just part of a clip is selected. In that case, the Split Clip command behaves normally, and slices up the clip along the yellow selection borders.

Cutaways

A *cutaway* is an important, basic editing technique. That's when someone on camera begins talking…and you hear him *keep* talking, even as the video switches to something different (that illustrates what he's saying). You see cutaways all the time on the nightly news, and in every documentary you've ever seen.

Creating cutaways before iMovie '09 was tricky. It involved separating audio from the person-talking video, cutting out a chunk of that video, trimming the replacement (cutaway) video to just the right length, and then sticking that into the gap in the person-talking video. You might as well be trimming an actual film reel and piecing it back together with tape!

Luckily, iMovie '09 makes cutaways ridiculously easy. Before you start, turn on the Advanced Tools (page 80), if you haven't by now. In the following discussion, you'll be working with what the pros call *A-roll* (the beginning video, usually of the person talking) and the *B-roll* (the soundless footage that illustrates what he's talking about). Then, to make a cutaway:

1. **Select your B-roll footage from the Event Browser.**

   This is whatever footage you want to cut away *to* while the audio of the A-roll plays underneath.

2. **Drag the B-roll selection onto your A-roll filmstrip in the project.**

When you do, the Drag and Drop shortcut menu appears.

3. **Click Cutaway.**

The B-roll clip is now glued to the top of the A-roll clip (Figure 3-15).

Figure 3-15:
Cutaway shots appear like gray-bordered clips casting a shadow on the main clip underneath. These are great for documentary-style interviews or news programs.

4. **Select your Cutaway clip, and then press Shift-⌘-M to mute it.**

You've just silenced any audio that came along with the B-roll clip, so it doesn't compete with the sound of the person talking.

Adjusting a Cutaway

To make adjustments to a cutaway clip, double-click it. The Inspector appears. Most of its controls are standard stuff for video clips—video effects (page 138), fast/slow/reverse (page 141), stabilization (page 154). But two of them are especially designed for cutaways, and they're very cool:

- **Fade in/Fade out.** You don't have to cut abruptly to the cutaway video; you can install a graceful crossfade into or out of it. If you click Manual, you can use the slider to specify how *quickly* it fades in and out.

- **Opacity.** Your cutaway video doesn't have to replace the talking-person video completely; it can, if you wish, appear *superimposed* on the talking-person video, as though it's translucent. It's a special effect you won't use often, but it's good to know it's there. Drag the Opacity slider to control *how* see-through the superimposed video looks.

When you're finished making these changes, click Done.

Removing a Cutaway

Just select the cutaway clip in your project and press Delete to get rid of it.

The Precision Editor

In editing jargon, a *cut* is the place where one clip ends and another begins—the crossroads where clips meet. A well-designed cut looks very professional, even if it's subtle. For example, you might cut between two birthday parties that happened in the last year. To make the cut really cool, you could move from one birthday to the next using the exact moment when the candles are blown out. One of your kids would lean down to blow out the candles, and the other would stand up smiling. The effect forges a connection between the two birthdays, even though they happened at different points in the year.

The Precision Editor, an innovative tool debuting in iMovie '09, makes cuts like these—cuts that would involve many steps in a professional editing tool—remarkably simple. Assuming you already have two clips needing a refined cut between them, using the Precision Editor on a cut would go something like this:

1. **Call up the Precision Editor.**

   You can get to the Precision Editor in several ways. The easiest way is to double-click the space between two clips. But if a clip is already selected, you can also choose Window → Precision Editor or press ⌘-/. You get the same effect by clicking the ✿ icon on the clip itself and choosing Precision Editor.

   NOTE   If you placed a *transition* between two clips (page 113), double-clicking the transition's icon brings up the Inspector for the transition. To get the Precision Editor instead, double-click the empty space just *above or below* the transition icon.

   The Precision Editor drops in, covering up your Event Library. What you see is a layered representation of your cut just like the one shown in Figure 3-16.

Show Extras   Show audio clip

Figure 3-16:
Behold the Precision Editor! The top layer holds the clips leading into a cut. The bottom layer contains the clips trailing the cut. Adjust the cut spot by dragging the vertical blue line. Adjust the clips surrounding the cut by dragging the clips themselves. The faint dots running along the bar between the layers represent the different cuts in your project.

2. **Adjust the cut point.**

The blue vertical line with the dot in the middle is the cut line; it represents the cut itself. You can drag it left or right to adjust its timing. Dragging to the right extends the leading clip and shortens the trailing clip. Drag left for the opposite effect.

3. **Adjust the clips surrounding the cut.**

You may like where the leading clip cuts out, but not where the trailing clip comes in. To adjust the clip itself, drag the clip left or right.

4. **Overlap the audio, if you like.**

Let's pretend the leading clip has someone describing a fun memory in Grandma's backyard, while the trailing clip shows the next generation running out of Grandma's backdoor to play. Click the Audio Tracks button to see the sound from the two clips, making them available for independent editing.

If you point to the spot where the blue line crosses the audio track (without clicking), you can sort of snap off that part of the cut line. Dragging the snapped-off part lets you specify where the audio should cut out. This means you can take the audio of the leading clip (memory about Grandma's backyard) and extend it into the video of the trailing clip (kids running out the backdoor to play) for a very nice effect. (Basically, this is another way to do the Cutaway audio trick just explained on page 94.) You can see all this in Figure 3-17.

Figure 3-17:
You can change the cut point for audio so that it comes in or leaves independently of the video. This kind of edit connects the two clips in a way that a regular cut can't. You might do this if you shot an interview, but you want the person's voice to start before she actually shows up on screen.

5. **Adjust the "extras."**

Not everything involved in a cut is video. You may have titles, songs, or photo cutaways involved in your cut masterpiece. Clicking the Show Extras button, identified in Figure 3-16, displays all of the other stuff involved in the edit. You can drag these elements left or right to adjust their timing, just as you can audio or video.

6. **Preview your edit.**

Previewing in the Precision Editor is just like previewing everywhere else. You can skim and play with all of the same commands covered on page 84.

NOTE   When skimming in the Precision Editor, be careful where you skim. Skimming over the grey middle bar shows you the cut. Skimming over a clip previews just the clip. Don't skim one of the clips, thinking you're seeing the cut!

7. **Go to the next cut, or click Done.**

Now that you have your cut worthy of an editing Oscar, you can go to other cuts by clicking the right or left arrow buttons, or by clicking the grey dots that run along the middle bar. Each dot represents a different cut.

If you're finished, just click Done or hit the Esc key on your keyboard.

Video Chunks: Keywords, Favorites, and Rejects

In iMovie '09, all the imported footage on all your hard drives is sitting there, like paints on a palette, to inspire your editorial brilliance. But that blessing is also a curse, because it's such a huge pile of video to manage—and a lot of it's dreck.

Fortunately, iMovie comes with a set of tools—unusual in a video editing program—that are specifically designed to help you sort and manage these vast chunks of video. Working in the Event browser, you can:

- Flag pieces of clips as your favorites, to make them easy to find.

- Flag pieces of your clips as rejects—bad footage that you'll either *probably* or *definitely* never want to incorporate into an edited project.

  The "probably" stuff you can just hide from view. The "definitely" stuff you can tell iMovie to delete, freeing up space on your hard drive, even if that entails snipping off only portions of clips.

- Flag pieces of clips with *keywords* of your choosing—your children's names, adjectives, characterizations like "action" or "moody"—whatever you like. Later, you can summon all matching keywords with a single click.

This short chapter explores these clip-flagging tools, and also describes the proper way to get rid of bad shots forever.

Marking Favorites and Rejects:
Two-Step Method

Most people, most of the time, flag a clip, or a piece of one, as a favorite or a reject using this technique:

1. **In the Event browser, select the video you like (or don't like).**

   You can use any of the selection techniques described on page 71. That is, you can select an entire clip, multiple clips, or only part of one.

2. **Flag it.**

   To flag the selection as a favorite, click the black star button (Figure 4-1) or just press the letter F on your keyboard.

   To flag it as a reject, either click the X icon, press the letter R key, choose Edit → Reject Selection, or press the Delete key.

   > **TIP**   You can also choose Edit → Reject Entire Clip (or press Option-Delete) to flag the *entire* clip as worthless. This method saves you a little time, because it means that you can select any old sloppy slice of the clip first, rather than highlighting the entire thing.

If you flag something as a favorite, it sprouts a green line across the top edge (Figure 4-1).

If you mark something as a reject, it sprouts a *red* line across the top edge—and promptly disappears from view. (If it doesn't disappear, you must have changed the pop-up menu shown in Figure 4-3 to say Show: All Clips.)

Figure 4-1:
Select some video and then click the black star button identified here. iMovie adds a green stripe, which designates a favorite shot.

Marking Favorites and Rejects:
One-Step Method

The usual method of flagging your best and worst footage takes only two steps. But believe it or not, even that's excessive in the eyes of Apple's Faster Editing team.

Hidden in the motley assortment of options known as the iMovie Advanced Tools lies another method, which reduces the favoriting and rejecting process down to *one* step.

To set up this method, turn on "Show advanced tools," as described on page 80.

Now have a look at the horizontal toolbar that divides the iMovie screen. It has sprouted a few additional tools, as shown in Figure 4-2. But you're not interested in the new icons. You're interested in the new behavior of three *original* buttons, the ones near the center—solid star, hollow star, and X. They now represent virtual *paintbrushes* that turn anything you touch with your cursor into a favorite or a reject.

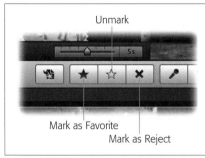

Unmark

Mark as Favorite

Mark as Reject

Figure 4-2:
The three icons identified here let you "paint" portions of your Event browser filmstrips with green highlighting (meaning "favorite") or red highlighting ("reject"). You don't have to select and then click the button.

For example, here's an amazingly fast way to zoom through a freshly imported pile of footage, marking favorite scenes as you go:

1. **Click the Favorite button (the black star), or press the letter F key.**

   The black star icon darkens to show that you've selected it. Your cursor is now loaded with green favorite paint, so be careful.

   Take a moment to skim (move your cursor over the filmstrip without clicking) and play (tap Space) to identify the good parts, and then:

2. **Drag across the filmstrip to indicate the good stuff.**

   The green "favorite" stripe appears instantly. Instead of "select, then flag as favorite," you've managed to select and flag-as-favorite all in one stroke.

Marking sections as rejects is just as easy, except you click the X button in step 1 (or press the letter R key). Now, when you drag across filmstrips in step 2, they instantly become rejects, which usually means that they disappear from view.

> **TIP** To mark an *entire* clip as a favorite or a reject, Option-click it. That's a lot faster than dragging.

For best results, then, you should plow through your footage, riding the F and R keys (favorite and reject modes), painting across good and bad sections of video as you go. Later, this prescreening process makes assembling your movie a heck of a lot easier and faster.

NOTE   If you mark something as a reject or a favorite by mistake, you can unmark it quickly: hold down the ⌘ key. iMovie switches temporarily to the Unmark tool described in the next section, just long enough for you to paint over (or Option-click) the mismarked footage.

Release the ⌘ key to return to the tool you were using.

Unmarking

No matter which method you used to mark favorites or rejects, it's easy to change your mind later. Just repeat the original process, but use the hollow star (or the letter U key) as your paintbrush.

- To use the "select, then flag" method, select the piece of filmstrip that you want to unmark and then click the hollow-star icon (or press the letter U).

- If you prefer the Advanced-tools, "paintbrush" method, turn on the Advanced Tools. Then click the hollow-star icon (or press the letter U), and begin painting. When you drag your cursor across a piece of filmstrip, you remove *all* colored stripes from it—both the favorite and the reject stripes.

NOTE   Of course, you can't unmark rejected footage unless you can *see* it on the screen. The following section shows you how to bring hidden footage back into view.

Selecting Marked Footage

In time, your Event footage will be twinkling with green, red, blue, and even orange bars, corresponding to the various ways you've flagged or used your footage.

But these colored stripes aren't just labels; they're also handles. Carefully double-click directly *on* one of the colored stripes, and presto: iMovie neatly selects just the piece of filmstrip that's marked by that bar, ready for unmarking, cutting, deleting, placing in your project, or whatever.

Hiding and Showing Favorites and Rejects

Flagging clips as favorites and rejects wouldn't save you any time if all it did was draw colored stripes on your filmstrips. The real payoff comes when you tell iMovie to *hide* everything except your favorites or rejects, making it exceptionally easy to work with a big pool of extraordinary footage, or to review all the lousy footage before you delete it for good.

You can access these various hide/show modes in two places: in the View menu, or in the Show pop-up menu on the bottom edge of the iMovie window.

- **Show only favorites.** Choose Favorites Only, either from the View menu or the Show pop-up menu (Figure 4-3).

- **Show everything except rejects**. Choose Favorites and Unmarked, either from the View menu or the Show pop-up menu.

This is what you see most of the time: iMovie shows you everything that you've marked as favorite *and* everything you haven't marked either way. Only the rejects are hidden.

NOTE   Since this is the view Apple expects you'll use most often, it has a keyboard shortcut all its own: ⌘-L.

Figure 4-3:
When you choose Favorites Only from this pop-up menu, the Event browser hides all your rejects and all footage that you haven't marked at all. This feature should translate into even faster movie-building time, since you're working exclusively with clips you already know you love.

- **Show everything**. Choose All Clips, either from the View menu or the Show pop-up menu.

Now you're seeing everything: favorites, rejects, and unmarked. This can be a handy anti-desperation view when you can't find a certain shot that you're sure you had before. It rules out the possibility that you've flagged it as a favorite or reject and then hidden it.

- **Show only rejects**. Choose Rejected Only, either from the View menu or the Show pop-up menu.

Now you're seeing *only* the bad stuff. Everything else is hidden.

You'd summon this view when hunting for a clip you can't seem to find among the good stuff (maybe you rejected it by mistake), or when reviewing your rejected footage before deleting it for good, as described on page 108.

Keywords

In iPhoto, iMovie's sibling in the iLife suite, *keywords* play an important role in helping you manage tens of thousands of photos.

A keyword is a text label that you can slap on a picture, a tag that will help you pluck that photo (and ones like it) out of a haystack later. Some people make keywords for the people in the pictures: "Casey," "Mom," "Robin," and so on; others use them to identify what's going on in the photo: "Vacation," "Home," "Kids." Either way, the point is that if you're consistent in using keywords, you can later round up *all* photos bearing a certain keyword ("Robin") with one click.

Well, iMovie works with keywords as well, but you wouldn't know it at first. iMovie keywords belong to the handful of miscellaneous efficiency features that Apple calls the Advanced Tools, so most people don't even know that they exist. To make them appear, turn on Advanced Tools as described on page 80.

Now, if you look carefully, you'll see that a new button has appeared on iMovie's central toolbar—one that looks like an old-fashioned key. Click it to open the Keywords window (Figure 4-4).

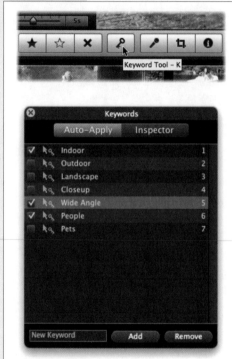

Figure 4-4:
Top: When the Advanced Tools are turned on, the Keywords button appears. Click it to open the Keywords window (bottom). You can now "paint" a selected keyword, or several, onto a filmstrip, using the Auto-Apply tab. Or, on the Inspector tab, you can select some video first on the filmstrip and then turn on the relevant keyword checkboxes.

You can see that Apple has started you out with several sample keywords: Indoor, Outdoor, Landscape, People, Pets, and so on. You can also see that the Keywords window has two tabs at the top, Auto-Apply and Inspector. They correspond to the two ways that you can apply keywords to your filmstrips: by "painting" across them, or using the select-then-apply method.

> **TIP** You can apply keywords to your filmstrips either in the storyboard or the Event browser.

Editing the Keyword List

To make up new keywords, click the Auto-Apply tab. Click in the Keyword box (lower-left), type a keyword, and press Enter. Type the next keyword, and press Enter. And so on.

To edit a keyword name, double-click it.

> **TIP** Be careful—keywords are case-sensitive. iMovie treats *kids* and *Kids* as two different keywords.

You can also rearrange the keyword list—to put the most common ones at the top, for example. (The top nine keywords get numeric keyboard shortcuts.) Just drag the keywords themselves up or down the list.

To remove keywords that you're not using, click the Auto-Apply tab, click the keyword you want to eliminate (*not* its checkbox) and then click Remove. If that keyword is actually in use—if you've applied it to some footage—iMovie warns you in a confirmation box. Click Yes to proceed with the keyword vaporization.

"Painting" Keywords onto Clips

This method is wicked fast. It's especially good if you want to apply the *same* set of keywords to a slew of different filmstrips. When you get back from your Disney World vacation, for example, chances are good that a lot of your video will fall into the categories "Vacation," "Family," and "Kids." Using this method, you can leave those keyword checkboxes turned on and then whip through the clips, "painting on" the keywords as necessary.

Start by opening the Keywords window and then:

1. **Click the Auto-Apply tab.**

   If you want to add a new keyword to the list, type it into the box at the bottom of the list and then click Add (or press Enter).

2. **Turn on the checkboxes for the relevant keywords.**

   As noted above, you can turn on as many as you like.

   > **TIP** See the little numbers 1, 2, 3, and so on, at the right side of the list? You can press these keys on your keyboard to turn keyword checkboxes on and off, for added speed.

3. **Drag across the filmstrip sections that should have those keywords.**

   As always, you can skim and play to review a clip before you paint the keywords onto it.

   As you drag, a blue line appears at the top of the filmstrip, indicating that you've applied keywords to it.

   > **TIP** *Option*-click a filmstrip to apply the selected keywords to the whole thing.

The Select-then-Apply Method

When you have a more motley assortment of video and you'll be applying a lot of different keywords as you go, it might make more sense to use this second method. Here, you highlight some video first and *then* turn on the keyword checkboxes.

Start by opening the Keywords window, and then:

1. **Click the Inspector tab.**

   The keyword list appears.

2. **Select some video.**

   You can use any of the techniques described on page 71. Of course, you can skim and play to see what you've got before you apply a keyword.

3. **Turn on the appropriate keyword checkboxes.**

   Click to select the checkboxes—or press the number keys on your keyboard that correspond to the numbers in the keyword list.

   Once again, a blue line appears at the top of the filmstrip, indicating that you've applied keywords to it.

   If you see a hyphen (-) in one of the checkboxes, it's because *part* of the selected video has that keyword, and part doesn't. Click that checkbox once to apply the keyword to the *entire* selection, or twice to remove the keyword from the entire selection.

   TIP   To apply a keyword that's not yet in the list, type the new keyword into the "Keyword" text box and then click Add to Clip (or press Enter). iMovie simultaneously adds the new keyword to the list *and* applies it to whatever's selected.

Now you can repeat steps 2 and 3, selecting, then applying keywords; selecting, then applying keywords.

Removing Keywords from Filmstrips

It's easy enough to strip away keywords that you've already applied. Just highlight the clip and then, on the Inspector tab, turn off the keywords you don't want. Or, if you don't want *any* keywords on your selected clip, click Remove All.

> **NOTE**   Whatever keywords are applied to a certain clip are visible in all projects. In other words, keywords are not project-specific.

The Keyword Filter

The payoff for painstakingly categorizing your footage with keywords comes when you need just the right clip, and you don't have time to review the 6 hours of footage you took during your 11-day cruise. You want to see all the footage of museums (or beaches, or shipboard fake Broadway shows), *now*.

That's easy. Choose Window → Show Keyword Filter, or click the magnifying-glass button under the Event Browser display. Either way, iMovie opens up a strange little keyword panel, wedged in between the Events list and the Event browser (Figure 4-5).

The minutes:seconds display down the right side is a cumulative tally of all the video in your library that bears each keyword.

Even handier are the red and green pill-shaped things down the *left* side. These traffic lights affect what footage you see in the Event Browser. When you click the green light, the Event browser shows *only* the clips marked by that keyword. The red light, naturally, has the opposite effect, *hiding* all clips with that keyword.

> **TIP** Clicking the keyword itself acts just like clicking the green light. A bigger target means more efficiency.

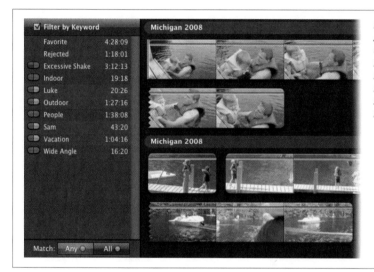

Figure 4-5:
As long as the master switch is turned on (Filter by Keyword), the traffic lights hide or show the video with matching keywords. When "Filter by Keyword" is off, the Event browser shows everything, regardless of keywords.

At least, that's what it does fresh from the factory. By clicking the buttons below the list, you can manipulate what's hidden and what's visible in several creative ways:

- **Any** means "show me video with *any* of the keywords I've selected." If you turn on Vacation and Kids, you'll see footage that has *either* of those keywords applied.

- **All** means "show me only the video that has *all* of these keywords." If you turn on Vacation and Kids, you'll see *only* footage to which you've applied *both* those keywords.

> **NOTE** Ordinarily, you can filter out shaky footage by clicking the red squiggly button below your event footage. When the Keyword Filter is turned on, however, that button disappears, replaced by a faux-keyword called Excessive Shake. Now you can not only hide shaky footage, you can also green-light it so you *only* see shaky footage—the better to quickly reject all the blurry stuff.

Deleting Footage for Good

When you mark a shot as a reject, iMovie generally hides it from you, so that you can spend less time wading through mountains of video as you build your project.

But marking shots as rejects has another payoff, too: It's the gateway to iMovie's video *deletion* feature. If a shot is really bad, and you're sure you'll never need it again, you can delete it from your Mac completely, thereby reclaiming a substantial amount of hard drive space.

iMovie '09 can even delete *part* of a clip on the hard drive, leaving the rest for you to work with. Technically speaking, that's quite a trick. (See the box on page 110.)

To purge your rejected clips and clip portions, do this:

1. **Choose View → Rejected Only.**

   As shown in Figure 4-6 (top), the Rejected Clips window appears. Skim or play these clips to double-check their worthlessness. The point is to review the rejects to make sure you're not about to nuke anything you'll regret losing.

   NOTE   If you spot an *orange* stripe on any of these clips, then you've actually used that video in a project—you must have marked it as rejected *afterward*—and iMovie won't let you delete it. Remove it from your project first, or unmark it as a reject.

2. **Click "Move Rejected to Trash".**

   You'll find this button in the upper-right corner of the Rejected Clips window. iMovie immediately asks if you're sure (Figure 4-6, bottom).

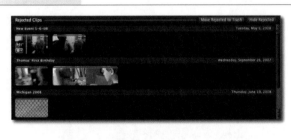

Figure 4-6:
Top: The Rejected Clips window shows you everything you've indicated is destined for the cutting-room floor. Here's your last chance to look it over before deleting it forever.

Bottom: When you click "Move Rejected to Trash", this confirmation box appears. Click "Move to Trash".

3. **Click "Move to Trash".**

After a moment of processing, iMovie places all of the rejected footage in your *Macintosh* Trash. The filmstrips disappear from the window before you.

NOTE At this point, the video isn't yet gone from your hard drive. You have one last, desperate chance to resurrect it. Click the Trash icon on your Dock, and then open the iMovie Temporary Items folder within. There you'll find both the deleted clip and the mini filmstrip movie thumbnail that iMovie '09 generated for it.

To rescue some video, drag it out of this Trash folder and back into the appropriate folder in your Movies → iMovie Events folder. (Refresh your memory on how these folders work on page 53.) The next time you open iMovie, you'll see it listed in the Event browser.

4. **Empty your Macintosh Trash.**

In other words, switch to the Finder (click the first icon on your Dock), and choose Finder → Empty Trash. Or, if you can see the Trash icon on your Dock right now, hold down your cursor on it; from the shortcut menu, choose Empty Trash.

Space Saver

Now you know how to permanently vaporize all the footage you've flagged as useless. But as it turns out, iMovie offers an additional tool for reclaiming hard drive space—a little something called Space Saver.

It's a little complicated, thanks to the double-negative wording of its options ("Reject if a clip is *not* this"), but here goes:

Space Saver's function is to mark *all* unused, unfavorited, or unkeyworded video in an Event as rejects, all in one fell swoop. That way, you can use the previous steps to empty your Rejected Clips window and get a *lot* of hard drive space back.

The most useful application of this powerful command is to purge your Event of leftover footage after you're really, truly finished editing a project. Space Saver can help you throw away *all* of the imported video that didn't wind up being used in the project. In essence, you're locking down your project in its current form, removing any chance of expanding the clips you've used in it—but you're getting a lot of hard drive space back.

NOTE If you have a tape camcorder, and you still have the original tape, this is a no-lose, no-risk proposition. If you're ever desperate to re-edit your movie years from now, you can always reimport the original clips from the tape. In the meantime, you're not filling up your hard drive with a lot of video deadwood.

GEM IN THE ROUGH

Deleting Partial Clips: The Mixed Blessing

iMovie '09's ability to delete *pieces* of clips from your hard drive certainly seems, at first glance, like a refreshing change from previous versions of iMovie.

In iMovie 5 and 6, you'd reclaim hard drive space only if you deleted an *entire* clip. If you'd incorporated even one second of a clip into your project, iMovie retained the entire clip on your hard drive, even if it was many minutes (and megabytes) long. As a result, even short iMovie projects could occupy many gigabytes of disk space.

Apple's justification for this behavior was, "Well, you might want to change your mind. You might want to re-edit this movie later and use *more* of that clip in your project." And that was true; it's frequently convenient to

tinker with your edit by dragging the outer edges of already-placed clips to bring more of those shots into view. That trick's possible only if you haven't *deleted* the hidden part of a clip.

All of this history is printed here for one purpose: To remind you that partial-clip deletion is a mixed blessing. iMovie '09 can save you an *enormous* amount of hard drive space if you diligently reject, and then delete, the footage that you're certain you'll never want anyone to see.

But keep in mind that when you do that, you lose the flexibility to change your mind.

To get started, choose File → Space Saver. The dialog box shown in Figure 4-7 appears. It's offering to mark *everything* as a reject unless it's:

- **Part of a project.** This is the example described in the box "Deleting Partial Clips: The Mixed Blessing." Turn on "Not added to any project" if you want to get rid of all video clips in this Event that you haven't used in any movie project.

- **One of your favorites.** If you've been using the Favorites feature religiously, and have marked *all* usable video as Favorite, then you can turn on "Not marked as Favorite". Anything you did *not* mark as a favorite now becomes a reject. (Pretty harsh!) The only footage left in this Event will be your favorites.

- **Categorized with a keyword.** This option is for people who categorize *everything* useful with one keyword or another, as described on page 103. Turning on "Not marked with a keyword" marks *everything else* as a reject, and puts it on the road to deletion.

There probably aren't very many people who always keyword *everything* that's useful, which is why the factory setting for this checkbox is off.

Once you've made your selections, click Reject and Review. You arrive in the Rejected Clips window (Figure 4-6, top), where you'll see all the clips that Space Saver has marked for termination.

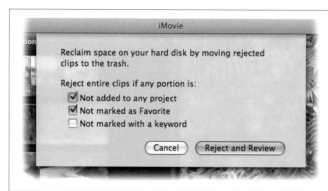

Figure 4-7:
iMovie can save you time and disk space if you let it reject whole categories of clips at a time.

If you're puzzled by what's here and what's not, keep these eccentricities in mind:

- Space Saver marks a clip as a reject only if *the entire thing* meets the criteria you selected. If part of it is flagged as a favorite, for example, and you've selected "Not marked as Favorite", then no part of the clip will be moved to the Rejected Clips window.

- The checkboxes are cumulative. You can turn on as many of the Space Saver checkboxes as you like. But in keeping with Space Saver's double-negative thinking, turning on *more* checkboxes rejects *fewer* clips. That is, if you turn on all three boxes, a clip won't be deleted unless it's unused in a project *and* not a favorite *and* doesn't have a keyword. This quirk, too, may explain why some clips don't wind up in the Rejected Clips window when you expected them to.

Once you've skimmed or played the filmstrips in the Rejected Clips window, and you've assured yourself that they're all expendable, you can delete them just as you'd delete any rejected clips. Page 108 has the full details, but the gist is this: Click "Move Rejected to Trash", click "Move to Trash" in the confirmation box, and then empty the Macintosh Trash.

Transitions, Themes, and Travel Maps

Cutting and ordering your clips makes them infinitely more entertaining than the hours of dreck you'd have otherwise. But why stop there? This is *computer* video editing, after all. The next two chapters cover what you can do *between* your clips (this chapter) and what you can do *to* your clips (Video Effects) to make your whole project more vivid.

Impressively enough, there's no *rendering time* required by iMovie—no delay while the program computes the effect you're creating—as there is in most other video-editing programs. You see the effect instantly.

About Transitions

What happens when one clip ends and the next one begins? In about 99.99 percent of all movies, music videos, and commercials—and in 100 percent of camcorder movies before the Macintosh era—you get a *cut*. That's the technical term for "nothing special happens at all." One scene ends, and the next one begins immediately.

Professional film and video editors, however, have at their disposal a wide range of *transitions*—special effects that smooth the juncture between one clip and the next. For example, the world's most popular transition is the *crossfade* or *dissolve*, in which the end of one clip gradually fades away as the next one fades in. (See Figure 5-1.) The crossfade is so popular because it's so effective. It gives a feeling of softness and grace to the transition, and yet it's so subtle that the viewer might not even be conscious of its presence.

Figure 5-1:
The world's most popular and effective transition effect: what iMovie calls a Cross Dissolve.

Like all video-editing programs, iMovie offers a variety of transitions, of which crossfades are only the beginning. You'll find a catalog of them starting on page 124. iMovie makes adding such effects incredibly easy, and the results look awesomely assured and professional.

When Not to Use Transitions

When the Macintosh debuted in 1984, one of its most exciting features was its *fonts*. Without having to buy those self-adhesive lettering sets from art stores, you could make posters, flyers, and newsletters using any typefaces you wanted. In fact, if you weren't particularly concerned with being tasteful, you could even combine lots of typefaces on the same page—and thousands of first-time desktop publishers did exactly that. They thought it was exciting to harness the world of typography right on the computer screen.

You may even remember the result: a proliferation of homemade graphic design that rated very low on the artistic-taste scale. Instead of making their documents look more professional, the wild explosion of mixed typefaces made them look amateurish in a whole new way.

In video, transitions present exactly the same temptation: If you use too many, you risk telegraphing that you're a beginner at work. When you begin to polish your movie by adding transitions, consider these questions:

• **Does it really need a transition?** Sometimes a simple cut is the most effective transition from one shot to the next. Yes, the crossfade lends a feeling of softness and smoothness to the movie, but is that really what you want? If it's a sweet video of your kids growing up over time, absolutely yes. But if it's a hard-hitting issue documentary, then probably not, as those soft edges would dull the impact of your footage.

Remember, too, that transitions often suggest the *passage of time*. In movies and commercials, consecutive shots in the same scene never include such effects. Plain old cuts tell the viewer that one shot is following the next in real time. But suppose one scene ends with the beleaguered hero saying, "Well, at least I still have my job at the law firm!"…and the next shot shows him operating a lemonade stand. (Now *that's* comedy!) In this case, a transition would be especially effective, because it would tell the audience that we've just jumped a couple of days. Learn taste in transitions. They should be done *for a reason*.

- **Is it consistent?** Once you've chosen a transition-effect style for your movie, stick to that transition style for the entire film (unless, as always, you have an artistic reason to do otherwise). Using one consistent style of effect lends unity to your work. That's why interior designers choose only one dominant color for each room.

- **Which effect is most appropriate?** As noted earlier, the crossfade is almost always the least intrusive, most effective, and best-looking transition. But each of the other iMovie transitions can be appropriate in certain situations.

The catalog on page 124 gives you an example of when each might be appropriate. Most of them are useful primarily in music videos and other situations when wild stylistic flights of fancy are more readily accepted by viewers.

TIP   The Fade Through Black transition in iMovie is exempt from the stern advice above. Use it at the beginning of *every* movie, if you like, and at the end. Doing so adds a fade in and fade out, lending a professional feeling to your film. But it's so subtle, your audience will notice it only subconsciously, if at all.

Two Ways to "Transish"

You can insert iMovie's transition effects one by one, placing them between scenes only where appropriate, and hand-tailoring each one. That's the way you do transitions in most programs, including the old iMovie.

But lurking one millimeter beneath iMovie's surface at all times is its primary mission: letting you assemble edited video *fast*, automating *everything*. For that reason, iMovie '09 also lets you turn on *automatic, global* transitions. (Great for slideshows!) The following sections cover both methods.

Creating Individual Transition Effects

To see the 20 transitions iMovie offers, click the Transitions button, which is identified in Figure 5-2. Point to a transition's name (like Cross Dissolve) without clicking to see a small animated preview of it.

Once you've found a good effect, drag its icon *out* of the Transitions panel and directly into the storyboard area, in the vertical gap between the two filmstrips that you want transitioned. Figure 5-3 shows the technique.

NOTE   Most people think of putting transitions *between* two clips. But if you drag one to the *beginning* of your storyboard, the transition works just as well—except that it transitions out of blackness. Fade Through Black and Circle Open work especially well to begin a movie.

The same happy surprise awaits if you drag a transition to the *end* of the movie. iMovie wipes, fades, or ripples from the final shot into blackness.

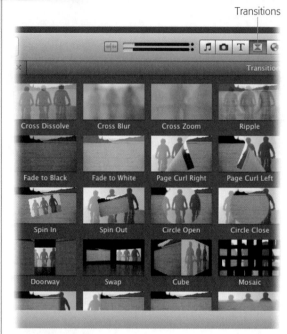

Transitions

Figure 5-2:
When you point to a transition's icon, you get to see a small preview right on its icon. Click to pause the tiny playback loop at any point, or double-click to reset the animation to its first frame.

Transition icon

Figure 5-3:
Insert a transition by dragging its icon out of the Transitions palette and in between two clips (or at either end of your movie). In the storyboard, a transition shows up as a tiny icon. You can even tell what kind of transition it is by the little logo on that icon.

Once you've dropped a transition into place, you can look over the result easily.

- To watch just the transition itself, click its icon in the storyboard (it sprouts a yellow border to show that it's highlighted) and then press the / key. That's on the bottom row of the keyboard, and it always means "play the selection" in iMovie.

- It's a good idea to watch your transition by "rewinding" a few seconds into the preceding footage, to get a sense of how the effect fits in the context of the existing footage. To watch the transition *and* the clips that it joins together, point to a spot just before the transition, and then hit the space bar. Alternatively, hit the [or] key to preview the three-second or six-second video chunk that surrounds the transition.

- If you think the scene seam looked better without the transition, choose Edit → Undo (⌘-Z).

You'll discover that the audio from the clips on either side of a transition still plays—you hear the sounds overlapping for a moment—but iMovie gradually crossfades the two.

> **TIP** If you want transitions on *most* of your scene seams, turn on the Automatic Transitions feature described on page 123. Then, using the Tip on that page, you can turn all those iMovie-generated transitions into manually editable ones. In other words, you can delete just the transitions you don't want.

Changing or Deleting a Transition

If you like the *idea* of a transition but you just don't like the one you put there, there are two ways to replace it.

- Drag a different one out of the Transitions panel right on top of the old one.

- Double-click the transition; the Inspector window appears. Click the Transition button labeled with the name of your current transition. The Inspector flips around and reveals skimmable previews of all 20 transitions. Select the new transition by clicking it. Once you've clicked a good one, click Done.

To get rid of a transition, even months or years later, highlight its icon and then press the Delete key. Your original clips return instantly, exactly as they were before you added the transition.

A Long Discussion of Transition Lengths

In iMovie HD and previous editions, you specified how long each transition effect lasted before you even put it into your movie. iMovie '09 thinks that *that*—choosing durations each time—is a nuisance. Every transition you insert starts out with the same length (which you can specify in the project properties). iMovie is not a complete tyrant, however; it does let you set individual transition lengths.

There are three ways to adjust the durations of your transitions. Two of these involve a visit to the Project Properties dialog box (see Figure 5-4). Here, you'll find a Transition Duration slider (whose settings range from .5 seconds to 4 seconds) and several options that affect it:

- **Change all transition durations at once.** If you select "Applies to all transitions," then the Duration slider affects all transitions simultaneously. Taking this road ensures consistency and minimizes the amount of effort you have to expend. For best results, choose something between 1 and 2 seconds.

  NOTE If you've manually set the durations of individual transitions, as described in the following paragraphs, be careful. Using "Applies to all transitions" wipes out all of the handwork you've done.

- **Change transition durations from here on.** The weird little option labeled "Applies when added to project" actually means "Whatever duration you choose on the Duration slider applies to the *next* transition you drop into the storyboard—and all future ones."

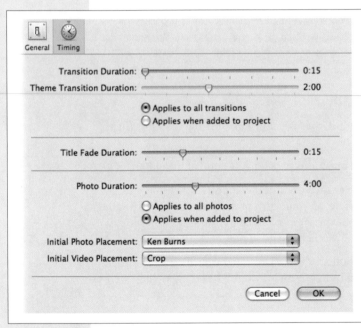

Figure 5-4:
Choose File → Project Properties and then click the Timing tab. In this dialog box, drag the slider to indicate how long you want each transition effect to last. If "Applies to all transitions" is selected, then, by golly, this slider affects all transitions in your project at once.

So you choose this option, you adjust the Duration slider, and finally you click OK. You've just preserved the durations of all *existing* transitions in your project, but changed the standard timing for all *incoming* transitions.

Here again, iMovie is trying to enforce a standard duration, albeit a different one, and trying to remove all necessity for you to manage your durations one by one.

- **Change individual transitions.** Fortunately for control freaks, you can also change transition durations on a one-at-a-time basis. When you double-click a transition icon, the Inspector appears; it offers a Duration slider (Figure 5-5). Type in the number of seconds you want for the transition. Whereas iMovie's automatic Duration slider limits your transitions to lengths between .5 and 4 seconds, this time, you have much greater creative latitude. You can type in anything between .25 (one-quarter second) and 60 (a whole minute, although, frankly, transitions longer than a couple of seconds are excruciating to watch).

NOTE   You can type decimals here. If you want a 2.1-second transition, then, by all means, type *2.1*.

Figure 5-5:
Type in the number you want, and then click OK. (This box, as you can see, offers a second way to change the durations of all transitions in your project so far.)

Why You Don't Always Get What You Want

Even after you've mastered all of the transition-duration permutations described on the previous pages, you may find yourself thwarted by iMovie itself. You may indicate that you want a 2-second transition, but iMovie may give you a half-second one, no matter how many things you try. That's because iMovie enforces its own Law of Reasonable Durations, which states that *no transition effect may consume more than half the length of a clip.* Figure 5-6 shows the problem, and the result.

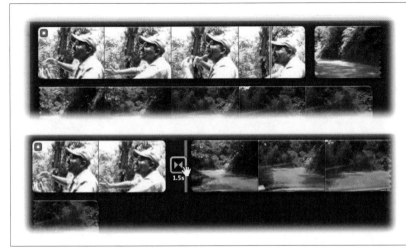

Figure 5-6:
Top: One of the clips involved in the transition is only 3 seconds long. You try to add a 2-second transition.

Bottom: iMovie gives you only a 1.5-second transition, because that's half of the clip's 3-second length—and iMovie won't let you add a transition longer than half the clip's length.

NOTE   If you can't manually change the durations of *any* transition, it's probably because you've got Automatic transitions turned on (see page 123).

How Transitions Affect the Length of Your Movie

As you can see by the example in Figure 5-7, transitions generally make your movie *shorter*. To superimpose the ends of two adjacent clips, iMovie is forced to slide the right-hand clip to the left, making the overall movie end sooner.

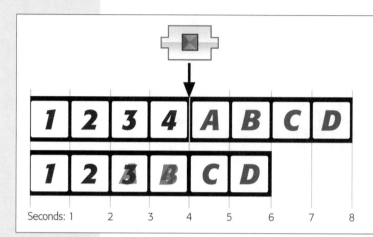

Figure 5-7:
When you insert a 2-second transition (top) between two clips, iMovie pulls the right-hand clip 2 seconds to the left so that it overlaps the end of the left-hand clip. The result (bottom): The entire movie is now 2 seconds shorter.

Under most circumstances, there's nothing wrong with that. After all, that's why, when importing your clips, you wisely avoided trimming off *all* of the excess leader and trailer footage (known as *trim handles*) from the ends of your clips. By leaving trim handles on each clip—which will be sacrificed to the transition—you'll have some fade-in or fade-out footage to play with.

Sometimes, however, having your overall project shortened is a serious problem, especially when you've been "cutting to sound," or synchronizing your footage to an existing music track. Even if you use the "Snap to Beats" feature covered on page 207, any transitions you add later will throw off the timing. (At least iMovie duly warns you of this potential disaster.)

In iMovie '09, there's no good solution to this problem if you've opted for manual control over transitions. (The *automatic* transition feature, which puts a transition in between every single scene seam in the entire movie, offers a semi-solution; see below.)

Automatic Transitions

If you're really in a hurry to crank out your edited movie, like the now-legendary Apple programmer who wound up writing iMovie '09 so he could whip out highlight reels without hand-tweaking everything, then you're in luck. You don't have to bother placing transitions one at a time. Using the Automatic feature, you can tell iMovie to put the same, identical, fixed-length transition effect between *all* clip seams. Figure 5-8 shows the idea.

Figure 5-8:
The Automatic feature takes your rough edit (top) and inserts identical transitions everywhere (bottom), masking the divider between every pair of clips.

This feature is OK *if* all of this is true:

- You choose a nontacky transition effect, like the cross dissolve.

- You set the duration to something short, like 1 second.

- You're creating a highlight reel, a sequence of shots that aren't intended to tell a story.

If you're not careful, these frequent transitions can get annoying or cloying, and they'll lose their impact in a hurry. You should also note that turning on the Automatic feature *removes* any customization you've done using the individual-transition feature described on the preceding pages. All of your duration adjustments are wiped away.

> **TIP** There is, however, a way to turn all of these automatic transitions into *individual* transitions that you can edit separately; see page 123.

Still interested? Then proceed like this:

1. **Choose File → Project Properties, and then click the General tab.**

   Alternatively, press ⌘-J. Either way, the Project Properties screen appears (Figure 5-4).

2. **Turn on "Automatically add." From the pop-up menu, choose the transition style you want.**

This time, you don't get the handy self-illustrating icons that show you what the effect will look like. It doesn't matter; the only one you'd ever use without looking amateurish is the Cross Dissolve. (Right?)

3. **Choose either "Overlap ends..." or "Extend ends..." and click OK.**

Once you click the box in step 2, a weird little question pops into the window (Figure 5-9). It's asking how you want these transitions to affect the overall timing of your movie.

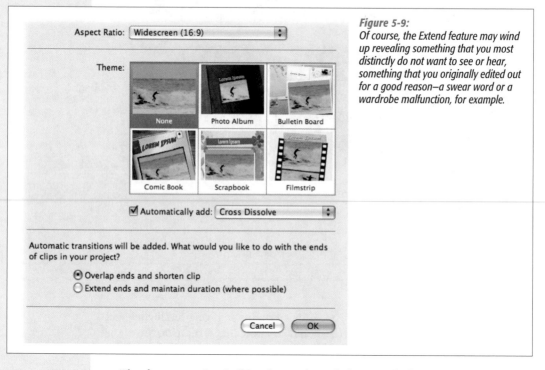

Figure 5-9:
Of course, the Extend feature may wind up revealing something that you most distinctly do not want to see or hear, something that you originally edited out for a good reason—a swear word or a wardrobe malfunction, for example.

The factory setting is "Overlap ends and shorten clip". As the discussion on page 120 makes clear, your movie will get shorter. iMovie slides every clip slightly to the left so that it can overlap the preceding one. That's usually fine— *except* when you've got the whole thing carefully timed to a music track, which will now be totally out of sync with the video.

The alternative is "Extend ends and keep duration the same (where possible)." Here, iMovie is proposing *not* shortening your movie. You'll still see every frame of the clips that you're seeing now. But to provide "trim handles" for the transition, iMovie automatically *lengthens* the clips in your storyboard. It reveals footage on either end that you had, in the process of choosing excerpts from the raw footage, previously hidden.

"Where possible" means that if iMovie encounters a clip that was *not* edited down from a longer one, it can't help you. It has no choice but to add a transition that eats into the clip, using up some of its frames, and shortening your movie overall.

4. **In the Timing tab, use the Transition Duration slider to specify the length of the transition itself.**

One second or less is a good bet.

5. **Click OK.**

You return to your project, where the icons for iMovie's automatic transitions now appear in place. Play back the movie to enjoy the effect, keeping in mind that you can't edit, change, or delete them *individually*, only en masse.

NOTE If you add any new clips to your movie, iMovie adds transitions to them automatically.

Adjusting the Automatic Transitions

You can change the uniform length or uniform style of *all* those auto-transitions, but you can't edit them individually. Just choose File → Project Properties (⌘-J). In the dialog box (Figure 5-4, page 118), you can change the Duration slider or, using the pop-up menu, the transition style. Any change you make here affects *all* of the transitions.

Turning off Automatic Transitions

If you decide that the all-at-once approach is a bit much, you can turn off the automatic-transitions feature. Choose File → Project Properties (⌘-J) and just turn off "Add transitions automatically." When you click OK, iMovie has one more bit of business to take care of: what to do about that messy overlapping-ends affair. A message now appears at the bottom of the window asking what you want to do:

- **Remove transitions and extend clip ends.** This option leaves in place whatever footage is now being used by the transition. For example, if you had an 8-second clip with a 1-second transition at the end, the clip will wind up being about 9 seconds long.

- **Remove transitions and maintain clip durations.** If you've spent a lot of energy working out timings, maybe to match a soundtrack, you'll probably want this choice. Now, that 8-second clip will still be 8 seconds long after the transitions are removed. The video that *was* being used in the transitions is hidden once again.

- **Leave transitions in current locations.** This handy option turns off automatic transitions, but leaves the actual transition icons in place. They've now turned into *individual* transitions, which you can now delete or edit on a one-at-a-time basis.

TIP This option can be a terrific help when you want transitions on *most* of your clips, but not all. You can turn Automatic Transitions on, and then choose this option as you turn them off again. Now you have a storyboard full of *manual* transition icons. Just delete the ones you don't need.

Transitions: The iMovie Catalog

Here, for your reference, is an explanation of each transition, and what editing circumstances might call for it.

Circle Open, Circle Close

This effect, called *iris close (iris open)* or *iris in (iris out)* in professional editing programs, is a holdover from the silent film days, when, in the days before zoom lenses, directors used the effect to highlight a detail in a scene.

It creates an ever-growing (or opening) porthole, with the first clip inside and the second clip outside. It's useful at the beginning or end of the movie, when the second clip is solid black and the subject of the first clip is centered in the frame. In that setup, the movie begins or ends with a picture that grows or shrinks away to a little dot. (If the subject in the center waves goodbye just before being blinked out of view, this trick is especially effective.)

Circle Opening

Cross Blur

Like an autofocus gone awry, the first clip gets blurry, only to have the focus return with the second clip now on the screen.

Cross Dissolve

The crossfade, or dissolve, is the world's most popular and effective transition. The first clip gradually disappears, superimposed on the beginning of the second clip, which fades in. If you must use a tarnsition at all, you can't go wrong with this one.

TIP You can use a very short cross dissolve to create what editors call a "soft cut." When the footage would jump too abruptly if you made a regular cut, put in a 10-frame cross dissolve, which makes the junction of clips *slightly* smoother than just cutting. Soft cuts are very common in interviews where the editors have deleted sections from a continuous shot of a person talking.

Cross Zoom

For anyone who's experienced jumping into hyperspace, this transition will look very familiar. The first clip turns into a streaky tunnel, giving the illusion of speeding into the video, only to come out on the other end with the second clip. This transition emphasizes what's at the end of the wormhole.

Doorway

Here's another effect that takes full advantage of the three-dimensional powers built into your Mac. The first clip splits in half, and the two halves swing open like double doors. The second clip charges through the doors, filling the screen.

Fade Through Black, Fade Through White

Use this effect at the beginning and end of every movie, for a handsome, professional fade in/fade out. Or use it at the start of any scene that begins in a new place or time. In that situation, it makes the first scene fade to black momentarily, and then the next one fades in.

Fade Through White is the same thing, with one big difference: It fades out to, and then in from, *white* instead of black. Fading in and out to white, an effect first popularized by Infiniti car commercials in the early 1980s, lends a very specific feeling to the movie. It's something ethereal, ghostly, and nostalgic. In today's Hollywood movies (including *The Sixth Sense*), a fade to white often indicates that the character you've been watching has just died.

The fade through white is an extremely popular technique in today's TV commercials, when the advertiser wants to show you a series of charming, brightly colored images. By fading out to white between shots, the editor inserts the video equivalent of an ellipsis (…like this…), and keeps the mood happy and bright. (Similar fade-outs to black seem to stop the flow with more finality.)

Fade Through White/Black

TIP   If you'd rather fade to black and then *hold* on the black screen for a moment, use the transition between your video and a *black clip*. See page 241 for details on making a black clip.

Mosaic

Like an impatient game of Memory, iMovie breaks your first clip into a bunch of little cards, and then flips them all over to reveal the second clip. The flipped cards blend together to finish the effect.

Page Curl

Here's another slightly tacky transition: the page curl. It makes the upper-right corner of the video frame appear to curl inward and toward you, and then peel down and to the left, as though it's a giant Post-it note being ripped off a pad. The clip that follows is revealed underneath.

Page Curl

Ripple

This effect is gorgeous, poetic, beautiful—and hard to justify. Ripple invokes the "drop of water on the surface of the pond" metaphor. As the ripple expands across the screen, it pushes the first clip (the pond surface) off the screen to make way for the incoming new clip (the expanding circular ripple). It's a soothing, beautiful effect but unless you're making mascara commercials, it calls a little too much attention to itself for everyday home movies.

Ripple

Spin In, Spin Out

Did you see *Superman 3*? That's the one where General Zod and his cronies end up in a space jail that looks like a playing card flipping through space. Now you too can create that visual effect. Amaze your friends!

With Spin In, the second clip looks like a card that zooms forward from the middle of the screen, eventually filling the frame. Spin Out looks similar, but the first clip looks like a card zooming off, while the second clip serves as a backdrop. Spin In emphasizes the clip coming in, while Spin Out keeps you dwelling on the departing clip.

Swap

This transition leaves no doubt that you're changing clips. Again harnessing your Mac's ability to animate in 3D, the first one slides backward and to the left, as the incoming clip slides in from the right, then comes forward to fill the screen. Several of these in a row would leave an impression of some sort of assembly line.

Wipe Down, Up, Left, Right

In this transition, the incoming clip *covers up* the outgoing clip, as though it's being shoved into the frame on a cookie sheet. (A cookie sheet with a soft, slightly blurry leading edge, that is; iMovie doesn't *do* hard transition edges.) You could use it to simulate an old-style projector changing slides, or when filming a clever, self-aware documentary in which the host (who first appears in the second clip) pushes his way onto the screen.

Wipe

Themes

Themes are transitions with graduate degrees. If you had experience with Themes in iMovie HD, you already know what they are: sets of professionally designed and animated transitions and titles that run throughout your movie, usually an opening-credit sequence, a special transition style, and a closing-credit sequence. Themes in iMovie look and work a lot like the cool animated DVD menus you can make in iDVD (Chapters 16 and 18). But iMovie themes don't require a DVD player; they're built right into your movie with all the same cool artwork and animations.

---

iMovie has five themes: Photo Album, Bulletin Board, Comic Book, Scrapbook, and Filmstrip. Each one includes custom transitions and titles.

Choosing a Theme

Anytime you create a new project, iMovie gives you the chance to apply a theme to it. The new project dialog box, shown in Figure 5-10, lines up the theme choices in a grid of skimmable previews. You can skim them to get some sense of what each theme has to offer.

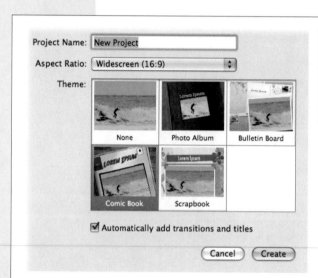

Figure 5-10:
Each of these themes has its own character and style. You can skim across them to get an idea of what your project will look like. If you want iMovie to automatically insert theme elements as you go, check the box "Automatically add transitions and titles" that appears when you click your chosen theme.

Once you click a theme in this window, you're offered the option of having iMovie automatically add transitions and titles for you. With the "Automatically add transitions and titles" box turned on, each new clip or picture you add to your storyboard comes along with some sort of added transition or title, either from those specific to the theme or from the standard list of transitions. Whether it's a simple cross dissolve or an animated photo album, iMovie mixes things up and avoids too many similar transitions in a row.

You can always change your mind. The moment you add your own transition, however, iMovie warns you that you'll need to turn off automatic transitions to proceed (Figure 5-11).

> **TIP** Don't forget the handy trick you learned in "Turning off Automatic Transitions" on page 123. That is, you can avoid having to insert transitions individually by letting iMovie do the work for you. Once all the transitions are in place, you can change them to your heart's content.

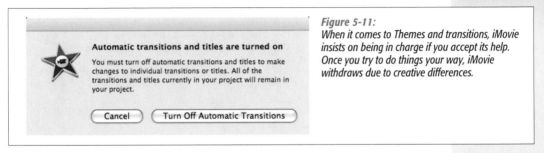

Figure 5-11:
When it comes to Themes and transitions, iMovie insists on being in charge if you accept its help. Once you try to do things your way, iMovie withdraws due to creative differences.

If you turned off the automatic transitions and decide that you really were better off with iMovie in charge, go to File → Project Properties. On the General tab, you can turn automatic transitions back on. Click OK and iMovie promptly scraps your custom transitions and sets them back to its liking. Remember, though, that turning automatic theme transitions on and off sends you through the same Extend Clips rigmarole covered on page 123.

Custom Theme Transition and Titles

If you choose a project theme, iMovie offers you additional transitions and titles available only to that theme, as shown in Figure 5-12. If you choose "None" for your theme, these transitions and titles don't show up in your list of choices.

> **TIP**   If you like having options but don't want your movie dominated by a theme, go ahead and pick a theme—but leave the automatic transitions and titles turned off. You can still add them manually.

Figure 5-12:
With a chosen theme assigned to your project, iMovie offers four more transitions and eight more titles than before. If you don't like the theme itself, just click the Set Theme button to change it.

On the other hand, if you choose a theme, you're locked out from the custom stuff available to the *other* four themes. (Maybe that's for the best. Mixing themes could look pretty ugly anyway.)

Changing a Theme

iMovie is very generous to the wishy-washy. Each theme has title and transition elements that correspond precisely to those in the other themes. When you change to a different theme, iMovie just replaces elements from the old theme with the matching elements from the new one.

To change a theme, choose File → Project Properties and click the new theme you want. Once you click OK, iMovie takes a moment to update all of the corresponding elements. Everything else, like timing and the clips in the project, stays the same.

> **TIP**   You can also change a theme by clicking the Set Theme button at the top of either the Titles or Transitions window. Clicking the button brings up a dialog box just for changing themes. Click the new theme you want, and then click OK.

Adjusting Theme Transitions

You can adjust a theme transition's length the same way you adjust a regular transition's length (page 117): Point to the transition and click the ✿ badge on the transition's icon. From the menu that appears, choose Transition Adjustments. The Inspector pops up; here, you can type in a new duration (in seconds and tenths of seconds). Click Done.

But one of the coolest things about themes is that they incorporate your pictures and video *into* the neat animations that go between clips. The animated photo album, for example (Figure 5-13), displays your video and photos as though they were actual photos in the album.

Figure 5-13:
Your movie looks professionally designed thanks to the way iMovie inserts your photos and videos into theme transitions and titles, like this transition from the Photo Album theme.

iMovie automatically chooses what clips go where in the animation, but you can have some influence on the outcome. (This may be especially useful if iMovie happened to choose the part of the clip where you are shoveling birthday cake into your mouth.) To make a more dignified appearance in theme animations:

1. **Click the animated transition you want to adjust.**

   When you click the theme transition that needs changing, orange numbers hover above various points in your storyboard. The little orange numbers represent different frames in the animation and are identified in the preview window. (See Figure 5-14.)

   NOTE   If you don't see the orange numbers, one of two things may be going on. First, some transitions just aren't editable. Second, there are often canned *portions* of editable ones.

2. **Drag the numbers where you want them.**

   As you drag the numbers to different points in your storyboard, iMovie updates the frames to show whatever image is under the corresponding number. This is how you'd drag the number away from *your* cake-stuffed face to your *brother's* cake-stuffed face.

3. **Preview your changes.**

   As with most editable iMovie elements, such as titles or photos, you can preview your changes by clicking the arrow in the top right corner of your preview window.

4. **Click Done.**

   iMovie displays the transition with the updated images.

   NOTE   If you've used themes in iMovie HD, you know that the old iMovie theme elements could use *any* photos and videos, even if they didn't show up anywhere else in your project. iMovie '09 isn't as generous. iMovie '09 themes point only to parts of photos or clips that are actually in your storyboard. Anything that isn't going to be shown full screen isn't going into the theme transitions, either.

Removing a Theme

You may come to the realization that a particular project is worse off with a theme applied to it. If this happens, you can always remove the offending theme. Click File → Project Properties; on the General tab, click None, then OK. iMovie sweeps away all the theme-related titles and transitions, leaving you with a decidedly less themey project. (Non-theme transitions, like cross dissolves, survive iMovie's sweep.)

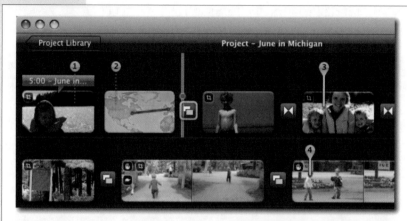

Figure 5-14:
Some theme transitions can be adjusted so that the images in the animation show the part of the project you choose. Dragging the orange numbers around in your project changes the corresponding frame.

Travel Maps

Just in case you didn't get the memo, here's some big news: iMovie loves travel footage. Maybe Apple did some rigorous focus-group research, or maybe the Apple programmer behind iMovie '09 just loves to travel. Whatever the reason, if you travel, iMovie has a special place in its heart for you.

Travel Maps are the grandest token of iMovie's travel-love. These are basically animated maps that take viewers from Point A to Point B with a snaking, animated red line across a map or a globe, à la the Indiana Jones movies. They're great for conveying your itinerary details in a quick, visually compelling way. Although you might think of them as transitions—after all, they fill the space between things, in this case places, much as transitions do—iMovie doesn't think of them that way. To iMovie, they're specialized video clips.

Adding a Travel Map

In the middle toolbar, on the far right, is a button with a globe icon (see Figure 5-15). Click it to open the Maps and Backgrounds pane. At the top of the list are eight different animated map options: a globe version and a flat version of four different map styles. There are also non-animated versions of each map style you can stick in your project as images. Scrolling down, you'll find a bunch of images that look nothing like maps (hence the "and Backgrounds" part). These are just pictures that you can use, for example, as backgrounds for titles.

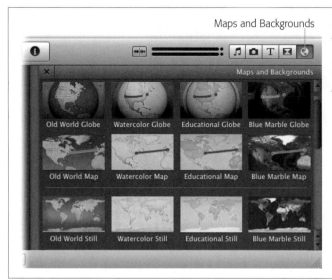

Maps and Backgrounds

Figure 5-15:
At the top of the Maps and Backgrounds window are eight different animated map options, four globes and four flat maps, to choose from. To add one of these to your project, just drag it in.

Adding an animated travel map to your project is a matter of dragging one of the eight icons into your project, just as you would a transition or a video clip. iMovie generates a specialized video clip that you can now customize.

Changing Travel Points

As soon as you drag a map icon into your project, the Inspector window appears. (If you don't see it, point to the map clip and click the ✿ badge. From the menu that appears, choose Clip Adjustments.) That's fortunate, because the first order of business is to change the endpoints of your new animated map. After all, showing the dramatic flight from Topeka to Tangiers is why you're putting this thing into your movie to begin with. You can choose your departure and destination points from a list of hundreds of preset locations (Figure 5-16).

To change a location, click the San Francisco button (or whatever it says next to Start Location). The Inspector flips around to reveal a huge list of cities and airports. You can winnow down the list by typing a destination's name into the box at the top of the window. Click to highlight the desired location, and then click OK.

Figure 5-16:
iMovie offers hundreds of potential destinations for your travel map. If you don't see the place you need, you can choose a nearby location, and then change the display name of that spot.

Repeat the process for the End Location, and then click Done once your locations are set.

> **TIP** If the list doesnÕt offer the location you want, you can type in the decimal coordinates (for example, *44.768056, -85.622222* points to Traverse City, MI.) You can get these coordinates at *www.itouchmap.com/latlong.html*. Then just edit the "Name to display" text at the bottom of the Inspector window.

Changing a Map's Style

If you started with a globe map and decide you prefer a flat map, or if you started with the Educational Map and like the Watercolor Map better, you can easily change it. Just drag a new map from the Maps and Backgrounds pane onto the map that needs replacing. iMovie preserves locations and the length of the animation.

> **TIP** Because iMovie treats a travel map like a clip, you can apply most video effects to the map as well. You might do this to match a map's style to the rest of your video. If you bring up the Inspector window (select the map and click the ❶ button in the middle toolbar), you see an option for video effects. Click None and iMovie shows you skimmable previews of 20 effects you can apply to your map. Click an effect and then click Done.

Changing a Map's Timing

If a map's animation is too slow or too fast, you can adjust it using one of three methods.

- **Use the Inspector.** Start by bringing up the Inspector (click the map icon in your project and then click the ❶ button in the middle toolbar). Here, you can type the duration you prefer, in seconds and frames, into the Duration text box. Click Done.

POWER USERS' CLINIC

Adding Locations to iMovie

If your destination isn't in iMovie's permanent list, you can make a permanent addition for each location you will use a lot, like Grandma's house. You can go into the file that tells iMovie where these places are and add your own. But proceed at your own risk! This trick is pretty advanced, so try it only if you're comfortable mucking about in files Apple didn't intend for amateurs to muck about in.

Find the iMovie icon in the Applications folder. Control-click (or right-click) it and choose Show Package Contents. In the resulting window, open the Contents → Resources folder. Find the file called *WorldLocation.txt*. Make a safety copy of this file, and then double-click the original. Unless you've hacked your Mac's document-to-program relationships, this file opens in TextEdit, revealing a list of map locations.

This is a tab-delimited list. That is, each location is listed something like this: *City TAB State TAB Country TAB Latitude and Longitude.* Feel free to add your custom location to the bottom of the list, following that pattern. For

non-US locations, you can replace the State with a region or province. (Or you can leave it blank. Just press Tab twice to skip that part.) Latitude and Longitude need to be separated by a comma and no spaces. If you need to look up the coordinates for a given location, use Google to help you.

Finally, save the changes to WorldLocations.txt and restart iMovie. The next time you go into your list of locations, the location you added now appears in the list. Adding it to a travel map works just the same as the locations iMovie came with.

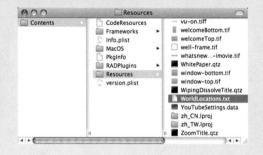

- **Extendo Buttons.** iMovie offers the same Extendo buttons it does to project clips. Click one of the double-arrow icons that appear in either corner when you point to the map clip in your project. An orange handle appears, which you can use to lengthen or shorten the clip by up to one second. It doesn't matter which end of the map you use. Either end will have the same effect on the map.

- **Select a Range and Delete.** This option can only *shorten* a map. Drag across a segment of the map clip's icon, and then press the Delete key. The map animation will still draw a line from Point A to Point B, but faster than before. Beware, though: If you select a middle portion of the map and delete that, iMovie makes *two* maps, each of which draws the line to its destination.

Removing a Map

To remove a map, just select its clip icon in the storyboard and hit the Delete key.

Video Effects, Slo-Mo, Green Screen, and Picture-in-Picture

It's a funny thing that we'll take pristine HD video and make it look old and grainy. On purpose. But video effects, like the popular Aged Film effect, create a mood that can't really be communicated in any other way.

That's why so many people were outraged to find that iMovie '08 came without any built-in video effects. You couldn't even slow clips down or speed them up. These newfangled boxes we call computers were supposed to make advanced video effects easy, not nonexistent. To make matters worse, you couldn't install new effects into iMovie '08 in the form of plug-ins from other companies, as you could in the old iMovie. A lot of people swore off iMovie '08 altogether as a result.

If you're reading this book, it may even be because you've heard the good news about iMovie '09: Apple brought back all of those missing effects. Slo-Mo is back. Reverse motion is back. Aged film is back. Apple even added new effects that iMovie has never had before, like Picture-in-Picture and Green Screen. (Still no plug-ins, though.)

And maybe best of all, you don't even have to wait for the software to *render* (process) an effect. Everything described in this chapter is immediately viewable in your project. This new state of video effects in iMovie is pretty compelling, even if it took a detour to get here.

Video Effects

What iMovie calls Video Effects may be better described as video filters. They don't insert lightning bolts or fairy dust, as iMovie effects have done in the past. Video filters in iMovie '09 generally change only the color and definition of the underlying video. (The one notable exception to this is the Flipped effect, which displays a mirror image of your clip.)

The difference between these filters and the Rain and Lens Flare effects of yesteryear isn't just technical, but also stylistic. Apple decided, rightly or not, that the old, gimmicky effects didn't do much to make your movies better. (Never mind the fact that you may have had *fun* using them.) The new filters are much more subtle and nuanced.

The Effects

A rundown of iMovie's video effects is in order (Figure 6-1). Some of these effects will sound familiar if you're a veteran of the original iMovie.

Figure 6-1:
Most video effects in iMovie are really video filters, each of which adds a unique style to your movie. This image demonstrates some of the effects. Clockwise from top left: The original clip, Cartoon, Vignette, X-Ray, Heat Wave, and the much adored Aged Film.

- **Flipped**. Turns your clip into a mirror image of itself.

- **Raster**. Covers your clip with horizontal scan lines like you'd see on an old TV.

- **Cartoon**. Smoothes the different colors in your clip to make it look like the clip was taken from a comic book.

- **Aged Film**. One of the most popular effects, Aged Film applies a sepia tone (see below) and film noise to make your clip look like an old, worn-out filmstrip.

- **Film Grain**. Applies a mild sepia tone and adds tiny speckles that look like grainy film.

- **Hard Light**. Overexposes the light colors and darkens the dark colors.

- **Day into Night.** Darkens the whole clip with a bluish hue, as though shot at night.

- **Glow.** Overexposes the light colors *without* darkening the dark colors.

- **Dream.** Blurs the clip and washes out its colors, to convey the idea that you're dreaming.

- **Romantic.** Blurs just the edges of the clip, so your focus rests on whatever's in the center of the clip (presumably the object of your desire).

- **Vignette.** Instead of blurring the edges, this effect fades the edges to black, not unlike what you'd see in studio photography from the 1980s.

- **Bleach Bypass.** Washes out colors, just like bleach.

- **Old World.** A sepia tone and a glow combined. Yet another way to make that high-tech footage look low-tech.

- **Heat Wave.** This is what your clip would look like under the punishing desert sun, yellow and overexposed.

- **Sci-Fi.** If you've seen the *Matrix* movies, you know exactly what Sci-Fi looks like. It applies a green hue to everything.

- **Black & White.** The old classic.

- **Sepia Tone.** The other old classic. Applies a brownish hue to everything, making it look like ancient photographs or films from the turn of the century (the turn of the *previous* century).

- **Negative.** Inverts all the colors in your clip by replacing them with their color-wheel opposites.

- **X-Ray.** Turns everything into shades of greenish-gray, with lights and darks inverted. Presumably, this is what your movie would look like if you filmed the whole thing with an X-ray machine.

Applying a Video Effect

You can apply video effects to any clip or photo in your project, even cutaways and travel maps. Start by double-clicking the clip (or, if it's selected, clicking the ❶ in the middle toolbar) to open the Inspector panel. Click the None button next to the Video Effect label.

The Inspector flips around, revealing a bunch of little thumbnails that show what your clip would look like with the video effect applied (Figure 6-2). As you skim across each thumbnail, the preview window demonstrates the effect. To finally apply an effect, click the thumbnail itself. When the Inspector flips back around, click Done.

POWER USERS' CLINIC

QuickTime Video Filters

The old iMovie effects haven't all disappeared; some just went into hiding.

In Chapter 14, you can read about exporting iMovie projects as *QuickTime* movies—digital movie files on the hard drive. During that exporting process, you'll have the opportunity to apply the special effects that are still around. These *filters*, as they're called, can process your footage in ways like these:

Blur softens the look of the video.

Edge Detect creates outlines of the subjects in your footage.

Emboss makes your footage look like it was carved into a sheet of metal.

Sharpen makes blurry footage sharper (as much as is possible anyway).

Color Tint makes your footage turn black-and-white, sepia tone, cobalt, or negative image.

Film Noise adds scratches, dust, and rot to otherwise modern footage.

Lens Flare adds a cool-looking light flare that progresses across your footage as though caught in the lens of your camera.

Unfortunately, you have to apply these filters at the moment you export a project as a QuickTime movie—and that means the filter has to apply to your *entire* movie.

So what if you want to apply one of these filters to just *one* clip within a movie? The trick: Create a separate project containing only that one clip. Export the one-clip project using the steps on page 292.

When it's all over, you'll have a QuickTime file on your hard drive, which you can bring right back into iMovie using the File → Import Movies command. Once the filtered footage is back in your Event library, just add it to your main project.

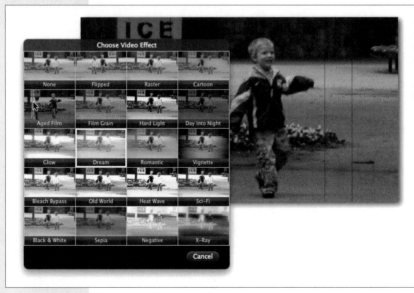

Figure 6-2:
iMovie's video effects generally affect the color and clarity of your clips. You can preview them by skimming over the little thumbnails.

TIP   You can also play the clip (with the effect applied) by tapping the space bar while you're previewing the video effects. iMovie plays the clip repeatedly while you make up your mind. As your clip plays back, you can point to other effect thumbnails in the preview window (without clicking) to see what they'd look like when applied to your looping video.

Adjusting a Video Effect

You can't make any adjustments to iMovie's video effects as you could in previous iMovie versions. If you don't like the exact way the effect comes from Apple, you're out of luck.

Removing a Video Effect

To remove a video effect, pull up the Inspector again, click the button that identifies the current effect, and then click the None thumbnail. The Inspector flips back around. Click Done.

Fast/Slow/Reverse

Whether you're mimicking *Chariots of Fire* or Buddy Hall, you can add a lot to your movie by changing the speed of your footage. Slowing a clip down emphasizes the drama of the moment. Speeding a clip up conveys urgency, depicts the passage of time, or just makes it funny.

Another new iMovie '09 trick is changing the speed and direction of your footage. Actually, since the old, original iMovie had these features, you could say that Apple is teaching a new dog old tricks.

Changing a Clip's Speed

To make a clip play back faster or slower, double-click it to open the Inspector panel. In the middle of this panel, you'll see one of two things:

- **Convert Entire Clip.** Ordinarily, Apple hides ugly technical underpinnings from you. If you want to play with the speed or direction of a clip's playback, however, you come face-to-face with one unfortunate technicality: iMovie can't adjust the speed or direction of a clip unless, as it sits there on your hard drive, it happens to be in a particular file format. (It's the aforementioned Apple Intermediate Codec [page 43] format, in case you're wondering.)

   NOTE   The Convert Entire Clip conversion step isn't necessary if you're editing footage imported from an *AVCHD* camera (page 7). That's because iMovie has *already* converted your footage into the same format it uses for fast/slow/reverse.

   If you see the Convert Entire Clip button, click it (Figure 6-3).

   NOTE   When iMovie says Convert Entire Clip, it means the *entire* clip. Even if you've used only part of a clip from your Event Browser, the conversion process makes a speedable copy of the entire thing.

CHAPTER 6: VIDEO EFFECTS, SLO-MO, GREEN SCREEN, AND PICTURE-IN-PICTURE

Figure 6-3:
Top: You'll need to convert this clip before you can change its speed or direction.

Bottom: The conversion process may take a minute or two, depending on the length of your source clip.

• **Speed slider.** If a clip is speed-adjustable (either you've already converted it, or it didn't need conversion), you see a slider in the middle of the Inspector panel, depicting a tortoise and a hare (Figure 6-4). (The hare's winning for the time being, but we can assume it's early in the race.)

Dragging the slider closer to the tortoise slows your clip. Dragging the slider to the hare speeds it up.

Figure 6-4:
Change the speed of your clip by dragging the Speed slider. You can make your clip up to eight times faster or eight times slower. If you want to be really precise, type the percentage change or the desired length in the corresponding text boxes next to the slider.

Reversing a Clip's Playback Direction

Playing a clip backward has been a comedic staple since the time film was born. To do it in iMovie, all you need to do is check a box.

Double-click the clip to open the Inspector window (or click it and then click ❶ on the toolbar). Assuming you've converted the clip as described above, a Reverse checkbox appears beneath the Speed slider. Turn it on (Figure 6-5) to make the video play backward. (You'll also notice that the tortoise is now winning the little race, which is as it should be. The two animal icons have flipped themselves around to face the opposite direction. Cute.)

Figure 6-5:
In this example, you've reversed a clip and slowed it down.

Removing Speed and Direction Changes

If you've *just* fooled with a clip's speed or playback direction, you can bring it back to normal by choosing File → Undo or pressing ⌘-Z.

If it's too late for that, select the clip, open the Inspector, drag the Speed slider back to the middle position, and turn off Reverse. There. Time and space are back to normal.

Green Screen

iMovie has opened the door to all kinds of fun with this one. Why film your kids playing in the backyard, when you could film them playing on the *moon*? Or wherever.

The Green Screen effect lets you superimpose your subjects on whatever background you can think up, just as they've been doing in Hollywood for decades. With a little preparation, you could film things that were otherwise impossible to shoot (Figure 6-6).

Figure 6-6:
Top: This is what your kids look like in front of a green screen.

Bottom: This is what your kids look like hurtling through space. Pretty cool.

Preparing the Green Screen

Professional green screens can cost hundreds to thousands of dollars, which is *way* too much to pay for something you're editing in iMovie. The brains behind iMovie get this, so they've designed the Green Screen to work with some pretty common, inexpensive materials.

You can try almost any kind of green background, as long as it's a bright, pure green color (no limes, turquoises, or pines) and isn't too shiny (see below). Fabric stores are a good bet, as are hardware stores that carry broad paint selections. Figure 6-7 shows how you can fake it.

How Green Screens Work

Green screen (like its predecessor, *blue screen*) is another term for an editing technique that the Hollywood pros call Chroma Key. The idea is that you tell your computer to replace every pixel of a certain color (like vibrant green) with new footage. In other words, anything that's *not* green (like the actor) gets superimposed onto the background stuff.

This is how Superman flew, how Neo dodged bullets in *The Matrix*, how *The Daily Show* correspondents seem to be in Paris or Iraq or Washington, and how TV actors never seem to hit anyone when they're in driving scenes and paying no attention to the road. The actors performed their scenes with smooth green fabric filling the car windows; later, editors (and their computers) replaced all patches of green with passing scenery. Watching actors in front of a green screen can be quite funny. They have to pretend they're being chased through the jungle by a dinosaur, when in fact they're sitting in a nondescript studio with its walls painted green, without so much as a vine in sight.

Green replaced blue as the most popular color for this technique because digital cameras are most sensitive to green. (Blue remains the runner-up, which is why it's sometimes used in place of green. But in iMovie, green is your only option.) Of course, this also means you can't wear green clothes in the shot, unless you are intentionally going for the floating-disembodied-head-thing.

TIP   A popular, low-budget approach is to buy some green fabric and attach it to a frame you make from plastic pipes or wood slats. If you don't glue the pipe joints, you can even make it collapsible. Use green paint only if you have a stiff, smooth surface that can be green, like the wall in your basement or garage. Keep in mind that surfaces like this are probably less mobile.

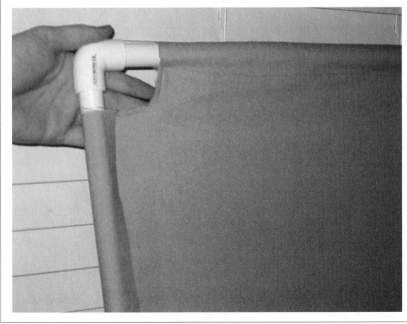

Figure 6-7:
This poor man's green screen cost $20, and was made with four yards of fabric from a fabric store, 24 feet of plastic pipe, and four "L" joints.

Getting the Shot

Besides having the right color of green, here's a short list of other tips that will make a world of difference in your Green Screen shots.

- **Good lighting.** The last thing you want are shadows on your green background, because shadows change the color your computer sees and ruin the seamless effect. Shadows cast by the actors themselves are particularly frustrating. The best bet is to light the background and the actor with separate light sources.

- **Lots of space.** Whether or not you have great lighting (but especially if you don't), keep lots of space between your actors and the green background. Four feet is a decent rule of thumb. This reduces the likelihood of shadows messing up the effect your computer will apply.

  NOTE   Good lighting and lots of space also helps you avoid the dreaded halo. When the lighting's poor or the actors are too close to the green screen, green light can reflect off your subjects. The outcome is a strange halo effect that makes it easier to tell that the subject isn't *really* flying through outer space.

- **No shine.** Some green materials, like poster board, come in the right color but if they're shiny, they reflect white light in addition to green. Green fabric is preferable, because it diffuses light and minimizes reflections. If you're using poster board, just make sure you don't see any glare.

- **No bumps or wrinkles.** We're not talking about your actors here. To eliminate shadows, the green surface has to be smooth. Wrinkles and bumps make the computer-added background look wrinkled and bumpy, too.

- **No other greens.** Don't let your actors, or anything else you want in the shot, wear green.

- **Get a key shot.** At the end of your shot, shoot just a few frames of the green background without your subjects in it. You can use it later to help iMovie figure out what belongs and what doesn't. Don't stop the camera before the actors exit, however; if you do that, iMovie imports the key shot as a separate clip, ruining your chances of putting it to any use. (See "Using a Key Frame" on page 149.)

Inserting a Green Screen Effect

Now that you've shot your green screen footage and imported it into iMovie, the rest is refreshingly easy. Before you do any of this, in the iMovie preferences, turn on Advanced Tools (page 80).

1. **Choose your background footage and add it to your project.**

   You can choose a still image or video footage, but avoid using backgrounds that distract from the subjects in the foreground. Be especially aware of scale; for example, close-up footage of garden flowers will make your actors looks unnaturally small. (Of course, you may be going for that *Honey, I Shrunk the Kids* look on purpose.)

If you're using moving footage, consider two things. First, because your subjects were lit a certain way, try to shoot a background with similar lighting. (Or try to shoot your actors with similar lighting, like daylight for daylight.)

Second, make sure that you've filmed *enough* background footage to cover the duration of your actors' scene. Or just repeat the background footage—loop it—by adding it to your project several times over.

2. **Select your green screen footage. Drop it onto your background clip.**

When you drag it and drop it onto your background, the Drag and Drop menu appears (Figure 6-8).

3. **From the shortcut menu, choose Green Screen.**

iMovie superimposes your green-screen clip onto the underlying background. In the storyboard, the green screen clip has a green border and floats on top of the background clip.

4. **Crop your green screen clip.**

While your green-screen clip is selected, the preview window offers some draggable points. Drag them until they tightly surround your subject. Everything outside the points will show your background, whether it was green or not, so those are areas where you don't have to worry about shadows, lighting, or wrinkles. Just be careful, when you drag the boundaries, to not eliminate an area where your actors will be at some point or they'll wind up losing body parts in a most unnatural way. (To check, play the entire clip by clicking the |▶| button in the preview window.)

Adjust the points accordingly, and click Done.

5. **Adjust the timing.**

You can drag the green-screen clip (the upper one in the storyboard) left or right to adjust its playback relationship to the background clip. When that green-screen clip isn't selected, you can also drag its ends to move it. To get really specific about the clip's timing, use the Clip Trimmer (page 90).

6. **Adjust the sound.**

You can use Ducking, the Volume slider, or any of the other volume-adjustment tricks described in Chapter 9.

Adding Effects to a Green Screen Effect

You can stabilize a green-screen clip and change its speed or direction. You can do anything to it that you can do to a regular clip, *except* add a video effect.

That's a shame, really. Imagine how fun it would be to have the green-screen actors look like X-rays of themselves while talking to other actors you put in the background shot. Alas, it's not to be.

You can add video effects to the *background*, though. That, at least, has potential.

Figure 6-8:
Top: Adding a green screen effect uses the highly touted Advanced Drag and Drop feature.

Bottom: The storyboard displays your green screen clip hovering over the background clip.

Removing a Green Screen Effect

To remove a green screen, just select the green-screen clip and press the Delete key.

Picture-in-Picture (PiP)

Picture-in-Picture is the effect that lets TV junkies watch two channels at once. The football game fills the big screen, but *60 Minutes* plays in a small inset window in the corner.

POWER USERS' CLINIC

Using a Key Frame

If iMovie knows *exactly* what your green-screen background looks like, shadows and all, it can do a much better job of creating the effect, because it knows exactly what elements to remove.

That's why, when you film your actors in front of a green screen, it's a good idea to include (in the same shot, without stopping the camera) some video of the motionless green background all by itself, with the actors out of the frame.

(Why is it so important to shoot the empty-background video without turning off the camera? Because if you stop the camera, you'll get separate clips in iMovie—and you can't merge Event clips in iMovie. The moving-actors video

and the empty-background video must be part of the same clip.)

Then, once in iMovie, open the Inspector window. Turn on "Subtract last frame".

That doesn't mean iMovie is going to *delete* the last frame. It means, instead, "Subtract this *image* when superimposing the green-screen video." That is, by comparing the moving-actor footage with the still-background footage, iMovie knows what's background and what's actor. (This background-only portion of the clip doesn't have to appear in your project. As long as it was there at the end of the original, untrimmed clip, iMovie can use the "Subtract last frame" feature.)

In its heyday, PiP was a boon to those who hated commercials. When the ads came on, you could swap to another show, all the while keeping your eye on the channel carrying the game. The moment commercials ended, click, you were back.

Commercials are obviously not why you would use Picture-in-Picture effects in your movie. It's more likely that you'll use it to recreate the effect on the nightly news (or *The Daily Show*), where a magic box floats over the anchor person's shoulder to display some corny graphic to go along with the story. The PiP box in this case is *supplemental.*

iMovie's PiP effect lets you do the same kinds of things. It might be a family member narrating that great hit from the reunion softball game. It might be a shot of the crowd as your kid takes her bows at her recital. Whatever the reason, the primary footage stays primary, while the PiP box helps it along.

Inserting a PiP

Before the Picture-in-Picture feature can work, you need to turn on Advanced Tools, as described on page 80.

Now drag some Event footage to the storyboard and drop it onto one of your clips. When the shortcut menu appears, choose Picture-in-Picture. iMovie adds a whole new row above your normal project footage and sticks the added clip there (Figure 6-9).

> **NOTE**   At a glance, PiP clips in your storyboard may seem indistinguishable from cutaway clips (page 94) or green-screen clips but the color-coding can help you out. PiP clips have turquoise borders, cutaway clips have gray borders, and green-screen clips have (what else?) green borders.

Figure 6-9:
Top: When you add footage on top of a project clip, iMovie offers the Picture-in-Picture feature as an option (assuming the Advanced Tools are turned on).

Bottom: PiP clips in the storyboard cast a shadow on the clips underneath.

Adjusting the PiP Size and Position

On a TV, PiP boxes are relegated to one corner of the screen and usually have a fixed size. If iMovie insisted on such behavior, a PiP box might cover up Aunt Bertie's face the entire time. (Of course, that might not be such a bad thing.) The point is that when it comes to PiP placement, iMovie is much more flexible than your TV.

When you select the PiP clip in your storyboard, look at the preview window to see the effect. Notice the inset picture? You can drag that box anywhere in the frame. You can also resize it by dragging one of the corners inward or outward. In fact, you can, if you want, make the box big enough to cover *all* of Aunt Bertie. (Of course, if you're going to make the PiP box fill the whole screen, it may make more sense to use a Cutaway [page 94]).

> **NOTE** Although you can change the size and position of a PiP box, you can't change its *dimensions*. The box will always have the same proportion of height to width—4:3 or 16:9. (See page 56 for a primer on aspect ratios.)

Changing the PiP Appearance

There's more to a PiP box than just size and position. You can actually change quite a few other aspects of its appearance. Each of these involve a trip to the Inspector panel, which appears when you double-click the PiP clip (Figure 6-10).

- **Change the PiP effect.** Using the PiP Effect pop-up menu, you can control how the smaller, inset video makes its appearance. None means it simply blinks onto the screen. Dissolve makes the inset fade in and out. Zoom makes the PiP box zoom forward to its spot, then, at the end, zoom back to its original location. Swap makes the two clips trade places, so that the underlying footage becomes the PiP). Adjust the PiP Effect slider to control the speed of these transitions.

- **Change the box border.** The Border Width and Border Color options control the outline that appears around the inset video. Your width options are none, thin, or thick. Choose any color you like for the border color, as long as it's black, gray, or white.

- **Add a drop shadow.** Turn on Drop Shadow to make the inset cast a subtle shadow on the underlying video, as though it's floating just above.

- **Change it just like a regular clip.** Even though it's a PiP clip, you can still do everything else to it, like stabilize it, add a video effect to it, or speed it up and slow it down. You may need to make these adjustments to get the clip to look more like the rest of your project.

Figure 6-10:
This PiP clip has a thin, white border, a drop shadow, and will fade in and out.

Mixing PiP Audio

There are a lot of reasons to use a PiP effect, and *none* of them involve having the audio from both clips on full volume. You want either the underlying clip *or* the PiP clip to be heard.

Fortunately, you can control their relative volume levels just as you would any clips, using the Volume slider or the Ducking feature. Both are described on page 219.

Moving and Trimming a PiP Clip

The odds are that you didn't get your PiP clip into *exactly* the right place when you dropped it in your storyboard. You can fix its position by grabbing any space inside the yellow selection border and dragging it to the correct spot.

> **NOTE** If your PiP clip covers a transition, the transition won't work. iMovie creates a clean cut between the clips instead.

You may also have to adjust the *length* of your PiP clip. You don't want too much or too little of the clip to play. While the PiP clip is *deselected* (the border is turquoise, *not* yellow), grab either end of the clip and drag it to make the clip longer or shorter.

> **TIP** To get *really* precise with the length and content of your PiP clip, use the Clip Trimmer (page 90) instead.

Removing a PiP Clip

Change your mind? Just select the PiP clip and hit the Delete key.

Stabilization, Color Fixes, Cropping, and Rotating

Not every piece of video needs fancy effects. In fact, most video is probably better without a Dream filter and Picture-in-Picture. The unadulterated stuff straight from your camera usually looks best.

In fact, if your footage needs any help at all, it's probably in the cameraman department. Don't take this personally. Handheld shots, the most common kind of home video, are notoriously unstable, and that's an instant giveaway that you're an amateur. You can have the hands of a surgeon and still end up with shaky footage. This is true even with all the newfangled image stabilization technology that comes in the latest cameras.

Don't give up (and don't resort to carrying a tripod everywhere). iMovie '09 can stabilize your video *after the fact,* using one of its most amazing new features.

That's not the only way iMovie can fix your footage, either. The Video Adjustments panel lets you make slight or gigantic changes to the brightness, contrast, white balance, saturation, and other image qualities of any clip.

For example, if a shot looks too dark and murky, you can bring details out of the shadows without blowing out the highlights. If the snow in a skiing shot looks too bluish, you can de-blue it. If the colors don't pop quite enough in the prize-winning soccer goal shot, you can boost their saturation levels.

In addition, the new program offers two features that the old iMovie versions couldn't even fantasize about:

- **Cropping**. Cropping video means to use only a portion of the frame, like an artificial zoom.

- **Rotation**. You can turn the entire video image 90 degrees, or even upside-down.

Coolest of all, iMovie does all of this—picture adjustment, cropping, and rotating—*instantaneously and nondestructively*. That is, there's no waiting around while iMovie renders (processes) the changes you make, which makes joyous, real-time experimentation possible. (Stabilization is the major exception to the instantaneous thing, but that doesn't make the results less impressive.) Furthermore, you're never actually making changes to the original clips. You can restore the original video any time you like.

This chapter introduces you to all of iMovie '09's more subtle video effects.

Video Stabilization

Say what you will about the new iMovie, one thing's for sure: It has powers that leave other "beginner" video-editing programs panting with envy. It's filled with tools that have historically been found only in professional editing programs. iMovie's stabilization feature, for example, is inherited from Apple's $1,000 Final Cut Pro software.

It works by analyzing every single frame in a clip, recognizing the changes in both camera position (movement up, down, left, or right) and camera rotation. Once it figures that bit out, it knows how to slide and rotate your clips to iron out the shakes.

Unfortunately, this sort of analysis takes a *very* long time—roughly ten minutes for every minute of video (more or less depending on your Mac's speed).

The results, however, are worth it. The stabilization feature works absolute magic on most jerky, bumpy handheld footage. It works so well, in fact, that it can look positively creepy, as though you were floating along on a magic carpet. Fortunately, there's a slider that lets you control how much stabilizing goes on.

Four Ways to Trigger Stabilization Analysis

Before iMovie can stabilize your video, it has to perform the abovementioned analysis, which takes a long time. Fortunately, you have a lot of control over when the program does this processing:

- **Stabilize during import.** You're offered the opportunity to perform the analysis when you bring the footage into your Mac, as described on page 30.

- **Stabilize selected clips.** You can analyze certain clips at any time. Select one, or a group of them, and then choose File → Analyze for Stabilization.

- **Stabilize an entire Event.** In the list, click an Event's name and then choose File → "Analyze for Stabilization". This option is great if the Event in question is someone jumping on a trampoline during an earthquake.

- **Stabilize a clip in the Event Browser.** Double-click the clip to open the Inspector panel. Click Analyze Entire Clip (Figure 7-1).

UP TO SPEED

Two Stabilization Weaknesses

The iMovie stabilizing feature is impressive, but it isn't magic. In fact, two common distortions that come from camera shake are unfixable. And iMovie makes these distortions look *worse* because it takes away the shake they like to hide in.

The first distortion is *Motion Blur*. Unless you have a camera that shoots at really high frame rates, it's possible to swing your camera around so fast that the pixels actually become *blurred*. Although iMovie can stabilize the frames relative to each other, it can't sharpen the blurriness in individual frames. When you play back stabilized footage with blurry frames, it looks like the camera is moving in and out of focus.

The second distortion, *Video Jelly*, can arise when you shoot with a camera that contains a so-called CMOS light-sensor chip. Some still cameras, like the Nikon D90, and many newer AVCHD cameras, contain this sort of chip.

Unfortunately, CMOS cameras use a rolling shutter, which means the sensor data starts recording at the top of the sensor working down to the bottom, really fast. If the camera is moving too much during filming, the subject gradually shifts left or right during that pass down the sensor.

Already, that effect makes the world look a little like it's suddenly made of jelly, but stabilization makes the jelly-effect stand out and look especially jiggly.

Fortunately, most video cameras and still cameras that shoot video still use CCD sensors rather than CMOS sensors, so you may never see the jelly problem.

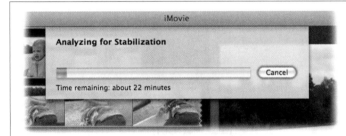

Figure 7-1:
Be prepared for a wait when you decide to analyze a clip. Depending on the speed of your computer, it can take between five and twelve minutes (or longer for older Macs) for every minute of footage stabilized. If you have a lot to analyze, let the Mac do its job overnight while you get some beauty sleep.

- **Stabilize a clip that's already in the storyboard.** Point to the clip, and then from the ❖ menu, choose Clip Adjustments. On the panel that appears, turn on "Smooth clip motion". This is a great trick when you're looking over a project in progress and discover that one particular jerky shot is ruining the flow. It can also save you a lot of time, because iMovie stabilizes only the 20 seconds of a clip that you've actually *used*—plus an additional second on either side—rather than processing the 15-minute original (see Figure 7-2).

If you later decide to lengthen the clip you stabilized (by more than a second), you'll need to do more analyzing. The once-checked checkbox in the Inspector will require rechecking. Fortunately, iMovie analyzes only the new part you added that wasn't already analyzed.

Then go knit a sweater while you wait for your Mac to analyze your footage.

Figure 7-2:
A stabilized clip in your project displays a checkmark in the Stabilization box, plus the Maximum Zoom slider. Turn Stabilization on and off all you like; iMovie never has to analyze a clip but once.

POWER USERS' CLINIC

Hide Shaky Footage

If you're in the habit of analyzing Event footage, you'll probably see swaths of red squiggly lines all over the clips in your browser. Most of this stuff is pure dreck—so jerky, it's beyond iMovie's capacity to stabilize it, and unworthy of any project you may create. If you agree, and you're sure you have no use for it, you can hide excessively shaky video from view so none of it ever sneaks into your storyboard.

Underneath your Event Browser, next to the Favorites filter menu, there's a red squiggly button that matches the red squiggly line branding all of your shakiest footage. Click this button to make all of the shaky stuff invisible.

Because shaky footage sneaks into the middle of clips, many of your Event clips will be split into smaller pieces as a result, but it's not permanent. Click the button again, turning the gray line red, to make the shaky footage reappear. Your clips are whole once more.

Note that the button disappears when you're using the keyword filter, as covered on page 108. In that case, you make shaky footage invisible using the Excessive Shake keyword.

Degrees of Stabilization

Once you've stabilized some video, you may be delighted and amazed at how professional and smooth it looks. You might ask yourself "Was I wearing a Steadi-Cam?" (those gyro-mounted camera harnesses the Hollywood pros wear for stability). Or not.

You may be a little alarmed by how fake it looks. You were running down a flight of stairs, for crying out loud. It should look a *little* like you were on foot, not like you were gliding down a sheet of ice.

For that reason, you can *throttle back* the amount of stabilizing that iMovie does. Double-click the stabilized clip to open its Inspector panel, where you'll see the Maximum Zoom slider (Figure 7-2).

Why is it called Maximum Zoom? Because iMovie does its work by shifting the whole picture around in the frame, counteracting your hand shakes pixel by pixel. This means, however, that you would see momentary glimpses of black emptiness between the video and the frame around it, which would be even more distracting than the shaky video. So iMovie conceals those slivers of blackness by enlarging the video just enough to fill the frame and eliminate the exposed black emptiness.

Of course, magnifying a photo (or a video frame) also reduces its resolution, and therefore its quality. It's very unlikely that you'll actually see the quality degrade but if you think you do, here's another reason for the Maximum Zoom slider: It can reduce the zooming. In other words, Maximum Zoom limits both the stabilizing effect *and* the zooming that goes along with it.

And now some stabilization notes:

- The more shake in your footage, the more zoom iMovie offers.

- As you zoom out, you may see the shaky-hand badge on your clip change colors. Zooming out on a black-badged clip, for example, may turn the little hand orange.

- If you crop away the shakiest part of a clip, iMovie may do a better job of stabilizing the rest. That's because iMovie figures out exactly how far it needs to zoom for the *shakiest part* of a project clip, and then applies that zoom amount to the whole clip.

If you see red squiggles painted across the bottom of your clip (see Figure 7-3), those sections are just too shaky for iMovie to be of any help. This is because no amount of tweaking the zoom, position, or rotation will rescue the video.

Removing Stabilization

You may change your mind and decide that a clip looks better without stabilization. It can happen (see box on page 155). Just double-click the clip to open the Inspector, and then turn off the box that says "Smooth clip motion". The shake comes back.

And don't worry about having to reanalyze footage if you change your mind again. It bears repeating: Once analyzed, always analyzed.

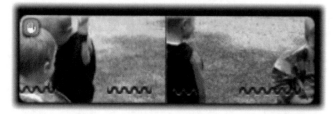

Figure 7-3:
Each of these three clip badges represents different levels of shake in your clip. From top to bottom: The black badge indicates very little to no shake. The orange badge tells you that there is moderate shake. The red badge means that the clip is very shaky. A red badge with a line through it is the sign that your clip is beyond hope. Clips tagged with this red badge also have red squiggles in them, painted on the specific parts that are too shaky to fix.

Color Fixes

iMovie can apply some awesome color-correction effects to your video. Here's the rundown.

Phase 1: Select the Clip, Find the Frame

iMovie can apply color fixes only to an entire clip at once. You can't make the effect fade in or out, you can't apply it to just a portion of a clip, and you can't apply it to multiple clips at once (although you *can* copy and paste the adjustments you make).

Before you apply an effect, therefore, you may want to start by isolating the piece you want. You can always chop up a clip into smaller pieces (page 93).

Then click the clip that needs help. You can click a filmstrip anywhere:

- **In the Event Browser.** If you click a raw source clip here, then the changes you make appear in *every project* that incorporates that clip.

• **In the project storyboard.** If you click a clip you've already placed into the storyboard, the changes you make affect that video *only in this movie*. The original, underlying source clip in the Event Browser remains unchanged.

(Of course, the truth is, you're never *really* changing anything at all. You can remove all your changes and revert to the original camcorder-captured clip at any time, even months or years from now.)

Once you've selected a clip, you see a still image of it in the Viewer window.

Phase 2: The Video Adjustments Panel

Now you're ready to open the Video Adjustments panel. Do that by pressing the V key on your keyboard, by clicking the ❶ button followed by the Video tab (Figure 7-4), or by clicking the ✿ on every filmstrip and selecting Video Adjustments from the shortcut menu.

Open Video Adjustments panel

Figure 7-4:
The Video Adjustments panel is part of the Inspector. You can drag it anywhere on the screen, and—here's the part that may not occur to you—you can move on to a different clip without having to close the panel first. (Click another clip from your filmstrips.) Also note that you can drag the tiny red dot to move around in the clip as you work.

If you've ever adjusted the colors of a picture in iPhoto, these controls should look familiar. They affect your video here exactly as they affect a digital photo in iPhoto.

Don't overlook the tiny red dot on the filmstrip itself (Figure 7-5). Using this dot, you can move around *within* the clip to find a better representative frame as you work. (That's important, because once the Video Adjustments panel is open, you can no longer skim in the usual way.)

Introduction to the Histogram

Learning to use the Video Adjustments panel effectively involves learning about its *histogram*, the colorful little graph at the top of the panel (visible in Figure 7-4).

The histogram is a self-updating visual representation of the dark and light tones that make up your video clip. If you've never encountered a histogram before, this may sound complicated. But the histogram is a terrific tool, and it'll make more sense the more you work with it.

Within each of the superimposed graphs (red, blue, and green), the scheme is the same: The clip's darker shades appear toward the left side of the graph; the lighter tones are graphed on the right side.

Therefore, in a very dark clip—a coalmine at midnight, say—you'll see big mountain peaks at the left side of the graph, trailing off to nothing toward the right. A shot of a brilliantly sunny snowscape, on the other hand, will show lots of information on the right, and very little on the left.

The best-balanced shots have some data spread across the entire histogram, with a few mountain-shaped peaks here and there. Those peaks and valleys represent the really dark spots and bright spots. Those mountains are fine, as long as you have some visual information in other parts of the histogram, too.

The histogram for a *bad* shot, on the other hand—a severely under- or overexposed one—has mountains bunched at one end or the other. Rescuing those pictures involves spreading the mountains across the entire spectrum, which is what the Video Adjustments palette is all about.

Three Channels

As you can see, the histogram actually displays three superimposed graphs at once. These layers—red, green, and blue—represent the three "channels" of color video.

When you make adjustments to a clip's brightness values—for example, when you drag the Exposure slider just below the histogram—you'll see the graphs in all three channels move in unison. Despite changing shape, they essentially stick together. Later, when you make color adjustments using, say, the Saturation slider, you'll see those individual channels move in different directions.

> **TIP** As you work, don't forget to spot-check your adjustments by moving the tiny red dot on the filmstrip itself (see Figure 7-5).

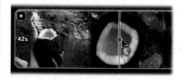

Figure 7-5:
The red dot lets you choose the representative frame you want to see in the Viewer. You should check a number of different frames within each clip to make sure that the change you're making looks good all the way through the shot.

Exposure

Most of the sliders in the Video Adjustments panel affect the histogram in some way. But where do you begin?

Here's a general suggestion: Make exposure adjustments first. In the simplest terms, the Exposure slider makes your video lighter when you move it to the right and darker when you move it to the left.

Watch the data on the histogram as you move the Exposure slider. Make sure you don't wind up shoving any of the mountain peaks beyond the edges of the Histogram box. If that happens, you're discarding precious image data and you'll see a loss of detail in the darks and lights.

The first step in fine-tuning a clip, then, is to drag the Exposure slider until the middle tones of the footage look acceptable to you. You can't add details that simply aren't there, but brightening a dark, shadowy image, or deepening the contrast on a washed-out shot, can coax out elements that were barely visible in the original.

If the dark and light areas aren't yet perfect, don't worry; you'll improve those areas next with the Levels control.

Adjusting the Levels

After you've spent some time working with the middle tones of your clip, you can turn your attention to the endpoints on the histogram, which represent the darkest and lightest areas of the clip.

If the mountains of your graph seem to cover all the territory from left to right, you already have a roughly even distribution of dark and light tones in your picture, so you're probably in good shape. But if the graph comes up short on either the left (darks) or the right (lights) side of the histogram, you may want to make an adjustment.

To do so, drag the right or left pointer on the Levels slider *inward*, toward the base of the mountain. If you're moving the right indicator inward, for example, you'll notice that the whites become brighter, but the dark areas stay pretty much the same. If you drag the left indicator inward, the dark tones change, but the highlights remain steady (Figure 7-6).

Brightness and Contrast Sliders

Once you've massaged the Exposure and Levels controls, the overall exposure for a clip usually looks pretty good. In effect, you've managed to create a full range of tones from dark to light.

So why, then, does Apple include Brightness and Contrast sliders, which govern similar aspects of the video's appearance? Because they're not quite the same as Exposure and Levels.

- **Brightness.** When you move the Brightness slider, you're making the *entire* image lighter or darker. You're literally sliding the entire histogram to the left or right without changing its shape. (Remember that the Exposure and Levels controls affect the midtones, highlights, and shadows independently.)

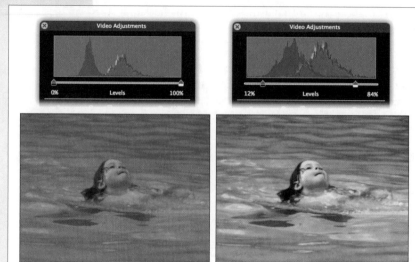

Figure 7-6:

Left: There's something wrong with the exposure of this clip.

Right: Drag the handles of the histogram inward to brighten the brights and darken the darks. Avoid moving the handles inward beyond the outer edges of the mountains. You'll throw away data outside the handles, which degrades the image quality.

In other words, if the shot's contrast is already exactly as you want it, but the whole clip could use darkening or lightening, Brightness should be your tool of choice.

- **Contrast.** The Contrast slider, on the other hand, *does* change the shape of the histogram. Contrast is the difference between the darkest and lightest tones in your clip. If you increase the contrast, you stretch out the shape of the histogram, creating darker blacks and brighter whites. When you decrease the contrast, you're scrunching the shape of the histogram inward, shortening the distance between the dark and light endpoints. Since the image data now resides in the middle area of the graph, the overall tones in the video are duller. Video pros might call this look "flat" or "muddy." (See Figure 7-7.)

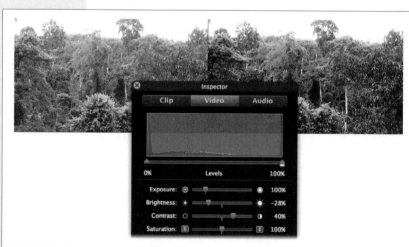

Figure 7-7:

Here's another way to fiddle with the darks and lights of your video—use the Brightness and Contrast sliders manually. The somewhat washed-out vista at left looks a lot better with the contrast goosed and the brightness toned down a tad.

Automatic Correction

Dragging the Levels, Exposure, and Brightness sliders by hand is one way to address color imbalances in a clip. But there's an easier way: iMovie can also adjust all three sliders *automatically*.

Just click the Auto button at the bottom of the Video Adjustments palette. Watch the results in the Viewer.

Amazing, isn't it? You'll be stunned at how much better your camcorder video can look with this one-click trick (Figure 7-8).

> **NOTE** To compare the before and after looks of your clip, press ⌘-Z and then Shift-⌘-Z, which correspond to the Undo and Redo commands. For added fun, go back and forth a few times.

Figure 7-8:
The before (left) and after shots of a clip that needed help. The only difference between the two is one click on the Auto button. (It affects only the brightness, contrast, and exposure. It doesn't attempt to fix color problems.)

Color Balance

Camcorders don't always capture color very accurately. You may encounter scenes with a slightly bluish or greenish tinge, dull colors, lower contrast, or sickly-looking skin tones. And you may wish you could fix it.

Or maybe you just want to take color adjustment into your own hands, not only to get the colors right, but also to create a specific mood for an image. Maybe you want a snowy landscape to look icy blue, so friends back home realize just how freakin' cold it was.

The Video Adjustments panel offers three controls that wield power over this sort of thing: Saturation, White Balance, and individual sliders that control the intensity of red, green, and blue.

- **White Balance.** Different kinds of light—fluorescent lighting, overcast skies, and so on—lend different color casts to video footage. White balance is a setting that eliminates or adjusts the color cast according to the lighting.

If you find a clip with such a color cast, it's easy to fix. Move your cursor into the Viewer window and find a spot that's *supposed* to be pure white or gray. (It might help to press ⌘-9 or ⌘-0 to enlarge the frame first.) The instant you click that white point, iMovie suddenly understands exactly what the nature of the color cast is—and adjusts *all* the colors accordingly. Often, that one click does the trick and fixes the entire clip (Figure 7-9).

Other times, you have to click around a few more times until you find a spot that makes the color cast go away.

As a last resort, you can try clicking inside the White Point color wheel *manually*, watching the results in the Viewer as you go.

• **Saturation**. Once you're happy with the color tones, you can increase or decrease their intensity with the Saturation slider. Move it to the right to increase the intensity and to the left for less saturation.

Figure 7-9:
In the Viewer, the cursor is a tiny eyedropper. (When you click a spot that's supposed to be white, the whole scene's color tint changes. You'll also see the tiny circle in the White Point color wheel shift to a new location, indicating its new understanding of the color cast.)

When you increase the saturation of a clip's colors, you make them more vivid; essentially, you make them "pop" more. You can also improve clips that have harsh, garish colors by dialing *down* the saturation, so that the colors end up looking a little less intense than they appeared in the original footage. That's a useful trick in shots whose composition is so strong that the colors are almost distracting.

Individual Channel Sliders

It's hard to imagine that any iMovie aficionado would need any more control over the colors in a shot than what's provided by the White Point and Saturation controls—especially in a program that's so simple and limited in so many other ways.

But believe it or not, iMovie can also offer you three individual sliders for red, green, and blue. You can use these sliders to correct color-tint problems manually, or you can use them to create crazy special effects like "Kids on Mars" or "I'm Feeling Really, Really Blue."

> **NOTE** You may be tempted to use the channel sliders to turn a clip from color to black-and-white. Save yourself the trouble. iMovie offers a Black & White video effect, which you can read more about on page 139.

So how come you don't see these sliders? Because they're hidden. They don't appear unless you've turned on Advanced Tools, as described on page 80.

As you know from Chapter 3, the advanced tools are a motley assortment of hidden editing features. What the dialog box *doesn't* tell you is that it makes these three sliders magically appear in the Inspector's Video Adjustments panel: Red Gain, Green Gain, and Blue Gain (Figure 7-10).

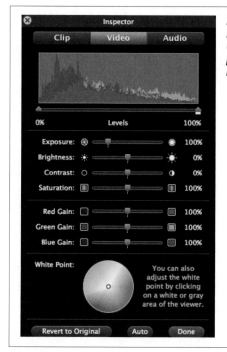

Figure 7-10:
In Preferences, you can turn on the secret on/off switch for the three color Gain sliders. These new, bonus sliders control the amount of each color present in the clip. (Compare with the standard Adjustments panel shown in Figure 7-4.)

Use these sliders to adjust the color mix of the clip. For example, if a scene is too bluish (because it was shot under fluorescent lighting, for example), you can nudge the Blue Gain slider a bit to the left.

Move the Red Gain slider to the right to warm up the tones, making them more orange-ish—a particularly handy technique for breathing life back into skin tones that have been bleached white with a spotlight or flashlight.

Removing or Adjusting Adjustments

NOTE Whenever you unleash the awesome powers of the Video Adjustments panel on a clip, you leave that clip branded—with a tiny sun icon in the upper-left corner of its filmstrip. That's to remind you, "Hey, I didn't always look like this."

None of the changes you make in the Video Adjustments panel are permanent. You can return at any time—minutes, days, or years later—and adjust them or remove them entirely.

- **Adjusting changes.** Click a clip, open the Video Adjustments panel, and make any changes you'd like.

- **Removing changes.** If you click a clip and then click Revert to Original (at the bottom of the Video Adjustments panel), you're saying, "Throw away *all* the changes I've made. Bring back my original, unmodified clip." iMovie instantly reinstates the original clip.

Copying and Pasting Adjustments

All of the fun you might be having in the Video Adjustments panel comes to a crashing halt the minute you realize one massive bummer in iMovie '09: You can adjust color on only one clip at a time. You might have just spent 15 minutes tweaking the color of your opening ski-school clip into submission, but what about the other 25 skiing shots in your montage? Are you condemned to repeating all of that handwork 25 more times?

Fortunately, no. While you can't edit multiple clips at once, you *can* copy and paste *just* the video adjustments between clips. Once you've got the blue cast worked out of the first skiing shot, you can wipe it out of each additional shot with a single command. Figure 7-11 shows the drill.

NOTE If you're the kind of person who plans ahead, consider this: If you intend to excerpt several clips from a single, long, master clip in the Event Browser, you'll save time by fixing *the original clip* before you start adding clips to your storyboard.

The reason: If you make color adjustments to the master clip *before* you grab chunks of it, the pieces inherit the fixes. If you adjust the master clip *after* you've placed some pieces of it into the storyboard, then the pieces won't change. (You can always use the Paste Adjustments command at that point, of course, but that's still more steps.)

Cropping Video

The Video Adjustments panel is only one example of the incredibly sophisticated, pro-level features that you stumble across in this supposedly simple, idiot-proof program. Another example is the Cropping tool, which was previously relegated to the stratosphere of professional, $1,000 video-editing programs like Final Cut Pro.

Figure 7-11:
Click the clip that you've already got looking good. Then choose Edit → Copy (⌘-C). Now click the next clip that needs the same touch and choose Edit → Paste Adjustments → Video (or press Option-⌘-I). Proceed through all the clips that were filmed under the same lighting conditions: Paste, paste, paste. You've just saved a heck of a lot of time.

This tool lets you crop a video clip the same way you'd crop a photo; that is, you can chop off the edges of the video frame. Figure 7-12 shows the idea.

Cropping isn't something you'll do every day. But it can be handy in situations like these:

- **You're adding a clip that's got the wrong aspect ratio to a project (page 56).** For example, you're creating a regular, squarish, standard-definition movie, but you want to place a widescreen clip into it. The Cropping tool lets you lop off the sides of that widescreen clip so it fits perfectly into the squarish frame without any black bars.

- **There's something at the margins of the picture that you want to get rid of.** Maybe your finger was in the lens. Maybe there's some ugly pipe or wire that you didn't notice. Maybe a telephone pole appears to be sticking out of your interviewee's head. Or maybe you just want to crop out the bonehead who kept trying to get on camera.

- **The scene is off-center.** Maybe the camera was on a tripod, self-running, when you and a buddy did your comedy schtick, but the whole thing wasn't framed right. By cropping away the empty part of the frame, you can recenter the whole thing.

- **The subject of the shot isn't prominent enough.** This happens often with accidental footage: That is, you were filming your Uncle Ned reminiscing about his days working for the National Guard when, *bam!*, there's a three-car collision in the intersection behind him. By cropping away Uncle Ned, you can isolate the car-crash portion of the frame. It now fills the screen; in effect, you've created an artificial zoom.

Whenever you crop out some video, you're leaving fewer pixels behind. You're therefore losing resolution and creating a less sharp picture. If you crop away a *huge* amount—more than half of the frame—you may wind up with noticeable pixellation and graininess.

If that happens, you can either live with it or use Undo.

Figure 7-12:
Top: Suppose you were too far away from the subject, or your zoom wasn't powerful enough.

Middle: Adjust the green rectangle so that it encloses the portion of the video you want to keep. The rectangle is either squarish or wide, depending on whether your project has the standard 4:3 aspect ratio or is widescreen. (See page 57 for details on aspect ratios.)

Bottom: After the cropping, the smaller portion of the frame expands to fill the entire frame. You lose some resolution in the process, of course, but you won't notice any graininess unless you crop out a lot of the original image.

In any case, here's how you crop in iMovie:

1. **Select the clip you want to edit, and the frame.**

   If the clip is in the Event Browser, then your crop applies to this clip every time you use it in a project, from now on. If the clip's already in the storyboard, then you're cropping it only there.

   Find a good representative frame of the clip to work with in the Viewer. Do that by dragging the red dot across the filmstrip itself (Figure 7-5). Remember, you're working with video here, so things do tend to move around on the screen, but the iMovie cropping area *doesn't* move. You don't want to crop the clip in a way that centers your subject nicely on frame 50, but cuts it out completely on frame 100.

TIP   You'll find this action a lot easier if you magnify the image. Choose Window → Viewer → Large, or press ⌘-0.

2. **Press the letter C key on your keyboard, or click the Crop button on the toolbar, or double-click the faint crop *badge* that sometimes appears when you point to a clip (Figure 7-13).**

Now the Viewer window sprouts a few new controls at the top, like Fit and Crop (Figure 7-13). The Crop button is already selected.

NOTE   The crop badge always appears on photos in your project, but appears on video clips only if you've already cropped them.

Figure 7-13:
Top: Click the Crop icon, or press the letter C, or click the tiny Crop badge on any clip.

Bottom: A little icon appears on the filmstrip to show that it's been cropped.

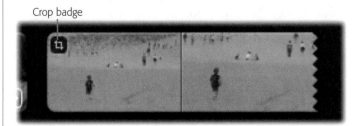

Crop badge

3. **Drag across the Viewer window to indicate what you want to keep.**

As you drag, you create a green rectangle. Everything outside it will be thrown away when the cropping is over.

As you work, you can drag inside the rectangle to move it around on the video. And you can drag any of the four corners to make the rectangle bigger or smaller. (You can't crop away more than half of the video area.)

Don't forget to move that little red dot on the filmstrip itself to spot check different places in the video to make sure you're not cropping out anything important somewhere else in the clip. Or just click the Play button, or press your space bar, to play the clip from the beginning.

4. **Press Enter (or click Done).**

The cropping is complete.

Adjusting or Removing the Crop

Cropping, like any iMovie edit, is nondestructive. That is, you haven't done anything permanent to the video on your hard drive, and you can adjust or remove the cropping at any time.

To do that, just click the Crop badge on the clip (Figure 7-13), or select the clip and then click the Crop tool (or press the letter C), and redo the cropping in the Viewer. For example, you can adjust the green boundary rectangle.

To remove the cropping altogether, click the Fit button in the Viewer. Then press Enter (or click Done).

Rotating Video

If there's any iMovie feature you'll use even less often than cropping, it's rotating. But sure enough, iMovie lets you rotate a clip by 90 degrees, or even upside-down.

When would you use this? OK, the answer is "almost never," but here are a couple of remote possibilities:

- Somebody actually filmed the scene with the camera turned 90 degrees. (This sometimes happens when people record video with a digital *still* camera, which they're used to turning 90 degrees for capturing tall subjects. Sometimes people forget that they can't rotate the camera that way when they're shooting *video*.)

- You shot a kid crawling along the rocks and want to make it look like he's mountain-climbing, vertically, straight up a cliff.

- You're making some strange, avant-garde film, and you're hoping to intentionally disorient your audience.

Anyway, if you're reading this, then you must have your reasons. Here's how you do the rotation:

1. **Select the clip you want to edit, and the frame.**

As usual, if the clip is in the Event Browser, then the rotation applies to this clip every time you use it in a project from now on. If the clip is already in the storyboard, then you're rotating it only there.

You can also move the red dot in the filmstrip itself (Figure 7-5) to find a good representative frame of the clip to watch in the Viewer.

2. **Press the letter C key on your keyboard, or click the Crop icon.**

   So far, this is exactly like the cropping procedure.

3. **Click one of the Rotate buttons at the top of the Viewer (Figure 7-14).**

   With each click, the entire video image rotates by 90 degrees in the corresponding direction. If you click twice, you flip the whole picture upside-down.

   If you rotate the image only 90 degrees, of course, the video no longer fits in the frame and black bars appear on either side. At this point, you have two options: You can either leave it like that, or you can crop it so that it fills the frame.

   To do that, click the Crop button in the Viewer, and then drag the green rectangle exactly as described in the previous section.

Figure 7-14:
With each click of the rotation arrows, you rotate the image 90 degrees. Use for special effects, or just for fun.

4. **Press Enter (or click Done).**

   The rotation is complete.

The little Crop icon appears in the upper-left corner of the clip's filmstrip (Figure 7-13). OK, you haven't necessarily *cropped* the video, but in iMovie's head, rotation is close enough for cropping for icon purposes.

Adjusting or Removing the Rotation

When you rotate your video, you're not changing the underlying footage. You can adjust or remove the rotation at any time.

Just click the clip, click the Crop tool (or press C), and then click those rotation arrow buttons again until the video looks the way you want it. Then press Enter (or click Done).

Titles, Subtitles, and Credits

Text superimposed over footage is incredibly common in the film and video worlds. You'd be hard-pressed to find a single movie, TV show, or commercial that doesn't have titles, captions, or credits. In fact, one telltale sign that you're watching an amateur video is the *absence* of superimposed text.

In iMovie, the term *title* refers to any kind of text: credits, titles, subtitles, copyright notices, and so on. You don't need to be nearly as economical in your use of titles as you are with, say, transitions. Transitional effects interfere with something that stands perfectly well on its own—the footage. When you superimpose text, on the other hand, the audience is much more likely to accept your intrusion. You're introducing this new element for its benefit, to convey information you couldn't transmit otherwise.

Moreover, as you'll see, most of iMovie's text effects are far more focused in purpose than its transition selections, so you'll have little trouble choosing the optimum text effect for a particular editing situation. For example, the Scrolling Credits effect rolls a list of names slowly up the screen—an obvious candidate for the close of your movie.

Setting Up a Title

Adding some text to your movie requires several setup steps:

1. **Choose a title style (centered, scrolling credits, or whatever).**

2. **Drag the title into position in the storyboard.**

3. **Type the text.**

4. **Choose a font, color, and type size.**

Here are these steps in more detail.

Choose a Title Style

Start by choosing Window → Titles (⌘-3), or clicking the T button just below the Viewer. The Titles panel appears (Figure 8-1).

Figure 8-1:
The icons here represent the various title styles. iMovie '09 has added quite a few over its predecessor.

Figuring out what each title style is for isn't rocket science, but here's a quick run-down:

- **Centered.** The Centered title may be the most useful of all iMovie text effects. It produces a single line of text (or two lines, if you take advantage of the subtitle option), fading in, staying onscreen for a moment, then fading out, making this effect ideal for displaying the title of your movie. This is a tasteful, professional, and powerful effect.

TIP You can always string together several consecutive Centered titles to imitate the way a movie's major stars' names appear at the beginning of a typical Hollywood movie.

- **Lower Third.** That's what it's called in the TV business—meaning the lower third of the TV screen—but the common name for this is *subtitle*. On TV, they usually use a lower-third title to identify the talking head on the screen ("Harold P. Higgenbottom, GrooviTunes CEO"). You can use it that way, or to identify the location of a scene, or to translate what the person or baby is saying.

- **Lower.** This title hovers in the bottom-right corner of the screen, like an MTV music video, but on the wrong side. (But see the Tip below.)

- **Upper.** This one gives you Lower's exact opposite: The text appears in the upper-left corner.

TIP You can change these Lower and Upper titles to appear in the other corner by changing the justification of the text. Press Shift-⌘-[to move the Lower title to the left corner. Press Shift-⌘-] to move the Upper title to the right corner.

- **Echo.** This unusual title style features a title, a subtitle, and an *echo* of the main title. An enormous, semitransparent, all-caps version of the main title also appears *behind* the text, almost as a graphic element.

- **Overlap.** Two bits of text, one red and one white, meet briefly in the middle on the bottom of the frame, then keep going their merry way. If you place several Overlap titles consecutively, they'll alternate colors.

- **Four Corners.** A very colorful series of titles, where the text swoops from different sides to meet in the middle before swooping out again. Each time you add one of these titles, the entry points and colors of the text change, with up to four different versions.

- **Scrolling Credits.** This effect produces two columns, like *Director…Steven Spielberg* and *Writer…Robert Towne*, or *character name…actor name* (Figure 8-2).

Be careful when using this effect, for two reasons. First, iMovie automatically adjusts the speed of scrolling to fit all the names you've typed into the duration you've specified. If the title effect is too short, they'll scroll by too fast to read.

Second, the type is fairly small, which could be a problem if you intend to save your movie as a QuickTime file.

NOTE Setting up this title style requires special instructions, which appear on page 182.

- **Drifting, Sideways Drift, Vertical Drift.** Three different versions of the same basic idea: The text zooms into the screen, decelerates as it gets to the middle, and then speeds up to leave the frame, never really coming to a full stop. If your clip were a stop sign, these titles would probably get a ticket.

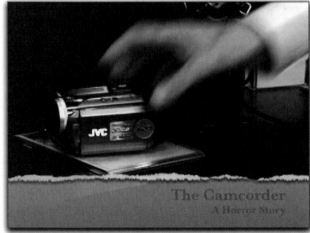

Figure 8-2:
Top: You control the speed of Scrolling credits by controlling the length of the title strip in your storyboard.

Bottom: These subtitle variations all include an opaque or semi-opaque background to make your text stand out against the video. You can change the color of that background bar by simply clicking it.

- **Zoom.** Like a centered title, but subtly grows (slightly) bigger.

- **Horizontal Blur.** This effect simulates your two eyes coming into focus to see the title, then going out of focus again.

- **Soft Edge.** Another very subtle effect. The text drifts slightly right; a magic eraser wipes it into existence, and then promptly erases it again.

- **Lens Flare, Boogie Lights, Pixie Dust.** These titles all use something shiny to announce themselves to the world (Figure 8-3). Definitely useful when you want something flashy.

Figure 8-3:
The Boogie Lights title exemplifies the cool, new animated titles in iMovie '09.

- **Pull Focus.** If you play around much with the manual focus on a camera, this one will look familiar. As the text comes into focus, the background goes blurry. At the end of the title, the background comes back into focus, only to have the title get blurry and disappear.

- **Organic Main and Organic Lower.** These are both very elegant titles, the kind you would love to have in a wedding video. Both involve delicate, viney animated plants that grow along with the title before fading away.

- **Ticker.** You know how cable-news channels run breaking news headlines across the bottom of the screen? In the same way, the Ticker title runs text, right to left, across the bottom. It's much more plain, however, than what you see on CNN.

- **Date/Time.** The only entirely uneditable title. When you select it, the preview window denies you access. It just sits there, impervious to clicking. This title's only job is to display the date and time of the underlying clip, something you generally want done automatically.

> **TIP** OK, this style isn't *totally* uneditable. You can change the date and time of your footage, as described on page 61.

- **Clouds.** This is a whimsical, animated, lower-third title. Two clouds, one blue and one pink, bounce up into the frame, carrying some equally whimsical text.

- **Far Far Away.** For all the budding George Lucases out there, this title displays text in the iconic, scrolling *Star Wars* style.

> **TIP** For added fun, you can add this title on top of the starscape image that comes with iMovie '09. See the next section for details.

- **Gradient, Soft Bar, Formal, Torn Edge, Paper.** These are all variations on the Lower Third style. The only difference is what's *behind* the text. You have a choice of various semi-opaque backgrounds to make the text more readable and to make it stand out more from the video playing behind it.

> **TIP** In these styles, the background behind the text—the transparent bar, the torn-edged paper, and so on—starts out black, white, or tan. You can, however, choose *any* color for this background bar (Figure 8-2).
>
> When you're editing the text, click anywhere *on* that background bar to open the Color Picker. (The Color Picker is described on page 190.)

Theme-based titles

If you've added a theme to your project (page 127), iMovie lists eight additional title styles at the top of your Titles pane (Figure 8-4). Four of them are heavily animated, embedding your clip into a shot of a photo album, for example. The other four titles are simpler, but stylistically designed to match your theme.

Figure 8-4:
These titles appear only if you apply a theme to your project (page 127). Each title is designed around the theme's style. In this case, the style is like a comic book.

You can use theme titles only if you've applied a theme to your project. This also means you can't use titles from multiple themes in a single project.

TIP   Want a particular theme title, but not the entire theme itself? Just make sure that when you add a theme (page 128), you *turn off* the box that tells iMovie to automatically add transitions and titles. That way, your movie uses only the theme elements *you* choose, even if you end up using just one theme-based title in your entire project.

Drag the Title into Position

Once you've chosen a title style, drag its icon directly into the storyboard. While you're still dragging (and the mouse button is down), you see blue highlighting on the filmstrip that will be covered by the text (Figure 8-5). That's iMovie's way of helping you pinpoint where the text will *first appear.*

As you'll soon see, knowing where the title is going to land in your storyboard is extremely important. You'll feel it snap into four places as your cursor moves:

- **At the beginning of the clip.** As the blue highlighting illustrates (Figure 8-5), iMovie proposes covering the *first third* of the filmstrip with the title. The text appears with moving video behind it.

- **Over the middle of the clip.** If your cursor winds up here, the title covers *the entire clip*, beginning to end.

- **At the end of the clip.** If your cursor falls here, the title stretches over the *final third* of the clip.

- **Between clips.** Under normal circumstances, iMovie text gets superimposed over the video picture. Particularly when you're creating opening or closing credits, however, you may want the lettering to appear on a nice background, such as black, for a striking and professional-looking effect.

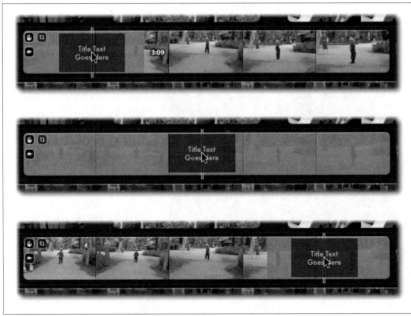

Figure 8-5:
As you drag a title onto a clip, the blue highlighting shows how long the title will last. It snaps into three positions relative to the clip, shown in these three examples.

Top: If you drag toward the beginning of the clip, the title covers the first third of it.

Middle: If you drag over the middle, the title covers the entire clip.

Bottom: if you drag toward the end of the clip, the title covers the final third of it. Of course, you can adjust any of this later.

In those cases, drag the title to the gap *between* filmstrips. iMovie surprises you (the first time, anyway) by displaying a palette of background images for your title.

These are the same background images available in the Maps and Backgrounds panel, discussed later on page 231. They let you place the text against a solid color, a photograph of red velvet curtains, or another attractive backdrop.

In professional movie editing, the Black background is by far the most common. It gives a title *over black* (rather than superimposed over your video). (There's no longer a checkbox for "Over black," as in previous iMovie versions; you must simply drag the title between two clips, or to the very beginning or end of the storyboard. See Figure 8-6.)

This option is attractive for three reasons. First, it looks extremely professional. Second, the high contrast of white against black makes the text very legible. Third, the audience will *read* it, instead of being distracted by the video behind it.

NOTE When you create a title over a background, you *add* to the total length of your movie. You force the clips to the right of your title to slide further rightward to accommodate the credit you just inserted. That's just a reminder to anyone who's editing a video to be in sync with music. (When you insert text over video, by contrast, you don't change the overall length of your movie.)

Figure 8-6:
Top: If you drag a title in between two filmstrips, iMovie asks you to pick a background image (bottom left), even if you just want black.

Bottom right: You can adjust the title's time on the screen by dragging the ends of its blue stripe. You can adjust the background clip's timing by double-clicking it and typing a new length into the text box in the Inspector.

Adjust the Timing

Once you've dropped the title into place, it turns into a blue stripe over the film-strip. (This, as it turns out, will become a familiar element in iMovie. Audio such as background music is represented with draggable strips, too.)

The stripe indicates how long the text appears on the screen. As you can see in Figure 8-7, this stripe can straddle part of a clip, a whole clip, or many clips, which gives you a huge amount of flexibility.

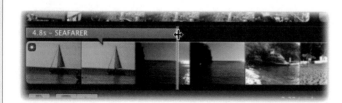

Figure 8-7:
When your cursor approaches either end of a title stripe, it changes to a double-headed arrow. That's your cue that it's OK to start dragging the stripe's endpoint horizontally to make it longer or shorter.

TIP iMovie doesn't let you overlap titles. You can, however, have more than one title on the same clip. Drag one onto the front third and another on the back third of the clip, for example. Then move those away from the ends and add even more titles, always using the ends of the clip as landing spots. The only rule is that titles can't overlap.

You can adjust this stripe in three ways:

- **Adjust the starting point** by dragging the left edge of the stripe.

- **Adjust the ending point** by dragging the *right* end of the stripe.

   NOTE Adjusting either end of the stripe also changes its duration.

- **Move the entire title in time** by dragging horizontally *anywhere else* on it.

As you make the adjustment, take into account your viewers' reading speed. There's only one thing more frustrating than titles that fly by too quickly to read, and that's titles that sit there onscreen forever, boring the audience silly. Many video editors use this guideline: Leave the words onscreen long enough for somebody to read them aloud twice.

Also consider the location of your title carefully. If you're superimposing it on a solid-colored background or a still image, no problem. But if you're planning to superimpose it on moving video, choose a scene that's relatively still, so that the video doesn't distract the audience from the words onscreen.

Be particularly careful not to superimpose your titles on an unsteady shot; the contrast between the jiggling picture and the rock-steady lettering on the screen will make your audience uncomfortable.

   NOTE The beauty of titles in iMovie '09 is that there's no rendering (computing) time. They appear instantly. So you can freely adjust the placement and timing of your titles as often as you like.

Type the Text

Unless the name of your movie is, in fact, "Title Text Here," you'll probably want to edit the dummy placeholder text of your newly born title.

To edit the text, click the blue stripe in the storyboard to select it. In the Viewer, text boxes appear, ready to edit.

   TIP Enlarge the Viewer (Window → Viewer → Large, or ⌘-0) for easier access to these text boxes.

In most styles, you actually see *two* text boxes: a main title, and a subtitle. Just click inside one of these boxes to edit the dummy text.

   TIP You don't have to type text into both of these boxes. The subtitle box underneath is there solely for your convenience, for those occasions when you need a second, smaller line of type underneath the larger credit. If you don't need text there, just delete the placeholder text.

All of the usual Mac OS X text-editing tricks apply in the text boxes. For example:

- Double-click a word to highlight it.

- Triple-click inside the text box to select the entire title; at this point, you can just begin typing to replace the placeholder text.

- Press Option-arrow key (left or right) to jump one word at a time.

- Press Control-arrow key to jump to the beginning or end of the text box.

- Add Shift to those keystrokes to jump *and* select the intervening text simultaneously. For example, Shift-Option-right arrow highlights the word to the right of your insertion point.

- Cut, Copy, and Paste work the way you'd expect.

- Press Tab to jump between text boxes.

When you're finished editing (and formatting, as described next), click Done in the Viewer.

Special Notes on Scrolling Credits

When you click the blue stripe representing a Scrolling Credits title, you see place-holder text snippets like the one shown in Figure 8-8.

To replace the dummy text with the actual names of your actors and characters, heed these notes:

- First, double-click where it says "Starring." Now you can type something new in its place, like "Featuring" or "Cast."

- When you see a dotted red underline, iMovie is warning you of a misspelling. Control-click (or right-click) the word to see spelling alternatives.

- Next, drag diagonally through the scrolling list of placeholder names. Once they're highlighted, you can begin typing your own cast list: the character name ("Raymond," for example), then press Tab, and then type the actor's name ("Dustin Hoffman," for example). Press Tab to go to the next row. Type the next character name, press Tab, and then add that actor's name. And so on.

- As you go, you can create headings like the ones shown in Figure 8-8 by pressing the Enter key at the end of a row. iMovie places the insertion point at the *left* side of the frame, so that you can type the heading (like "CREW" or "SECOND UNIT").

- You can create a blank line in the credits by pressing Enter, Enter, and then Tab.

> **TIP** Using the Font panel, you can control the spacing between the lines of credits. See the Tip on page 189.

Figure 8-8:
Figure 8-8:
Press Tab between names for one big scrolling list. Press Enter after a row to create a left-justified heading. After you type the heading, press either Tab (to list another name on the same row) or Enter, and then Tab (to leave the heading on a row by itself).

If you have too many names to fit on one screen, don't worry; the list scrolls automatically when you reach the bottom of the frame. You can keep typing until you've given credit to every last gaffer, best boy, and caterer. (You can scroll back up again by holding down the up arrow key.)

Font, Size, and Style

iMovie's creators are rather fond of Gill Sans; that's the typeface used in most of the title styles. It looks great, but it also looks like everyone *else's* iMovie '09 videos.

> **NOTE** Unfortunately, some titles are impervious to font changes, thanks to the way they've been animated. You can tell if a title's font can be changed if the Show Fonts button appears in the top-left corner preview window (Figure 8-8). If there's no Show Fonts button, your title is a one-font pony.

Fortunately, for most titles you have a surprising amount of typographical flexibility at your command. That may come as a surprise, considering that *no* font, size, style, or justification controls are visible when you create a title.

The most basic style options are available in the Text menu.

Start by highlighting the text you want to change. That is, click the blue stripe of a title you've already placed. Then drag through some of the text in the text boxes in the Viewer.

> **NOTE** For most titles, iMovie '09 doesn't limit you to a single font and size. You can use different fonts within a single text block, if you must. You can even use a different font for *every letter*, if you so desire (or if you're making a ransom-note video).

Now you can choose a style from the Text menu. Your options include:

- **Bold, Italic, Underline, Outline.** Avoid Underline; it looks cheesy. In a document, Outline usually looks cheesy, too. But in iMovie, it's a terrific help. It means that each letter has a fine hairline around it, to help set it off against the video background. If the lettering is white, for example, it would otherwise disappear against white parts of the background.

- **Bigger, Smaller.** Here's a quick way to enlarge or shrink the highlighted text.

- **Align.** This submenu refers to the horizontal alignment of the text within its text block. You can choose Left (against the left side), Center (centered), or Right (against the right side). (The final choice, Justified, does nothing in iMovie.)

- **Kern.** *Kerning* is the typographical process of squishing characters closer together. Sometimes doing that makes a title more readable, more artistic, or just fit better in a small space. The commands in this submenu let you either tighten or loosen the spacing a tiny bit at a time.

- **Ligature.** *Ligatures* are character pairs, usually beginning with the lowercase *f*, that are artistically fused into a single symbol. For example, the word "figure," with ligatures turned on, becomes *figure*. To turn ligatures on, highlight the text that contains the ligature-able pair (fl, fi, oe, or ae) and then choose Text → Ligature → Use All. To turn ligatures off, highlight the text and choose Text → Ligature → Use None.

- **Baseline.** The *baseline* is the invisible horizontal line on which text sits. Using this control, you can raise or lower some text, like this, or even create superscript (2^2) or subscript (H_2O) characters. (Use Default restores the text to the original baseline.)

- **Justification.** Press Shift-⌘-[to align the text with the left side of the text box, Shift-⌘-] for the right side, or Shift-⌘-\ to center it.

Figure 8-9 shows examples of many of these styles in use at once in a single, truly hideous opening credit.

> **TIP** Most of the commands in the Text menu have easy-to-remember keyboard shortcuts. It's always Shift, ⌘, and the first letter: B for bold, I for italic, + for bigger, – for smaller, and so on.

The iMovie Font Panel

The iMovie Font Panel is new in iMovie '09. It's a creative and simplified approach to changing your title's style. (This window is different from the System Font Panel described below.) The idea is to put the most common fonts and colors at your fingertips.

Select a title in your storyboard, and then click Show Fonts in the preview window.

Figure 8-9:
You would never use all of iMovie's typography variations in a single title. But you could.

An Inspector-like window appears, but you can tell at first glance that it has a unique purpose. The window contains a big grid with three distinct columns. The first column contains a list of title fonts. The second offers an array of colors. The last column shows type-size numbers, one through nine. Take a look at Figure 8-10 to see it in action.

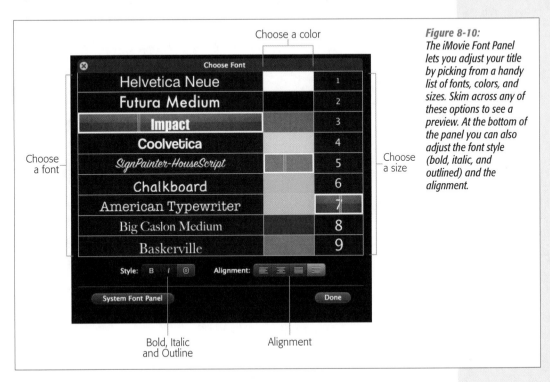

Choose a color

Figure 8-10:
The iMovie Font Panel lets you adjust your title by picking from a handy list of fonts, colors, and sizes. Skim across any of these options to see a preview. At the bottom of the panel you can also adjust the font style (bold, italic, and outlined) and the alignment.

Choose a font

Choose a size

Bold, Italic and Outline

Alignment

As you run your mouse over the grid, you can see the changes to the font, color, and type size of your title immediately, even without clicking. When you see one you like, click to lock in that font, color, or size.

You can also turn certain font styles (bold, italic, and outline) on or off by clicking the buttons at the bottom. You can adjust the title's paragraph alignment (left-justified, centered, right-justified, fully justified) by clicking the little icons, too (Figure 8-10).

Click Done when your title looks just right.

The System Font Panel

Handy as the iMovie Font Panel may be, it offers only a tiny slate of options. Nine typefaces, nine colors. What is this, graphic-designer preschool?

Fortunately for control freaks, iMovie also gives you full access to the System Fonts Panel, a standard Mac OS X feature that puts all typographical controls into a single place.

POWER USERS' CLINIC

Choose Favorite Fonts and Colors

As naturally stylish as Apple employees are, you may disagree with their default font and color choices in the iMovie Font Panel. Hot Pink, for example, may never make it into the titles of any of your movies. Luckily, you don't have to go through life with Hot Pink wasting space on the iMovie Font Panel.

To customize the default fonts and colors in the iMovie Font Panel, choose iMovie → Preferences, and click the Fonts tab. It lists all of the fonts and colors that appear in the iMovie Font Panel.

To change a font, click the tiny arrows next to it, and then choose from the very large Font menu that appears. You've just replaced that standard font on the iMovie Font Panel.

To change a color, click the color needing replacing, and the Color Picker panel (page 190) appears. Choose a color, and keep choosing until you find the one you like. When you do, close the Color Picker.

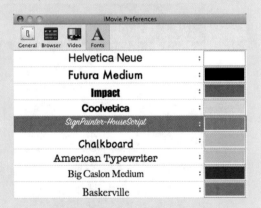

Suppose you've just highlighted a title block, and now you want to choose an appropriate typeface for it. If the iMovie Fonts Panel is open, click the button in the bottom-left that says System Font Panel. If not, choose Text → Show Fonts (⌘-T).

Here's what you'll find there (Figure 8-11):

- **Collections.** The first column lists your *collections*, which are canned sets of fonts. Apple starts you off with collections called things like PDF (a set of standard fonts used in PDF files) and Web (fonts you're safe using on Web pages—that is, fonts that are very likely to be installed on the Macs or Windows PCs of your Web visitors).

> **TIP** You can create your own collections called, for example, Headline or Sans Serif, organized by font type. Then you can switch these groups of fonts on or off at will, just as though you'd bought a program like Suitcase. You use Mac OS X's Font Book program for this purpose.

- **Family, Typeface.** The second column shows the names of the actual fonts in your system. The third, Typeface, shows the various style variations—Bold, Italic, Condensed, and so on—available in that type family. (Oblique and Italic are roughly the same thing; Bold, Black, and Ultra are varying degrees of boldface.) Just click the font you want to use in your iMovie title.

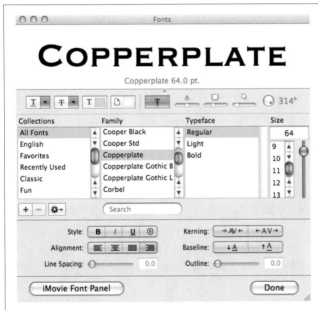

Figure 8-11:
The Fonts panel, available in many Mac OS X programs, offers elaborate controls over text color, shadow, and underline styles. It also contains some of the genetic material of old-style programs like Suitcase and Font Juggler. See the handy font sample shown here above the font lists? To get it, choose Show Preview from the Action (✿) pop-up menu at the bottom of the panel. Or use the mousy way: Place your cursor just above the headings (Collections, Family, and so on) and drag downward.

- **Size.** The last column lists a sampling of point sizes. You can use the size slider, choose from the point-size pop-up menu, or type any number into the box at the top of the Size list.

Underline, strikethrough, color, shadow

At the top of the Font panel are five rectangular buttons. Each is a pop-up menu that gives you an even more ridiculous amount of typography control:

- **Underline.** You can choose how you want the selected text to be underlined: with one underline, two, or none. If you choose Color, then the Mac OS X Color Picker appears (Figure 8-12), so that you can specify what *color* you want the underlines to be.

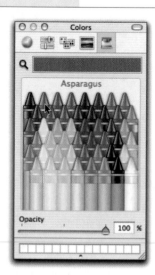

Figure 8-12:
Some of the typographical options can get ridiculous. When you request a different color for an underline or strikethrough, you get the Mac OS X Color Picker dialog box, which gives you a million different ways to dial up a precise shade.

- **Strikethrough.** This option draws a line through your text, as though you've crossed it out. These days, there's really only one situation when you might find it useful: the way bloggers indicate a correction, either a real one or a fake one done for humorous purposes. You know: "Cellphone Companies Are ~~Greedy Slimebags~~ Profitable."

- **Text color.** The third pop-up rectangle opens the Color Picker dialog box. Here, you can specify what *color* you want the highlighted text to be. (See the box on page 190.) The important thing is to choose a color that *contrasts* with the footage behind the lettering. Use white against black, black against white, yellow against blue, and so on.

    NOTE iMovie doesn't limit you to TV-safe colors. But be careful. If colors are too bright (saturated), the edges of the letters can smear and tear when played back on a TV.

- **Document color.** The next pop-up rectangle is supposed to let you choose a background color for your text, but it doesn't work in iMovie.

- **Drop shadow.** The rightmost pop-up button is responsible for the shadow that iMovie adds to your titles to help them stand out from the background (Figure 8-13).

Figure 8-13:
The four tiny controls to the right of the Shadow button control the shadow itself: its opacity, degree of "spread," distance from the main characters (controls how far away the "page" looks from the text), and the angle of the light that's casting the shadow.

Secondary controls

At the bottom of the Fonts panel are controls for Bold, Italic, Underline, and Outline; Alignment; Kerning; and Baseline height. All of these duplicate the equivalent commands in the Text menu.

There are, however, two controls here that are *not* in the Text menu, and they can sometimes be very useful:

- **Line Spacing.** In a word processor, this slider would affect the distance between lines of text in a single paragraph. iMovie doesn't let you create paragraphs, of course—each text block contains only a single line of type—but this slider can still be helpful. It governs the distance between the main title and its *subtitle*, so that you can add some space between the two.

  TIP In the Scrolling Credits title style, this control lets you adjust the amount of vertical space between the rows of credits. Cool!

- **Outline.** This slider governs the thickness of the outline (when you're using the Outline font style). Make it thick enough, and you can create some truly, er, *unforgettable* effects.

TIP   Once you've got a piece of text formatted just the way you like it, you're not condemned to repeating all that work to format the *next* title. Instead, highlight some of the text that already looks good. Choose Text → Copy Style (Option-⌘-C). Then highlight the text that you want to match, and choose Text → Paste Style (Option-⌘-V). The second title now changes to match the formatting of the first one.

UP TO SPEED

The Color Picker

Here and there—not just in iMovie, but also in System Preferences, TextEdit, Microsoft Office, and many other programs—Mac OS X offers you the opportunity to choose a *color* for some element, like your desktop background, a window, and so on.

The Colors dialog box (Figure 8-12) offers a miniature color lab that lets you dial in any color in the Mac's rainbow. *Several* color labs, actually, arrayed across the top, are each designed to make color-choosing easier in certain circumstances:

Color Wheel. Drag the scroll bar vertically to adjust the brightness, and then drag your cursor around the ball to pick the shade.

Color Sliders. From the pop-up menu, choose the color-mixing method you prefer. *CMYK* stands for Cyan, Magenta, Yellow, and Black. People in the printing industry will feel immediately at home, because these four colors are the component inks for color printing. (These people may also be able to explain why *K* stands for *black*.)

RGB and HSV. *RGB* is how a TV or computer monitor thinks of colors: as proportions of red, green, and blue. *HSV* stands for Hue, Saturation, and Value—a favorite color-specifying scheme in scientific circles. In each case, just drag the sliders to mix up the color you want, or type in the percentages of each component.

Color Palettes. These palettes present canned sets of color swatches. They're primarily for programmers who want quick access to the standard colors in Mac OS X.

Image Palettes. Image palettes offer the visible rainbow arrayed yet another way—cloudy, color-arranged streaks.

Crayons. Now *this* is a handy tool. You can click each crayon to see its color name: Mocha, Cayenne, Fern, and so on. (Some interior decorator in Cupertino had a field day naming these crayons.)

In any of these color pickers, you can also "sample" a color that's *outside* the dialog box—a color in the video shot, for example, or one that you found on a Web page. Just click the magnifying-glass icon and then move your cursor around the screen. You'll see the sliders and numbers automatically change inside the dialog box when you click.

Finally, note that you can store frequently used (or frequently admired) colors in the mini-palette squares at the bottom. To do that, drag the big rectangular color swatch (next to the magnifying glass) directly down into one of the little squares, where it will stay fresh for weeks.

General Guidelines

As you choose fonts and type effects for the various credits in your movie, consider these guidelines:

• **Be consistent.** Using the same typeface for all of the titles in your movie lends consistency and professionalism to the project.

- **Remember the QuickTime effect.** If you plan to distribute your finished movie as a QuickTime file—an electronic movie file that you can distribute by email, network, CD, disk, or Web page—use the biggest, boldest, cleanest fonts you have. Avoid spindly, delicate fonts or script fonts. When your movie is compressed down to a 3-inch square, what looks terrific in your Viewer will be so small it may become completely illegible.

Come to think of it, you might want to choose big, bold, clean fonts even if you're going to play the finished movie on a TV with a resolution far lower than that of your computer screen. Be especially careful when using one of the text effects that includes a subtitle, as iMovie subtitles often use an even smaller typeface than the primary title font, and may lose legibility if the font has too much filigree.

Finally, favor *sans serif* fonts—typefaces that don't have the tiny *serifs*, or "hats and feet," at the end of the character strokes. The typeface you're reading now is a serif font, one that's less likely to remain legible in a QuickTime movie. The typeface used in the Tip below is a sans serif font.

> **TIP**   Some of the standard Mac fonts that look especially good as iMovie fonts are Arial Black, Capitals, Charcoal, Chicago, Gadget, Helvetica, Impact, Sand, Techno, and Textile.
>
> Some of the fonts whose delicate nature may be harder to read are Monaco, Courier, Old English, Swing, Trebuchet, Times, Palatino, and Verdana.

The beauty of iMovie's titling feature is that the fonts you choose become embedded into the actual digital picture. In other words, when you distribute your movie as a QuickTime file, you don't have to worry that your recipients may not have the same fonts you used to create the file. They'll see on their screens exactly what you see on yours.

> **TIP**   Don't forget that you can superimpose text on a *still* image too (Chapter 10)—such as a photo or some gradient fill you've created in, say, Photoshop Elements.

Add Your Own Custom Title

Using the Titles feature isn't the only way to create text effects. Using a graphics program like Photoshop or Photoshop Elements, you can create text "slides" with far more flexibility than you can in the Titles feature. Using a title card that you import as a graphic, you're free to use any text color and any font size. You can even dress up such titles with clip art, 3-D effects, and whatever other features your graphics software offers. Figure 8-14 (bottom) shows the idea.

Creating a title like this involves creating an *alpha-channel PNG* file. A little Photoshop experience is helpful, but here's the gist:

Use the text tool to type and format the text in Photoshop. In the Layers palette, ⌘-click the text layer's thumbnail to select it. Then, at the bottom of the Channels palette, click the Save Selection as Channel button. Finally, choose File → Save As.

UP TO SPEED

Title Fade-In/Fade-Out Timing

There's an important setting for a title that doesn't always come to mind: How long does it take for my title to fade in and out? This doesn't occur to you until you want, for example, a title that cuts in suddenly for dramatic effect. A fading title just won't do.

Every iMovie project has a global setting for title fades, which can be set in File → Project Properties under the Timing tab. The Title Fade Duration slider controls how long every title takes to fade in and out.

If you want one title to pop and another to plod, you can override the global fade setting in the Inspector. To open the Inspector for a title, double-click its icon in the storyboard. Next to the Fade In/Out label, turn on Manual, and adjust the duration slider.

You can also just type a duration into the text box. Even though the slider goes up to only two seconds (and down to zero), you can actually type in a ridiculously long fade duration here. Want the title to take 20 minutes to fade in? Type *20.0.0* (for minutes.seconds.frames).

Because you're setting the *fade out* timing as well, you'd have to make your title at least 40 minutes long to accommodate this setting: 20 minutes for the fade in, and 20 minutes for the fade out.

You would also be insane.

Unfortunately, you can't set the fade out time independently. Whatever timing you set for your title fade affects the fades on both ends.

Also, don't bother trying to set the fade time for some titles, usually the ones that do something other than fading in and out. You can't adjust the timing on those.

Choose PNG as the format, and Photoshop makes you save the file as a copy. (Don't worry, the transparency should be preserved.) Name the title and save it to your desktop.

Now just drag the title graphic off your desktop and onto a title, as shown in Figure 8-14 (top). iMovie prompts you with the Drag and Drop menu, just like it does when you drag and drop a photo (page 233). Choose Cutaway; your PNG graphic will now look like a title to anyone who watches your movie.

NOTE   You won't see the Cutaway option unless you've turned on Advanced Tools (page 80).

Checking the Result

As you're editing the title, you can see how it looks in context by clicking the |►| button (upper right of the Viewer). Or, once your title is complete, point to a spot in the storyboard just before the title and then press the space bar to view the title in the context of the movie. You can also simply move your cursor back and forth across the title without clicking to see how it looks.

Figure 8-14:
Top: Drag your alpha-channel PNG title graphic right off the desktop and into a filmstrip, and then choose Cutaway from the Drag and Drop menu that appears.

Bottom: iMovie treats it like a cutaway to a photo, and superimposes it on your video. To the rest of the world, though, it looks like a snazzy title.

If the title isn't quite what you wanted—if it's the wrong length, style, or font, or if there's a typo, for example—you can change its settings as described in the next section. If the title wasn't *at all* what you wanted—if it's the wrong title style, for example—you can undo the entire process by highlighting the blue title strip and pressing the Delete key (or choosing Edit → Undo, if you added the title recently).

Editing or Deleting a Title

If you don't like the title style you chose, just drag another one from the Titles pane and drop it right on top of the one you want to replace. iMovie updates the title instantly to reflect the change.

Of course, you may be a window-shopper, someone who likes to see *all* of the choices before committing. If that's you, double-click the title's icon in your storyboard to bring up the Inspector. In the window that appears, click the button to the right of the Title label, labeled Lower (or whatever style the title has now).

The Inspector flips around to reveal skimmable previews of all the title styles, incorporating your own title text. You see exactly what you'll get from each title style. When you find the one you like, click it, and then click Done.

Making other changes to a title is easy:

- **Change the starting or ending points** by dragging the endpoints of the blue stripe in the storyboard.

- **Move the entire title earlier or later** by dragging its stripe left or right in the storyboard.

- **Edit the text or its typography** by clicking the title's blue stripe in the storyboard. The text boxes appear immediately in the Viewer. Press ⌘-T to open the Font panel if you need to change the color, font, or other typographical niceties.

- **Delete a title** by clicking its blue stripe and then pressing the Delete key.

Narration, Music, and Sound

If you're lucky, you may someday get a chance to watch a movie whose soundtrack isn't finished yet. You'll be scanning channels and stumble across a special about how movies are made, or you'll see a tribute to a film composer, or you'll rent a DVD of some movie that includes a "making of" documentary. Such TV shows or DVDs sometimes include a couple of minutes from the finished movie as it looked *before* the musical soundtrack and sound effects were added.

At that moment, your understanding of the film medium will take an enormous leap forward. "Jeez," you'll say, "without music and sound effects, this $100 million Hollywood film has no more emotional impact than...my home movies!"

And you'll be right. It's true that the *visual* component of film is the most, well, visible. The household names are the directors and movie stars, not the sound editors, composers, *foley* (sound effects) artists, and others who devote their careers to the audio experience of film.

But without music, sound effects (called SFX for short), and sound editing, even the best Hollywood movie will leave you cold and unimpressed.

Two Kinds of Audio

iMovie '09 doesn't have the timeline that's traditional in video-editing programs, and the one place you may miss it most is in editing audio.

Instead of that metaphor, iMovie's designers have designated two kinds of audio clips, which are (supposedly) focused on the way people actually use audio in home movies:

- **Background music** is a solid block of music that sits "behind" the clips in your project, playing through everything, no matter how you shuffle the video clips around. You can even line up a playlist of several songs; they play consecutively, crossfading nicely between songs.

- **Sound effects.** In this case, you attach an audio file to a specific spot in the video. It goes along for the ride as you rearrange your clips.

Now, the following gets confusing, so read it slowly: There's no difference at all between the *kinds* of audio that you can use in these two ways. *Any* audio, including sound effects, can be background audio; and *any* audio, including songs, can behave like a sound effect. You'll learn the details later in this chapter.

Audio Sources

Much like traditional film cameras, iMovie separates the audio and video into separate tracks, which you can view and edit independently. In iMovie, audio shows up as a colored stripe under or behind the filmstrips.

You can incorporate sound from any of these sources:

- **Camcorder audio.** You can extract the audio from a camcorder video clip to use as an independent sound clip, for use somewhere else in the movie.

- **iTunes tracks.** This, of course, is an example of what makes iLife a suite and not just a handful of separate programs: iMovie's integration with the other Apple programs. As described later in this chapter, iMovie displays your complete iTunes music collection, playlists and all. Adding background music to your flick is easy as can be.

- **Narration.** This can be anything that you record with your microphone.

- **Sound effects.** Choose these from iMovie's Audio palette (gunshots, glass breaking, applause, and so on).

NOSTALGIA CORNER

Importing Music from a CD

For several versions of iMovie, you could import songs from a CD directly into iMovie. You could just insert your favorite music CD (Carly Simon, The Rolling Stones, the Cleveland Orchestra, or whatever), choose the track you wanted to swipe, and the deed was done.

That feature mysteriously disappeared, starting in iMovie 6. Now you're supposed to switch into iTunes, import the CD into your music collection there, and then return to iMovie to import it.

- **MP3, WAV, AIFF, and AAC files.** iMovie can directly import files in these popular music formats. You can drag them in from the Finder or bring them in from iTunes.

This chapter covers all these sound varieties.

Adding Audio to the Storyboard

Nothing adds emotional impact to a piece of video like music. Slow, romantic music makes the difference between a sad story and one that actually makes viewers cry. Fast, driving music makes viewers' hearts beat faster—scientists have proven it. Music is so integral to movies these days that, as you walk out of the theater, you may not even be aware that a movie *had* music, but virtually every movie does—and you were emotionally manipulated by it.

Home movies are no exception. Music adds a new dimension to your movie, so much so that some iMovie fans *edit to music.* They choose a song, lay it down in the audio track, and then cut the video footage to fit the beats, words, or sections of the music.

> **TIP** Even if you don't synchronize your video to the music in this way, you may still want to experiment with a music-only soundtrack. That is, set the volume for your camcorder clips to zero (Volume Adjustments), so your movie is silent except for the music. The effect is powerful and is often used in Hollywood montage sequences.

The Music and Sound Effects Browser

Here's how you go about choosing a piece of music, or a sound effect, for your movie:

1. **Choose Window → "Music and Sound Effects" (or press ⌘-1).**

   Alternatively, click the musical-notes icon just beneath the Viewer. Either way, the lower-right chunk of your iMovie window is now filled with the Music and Sound Effects browser (Figure 9-1).

2. **Find just the right song (or sound).**

   The panel is filled with useful controls to help you find the right sound. Its listings include:

   iMovie '09 Sound Effects. This list includes about 100 handy sound effects like doors closing, trains passing, and animal sounds.

   iLife Sound Effects. This list represents another enormous collection of sound effects, organized into folders. Don't miss, in particular, the Jingles folder; it contains 200 pieces of terrific, professionally recorded, *royalty-free* background music in every style.

Figure 9-1:
*Welcome to the "Music and Sound Effects"
browser, which reveals your iTunes music
collection, your GarageBand masterpieces, and
several hundred sound effects. (If you don't see
the category you want, click the corresponding
flippy triangle at the top of the list.)*

GarageBand. Here's a nice perk of having an integrated suite of programs like
iLife: You can share the output of each program and touch it up in the others.
For example, any musical compositions you've worked up in GarageBand show
up here.

NOTE Actually, you see in this list only the compositions you've saved with what Apple calls an
iLife preview. To make sure your piece has this preview attached, open GarageBand → Preferences, click General, and then turn on "Render an audio preview when saving." This option makes
saving a GarageBand song take longer, but it's necessary if you want your musical masterpieces to
show up in iMovie.

iTunes. If you keep your music collection in the free iTunes software, you're in
luck; the entire assortment shows up right here, in the iTunes category. In fact,
if you've organized your iTunes music into *playlists* (subsets), you can scroll
through them right in the list. You can also use the Search box at the bottom of
the list, as shown in Figure 9-2.

To listen to a piece of audio in *any* of these categories (GarageBand, iTunes, and
so on), click its name, and then click the ▶ button beneath the list. Or, if you
think life is too short already, just *double-click* a song name. (To interrupt playback, either double-click a different song, double-click the same song, or click
the ▶ button again.)

Figure 9-2:
Choose any of your playlists to navigate your massive music collection. You can also click in the Search box. As you type a song or performer's name, iMovie hides all songs whose names don't match, so that you can quickly find a certain song or group of songs from among thousands. (To restore the entire list and delete what you've typed, click the little X button at the right end of the Search box.)

You can sort the list alphabetically by song name, artist name, or song length by clicking the appropriate heading above the list. (Ordinarily, you wouldn't think that it would be very useful to sort the list by track length. But remember that in the context of a video-editing program, finding a song that's exactly the right length for your video could wind up being more important than which band plays it.)

TIP   The playback controls on the Audio pane are independent of the playback controls in the Monitor window. You may find it useful, therefore, to play your movie *as* you listen to the different songs, so that you can preview how the music might sound when played simultaneously with the video.

The easiest way to experiment in this way is to click ▶ in the "Music and Sound Effects" browser at precisely the same instant that you press the space bar to begin the movie playback.

3. **Drag the music into your storyboard.**

Using the song's name as a handle, drag it directly out of the list and into the storyboard. Release the mouse when the song looks like it's in the right place.

And what, you may ask, is "the right place" to position a song? It turns out that where you drop the music is extremely important. If you release the mouse when the *entire background* of the storyboard has turned green (Figure 9-3), then you're creating what iMovie calls background music (see the next page for details).

NOTE   If your intention is to add background music, then you can actually drag *more than one* song from the Music and Sound Effects browser simultaneously. (To select more than one, click the first one, and then ⌘-click each additional one in the list.)

This presumes, of course, that there's enough video to cover them all. If there's not, iMovie won't play all of them. You'll need to either add more video or photos, or cut your songs shorter with the Clip Trimmer (page 203).

If you release the mouse when the pointer is on a filmstrip, then you're creating what iMovie calls a sound effect; page 206 has more information.

Figure 9-3:
Background music turns into a huge green puddle behind your filmstrips. Try skimming/playing the movie after you've placed the music. If it doesn't have quite the effect you thought it would, press ⌘-Z (Edit → Undo) and try another experiment.

Adding Audio from the Finder

The "Music and Sound Effects" browser is a great way to find music and effects for your movie—*if* they're listed there. You may very well have folders full of audio files that *didn't* come from iTunes, GarageBand, or Apple.

Fortunately, they're easy to incorporate; see Figure 9-4. Just keep in mind that *how* you drag files in from the desktop determines whether they become background audio (big green bubble) or sound-effects audio (horizontal stripes), just exactly as described above.

Figure 9-4:
If you have audio files on your Mac that aren't listed in the iMovie audio browser, make the iMovie window smaller (drag its lower-right corner inward) so you can see the desktop behind it. Open the desktop window that contains your audio clips, and then drag them into your storyboard.

POWER USERS' CLINIC

Adding or Removing Sound Effects

The list of sound effects in the Music and Sound Effects panel isn't magical. It's simply a listing of the sound files that come with iMovie. If you know the secret, you can delete, move, or rename your sound effects–or even install new ones. Here's how:

First, quit iMovie. In the Finder, open your Applications folder. Control-click (or right-click) iMovie's icon; from the shortcut menu, choose Show Package Contents.

The iMovie *package window* appears. You've just discovered, if you didn't already know, that many Mac OS X program icons are, in fact, thinly disguised folders (called *packages*) that contain dozens or hundreds of individual support files. You've just opened up iMovie for inspection.

Open the Contents → Resources folder. Welcome to the belly of the beast. Before you sit hundreds of individual files, most of them the little graphics that make up the various iMovie buttons, controls, and so on. (If you're really feeling ambitious, you can actually open up these graphics and edit them, completely changing the look of iMovie.)

The icon you want is the folder called iMovie '08 Sound Effects. (Yes, the folder still bears the '08 name, even though you paid for iMovie '09.) It's a folder full of individual sound files–in MP3 format–that make up the list you see in the Audio pane (Figure 9-2).

Feel free to reorganize these files. For example, you can throw away the ones you never use, or rename the ones you do. You can add new MP3 files to this list. You can even make new folders to categorize the selection. Later, you'll see them show up as subfolders of the iMovie '08 Sound Effects heading in the "Music and Sound Effects" browser.

(Looking for even more sound effects? The Internet is filled with downloadable MP3 files that you can use in your iMovie projects. You can start your search at *http://www.google.com*. Perform a search for *free sound effects*. Many are already in MP3 format; many others are in AIFF format, which you can convert to iMovie-friendly MP3 files using iTunes.)

Close all the windows. When you return to iMovie, you'll see, under the iMovie Sound Effects heading, the updated list of MP3 sound-effects files.

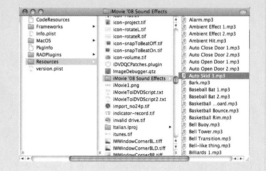

Background Music

If you drag a piece of music into the *background well* of your storyboard—basically, anywhere *except* onto a clip—the background of the entire storyboard area develops a broad green bubble. That's your clue that you've just installed a piece of what Apple calls background music.

Understanding what, exactly, Apple means by this term—and figuring out how it's different from the *sound effects*–style music—is not especially easy. This much, though, is clear:

- **Background music appears in the storyboard.** The music appears as a huge green or purple background bubble behind your filmstrips. (Sound-effects audio, on the other hand, appears as a skinny horizontal stripe under the filmstrip.)

- **The music ends at the end of your video, even if the song isn't over yet.** If the song is *longer* than the movie, a special vertical indicator bar appears after the last filmstrip to let you know. (It's a vertical dotted line with two musical notes.) And if you then add *more* video to the project, the background music auto-expands to include it. It's stretchy that way.

- **Background music generally plays from the beginning of your movie.** You can drag it into a different spot, however, as described on page 203.

- **If you place two pieces of background music right up against each other, iMovie plays them consecutively, with a crossfade in between.** You can add another piece the same way you added the first one: by dragging its name from the "Music and Sound Effects" browser. (Two pieces of background music can never overlap, though.)

FREQUENTLY ASKED QUESTION

Fun with Copyright Law

Don't I break some kind of law when I copy music from a commercial CD, or use iTunes Store music in one of my movies?

Exactly what constitutes stealing music is a hot-button issue that has tied millions of people (and recording executives) in knots. That's why some iMovie fans hesitate to distribute their iMovie films in places where lawyers might see them—like the Internet.

Frankly, though, record company lawyers have bigger fish to fry than small-time amateur operators like you. You're perfectly safe showing your movies to family and friends, your user group, and other limited circles of viewers. In fact, Apple *encourages* you to use iTunes Music Store purchases in your movies. After all, Apple is the one who made them available right in iMovie.

You'll risk trouble only if you go commercial, making money from movies that incorporate copyrighted music.

Still, if your conscience nags you, you can always use one of your GarageBand compositions. And even if you're not

especially musical, the world is filled with royalty-free music—music that has been composed and recorded expressly for the purpose of letting filmmakers add music to their work without having to pay a licensing fee every time they do so. Some of it's even free. You'll find 200 free musical pieces in the Jingles folder of your Music and Sound Effects browser, for example, ready to use.

Or check out *http://www.freeplaymusic.com*, a Web site filled with prerecorded music in every conceivable style, that you're welcome to use in your movies at no charge for noncommercial use.

If that's not enough for you, visit a search page like *http://www.google.com*, search for *music library* or *royalty-free music*, and start clicking your way to the hundreds of Web sites that offer information about (and listenable samples of) music that you can buy and use without fear. (Many of these sites require a RealAudio plug-in, an add-on for your Web browser that you can download and install from *http://www.real.com*.)

Pinning and Unpinning Background Music

When you drag music into the background of your storyboard, it starts out being *unpinned*. It's called unpinned because it's not attached to the video. You can add or delete chunks of video, but that good ol' music pad stays right where it is, unaffected. It's a steady stream of music that plays from the beginning of your movie. Unpinned background music has a green bubble.

There are times, however, when unpinned music can be a real pain. You might have a situation where you want to line up a certain video moment (like Bill-Gates-getting-hit-with-a-pie footage) with a particular audio moment (like a cymbal crash). You'll find that when you insert or delete some video footage *after* lining up audio with specific video moments, everything goes out of alignment. This syndrome can rear its ugly head in many video editing programs.

POWER USERS' CLINIC

The Clip Trimmer

Most people treat background music in iMovie as a set-it-and-forget-it affair. You drop it into the storyboard, it plays as long as necessary to cover your video, end of story.

Truth is, though, you have a little more control than that. Exhibit A: You can start any piece of music playing from someplace *other* than its beginning (and stop it before its end). If you have an iTunes track that begins with an annoying 35-second drum solo, for example, you can lop it out, so that the music (and your movie) begins with the actual hook of the song—the main part.

To edit background audio in this way, click anywhere on the green background bubble to select it (a yellow outline appears on it). Now click the ✿ button in the upper-left corner of the background audio bubble. From the shortcut menu, choose Clip Trimmer.

Suddenly, the Event Browser filmstrips disappear. They're replaced by the Clip Trimmer window, which you first read about back on page 90.

You're seeing the soundwaves that represent the background music. The soundwaves you'll actually hear are light green. If the music is longer than the video, the soundwaves you *won't* hear (because they would play after the video is over) are black.

Your job here is to adjust the position of the yellow vertical end handles. Drag the first one to the right if you want the music to begin at a point that's later in the song; drag the final one to the left if you want the music to end before the official end of the song. You can skim or play to hear where you are in the piece.

Click Done when you're finished adjusting the beginning and ending points.

Incidentally, this trick also works on sound-effects audio (page 206), narration, and so on. In those situations, begin with one click on the same ✿ icon at the beginning of the sound effect.

You may wind up playing a frustrating game of find-the-frame, over and over again, all the way through the movie, as you try to redo all of your careful audio/video alignments.

The solution is to *pin* the audio. Click carefully on the *name* of the background audio bubble, and drag it horizontally (Figure 9-5).

When you release the mouse, you'll see that the background audio bubble has turned purple. iMovie has locked the audio to the video at that frame, as indicated by the little pushpin (Figure 9-5, bottom). Even if the video later gets moved around in its track, or even if you later trim away some footage from the beginning of the video clip, the music will still begin at that point in the video.

Figure 9-5:

Top: These two consecutive green background songs are unpinned. They're floating, completely unaffected by your video editing.

Bottom: If you drag one of the bubbles to the right, you pin it to a particular video frame—which you'll know because of the purple coloring and the pushpin. You can add new video clips or take some away, but this audio will always begin playing at this spot in the video.

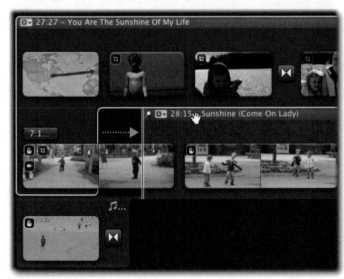

Once you've locked an audio clip to its video, you no longer have to worry that it might lose sync with its video when you edit your video clips.

By the way, pinning an audio clip doesn't prevent *you* from shifting it. Dragging the audio clip does *not* drag the attached video clip along with it. You're still welcome to slide the audio clip left or right in its track, independent of any other clips. Doing so simply makes iMovie realign the clip with a new video frame, lining up the pushpin accordingly. (If you *cut* the video clip, the background audio disappears entirely.)

> **TIP** You can overlap pinned background tracks if you want. Simply drag one background track over another one.

To *unpin* an audio clip, restoring it to its free-floating status, click it, and then choose Edit → Un-Pin Music Track. The audio bubble turns green again, and slams against the left side of the storyboard area (or against whatever background audio bubble is to its left). It's no longer attached to the video.

Rearranging Unpinned Background Music

If you understand the concept of unpinned, free-floating background audio (and you're forgiven if you don't), then you realize that these songs play consecutively, one after another. Unless you've dragged and pinned them, they stack up against each other, left to right in your storyboard, and play sequentially, with a 1-second crossfade between them.

Now suppose you want to rearrange them. How are you supposed to do that? If you drag them, you'll wind up pinning them, which changes their whole function. Fortunately, iMovie offers another way, a way that keeps them unpinned.

The trick is to choose Edit → Arrange Music Tracks. The weird little dialog box shown in Figure 9-6 appears.

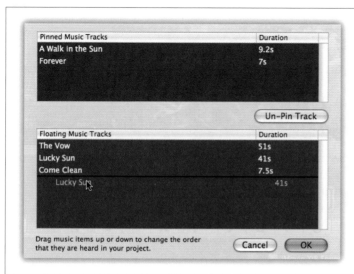

Figure 9-6:
The Edit → Arrange Music Tracks command is available only when you've added at least two background audio clips to your project. It opens this dialog box.

It's a master list of all the background audio clips you've added. Two master lists, actually, helpfully color-coded to match the background audio bubbles in the storyboard:

- **Pinned Music Tracks (purple).** This is a list of all the audio you've pinned to specific moments in the storyboard, complete with their durations.

  You can't do anything in this upper list *except* to click a song, and then click Un-Pin Track. Doing so makes the song leave the purple list and jump down to the green list of Floating Music Tracks. (Meanwhile, back in the storyboard, that bit of audio turns green and slams against the next available piece of green, floating background audio.)

  TIP   In all, there are three ways to unpin a piece of music. You can use the Un-Pin Track button described here; you can use the Edit → Un-Pin Music Track command; or you can Control-click (right-click) a piece of pinned, purple music, and, from the shortcut menu, choose Un-Pin Music Track.

- **Floating Music Tracks (green).** Here are all the background audio pieces that you *haven't* pinned to your video. These are the ones that "float" from the left side of your storyboard, playing sequentially, without any connection to the video.

  And here's the main idea behind this dialog box: You can drag the names of the floating tracks up or down in the list to rearrange them. (Music at the *top* of this list appears at the *beginning* of your project.)

When you're finished, click OK.

Deleting Background Audio

To remove a piece of background audio from your project, click its green or purple bubble once. When the yellow border appears, press the Delete key.

Sound Effects (Pinned Music)

As you now know, iMovie has two kinds of audio. What Apple calls background music is represented by a big green bubble *behind* your filmstrips. It's meant to play continuously as a background pad, regardless of the video that's playing. (Yes, yes, it's true, you *can* pin this type of audio to a specific video frame, but for the sake of clarity, let's ignore that.)

Apple calls the other type of audio *sound effects* audio, and it's specifically intended to be attached, or pinned, directly to a particular frame of a particular clip. If that clip gets pushed around in the storyboard during editing, the audio goes along for the ride.

There are three interesting things about sound-effects audio (Figure 9-7). First, it's represented as a green horizontal stripe below the filmstrip. Second, you can attach more than one of these stripes, stacking them up as high as necessary. Basically, you're overlapping them. And finally, you can move, shorten, or delete the sound-effect stripes by simply dragging.

> **TIP** Actually, there are two ways to adjust the length of a sound-effect stripe. You can drag its right end with your mouse, which is quick and direct. You can also click the ✿ button at the front of the stripe and, from the shortcut menu, choose Clip Trimmer. For details on using the Clip Trimmer window, see the box on page 203.

Figure 9-7:
You can attach multiple sound effects to a single clip and they all move when the video clip moves. To delete a sound effect, click its stripe, and then press the Delete key. To move it, drag the stripe horizontally. And to shorten the clip, drag either end inward.

Editing to the Beat

Without a traditional timeline in iMovie '09, you could pull your hair out trying to match a transition with a beat in the background music. To make sure you don't go bald, iMovie offers a subtle, but very powerful, tool called a Beat Marker.

Beat markers are not the same thing as chapter markers (page 326) or comment markers (page 88). Instead, they're specially designed indicators that correspond to particular musical moments in your background track. Video clips that you add to your project automatically snap against these beats, even resizing themselves if necessary. Later, adjustments you make in the Precision Editor will also snap to line up with the beats you mark.

The truth is, beat markers are the biggest iMovie improvement that no one's talking about. They're not even listed in Apple Marketing's short list of cool new features. What beat markers lack in publicity, they make up for in power. They'll save you huge swaths of time editing a movie to the beat of a song.

Before you do anything, go to View → "Snap to Beats" and make sure that "Snap to Beats" is enabled.

Phase 1: Add your Background Music

Start with a new project. Drop a background music track into your project, as described on page 201.

Now, at this point, you may protest, "Wait a minute! You told me songs won't play unless there are also video clips in place!" You have learned well, Grasshoppa. And your concern is justified. Your song appears like a lonely green blob in your time-line, and the movie won't play.

But your song *is* there. You can still edit the song itself with things like audio adjustments (page 218) and the Clip Trimmer (page 203). Besides, you have a great reason for putting the song in first: All of your added video and photos will automatically resize to match the beats you're about to mark.

> **NOTE** Beat markers work with projects you've already created, but they won't have any effect on the existing clips (like resizing them to fit the beats). You can still exploit beat markers in an existing project, however. The Precision Editor, described below, lets you drag video clips by hand into alignment with beat markers.

Phase 2a: Insert Beat Markers

Click the ✿ button on your lonely song's bubble. From the shortcut menu, choose Clip Trimmer. (The Clip Trimmer's power over music is described on page 203. This time, you're using it for a different purpose.)

In the Clip Trimmer, you can skim and play (by tapping the space bar). But notice the note among the buttons at the top of the Clip Trimmer. This little musical-note icon is a draggable beat marker, which you can grab and drop onto any point in your music track (Figure 9-8). The supply is unlimited, so you can drag as many as you want into your song.

> **NOTE** You can mark beats in *any* kind of audio track: pinned, unpinned, sound effect, or even a voiceover.

Mark any spot that needs special attention in your editing. Most of the time, these will be the beats to the music where you want one clip to cut to the next. But there could be some big musical swells or a key bit in the lyrics that also merit a mark.

The actual markers appear as thin, vertical, white lines with a dot in them (Figure 9-8).

> **TIP** The audio waveforms give you visual cues about what's going on with the music, and can guide you to the right spots in the song.

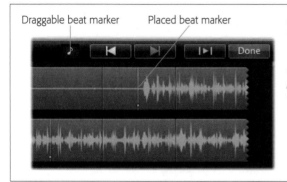

Draggable beat marker   Placed beat marker

Figure 9-8:
Using the note icon in the top-right corner of the Clip Trimmer, you can drag beat markers down into your song. The beat markers appear as thin, vertical, white lines with a dot in them. You can move beat markers after you've placed them by dragging them around. Delete them by dragging them past the bottom or the top of the Clip Trimmer.

Phase 2b: Tapping Out Beats

Dragging is great and all, but you'll find it a lot simpler to just hit the letter M key on the keyboard to add beat markers. (Alternatively, you can right-click [or Control-click] the spot you want to mark, and, from the shortcut menu, choose Add Beat Marker.)

Using your expertise with the M key, start the audio track playing from the beginning. As the song plays, tap the M key on every musical beat where you'll want the video to cut to a new shot. It's OK to boogie in your chair while you tap out the beats to the entire song; no one is watching.

Once you've tapped out the whole song, take a moment to fix your mistakes. Beat markers are draggable, even after you've placed them. You can remove one entirely by dragging it off of the top or bottom of the Clip Trimmer window. If you want to start over, just right-click (or Control-click) any point along your music track and, from the shortcut menu, choose Remove All Beat Markers.

> **TIP**   Usually, if you're cutting right on the beat, your cut will actually appear to be late. If you practice tapping the M key just barely *before* the beats, your cuts will look just right.

Also, don't group your beat markers too closely together unless you're trying to get a very fast-paced effect. If the video cuts happen *too* fast, your viewers won't be able to absorb them.

Once you're happy with all of the beat placements, click Done in the top-right corner of the Clip Trimmer.

Phase 3: Add Your Video Clips

You should be back in your Event Browser now, having a basically blank project awaiting some footage. Grab some video chunk from the Event Browser, and then add it to the project above.

Voilà: There it is. iMovie added your chunk to the project, but resized it to match the next closest beat marker. Try it with a photo now (page 233). Isn't that cool?

(If no auto-resizing seems to be going on, make sure that View → "Snap to Beats" is turned on.)

After very little work, your project will look something like Figure 9-9.

Figure 9-9:
A project that was edited to the beat. Each clip cuts out right in front of the next beat marker—with one exception. See how the beginning clip doesn't touch any beat markers and has the background audio pinned to it? This was done by pinning the background audio after placing the first clip, in spite of iMovie's warning (page 212).

Notice how the beat markers show up in your project to remind you why the cuts are taking place there. Seeing them in your project lets you keep them in mind should you want to edit around them, or want something in the middle of a clip to happen at the beat.

Snap to Beats in Your Project

With "Snap to Beats" turned on, your beat markers in place, and your footage added, you can start plugging in things like titles and sound effects. As you drag these other elements around, they, too, snap into position against beat markers, as though magnetically attracted. You can adjust their timing too, so they also match the beats in your project.

> **WARNING**   You can add all kinds of other project elements, but *transitions* will disrupt your timings, as described below.

Beat Markers in the Precision Editor

What if the video isn't showing exactly what you want when the cut takes place? What if you added your beat markers *after* putting in all of your footage? Not a problem. The Precision Editor knows all about beat markers.

To use the Precision Editor, double-click any empty space between two project clips. Page 96 covers the basics of the Precision Editor, but it offers some handy extras when you're working with beat markers.

First, make sure that you're seeing the background song. Click the Show Extras button, identified in Figure 9-10, to make sure it appears. (The Show Extras button changes from gray to blue when it's turned on.)

Your song appears on the bottom of the window, with all the beat markers standing at attention (Figure 9-10).

Show Extras

Figure 9-10:
With beat markers plugged into your song and "Snap to Beats" turned on, the Precision Editor takes on a new twist. As the cut line nears a beat marker, it snaps to line right up with the beat, turning yellow to let you know what happened.

Drag the cut line around. Each time it approaches a beat marker in the background song, the cut line turns yellow and snaps against the marker.

Here's a rundown of how you could use beat markers in the Precision Editor:

- You can go back through cuts you made before you added beat markers, lining them up to look good with your background song.

- You can ignore the snapping effect and line up a video moment in the *middle* of the clip, like the crack of a bat, with a meaningful moment in the music.

- You can line up other things, like a title, to match a beat.

WORD TO THE WISE

Beats and Transitions

Since you can save so much time using beat markers, you may decide to speed things up even more with automatic transitions, as described on page 120. If so, here is some timely advice.

A simple cut almost always looks good to a beat, because it's just as quick as the beat itself. They match up perfectly. But transitions, like cross dissolves (page 124), generally last *longer* than the beat. The musical beat won't line up as precisely as a regular old cut does.

You'll encounter this problem no matter which transition you use; iMovie can't read your mind to figure out where in the transition you want the beat to take place. As a rule, iMovie puts the beat in the *middle* of the transition. Knowing all this, if you still want to use automatic transitions with beat markers, make sure you've updated

iMovie to version 8.0.3 or later. Once that's done, all the same rules about automatic transitions apply, including the way they change the length of your clips.

In 8.0.3, there's one more oddity (probably a bug): Ordinarily—when you're not using automatic transitions—iMovie shortens each piece of footage so that it ends on the next beat. In other words, a ten-second selection might cut down to two seconds. If automatic transitions are turned *on*, though, iMovie may skip over beat markers entirely. (A ten-second video clip might skip three beat markers, ending with the beat marker closest to the end of the clip.) You'll have to cut your clips down to approximate size before you add them to your project.

CHAPTER 9: NARRATION, MUSIC, AND SOUND

The Beat Warning

With all of this work done, you may want to go back and tweak some things to your liking, such as throwing a transition into a few places or inserting a video clip between two others. As long as "Snap to Beats" is turned on in the View menu, iMovie plays the vigilant guard dog, yapping at you every time you attempt a change that will throw off the beat alignment (Figure 9-11).

Figure 9-11:
iMovie hates so desperately the thought of your project getting out of sync, it warns you anytime you attempt an edit that will mess up its timing. Turn off "Snap to Beats" to make the warnings disappear.

You can dismiss every single warning individually or, to put a permanent muzzle on iMovie, turn off "Snap to Beats" by choosing View → "Snap to Beats" (⌘-U).

FREQUENTLY ASKED QUESTION

Music Beyond the Video

How the heck do I make the music start before the video, or play on for a few seconds past the end of the video?

You're on to something here. There is no way to drag audio, of any type, to the *left* of the first filmstrip in your storyboard. And there's no way to make one extend to the *right* of the last one. Therefore, there doesn't seem to be any way to make the music begin before the movie, or play past the end of it. Ah, but that's what workarounds are for.

The solution, in this case, is simple: Insert a *black background* at the beginning or end of your movie. Fill the screen with nothingness. Your music will play happily,

since it *thinks* that it's playing under video but your audience will see a black screen as the music plays.

Details on background images appear on page 231.

Recording Narration

If anyone ever belittles iMovie for being underpowered, point out an iMovie feature that isn't even available in most expensive video-editing programs: the ability to record narration while you watch your movie play. If your Mac has a microphone, you can easily create any of these effects:

- **Create a reminiscence.** As the footage shows children playing, we hear you saying, "It was the year 2009. It was a time of innocence. Of sunlight. Of children at play. In the years before the Great Asteroid, nobody imagined that one 6-year-old child would become a goddess to her people. This, then, is her story."

- **Voiceover.** The technique of superimposing an unseen narrator's voice over video is called a *voiceover*. It's incredibly popular in TV, commercials, and movies (such as *Saving Private Ryan*, *Sin City*, and of course, the *Look Who's Talking* movies).

- **Identify the scene.** Even if your movie isn't one with a story line, iMovie's narration feature offers an extremely convenient method of identifying your home movies. Think about it: When you get photos back from the drugstore, the date is stamped across the back of each photo. In years to come, you'll know when the photos were taken.

  Video cameras offer an optional date-stamp feature, too—a crude, ugly, digital readout that permanently mars your footage. But otherwise, as they view their deteriorating VHS cassettes in 2025, most of the world's camcorder owners will never know where, why, or when their footage was shot. Few people are compulsive enough to film, before each new shot, somebody saying, "It's Halloween 2007, and little Chrissie is going out for her very first trick-or-treating. Mommy made the costume out of some fishnet stockings and a melon," or whatever.

  Using iMovie, though, it's easy to add a few words of shot-identification narration over your establishing shot. (To find out the time and date when the footage was shot, just double-click the clip.)

- **Provide new information.** For professional work, the narration feature is an excellent way to add another continuous information stream to whatever videos or still pictures are appearing on the screen. Doctors use iMovie to create narrated slideshows, having created a storyboard filled with still images of scanned slides. (See Chapter 10.) Real estate agents feature camcorder footage of houses under consideration, while narrating the key features that can't be seen. ("Built in 1869, this house was extensively renovated in 1880…"). And it doesn't take much imagination to see how *lawyers* can exploit iMovie.

To create a *voiceover* (a narration), follow these steps.

1. **Click the Voiceover button (Figure 9-12, top), or press the letter O key.**

   The Voiceover window appears (Figure 9-12, bottom).

2. **Choose a sound source, like your Mac's microphone.**

   Your Mac's microphone takes one of two forms: built-in, or external. The built-in mic, a tiny hole in the facade of the iMac, eMac, or MacBook, couldn't be more convenient. It's always with you, and always turned on.

If your Mac doesn't have a built-in microphone, you can plug in an external USB microphone, an old external iSight camera, or a standard microphone with an adapter (like the iMic, *www.griffintechnology.com*).

The Record From pop-up menu lists all the audio sources that the Mac knows about—Built-in Microphone, Built-in Input (meaning the audio-input jack on the back or the side), USB Microphone, or whatever you've got connected.

NOTE   The selection you make here is independent of the input that's currently selected in System Preferences. That's a welcome change from the old iMovie.

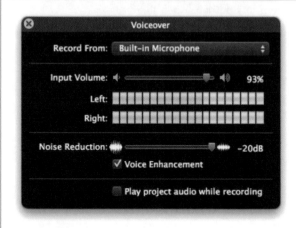

Figure 9-12:
Click the Voiceover button (top) to open the Voiceover window (bottom), where you set up the voice recording to come. Test your setup by speaking into the microphone. If the live VU meter twitches in response, and has a decent level, you're ready to record. When it's all over, your recording will look like the purple stripe below the filmstrip (top). It behaves just like the green stripes of other sound-effects audio.

3. **Set the input level.**

   That is, move close to the microphone and practice your spiel. If the level meter bars are dancing, but only partway across the graph (Figure 9-12), then your narration isn't loud enough. On playback, it'll probably be drowned out by the camcorder audio track.

If they're hitting the right end of the graph, on the other hand, those bars turn bright red to get your attention. In that case, the sound source is too loud, and the recording will have an ugly, "overdriven" distortion.

To increase the recording volume, drag the Input Volume slider to the right. (You can learn tricks for boosting the volume of audio tracks later in this chapter, but it's much better to get the level right the first time.)

4. **Adjust the Noise Reduction and Voice Enhancement controls, if you like.**

   The Voice Enhancement checkbox is supposed to electronically alter your voice to sound more smooth. The Noise Reduction slider is supposed to screen out ambient background noise. Neither one produces an earth-shaking effect, but you can experiment with them to see how you like the result.

5. **Turn the "Play project audio" checkbox on or off.**

   The question you're answering here is: Do you want to hear the audio from your movie playing back while you record? Usually, the answer is "Yes." That way, you can avoid talking over somebody's on-camera conversation, and you can time your own utterances to perfection. The problem is, your microphone *hears* the movie playback coming out of your Mac's speakers and records a second copy of it, or even triggers squealing feedback.

   Therefore, turn on "Play project audio" only if you're wearing headphones to monitor the playback.

6. **Find the spot where you want the narration to begin.**

   You can use all the usual navigational techniques to navigate your clips: skim (point without clicking), press the space bar to play the movie, and so on. Don't click the mouse; just skim and play.

7. **When you've found the spot, click the mouse.**

   Big red letters in the Viewer say, "Get ready…", and a big 3-2-1 countdown timer appears, accompanied by attention-getting countdown beeps. You even see preroll—the Viewer shows the three seconds of video that *lead up* to the point you clicked. All of this is intended to help you get ready to speak at the spot you clicked.

8. **When the Viewer says Recording, start talking. Press the space bar (or click anywhere) to stop.**

   Now a new, purple stripe appears below your filmstrip, already highlighted, bearing the name Voiceover Recording 1 (or 2, or 3), as shown in Figure 9-12. Point to a spot just before the beginning of the new recording, and then press the space bar to listen to your voiceover work.

9. **Close the Narration window.**

If the narration wasn't everything you hoped for, it's easy enough to record another take. Just hit ⌘-Z (Undo) or click the purple stripe, and then press Delete. Then repeat the process.

You can record as many overlapping narration takes as you like. The purple stripes just pile up and they behave exactly like the sound-effects stripes described on page 206. That is, you can:

- **Delete a stripe** by clicking it and then pressing the Delete key.

- **Shorten a stripe** by dragging its endpoints (or by clicking the purple stripe, and then using the Clip Trimmer as described on page 203).

- **Move a stripe** by draging it to a new spot, using the middle of it as the handle.

When you're finished, click the Voiceover button again, or hit the letter O again, to return to normal editing.

Extracting Audio from Video

iMovie is perfectly capable of stripping the audio portion of your footage apart from the video. The recorded audio suddenly shows up as an independent audio clip. Its pushpins indicate that it's locked to whatever spot on the video you've selected. Figure 9-13 shows the process.

Figure 9-13:
Top: Highlight part of a filmstrip in your Event Browser, and then drag the selection into your storyboard. When you let go, the Drag and Drop menu appears. Click Audio Only.

Bottom: The camcorder audio appears as an independent clip, which you can manipulate exactly as though it's any ordinary audio clip: delete it, shorten it, trim it, move it, and so on. You can create a reverb or echo effect by overlaying the same extracted audio several times.

The Audio Only command unleashes all kinds of useful new tricks that are impossible to achieve any other way:

- **Make an echo.** This is a cool one. Park the extracted audio clip a few frames to the right of the original, as shown at bottom in Figure 9-13. Use the Audio Adjustments panel (page 219) to make it slightly quieter than the original. Repeat a few more times, until you've got a realistic echo or reverb sound.

- **Reuse the sound.** You can put the extracted audio elsewhere in the movie. You've probably seen this technique used in dozens of Hollywood movies: About 15 minutes before the end of the movie, the main character, lying beaten and defeated in an alley, suddenly pieces together the solution to the central plot mystery, as snippets of dialog we've already heard in the movie float through his brain, finally adding up.

    NOTE   You may be tempted to extract audio for creating a *cutaway*, something like you see in documentaries. An interviewee starts on camera, but historical pictures soon replace the video while the interviewee's voice forges on excitedly about the history of dirt.

    But don't. Cutaways like these are much easier to make using the dedicated Cutaway feature, covered on page 94.

- **Grab some ambient sound.** In real movie editing studios, it happens all the time: A perfect take is ruined by the sound of a passing bus during the tender kiss moment and you don't discover it until you're in the editing room, long after the actors and crew have moved on to other projects.

    You can eliminate the final seconds of sound from the scene by cropping or splitting the clip, of course. But that won't result in a satisfying solution, and you'll have three seconds of *silence* during the kiss. The real world isn't truly silent, even when there's no talking. The air is always filled with *ambient sound*, such as breezes, distant traffic, the hum of fluorescent lights, and so on.

    Even inside, in a perfectly still room, there's *room tone*. When you want to replace a portion of the audio track with silence, what you usually want, in fact, is to replace it with ambient sound.

    Professionals always record about 30 seconds of room tone or ambient sound just so they'll have material to use in case of emergency. You may not need to go to that extreme; you may well be able to grab some sound from a different part of the same shot. The point is that by extracting the audio from another part of the scene (when nobody was talking), you've got yourself a useful piece of ambient-sound footage that you can use to patch over unwanted portions of the originally recorded audio.

• **Add narration.** The technique described on page 212 is ideal for narration that you record at one sitting, in a quiet room. But you can add narration via camcorder, too. Just record yourself speaking, import the footage into iMovie, extract the audio, and then throw away the video. You may want to do this if you're editing on a micless Mac, or if you want the new narration to better match the camcorder's original sound.

It's important to note that iMovie never *removes* the audio from the original video clip. You'll never be placed into the frantic situation of wishing that you'd never done the extraction at all, unable to sync the audio and video together again (which sometimes happens in "more powerful" video editing programs).

Instead, iMovie places a *copy* of the audio into the storyboard. The original video clip retains its original audio. As a result, you can extract audio from the same clip over and over again, if you like. iMovie simply spins out another copy of the audio each time.

Volume Adjustments

Ah, yes: volume adjustments…one of the most controversial aspects of iMovie '08 and '09.

It's true: There's no "rubber-banding" in iMovie '09, no little graph that represents the way a clip's volume rises and falls over its length, no way to make the music get softer at a point you select. The following pages provide instructions and workarounds.

Adjusting Overall Clip Volume

You should know from the start that you can't make manual changes to a clip's volume level along its length. You can, however, make the *entire* song louder or softer, raising or lowering all of its peaks and valleys simultaneously.

To do that, double-click the clip. It can be any kind of audio: a background audio bubble, a purple narration stripe, or a green sound-effect stripe. In fact, you can even click a *video* clip, with the understanding that you're about to adjust the camcorder audio's volume.

> **TIP** The clip can even be one that's still in your Event Browser, not even placed in a project yet. In that case, the audio changes you're about to make will affect that video selection in *every* project from now on.

The Inspector window appears. Click the Audio button (shown in Figure 9-14), or just press the letter A when your clip is selected. Immediately, the Audio Adjustments dialog box appears.

NOTE   Whenever you adjust the volume of a video clip, a tiny, faint ◀)) logo appears in the top-left corner as a reminder that you've fooled around with the audio. You can double-click it to open the Audio Adjustments panel, too.

Figure 9-14:
Click the ❶ *button to open the Inspector, and then select the Audio tab to make volume adjustments.*

There are four items of interest here:

- **Volume slider**. By dragging the Volume slider, you can adjust the overall volume level of the selected clip. You can mute it entirely (drag the slider all the way to the left), or make it twice as loud (all the way to the right).

  At this point, you *can't* skim your filmstrips to hear the changes you're making. Instead, to spot-check your work, click the filmstrip corresponding to the audio change you're making. Drag the little red dot handle to position the Playhead, and then press the space bar to start playback.

- **Ducking**. Apple's response to, "Hey, you took away manual audio controls!" is, "You don't need them. We'll do your mixing *for* you!" And that's the purpose of this intriguing checkbox. When you turn it on, you're saying, "The selected audio clip is the most important audio. I want to hear it above any other audio that's going on." This checkbox, in other words, makes all other simultaneous audio clips play softer. And using the slider, you can specify how *much* softer they get.

  In the film business, lowering the music volume so that you can hear the spoken dialogue is called *ducking*. What Apple is offering here is *automatic* ducking. For example, suppose you've cluttered up your storyboard with so many back-ground songs, crowd noises, and sound effects that you can no longer hear the dialogue in the original video. You can apply this option to the *video itself* (not one of the colored audio stripes or bubbles) to bring out the original filmed talking.

NOTE   You can't use this checkbox to boost the volume of background audio; it's dimmed and unavailable for background tracks. If you want to duck everything *but* the background track, you have to do it the old-fashioned way: Use the volume sliders to lower the volume on *other* tracks, and/or to raise the volume on the background audio track.

Overall, auto-ducking is not as flexible as having manual volume controls, but it's better than nothing.

- **Fade In, Fade Out**. Ordinarily, you hear the audio for a sound or video clip immediately. But if you click Manual, you can create a graceful audio *fade-in* or *fade-out* for the selected clip—even if it's a *video* clip from the camcorder. Use the slider to indicate how long you want that fading to take, in seconds (up to five seconds).

NOTE   The fade controls are available only for clips in your storyboard—not for clips in the Event Browser.

- **Normalize Clip Volume**. You may not have much call for this button, but it can be handy now and then. It's designed for situations when the clips in your project were recorded at different volume levels, resulting in some jarring unevenness during playback.

  iMovie can *normalize* the clips, so that all of them have roughly the same volume. Just click the clips containing volume that's out of whack, and then click Normalize Clip Volume. (For tips on selecting multiple clips, see page 74.)

iMovie takes a moment to compute the clip's new audio level. And then, just as a reminder that you've messed around with that clip, iMovie displays a tiny speaker icon near the beginning of it (Figure 9-15, bottom).

When you're finished fiddling, click Done. The dialog box goes away, and you return to the movie.

Copying and Pasting Audio Adjustments

It's very, very cool that Apple gave iMovie the ability to select more than one clip at a time. Yay, Apple! Unfortunately, that's of no help when it comes to audio. You can still select only one clip at a time to make volume adjustments. Boo, Apple!

So if you've got an interview with a 100-year-old man, interspersed with footage of the old town where he grew up, and his audio needs boosting *every single time* he's on camera, you may suppose that you're in for a bit of work. You'll have to click those clips, one at a time, and fix their audio. Right? Not quite. Fortunately, you can make the changes only once, and then *copy and paste* those changes to all the other clips.

Begin by boosting the overall clip volume, or applying the "Reduce volume of other tracks" option, or using the Normalize button, to *one* clip. Now highlight that clip, and then choose Edit → Copy (or press ⌘-C).

Figure 9-15:
Top: In the iMovie scheme, the ✿ badge gives quick access to audio adjustments.

Bottom: The upper clip's audio has been made louder or softer (the badge is now permanent, and shows round sound waves). The lower clip's audio has been normalized (straight sound waves). It may sound truly abnormal, but at least its audio levels are roughly even with the rest of the movie.

Volume has been adjusted

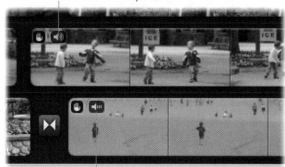

Volume has been normalized

At this point, you can select all of the other clips that need a change (see page 74 for multi-clip selection tips), and then choose Edit → Paste Adjustments → Audio (or just press Option-⌘-A). The appearance of the little icons shown in Figure 9-15 (above) lets you know that all of those other clips have now taken on the audio adjustments of the first.

Or you can plow through your storyboard, clicking and hitting Option-⌘-A, to apply the same settings to each additional clip. Either way, you can breathe a sigh of relief that at least you don't have to work through the Audio Adjustments dialog box each time.

Removing Audio Adjustments

As with all iMovie editing tools, the changes you make in the Audio Adjustments dialog box are nondestructive, meaning that you're never actually changing the underlying clips. You can undo or adjust your changes at any time, even years later.

Just click the clip you edited and then double-click the clip and select the Audio tab (or press the letter A, or double-click the tiny ◂» badge), and then click "Revert to Original". The clip now has its original audio levels back. (Finally, click Done.)

Editing Audio in GarageBand

Why do you suppose the audio-editing features in iMovie '09 are so much weaker than they were in iMovie 6? One possibility is that Apple said to itself, "Well, sheesh—if they want to edit audio, let them use an audio-editing program like the one that comes on *the same DVD as iMovie!*"

That would be a reference to GarageBand, the music composition program included with iLife. It offers all of the tools that iMovie lacks: rubber-band volume levels, multiple overlapping audio tracks, a convenient timeline, audio processing effects like reverb and a graphic equalizer, and much more.

Fortunately, you can export your movie into GarageBand to edit its soundtrack with these much more powerful tools. Don't read any further, however, until you've absorbed these two warnings:

- Your movie arrives in GarageBand with only a single, boiled-down audio track. You can't adjust the camcorder audio and the iMovie music independently. (That's a good argument for avoiding adding *any* music in iMovie. Wait until you're in GarageBand to add all music and sound effects.)

- The iMovie → GarageBand train goes only one way. Once you've worked with a movie in GarageBand, you can no longer return to iMovie for further edits. You *can* return to iMovie, edit the video, and re-export the thing, but of course then you lose all the audio work you'd done in GarageBand the first time.

GarageBand Basics

GarageBand is a music composition program, containing dozens of powerful tools. It lets you combine dozens of audio tracks, giving you fine control over each track's sound effects, volume, and even stereo panning.

But if you're like most people, you've never even set foot in GarageBand. (Apple says that GarageBand is the second least-used iLife program, second only to iWeb.) Here's a crash course:

1. **Export your movie from iMovie.**

   Either send it to the Media Browser (page 279) or save it as a QuickTime movie (page 292) in your Home → Movies folder. (GarageBand can import from either of these locations—the Media Browser or your Movies folder—without any digging around on your part.)

2. **Open GarageBand.**

   GarageBand's icon looks like an electric guitar; it's in your Applications folder.

3. **Create a new project.**

If this is your first time in GarageBand, a welcome screen greets you with a list of choices. If you *have* worked in GarageBand before, it opens the last project you worked on. Choose File → New.

In either case, select New Project from the list on the left, then scroll down and double-click the gigantic clapper icon labeled Movie (Figure 9-16).

Figure 9-16:
GarageBand appears to be designed for either the short-sighted or for those with really bad mouse-aim. Either way, double-click on the Movie icon to create a new movie project.

You're asked to name your project and save it *before* you start editing. Then click Create.

4. **Add your movie from the Media Browser.**

The Media Browser now appears. (If it isn't showing, for some reason, choose Control → Show Media Browser.) Find your movie on the Movies tab, either under the iMovie or Movies heading. Drag the movie into the GarageBand timeline, right into the movie track. (You can also drag a movie file in from the Finder.)

NOTE   You may have noticed that the Media Browser also gives you full access to everything in your Event Library. Theoretically, you can build your whole movie right here in GarageBand. Who needs iMovie? (Well, everyone who wants titles, transitions, clip trimming….but you get the idea.)

GarageBand creates its own thumbnails to represent your movie.

5. **Edit your movie's audio track.**

Once GarageBand has imported your movie, you'll see, directly under the video track, an audio track. This is the audio from your exported movie. It contains *all* of your movie's audio, all merged into one track. Now that it's in Garage-Band, you can manipulate the audio in a multitude of ways. At the left edge of the window, under the words Movie Sound, tiny icons let you mute, isolate, lock, and pan the audio (shift the stereo sound right or left). You can also make the volume rise and fall at particular points, as shown in Figure 9-17.

Figure 9-17:
To show the rubber band tool, click the button marked (A) to expand the volume graph (B). Drag any point on the graph to make the volume rise or fall. Using the pop-up menu (C), you can also plot a graph for the panning. Use the Add Automation menu item to add other sophisticated audio effects to control.

6. **Add audio tracks.**

Add additional tracks, if you like, by choosing Track → New Track (Option-⌘-N), or by clicking the + button on the toolbar. You might use these new tracks to create a custom score. (Read on.) In GarageBand, you can create as many parallel audio tracks as you like, although a huge number bring your Mac to a crawl.

You can also drag songs from the Media Browser (except, mysteriously, songs from iTunes) right into a blank area of the GarageBand window. GarageBand automatically creates a new track and places the song in it.

TIP   To get a song from iTunes into GarageBand, you have to take a trip through the Finder. While in iTunes, select the song you want and right-click (or Control-click) it. From the shortcut menu, choose Show In Finder, and a Finder window pops up with your song highlighted. Drag that file into your GarageBand timeline.

Copy-protected songs you bought from the iTunes Store won't work. GarageBand isn't on the guest list for protected songs (unlike iMovie which has an all-access pass).

7. **Export your movie.**

Once you've finished the audio editing, send the movie out into the world using the commands in the Share menu. For example, you can send the movie directly to iWeb, iTunes, or iDVD.

Or, if you choose Share → "Export to Disk", you can create a standalone Quick-Time movie file on your hard drive. In theory, you can actually import *that* movie *back* into iMovie, although the shuttling back and forth might be getting a little ridiculous at that point.

Scoring in GarageBand

Because GarageBand is a music program, its greatest strength is its ability to help you create a custom musical score for your movie. You can actually record or compose music that runs along with the video, turning you into a regular John Williams. (Actual musical ability may vary.) GarageBand shows the movie in the timeline, frame by frame, so you know exactly where to add the cymbal crash or guitar riff.

Here's a supercondensed review of the different tools for scoring:

- **Use prerecorded loops.** Click the eyeball icon to see all the different categories of prerecorded *loops* (musical building blocks) that you can drag directly upward into new tracks beneath your video. Once it's installed, you can drag the upper-right corner of a loop to make it repeat over and over, for as long as you drag to the right. (This works well with drum parts.)

- **Record a MIDI instrument.** If you have a MIDI instrument connected to your Mac (usually a musical keyboard or synthesizer), choose Track → New Track, click Software Instrument, and then click Create. Now you can choose an instrument sound from the list that appears at lower-right, and then click the round red Record button to begin recording as you play. You can even use the Tempo control (hold your mouse down on the digits) to make the movie play back more slowly, so that you have a better chance at a perfect performance. After you're finished playing, you can crank the tempo back up to its original speed.

- **Record a live instrument or voice.** GarageBand can record live sounds, like your own singing or saxophone playing. Choose Track → New Track, click Real Instrument, and then click Create. Next, choose a reverb preset from the list at lower-right (like Female Basic or Male Rock Vocals). Click the round red Record button to begin recording.

When the musical soundtrack is complete, export the result using the methods described on the previous page. With enough practice, you might eventually wind up on Steven Spielberg's speed dial.

Photos

You may think that iMovie's primary purpose is working with video. But the truth is, it's quite handy with still photos, too. You can bring in still images from iPhoto or from your hard drive, for use as slideshows. You can also turn individual frames of your movie *into* still images, for use as freeze-frames. And, if you know the secret, you can even *export* individual frames as graphics files to your hard drive, suitable for emailing or Web posting.

This chapter tells all there is to tell.

Importing Still Images

You may want to import a graphics file into iMovie for any number of reasons. For example:

- You can use a graphic, digital photo, or other still image as a backdrop for iMovie's titling feature (Chapter 8). A still image behind your text is less distracting than moving footage.

- You can use a graphics file *instead* of using the iMovie titling feature. As noted in Chapter 8, iMovie's titling feature offers a number of powerful features, but it also has a number of serious limitations. For example, you have only rudimentary control over the title's placement in the frame. (See Figure 10-1.)

  Preparing your own title "slides" in, say, Photoshop Elements or Photoshop gives you a lot of flexibility that the iMovie titling feature lacks. You get complete control over the type size, color, and placement, and you can also add graphic touches to your text or to the "slide" on which it appears.

• One of the most compelling uses of video is the *video photo album*: a smoothly integrated succession of photos (from your scanner or digital camera), joined by crossfades, enhanced by titles, and accompanied by music. Thanks to iMovie's ability to import photos directly—either from your hard drive or from your iPhoto collection—creating this kind of video slideshow is a piece of cake.

NOTE Of course, *iPhoto* can create video photo albums, too. And in iPhoto, you can opt to loop a slideshow (which iMovie can't do); rearranging and regrouping your photos is much easier than in iMovie, too.

But building them in a movie has several advantages. First of all, your audio options are much greater; you can record narration as you watch the slideshow, for example. You have a full arsenal of tools for creating titles, credits, and special effects, too.

Figure 10-1:
Preparing your "title cards" in a graphics program gives you far more typographical and design flexibility than iMovie's own titling feature gives you. Using separate graphics software, for example, you can enhance your titles with drop shadows, a 3-D look, or clip art.

As your life with iMovie proceeds, you may encounter other uses for the picture-importing feature. Maybe, when editing a home movie of your kids tussling in the living room, you decide it would be hilarious to insert some *Batman*-style fight-sound title cards ("BAM!") into the footage. Maybe you need an establishing shot of, say, a storefront or apartment building, and realize that you could save production money by inserting a still photo that passes for live video in which there's nothing moving. And maybe you want to end your movie with a fade-out—not to black, but to maroon (an effect described later in this chapter).

You have a delicious choice of two methods for bringing still photos into a project. The first and most convenient method is to choose the photo from among those you've organized in iPhoto, using iMovie's window into your picture collection. If you're not using iPhoto to organize your digital photos, you can also use the older method of importing pictures directly from the hard drive.

The Photos Browser

The more you work with iMovie and iDVD, the more you appreciate the convenience of the way Apple has linked them to the other i-programs, like iTunes and iPhoto. Here's a classic case:

When you open the Photos Browser (Figure 10-2), or choose Window → Photos, or press ⌘-2, you're shown what amounts to iPhoto Lite: a scrolling panel of thumbnail images reflecting the contents of your entire iPhoto Library. Using the navigation panel just above the thumbnails, you can browse your photos by event, album, folder, or according to the other iPhoto presets (like flagged photos or photos added in your last import). If you use Aperture, Apple's pro photo-organization program, its library shows up here, too.

> **NOTE**   Events in iPhoto are a lot like Events in iMovie. That is, iPhoto groups all the photos taken on the same day into an Event.
>
> Albums are the category containers that you can create in iPhoto by choosing File → New Album (or by clicking the + button at the lower-left corner). You can drag a single picture into as many of these albums as you like. Folders are simply larger structures that let you group albums together. Complete details are in *iPhoto '09: The Missing Manual*.

iPhoto albums, events, and groups   Photos browser

368 items

Show photos   within Event date range

Thumbnail size

Figure 10-2:
The Photos Browser shows all the pictures you've imported into iPhoto (or Aperture, if you have it). Use the navigation panel to limit the photo display to those in a certain album or folder. (The white lettering at the lower right tells you how many pictures are in that album or folder—or in your entire library, if that's what you're seeing.) Note the Search box. As you type into it, iMovie smoothly hides all photos except the ones whose names or keywords contain matching text. It's an amazingly quick way to pinpoint one photo out of several thousand. To clear the search box and return to viewing all photos, click the ⊗ at the right end of the box.

Here are four other handy Photos Browser tips:

- iMovie starts out showing you rows of photo thumbnails. You can control their size by dragging the slider below the browser.

- iMovie offers an alternative, and very useful, way to view your photos. Control-click (or right-click) anywhere in the Photos Browser. From the shortcut menu, choose "Display as List". iMovie changes the Photos Browser's display into columns, as shown in Figure 10-3.

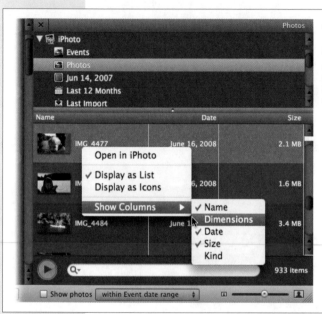

Figure 10-3:
The List view shows each photo, the day it was taken, and its size. An additional right-click lets you add even more columns that show the photo dimensions and file type. To return to icon view, right-click (Control-click) again and choose "Display as Icons".

- If you want to edit a photo before adding it to your movie, you don't have to fire up iPhoto manually. Just Control-click (or right-click) the photo, and from the shortcut menu, choose "Open in iPhoto". iPhoto opens and takes you directly to the photo you clicked. Once you make the necessary changes, iMovie returns and uses the updated version of your photo.

- Double-click a thumbnail to make that photo fill the *entire* Photos Browser for a much closer look. Then press the left and right arrow keys to walk through the adjacent photos at this larger size. Click a photo once to return to the thumbnails.

Photos from the Finder

If you haven't added the image you need to your iPhoto library, you can still add it to your movie project. All you have to do is locate it in the Finder and drag it into your project window.

Match Event Dates

It doesn't take long to get a full iPhoto library. A few soccer games, a couple of birthdays, a trip to Disney, and suddenly you feel like you're storing the Library of Congress on your computer. And then you have to scroll through all those thousands of pictures, represented as tiny icons, in iMovie.

You can drill down through iMovie Events to find the photos you want, or you can show some discipline and put those photos into albums. But you don't want to, so what now?

iMovie '09 kicks in this little freebie: You can tell it to match photos from iPhoto with the Event you are currently browsing in iMovie. This little stroke of genius makes a lot of sense, since both programs rely on the Event dates of your stuff (and since you probably took both stills and videos during that big day).

To turn on Event date matching, turn on the tiny Show Photos checkbox below your Photos Browser. Using the tiny menu to the right of it, you can limit the photos you see to those shot the same day as your iMovie Event, or those shot within a day, week, or month of your footage.

This is a great trick, mainly because a lot of special events involve footage *and* photos. This feature makes finding the right photos a piece of cake.

TIP iMovie can import graphics in any format that QuickTime can understand, which includes PICT, JPEG, GIF, PNG, Photoshop files, and even PDF files, for when an IRS form is exactly what you want to illustrate in your movie. Avoid the GIF format for photos, which limits the number of colors available to the image; otherwise, just about any format is good still-image material.

Once you've added a photo to iMovie, you don't have to keep track of the original. iMovie actually socks away a *copy* of any image that you import. Even if you delete a photo file from iPhoto or the Finder, iMovie still keeps a copy of it. (Just don't try this with video clips as iMovie treats them very differently!)

iMovie Backgrounds

Generations of iMovie fans have dressed up their opening credits and chapter titles by creating custom backgrounds, so that text appears in front of red curtains or a Hollywood opening-night spotlight instead of plain black. To save you that hassle, iMovie now comes with a handsome set of premade background images (Figure 10-4). Some are even animated; for example, the Underwater background shows shimmering rays of sunlight filtering through the water.

TIP You can use these images and animations as backgrounds for your green-screen work too (page 143). That is, instead of revealing your newscaster skit to have been shot in your pathetic basement, you can insert one of these much more handsome backgrounds.

Add Folders to the Photos Browser

Not everyone uses iPhoto. There are plenty of other good programs for organizing pictures. Plenty of people just store photos in folders in the Finder, and don't use any fancy photo-shoebox program at all.

Fortunately, you can still access them from within iMovie. You can add a folder, any folder, to your Photos Browser.

To do this, switch into the Finder. Find the folder that you want to add to your Photos Browser. Drag it directly into the list in the Photos Browser (where it now says iPhoto).

Now you have an additional item in your list called Folders. Click its flippy triangle to see what's in it—the folder you just dragged. You can add as many more photo folders as you like.

Figure 10-4:
Behold the reason this is called the Maps and Backgrounds Browser. If you count the maps, that's 24 high-quality image backgrounds that you can use to jazz up your project.

Even though these are basically image files, there are a few key differences:

- **iMovie knows these are backgrounds.** If you double-click one after you've placed it in your project, the Inspector appears, identifying it as such.

    TIP   In the Inspector, you can also click the Background button to get a skimmable palette of all the backgrounds. That's how you can swap one background image for another without having to re-place it in your project.

- **Backgrounds go between clips only.** This means you can't use backgrounds for cutaways, discussed on page 94.

- **Backgrounds are immune to video effects.** You can't crop or rotate backgrounds. You can't animate them with a Ken Burns effect. You can't adjust their colors or apply video filters. They just sit there.

To use a background, drag it out of the Maps and Backgrounds browser and into any empty area of your project (for example, between two clips, or following your clips). It appears as a four-second clip; double-click it to change its duration or style.

Two Ways to Add Photos

Adding photos to your project is a lot like adding music, in that there are two ways to go about it. If you're using photos from your iPhoto library or from the Finder, adding photos in iMovie behaves similar to adding titles, as described in Chapter 10. That is, there are two places to drag photos: between clips, or onto them. The results are quite different.

Photo Filmstrips

If you drag a photo *between* two filmstrips in your storyboard, you create a new *photo filmstrip* (Figure 10-5, top).

> **TIP**   You can add more than one photo at a time in this way—a handy trick if you're creating a slideshow. Select multiple photos in the iPhoto browser just as you'd select multiple icons in the Finder. For example, you can click the first one, then Shift-click the last to select a group, or ⌘-click individual thumbnails. You can even just drag an entire album from the album list.

In most regards, the photo now behaves exactly like a video filmstrip. You can crop it, rotate it, and make color adjustments to it, for example, exactly as described in Chapter 7. You can apply the snazzier video effects described in Chapter 6. You can superimpose titles and credits on it, just as described in Chapter 8. You can even use the Split or Trim commands on a photo.

Key differences: You can't adjust a photo's timing by dragging the clip ends or by using the Fine Tuning controls (page 92). Instead, you have to use the Inspector, described on page 237. You also can't make any audio adjustments because, well, you can't adjust what ain't there.

Photo Cutaways

Alternatively, you can drag a photo *on top of* a video clip (or photo filmstrip). At that point, the Drag and Drop menu appears (Figure 10-5).

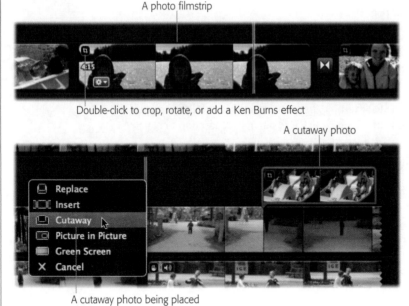

A photo filmstrip

Double-click to crop, rotate, or add a Ken Burns effect

A cutaway photo

Replace
Insert
Cutaway
Picture in Picture
Green Screen
Cancel

A cutaway photo being placed

Figure 10-5:
Top: Here's a photo you dragged between two other filmstrips. It turns into a photo filmstrip, which behaves in almost every way like a video filmstrip. (You can identify a photo filmstrip by the tiny badges that appear when you point to it without clicking. If it's a photo, there's no audio icon, and the Crop icon always appears, whether or not you actually cropped the photo.)

Bottom: If you drag onto part of an existing filmstrip, you can make a Cutaway, like the one shown here.

If you aren't inserting the photo or replacing something else with it, the most common and useful command in this menu is Cutaway. This is the documentary style effect discussed on page 94. When you use a photo as a Cutaway, iMovie sticks it right on top of the underlying clip in the timeline. (It even casts a shadow on the clip below it.)

> **TIP** Photo cutaways get close to full iMovie citizenship. You can crop, rotate, and apply effects to adjust colors of all photo cutaways. What you *can't* do is adjust audio or crop/trim a photo. Those two actions don't fit the concept of a photo cutaway.

Of course, it also covers up the video in the movie itself. So if the photo blocks the video, what good is it? Why not just create a photo filmstrip?

Actually, a photo cutaway has four advantages over a photo filmstrip:

- **Cutaways are much easier to adjust.** You can slide a cutaway left or right, earlier or later in the movie, with the touch of the mouse. And you can shorten or lengthen it by just dragging its ends. (Oddly, this last trick works only when the clip is *not* selected.)

- **You can make cutaways transparent.** Because iMovie lets you adjust the transparency of a photo cutaway, you can dial it back, turning the photo into a translucent layer. You might take a photo of clouds, dial back the opacity, and—bam!—you have fog covering the clip underneath. To adjust the transparency of a photo you've placed in your project, double-click the photo to open the Inspector, and then drag the Opacity slider (Figure 10-6).

Figure 10-6:
By dialing back the opacity of a photo cutaway, you can add cool effects, like the fog covering this clip. (Compare the top and bottom images.) The effect was created with a cutaway picture of clouds, set at half transparency. You can use this trick for your "Scooby Doo and the Haunted Forest" remake.

- **Cutaways are incredibly useful.** You've seen it a million times on TV. Someone starts talking; as the narration continues, the camera *cuts away* to a photo or another video clip; and then we return to the original person speaking.

  It's actually pretty remarkable how easy iMovie makes this. Instead of having to extract audio from your video clip and then create a still clip to plug in the middle, you just drop a photo over the video and choose Cutaway. The result is a cutaway (with a cross dissolve, if you like) that looks like it took a lot more work than it actually did.

- **You can poke holes in it.** This tip is for Photoshop (or Photoshop Elements) mavens, but it's wicked cool. It lets you create see-through *pieces* of a photo—and the video behind it plays through the holes. (It's not the same as the whole-photo transparency setting described above.) The steps for creating this fantastic effect appear in Figure 10-7.

  This trick opens up a host of effects that iMovie can't do with its built-in tools. You could make a black image with two holes. They'll show up in iMovie as though you're peering through a pair of binoculars. (A great way to pump up your ten-year-old's spy movie!)

  Use this trick to put a pair of nose glasses or a funny hat on someone. Or create text titles, like *Batman*-style "BAM!"s and "KAPOW!"s superimposed on your footage. As long as you use the PNG image format (which recognizes transparency), then a little creativity can lead to all kinds of cool effects. (iMovie '09 does *not* support transparency in TIFF files.)

Figure 10-7:
*This effect pops up often
in opening credits for TV
shows (at least ones
from the 1970s) and the
occasionally cheesy
movie.*

*Make a graphic in
Photoshop that contains
cutouts. Select the
pieces that you don't
want to be transparent;
⌘-click the "Save
selection as channel"
button on the Channels
palette, and save the
result as a PNG graphic
with an alpha channel.
Drag the resulting file
right off the desktop
onto any filmstrip in
iMovie. (Page 193
shows the effect.) Once
it becomes a photo
cutaway in iMovie, the
underlying video plays
through the holes!*

Timing Changes

The way you change the duration and position for a photo depends on what kind it is.

Photo filmstrips

A still image doesn't naturally have a *duration*, as a movie clip might. (Asking "How many seconds long is a photograph?" is like asking, "What is the sound of one hand clapping?")

Still, it's working like a clip, so iMovie has to assign it *some* duration. iMovie turns every filmstrip photo into a 4-second clip. If you prefer a different default timing, choose File → Project Properties (⌘-J), click the Timing tab, and then adjust the Photo Duration slider. You can change the default timing to as little as 1 second or as long as 10 seconds.

Actually, there are *three* ways to adjust filmstrip photos' durations:

- **Change all photo durations at once.** If, in the Project Properties dialog box, you select "Applies to all photos", then the Duration slider affects all photos simultaneously.

- **Change photo durations from here on.** The weird little option labeled "Applies when added to project" actually means "Whatever duration you choose on the Duration slider applies to the *next* photo you drop into the storyboard—and all future ones." It preserves the durations of all *existing* photos in your project, but changes the standard timing for all *incoming* photos.

- **Change individual photo durations.** You can also change photo durations on a one-at-a-time basis. Double-click the photo and the Inspector appears.

In the Duration text box, type in the number of seconds you want for the photo. You can make your photo appear on the screen for as little as .25 of a second (a favorite of subliminal advertisers) or as long as 10 minutes (a favorite of all other advertisers).

TIP   When you get right down to it, 10 minutes is just way too long for looking at one particular photo, no matter how good it is. Still, if for some bizarre reason you need it to last longer—perhaps because you're using it as a background for a long series of titles—you can always overcome the 10-minute limit by placing the same photo into your project over and over again, side by side.

Photo Cutaways

As noted earlier, changing the duration of a superimposed photo cutaway is much easier. Just drag the ends of the cutaway clip to make it longer or shorter. (You can even span more than one filmstrip.)

TIP   You've probably noticed that cutaway photos cut in and out at a set speed, that is, without a quick fade. If you prefer a cutaway to fade in slowly (or pop in dramatically), double-click it to open the Inspector.

Next to the Cutaway Fade label, turn on Manual and drag the slider to change the fade's duration (shown in the Inspector in Figure 10-6). (You can also just type the timing into the text box next to the fade slider. In fact, you can have it last ridiculously long, but never longer than your photo's actual duration.)

The Dimensions of an iMovie Photo

If you're designing a custom image for your movie, you'll generally want it to have the same dimensions as your video dimensions. Otherwise, iMovie crops the photo or inserts black bars to make it fit.

iMovie offers three standard aspect ratios for your videos: Standard (4:3), iPhone (3:2), and Widescreen (16:9). (See page 56 for a complete discussion.) For now, here's how big to make your photos so that they fit these movie frames:

- **Standard 4:3.** Make your image 640 pixels wide and 480 pixels tall. (Be aware that the outer edges may get chopped off on standard-definition TVs, as explained on page 324.

• **iPhone 3:2**. Make the photo 480 pixels wide and 320 pixels tall to fit the iPhone screen.

• **Widescreen 16:9**. Your imported photo should be at least 960 pixels wide and 540 pixels tall. (True high definition is more than that—1920 pixels wide and 1080 pixels tall—but Apple doesn't think you'll see much difference.)

If you have an image that wasn't born with the right dimensions, don't worry. The powerful Crop tool and the Ken Burns effect can help you compensate.

Crop, Fit, Rotate

One of iMovie's greatest virtues is its resolution agnosticism. You can combine widescreen footage from your new HD camcorder with standard-def footage from your old DV camera in the same movie; iMovie gracefully handles their different dimensions.

This adaptability also extends to photos. Chapter 7 contains a detailed discussion of cropping *video* to fit the frame (or to draw emphasis to a certain part of the picture), making it fit the frame by adding letterbox bars, and even rotating it.

Well, surprise, surprise: *Exactly* the same features are available for photo filmstrips. See the write-ups beginning on page 166 for the full discussion.

> **TIP** You can crop, fit, and rotate both photo *filmstrips* and photo *cutaways*. The process is exactly the same.

UP TO SPEED

Avoiding Pixellated Images

You may have tried adding an image to iMovie and found that it looked pretty rotten. Blurry, pixellated, or jagged images are ugly and quite jarring when they appear in a movie surrounded by pristine video footage.

Sloppy-looking images like these usually result from using a photo file whose resolution is too low to begin with. For example, you might have taken a hilarious little shot with your cameraphone—emphasis on little. Images downloaded from the Web often have very low resolution, too.

iMovie, thinking it's doing you a favor, stretches that photo larger than its original size to make it fit the movie frame, and ugly-looking coarseness results.

If you absolutely must use a small image, consider framing your picture inside a larger image of the proper dimensions. iMovie shows the small picture with the frame surrounding it, preventing the jagged, blurry resizing you would otherwise see.

The Ken Burns Effect

The only problem with using still photos in a movie is that they're *still*. They just sit there without motion or sound, wasting much of the dynamic potential of video.

For years, professionals have addressed the problem using special sliding camera rigs that produce gradual zooming, panning, or both, to bring photographs to life.

But this smooth motion isn't just about adding animation to photos for its own sake. It also lets you draw the viewer's attention where you want it, *when* you want it. For example: "Little Harry graduated from junior high school in 1963"—slow pan to someone else in the school photo, a little girl with a ribbon in her hair— "little suspecting that the woman who would one day become his tormentor was standing only a few feet away."

Among the most famous practitioners of this art is Ken Burns, the creator of PBS documentaries like *The Civil War* and *Baseball*, which is why Apple named the feature after him.

> **TIP** If you've updated iMovie to version 8.0.3, you can also apply the Ken Burns effect to *video*. You can create very smooth pans and zooms in footage where the camera didn't actually move an inch. Powerful feature!

Applying the Ken Burns Effect

iMovie '09's Ken Burns controls are totally different from what was in iMovie before. Here's how you use them:

1. **Click a photo filmstrip or cutaway.**

   A yellow border appears.

2. **Press the letter C key, or click the Crop icon on the toolbar, or click the tiny Crop badge that appears when you've already cropped a photo.**

   All three of these techniques open up the Crop/Fit/Rotate/Ken Burns window in the upper-right corner of the iMovie window.

3. **Click the Ken Burns button.**

   Now you see the outlines of two rectangles over your photo, one green and one red. They represent the framing of your photo during its short moment in the sun: the way it will first appear (the green box), and the way it will conclude (red). Basically, you're setting up the start frame and the end frame. iMovie automatically produces the animation required to smoothly pan and/or zoom between them.

4. **Set up the photo's starting point.**

   That is, select the green box by clicking it. Drag its corners to resize the box and drag in the middle to move it.

   > **TIP** Getting your hands on those boxes isn't always easy, since they're hugging the outer edges of the Viewer. Here's a tip: Try clicking the *word* Start or End. Then drag inside the frame, anywhere, to pull the box boundaries into view. Now you can drag the corners to make the box smaller.

   You're setting up the green box so it frames the photo as you'll want it to *start out*—the part that your viewers will see first. For example, if you want to zoom in on the photo, make the green box big. (Drag its corners to resize it.) If you want to pull back from the photo, make the green box small. See Figure 10-8.

NOTE In previous versions of iMovie, you could adjust your start or end points so that the picture slid into or out of the frame. Unfortunately, you can't do that in iMovie '09; a photo *must* begin and end in the frame.

Click "End" to adjust   Swap start/stop
stopping point   settings

Drag corners
to resize

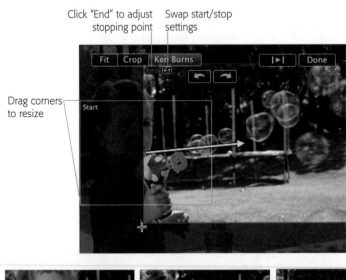

Figure 10-8:
Top: In this somewhat confusing display, you adjust the green box and then the red one, to show iMovie how you want to pan and zoom across the photo. A yellow arrow shows the current direction of iMovie's pan, from the green box to the red one, to help you visualize the motion of the shot.

Bottom: This three-frame sample shows a representation of the pan and zoom out that will be produced by the setup at top.

5. **Adjust your end point (the red box).**

   Click the red box, or the word End, to select it. Move and resize it just as you did with the green box.

   If you don't want your shot to zoom (but only to move), make sure that the red box is the same size as the green one. Line them up, match their sizes, and then move each where you want it. With the start and end points the same size, iMovie just pans from one to the other.

6. **Preview your effect and make adjustments.**

   Click the |►| button to preview your Ken Burns effect. If you don't like what you saw, adjust your green and red boxes accordingly.

   If you decide that you want to *reverse* what you've set up—you want to zoom out instead of in, or pan left instead of right—click the very tiny Swap button identified in Figure 10-8. That turns your green box into the red one, and vice versa.

7. **Click Done.**

You can always adjust the Ken Burns effect by selecting the photo filmstrip and pressing the letter C again.

TIP   If you drag a group of photos into your project all at once, iMovie creates automatic, *varied* Ken Burns effects, subtly panning and zooming in different directions for each one. Add a sweet little crossfade to all of them simultaneously (page 124), and you've got a gorgeous slideshow. (If you're a killjoy, you can always turn off the automatic Ken Burns feature. Choose File → Project Properties → Timing, and use the Initial Photo Placement pop-up menu.)

POWER USERS' CLINIC

The Fade-to-Black (or Fade-to-Puce) Secret

As noted in Chapter 5, it's easy to create a professional-looking fade-out at the end of your movie. But unlike professional movies, which fade to black and then hold for a moment, iMovie fades to black at the end of the movie and then stops playing, sending your viewers back to iMovie, your desktop, the football game, or whatever was on the computer or TV screen before you played the movie.

The solution is very simple, and well worth making a part of your regular iMovie repertoire. Here's the drill:

- Insert a black background just after the final fade-out. (Page 231 has the instructions.)

- Use the Cross Dissolve transition so that iMovie fades smoothly from the final footage of the clip into your black frame—and holds.

- Use the Inspector to make your black frame last as long as you desire.

Don't be content with fading to black. In fact, you can cross-dissolve to whatever color you want—white, blue, gray, anything. Instead of adding a black background, insert any other iMovie background or use a solid-colored image of your own creation.

Creating Still Images from Footage

iMovie doesn't just accept still photos; it can also *create* them for its own purposes. To do this, iMovie can pluck a frame out of any footage, whether it's in the storyboard or the Event Browser.

And why would you want to create a still from your video? Let us count some ways:

- **Create cool titles.** One of the best reasons to get to know iMovie's still-image feature is to supplement iMovie's built-in titling feature. Using still images as titles gives you the freedom to use any colors, type sizes, and positions you want.

  Since you know about Ken Burns, you can even animate them now that you know about alpha channels (Figure 10-7), and even make video play behind them (if they're cutaways).

• **The freeze-frame effect**. One of the most obvious uses of a still frame is the *freeze-frame* effect, in which the movie holds on the final frame of a shot. It's a terrifically effective way to end a movie, particularly if the final shot depicts the shy, unpopular hero in a moment of triumph, arms in the air, hoisted onto the shoulders of the crowd. (Fade to black; bring up the music; roll credits.)

• **Credits sequences**. If you were a fan of 1970s action shows like *Emergency!*, you may remember how the opening credits looked. You'd be watching one of the starring characters frantically at work in some lifesaving situation. As she looked up from her work, just for a moment, the picture would freeze, catching her by lucky happenstance at her most flattering angle. At that instant, you'd see her credit flashed onto the screen: "JULIE LONDON as Dixie McCall, RN."

That's an easy one to simulate. Just create a freeze-frame as described in the next section, and then add a superimposed title image.

• **The layered effect**. In many cases, the most creative use of still-image titles comes from using *several* of them, each building on the last. For example, you can make the main title appear, hold for a moment, and then transition into a second still graphic on which a subtitle appears.

If you have more time on your hands, you can use this trick to create simple animations. Suppose you were to create 10 different title cards, all superimposed on the same background, but each with the words in a different size or position. If you were to place each title card on the screen for only half a second (15 frames), joined by very fast crossfades, you'd create a striking visual effect. Similarly, you might consider making the *color* of the lettering shift over time. To do that, create two or three different title cards, each with the text in a different color. Insert them into your movie, join them with slow crossfades, and you've got a striking, color-shifting title sequence.

Creating a Still Frame

Here's how you go about extracting a still frame from your video.

1. **Position the Playhead on the frame you want frozen.**

   You can choose from any filmstrip in the Event Browser.

2. **Right-click (or Control-click) the filmstrip at the spot from which you want to extract the still. From the shortcut menu, choose "Add Still Frame to Project". See Figure 10-9.**

   This command directs iMovie to place a new photo clip at the end of the storyboard.

3. **Drag the still clip into the right place in your storyboard.**

   iMovie sticks the still frame at the end of your project. Drag it to the right spot, if the end isn't where you want it.

Figure 10-9:
"Add Still Frame to Project" is one of the very few iMovie commands that's available only in the shortcut menu—not in any of the main menus. Note that if you generate a still image from a filmstrip in your Event Browser, iMovie applies a subtle Ken Burns effect to the still image. If you captured the still from your storyboard, however, iMovie assumes that you wanted a freeze-frame effect. The still image will be still (unanimated).

4. **Adjust the still's duration, cropping, color, and so on.**

Your still frame behaves like any other photo. You can use the Ken Burns effect, for example, to zoom in on a meaningful part of the shot. (Ever seen a suspense movie, where the director zooms in on the once-vanquished villain watching the hero from the middle of a crowd? Works every time.)

Creating a Freeze Frame

A freeze frame is basically a still frame, but one that gets automatically inserted into the spot from which you took it. Confused? Why would you put a photo in the exact place you were taking it from?

Well, just imagine that moment when Baby Tommy *finally* smiles into the camera. You could freeze on that spot for a second or two, and then have your video keep going. The smile has ten times the impact if you can dwell on it just a little.

To make a freeze frame, follow the steps described above for creating a still frame—but use a *project* clip as the source material rather than an Event clip. (The shortcut menu command, in this case, says Add Freeze Frame.) iMovie inserts your photo on the spot, rather than shoving it in at the end.

> **TIP**   The inserted photo splits the clip surrounding it. If you delete the photo, your clip remains split in two. If you don't like the effect of the freeze-frame, choose Edit → Undo (⌘-U), instead, to keep your clip together.

Once the freeze frame's in place, you can apply to it color adjustments, cropping, duration adjustments, and so on.

TIP If you want to create a still from the first or last frame of a clip, point to a spot near that end of the filmstrip, and then hit the left or right arrow key. The Playhead jumps to the first or last frame of the clip.

Figuring out how to handle the *audio* in such situations is up to you, since a still frame has no sound. That's a good argument for starting your closing-credits music *during* the final clip, and making it build to a crescendo for the final freeze-frame.

Exporting a Still Frame

The still-frame feature is primarily designed for adding still shots of your footage within iMovie. But you may sometimes find it useful to export a frame to your hard drive as a graphics file—for emailing to friends, installing on your desktop as a background picture, posting on a Web page, and so on. An exported frame also makes a neat piece of "album art" that you can print out and slip into the plastic case of a homemade DVD.

The Resolution Problem

It's worth noting, however, that the maximum *resolution* for a standard-definition digital video frame—the number of dots that compose the image—is 640 across, and 480 down. As digital photos go, that's pretty pathetic, on a par with the photos taken by some cameraphones. One-third of a megapixel is a pretty puny number compared with the shots from today's five-, eight-, and ten-megapixel cameras. High-def video produces better stills, but it's nothing like what you'd get from a digital camera.

The low resolution of the video frame is only half the reason your captured pictures look so bad. Most camcorders capture images the same way television displays images: as hundreds of fine horizontal stripes, or *scan lines*. You don't actually see all of the scan lines at any one instant; you see odd-numbered lines in one frame, and even-numbered lines in the next. Because the frames flash by your eyes so quickly, your brain smoothes the lines together so that you perceive one continuous image.

This system of *interlacing* may work fine for moving video images, but it presents an unpleasant problem when you capture just one frame. Capturing a still image from this footage gives you, in essence, only half of the scan lines that compose the image. QuickTime does what it can to fill in the missing information. But as shown in Figure 10-10, the horizontal scan lines still cause a jaggedness problem.

Now that your expectations have been duly lowered, here's how you export a frame in iMovie. There's a short way that offers little control, and a long way with lots of control.

Figure 10-10:
Digital still frames you export from your DV footage suffer from two disadvantages. First, the resolution is comparatively low. Second, the horizontal scan lines of the original video may sometimes create subtle stair-stepped, jagged edges in the still.

The Short Way

Every time you make a still frame in iMovie, the software makes an actual image file that gets stowed away in the current project file. That project file is actually a Mac OS X *package* file—a folder that acts like a single file. (It's sealed up in this way to prevent novices from opening it, mucking around with its contents, and thereby unwittingly ruining the project. A *package* keeps all the pieces together.)

If you've already created a still frame, right-click (or Control-click) it. From the shortcut menu, choose Show in Finder. The Finder pops up, showing you the window that contains the package file for the project. No mucking necessary. The image being used for your still frame is highlighted, and ready to be copied elsewhere.

> **WARNING** Don't *move* this file; make a copy. If you move the original file, the still frame in your project will be broken.

The Long Way

If you use the short way, you have to accept what iMovie uses for its own purposes (in this case, a JPEG file). What if you want to create TIFFs instead? That's *just* the question for the Long Way.

1. **Create a new project.**

   You'll be exporting to QuickTime for this task, and iMovie can export only an *entire project* at a time. So you'll have to isolate the frame you want in a new, separate project.

TIP   Rather than creating another project every time you want to export a frame, consider creating a single project called Image Export. Use this project every time you want to export a still frame.

2. **Add the video frames you want to export.**

Here's where you get to practice your frame-accurate editing skills. In the Event Browser, select only the frame—yes, you can select a single frame—that you want to export as a still image. (See page 74 for details.) Actually, you can select a *several*-frame stretch of footage; you'll wind up with each frame as a separate graphic.

Add the selection to your new project by dragging it there or hitting the E key on your keyboard.

3. **Choose Share → Export Using QuickTime.**

The QuickTime export window appears, letting you adjust the myriad settings that come with a QuickTime export (Chapter 14).

As iMovie creates your pile of stills, it uses, as its naming scheme, whatever you type into the Save As box (Movie Frame 1, Movie Frame 2, and so on).

4. **From the Export pop-up menu, choose "Movie to Image Sequence".**

This setting tells iMovie to save a separate image for every frame. You might want to save these in a special folder. If you're exporting a lot of frames, they'll clutter your desktop pretty quickly.

5. **Click Options. In the next dialog box, click Settings.**

You now arrive at the mighty Export Image Sequence Settings box (Figure 10-11).

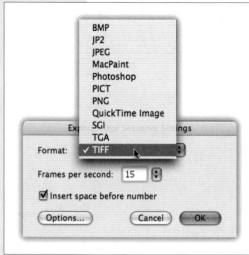

Figure 10-11:
Use this handy dialog box to specify the still-image format you want, and how many frames you want per second.

6. **From the Format pop-up menu, choose the graphics format you want for the exported frames.**

All the usual suspects are here: JPEG (great for Web posting and email), TIFF (higher quality, larger files, better for printing), and so on.

Also choose how *many* stills you want iMovie to pull from each second of video. For the greatest freedom in choosing just the right expression, you'll want to extract *every single frame* of the video. In that case, type *29.97* (to match standard North American video), *30* (for high-def video), or *25* (European video).

7. **Click OK, and then Save.**

Head over to your destination folder, where you'll find all of the images you exported, named and ready to be used in other applications.

TIP   If you plunked down the $30 for QuickTime Player Pro (Chapter 15), you can export a still with much greater efficiency. Find the source footage in the Finder. (Right-click or Control-click a clip and from the shortcut menu, choose "Reveal in Finder".)

Double-click it to open it in QuickTime Player Pro. Set the Playhead on the frame of video you want, and choose File → Export. The resulting dialog box looks much the same, but the Export pop-up menu offers a Movie to Picture option. You'll wind up exporting only the one frame you wanted.

Advanced Editing

Stumble around long enough with iMovie '09, and you'll be able to figure out most of its workings. But in this chapter, you can read about another entire level, another realm of power and professionalism, that would never occur to most people.

This chapter covers two advanced topics:

- **Advanced editing theory**. Where the preceding chapters covered the *technical* aspects of editing video in iMovie—what keys to press, where to click, and so on—the first part of this chapter is about the *artistic* aspects of video editing. It covers when to cut, what to cut to, and how to create the emotional impact you want.

- **Back and forth with iMovie 6**. It's a fact of life: iMovie '09 is not in any way a relative of iMovie 6. They're two different programs, designed for different purposes, with different kinds of people in mind. Each offers features that aren't found in the other.

  There's no reason you can't use *both* programs, swinging deftly back and forth, using each for what it's good for. In this chapter, you'll find out how and why.

The Power of Editing

The editing process is crucial in any kind of movie, from a home movie to a Hollywood thriller. Clever editing can turn a troubled movie into a successful one, or a boring home movie into one that, for the first time, family members don't interrupt every three minutes by lapsing into conversation.

You, the editor, are free to jump from camera to camera, angle to angle, to cut from one location or time to another, and so on. Today's audiences accept that you're telling a story. They don't stomp out in confusion because one minute, James Bond is in his London office, but shows up in Venice a split second later.

You can also compress time, which is one of editing's most common duties. (That's fortunate, because most movies tell stories that, in real life, would take days, weeks, or years to unfold.) You can also *expand* time, making 10 seconds stretch out to 6 minutes—a familiar effect to anyone who's ever watched a final sequence involving a bomb connected to a digital timer (and heroes racing to defuse it).

Editing boils down to choosing which shots you want to include, how long each shot lasts, and in what order they should play.

Modern Film Theory

When you're creating a rock video or an experimental film, you can safely chuck all the advice in this chapter—and in this book. But if you aspire to make good "normal" movies, designed to engage or delight your viewers rather than shock or mystify them, then you should become familiar with the fundamental principles of film editing that have shaped virtually every Hollywood movie (and even most student and independent films) of the last 75 years. For example:

Tell the story chronologically

Most movies tell the story from beginning to end. This part is probably instinct, even when you're making home movies. Arrange your clips roughly in chronological order, except when you're representing your characters' flashbacks and memories or deliberately playing a chronology game, as in *Pulp Fiction*.

Try to be invisible

These days, an expertly edited movie is one where the audience isn't even aware of the editing. This principle has wide-ranging ramifications. For example, the desire to avoid making the editing noticeable is why the simple cut is by far the most common joint between film clips. Using, say, the Circle Open transition between alternate lines of the vows at somebody's wedding would hardly qualify as invisible editing.

Within a single scene, use simple cuts and no transitions. Try to create the effect of seamless real time, making the audience feel as though it's witnessing the scene in its entirety, from beginning to end. This kind of editing is more likely to make your viewers less aware that they're watching a movie.

Develop a shot rhythm

Every movie has an editing *rhythm* that's established by the lengths of the shots in it. The prevailing rhythm of *Dances with Wolves*, for example, is extremely different from that of *Natural Born Killers*. Every *scene* in a movie has its own rhythm, too.

As a general rule, linger less on closeup shots, but give more time to establishing wide shots. (After all, in an establishing shot, there are many more elements for the audience to study and notice.) Similarly, change the pacing of the shots according to the nature of the scene. Most action scenes feature very short clips and fast edits. Most love scenes include longer clips and fewer changes of camera angle.

Maintaining Continuity

As a corollary to the notion that the audience should feel that they're part of the story, professional editors strive to maintain *continuity* during the editing process. This continuity business applies mostly to scripted films, not home movies. Still, knowing what the pros worry about makes you a better editor, no matter what kind of footage you're working with.

Continuity refers to consistency in:

- **The picture**. Suppose we watch a guy with wet hair say, "I'm going to have to break up with you." We cut to his girlfriend's horrified reaction, but when we cut back to the guy, his hair is dry. That's a continuity error, a frequent by-product of having spliced together footage that was filmed at different times. Every Hollywood movie, in fact, has a person whose sole job it is to watch out for errors like this during the editing process.

- **Direction of travel**. In the effort to make the editing as seamless as possible, film editors and directors try to maintain continuity of direction from shot to shot. That is, if the hero sets out crawling across the Sahara from right to left across the scene to be with his true love, you better believe that when we see him next, hours later, he'll still be crawling from right to left. This general rule even applies to much less dramatic circumstances, such as car chases, plane flights, and even people walking to the corner store. If you see her walk out of the frame from left to right in Shot A, you'll see her approach the corner store's doorway from left to right in Shot B.

- **The sound**. In an establishing shot, suppose we see hundreds of men in a battle-field trench, huddled for safety as bullets and bombs fly and explode all around them. Now we cut to a closeup of two of these men talking, but the sounds of the explosions are missing. That's a sound continuity error. The audience is certain to notice that hundreds of soldiers were issued a cease-fire just as these two guys started talking.

- **The camera setup.** In scenes of conversations between two people, it would look really bizarre to show one person speaking only in closeup, and his conversation partner filmed in a medium shot. (Unless, of course, the first person were filmed in *extreme* closeup—just the lips filling the screen—because the filmmaker is trying to protect his identity.)

- **Gesture and motion.** If one shot begins with a character reaching down to pick up the newspaper from her doorstep, the next shot—a closeup of her hand closing around the rolled-up paper, for example—should pick up from the exact moment where the previous shot ended. And as the rolled-up paper leaves our closeup field of view, the following shot should show her straightening into an upright position. Unless you've made the deliberate editing decision to skip over some time from one shot to the next (which should be clear to the audience), the action should seem continuous from one shot to the next.

NOTE When filming scripted movies, directors always instruct their actors to begin each new scene's action with the same gesture or motion that *ended* the last shot. Having two copies of this gesture, action, or motion—one on each end of each take—gives the editor a lot of flexibility when it comes time to piece the movie together.

This principle explains why you'll find it extremely rare for an editor to cut from one shot of two people to another shot of the *same* two people (without inserting some other shot between them, such as a reaction shot or a closeup of one person or the other). The odds are small that, as the new shot begins, both actors will be in precisely the same body positions they were in when the previous shot ended.

When to Cut

Some Hollywood directors may tell their editors to make cuts just for the sake of making the cuts come faster, in an effort to pick up the pace. The more seasoned director and editor, however, usually adopts a more classical view of editing: Cut to a different shot when it's *motivated*. That is, cut when you *need* to cut, so that you can convey new visual information by taking advantage of a different camera angle, switching to a different character, providing a reaction shot, and so on.

Editors look for a motivating event that suggests *where* they should make the cut, too, such as a movement, a look, the end of the sentence, or the intrusion of an off-camera sound that makes us *want* to look somewhere else in the scene.

Choosing the Next Shot

As you've read elsewhere in this book, the final piece of advice when it comes to choosing when and how to make a cut is this: Cut to a *different* shot. If you've been filming the husband, cut to the wife; if you've been in a closeup, cut to a medium or wide shot; if you've been showing someone looking off-camera, cut to what she's looking at.

Avoid cutting from one shot of somebody to a similar shot of the same person. Doing so creates a *jump cut*, a disturbing and seemingly unmotivated splice between shots of the same subject from the same angle.

Video editors sometimes have to swallow hard and perform jump cuts for the sake of compressing a long interview into a much shorter sound bite. Customer testimonials on TV commercials frequently illustrate this point. You'll see a woman saying, "Wonderglove changed…[cut] our lives, it really did…[cut] My husband used to be a drunk and a slob…[cut] but now we have Wonderglove." (Often, a fast cross dissolve is applied to the cuts in a futile attempt to make them less noticeable.)

As you can probably attest if you've ever seen such an ad, however, that kind of editing is rarely convincing. As you watch it, you can't help wondering exactly *what* was cut out and why. (The editors of *60 Minutes* and other documentary-style shows edit the comments of their interview subjects just as heavily, but conceal it better by cutting away to reaction shots—of the interviewer, for example—between edited shots.)

Popular Editing Techniques

Variety and pacing play a role in every decision the video editor makes. The following sections explain some common tricks of professional editors that you can use in iMovie editing.

Tight Editing

One of the first tasks you'll encounter when editing your footage is choosing how to trim and chop up your clips, as described in Chapter 3. Even when editing home movies, consider the Hollywood guideline for tight editing: Begin every scene as *late* as possible, and end it as *soon* as possible.

In other words, suppose the audience sees the heroine receiving the call that her husband has been in an accident, and then hanging up the phone in shock. We don't really need to see her putting on her coat, opening the apartment door, locking it behind her, taking the elevator to the ground floor, hailing a cab, driving frantically through the city, screeching to a stop in front of the hospital, and finally leaping out of the cab. In a tightly edited movie, she would hang up the phone and then we'd see her leaping out of the cab (or even walking into her husband's hospital room).

Keep this principle in mind even when editing your own, slice-of-life videos. For example, a very engaging account of your ski trip could begin with only three shots: an establishing shot of the airport; a shot of the kids piling into the plane; and then the tumultuous, noisy, trying-on-ski-boots shot the next morning. You get less reality with this kind of tight editing, but much more watchability.

Variety of Shots

Variety is important in every aspect of filmmaking—variety of shots, locations, angles, and so on. Consider the lengths of your shots, too. In action sequences, you may prefer quick cutting, where each clip in your Movie Track is only a second or two long. In softer, more peaceful scenes, longer shots may set the mood more effectively.

Establishing shots

Almost every scene of every movie and every TV show—even the nightly news—begins with an *establishing shot*: a long-range, zoomed-out shot that shows the audience where the action is about to take place.

Now that you know something about film theory, you'll begin to notice how often TV and movie scenes begin with an establishing shot. It gives the audience a feeling of being there, and helps them understand the context for the medium shots or closeups that follow. Furthermore, after a long series of closeups, consider showing *another* wide shot, to remind the audience of where the characters are and what the world around them looks like.

As with every film-editing guideline, this one is occasionally worth violating. For example, in comedies, a new scene may begin with a closeup instead of an establishing shot, so that the camera can then pull back to *make* the establishing shot the joke. (For example, closeup on main character looking uncomfortable; camera pulls back to reveal that we were looking at him upside down as he hangs, tied by his feet, over a pit of alligators.) In general, however, setting up any new scene with an establishing shot is the smart, and polite thing to do for your audience's benefit.

Cutaways and cut-ins

Cutaways and *cut-ins* are extremely common and effective editing techniques. Not only do they add some variety to the movie, but they let you conceal enormous editing shenanigans. By the time your movie resumes after the cutaway shot, you can have deleted enormous amounts of material, switched to a different take of the same scene, and so on. Figure 11-1 shows the idea.

The *cut-in* is similar, but instead of showing a different person or a reaction shot, it usually features a closeup of what the speaker is holding or talking about—a very common technique in training tapes and cooking shows.

Reaction shots

One of the most common sequences in Hollywood history is a three-shot sequence that goes like this: First, we see the character looking offscreen; then we see what he's looking at (a cutaway shot); and finally, we see him again so that we can read his reaction. This sequence is repeated so frequently in commercial movies that you can feel it coming the moment the performer looks off the screen.

Figure 11-1:

Top: You've got a shot of your main character in action.

Middle: We cut away to a shot of what he's looking at or reacting to.

Bottom: When you cut back to the main character, you could use a different take on a different day, or dialog from a much later part of the scene (due to some cuts suggested by the editor). The audience will never know that the action wasn't continuous. The cutaway masks the fact that there was a discontinuity between the first and third shots.

From the editor's standpoint, of course, the beauty of the three-shot reaction shot is that the middle shot can be anything from anywhere. That is, it can be footage shot on another day in another part of the world, or even from a different movie entirely. The ritual of character/action/reaction is so ingrained in our brains that the audience believes the actor was looking at the action, no matter what.

In home-movie footage, you may have been creating reaction shots without even knowing it. But you've probably been capturing them by panning from your kid's beaming face to the petting-zoo sheep and then back to the face. You can make this sequence look great in iMovie by just snipping out the pans, leaving you with crisp, professional-looking cuts.

Parallel cutting

When you're making a movie that tells a story, it's sometimes fun to use *parallel editing* or *intercutting*. That's when you show two trains of action simultaneously and you keep cutting back and forth to show the parallel simultaneous action. In *Fatal Attraction*, for example, the intercut climax shows main character Dan Gallagher (Michael Douglas) downstairs in the kitchen, trying to figure out why the ceiling is dripping, even as his psychotic mistress Alex (Glenn Close) is upstairs attempting to murder his wife in the bathtub. If you're making movies that tell a story, you'll find this technique an exciting one when you're trying to build suspense.

Back and Forth to iMovie 6

Owning a copy of the new iMovie used to mean that you got a free copy of iMovie 6. It was Apple's way of saying, "OK, look, we know that the new iMovie ('08) is, ahem, a work in progress. To tide you over, here's a link to download the old version."

That link, and that offer, are gone now. Clearly, Apple feels that in iMovie '09, all the necessary missing features have been restored (like fast/slow/reverse and special effects).

The following pages, therefore, are only for people who already have a copy of iMovie HD (or iMovie 6, as it's also known), sitting there in the Applications → iMovie (Previous Version) folder—or for people who know how to find a copy kicking around online.

So why do you care about iMovie 6? Because even though iMovie '09 brought back many iMovie 6 features, not all of them made the trip. The following leftover iMovie 6 features may tempt you to continue using iMovie 6:

- **Audio rubber-banding.** As shown in Figure 11-2, this term refers to manual volume adjustments on an audio track. It's like iMovie '09's *automatic ducking* feature (Volume Adjustments), except that it's not automatic; you get complete control.

  Of course, when you export your iMovie '09 movie to iMovie 6, your audio gets mashed down into a single track. So passing off the project to iMovie 6 doesn't mean you'll be able to do elaborate mix adjustments of the camcorder audio, the background music, and so on.

But you *can* do most of the editing in iMovie '09, using what *it's* good for: quick selection of shots, better-looking titles, superior color-correction tools, cropping and rotation of video, and so on—and then add your music and sound effects in iMovie 6.

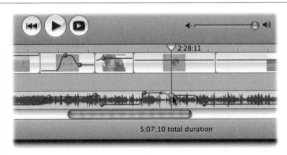

Figure 11-2:
In iMovie 6, you can adjust the audio volume manually along the length of a clip just by drawing in its volume graph, also known as "rubber-banding" because of the way the line snaps to the control points you create.

- **Audio effects**. iMovie '09 doesn't offer any audio effects at all. You can't add reverb or echo, adjust the pitch, change the audio speed, or tweak the sound with a graphic equalizer. But all of that *is* available in iMovie 6. It's another reason to do your *video* work in iMovie '09, and then export the result to iMovie 6 for audio editing and fine-tuning.

- **Video special effects**. iMovie '09 caught up to iMovie 6 in many ways—such as offering video filters, Slow Motion, Fast Motion, and Reverse Motion.

  iMovie 6, on the other hand, still beats the new iMovie with the *flashier* video effects like Lens Flare, Mirror, Crystallize, Glass Distortion, Water Color, and Rain. iMovie 6 can also accommodate *add-on* effects from other companies. (iMovie '09 can't.) If you invested a lot in third-party plug-ins, they can still do the job you paid for.

  So there's no reason you can't do most of your editing in iMovie '09, and then send the whole thing back to iMovie 6 to apply these effects.

- **Export to tape**. This one's *huge*. When you're finished with an iMovie '09 project, you can export it to the Web, burn it to a DVD, or export it as a Quick-Time movie. Unfortunately, *all* of those options involve some degradation of video quality. (Yes, even a DVD compresses the video somewhat.)

  In iMovie 6, there's an easy solution. You can preserve the really important videos, the ones you wanted to save forever with 100 percent of the original quality, on tape. iMovie 6 can play your finished masterpiece directly into a DV camcorder at full original quality—a great way to archive your masterpiece so that not even a hard drive crash can affect it.

  By exporting your movie from iMovie '09 into iMovie 6, you grant yourself the freedom to back up your best work onto tapes in just this way.

Transferring Your Project, iMovie '09 → iMovie 6

In all of the examples described above, it makes sense to begin your project in iMovie '09, and then to finish it up in iMovie 6.

Here's how you go about it. (For more explanation of what you're doing here, see Chapter 16, which goes into more detail about exporting iMovie projects as Quick-Time movies.)

1. **When you've gone as far as you can go in iMovie '09, choose Share → "Export using QuickTime".**

   The "Save exported file as" dialog box appears. Type a name for the intermediate transfer file you're going to create. In this example, suppose you call it *Transfer Movie*.

   Choose a location for the exported movie, as shown in Figure 11-3, top.

2. **Make sure the Export pop-up menu says "Movie to QuickTime Movie." Then click Options.**

   Now the Movie Settings dialog box appears (Figure 11-3, bottom).

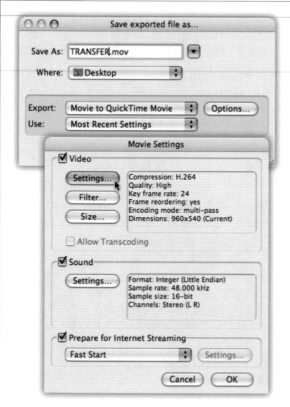

Figure 11-3:

Top: In this first dialog box, your job is to type a name for the exported movie. It doesn't really matter what you call it. Choose your desktop as the save location, but don't click Save yet.

Bottom: Here's where you specify a format for your exported QuickTime movie. Click Settings. Incidentally, you can also pass your iMovie '09 projects off to Final Cut Pro or Final Cut Express (page 413 has the details). That way, you can use iMovie for what it's good at (importing video from tapeless camcorders, and quickly choosing the best shots)—and then use Final Cut for what it's good for (everything else).

3. **Click the top Settings button.**

The Video Compression Settings dialog box appears.

4. **From the Compression Type pop-up menu, choose Apple Intermediate Codec.**

You can read more about this important format on page 43. In essence, it's a file format that's understood by all of Apple's video-editing programs, past and present, and retains 100 percent of the video quality of the original.

5. **Click OK, and then click OK in the next dialog box. Click Save.**

iMovie takes a few moments to export the video.

You now have on your desktop a QuickTime movie version of your project, named "Transfer Movie" (or whatever you called it in step 1).

6. **Open iMovie 6.**

It's probably in your Applications → iMovie (Previous Version) folder. Oh, and it's probably called iMovie HD. (And yes, it's perfectly OK to have iMovie '09 and iMovie 6 open at the same time.)

NOTE Apple is schizophrenic in its naming scheme. The icons for both iMovie 5 and iMovie 6 were named "iMovie HD."

7. **In iMovie 6, create a new, empty project. Name and save it. Choose File → Import (Shift-⌘-I). In the Open dialog box, find and double-click the exported movie file you created in step 5 ("Transfer Movie").**

The project shows up in iMovie 6 on the Clips shelf, as shown in Figure 11-4.

8. **Drag the Transfer Movie icon down to the Timeline at the bottom of the window.**

You're ready to edit it!

TIP iMovie 6, of course, is an entirely different ball of wax. Not to be totally mercenary here, but the best way to learn it is to read *iMovie 6 and iDVD: The Missing Manual*.

Transferring Your Project, iMovie 6 → iMovie '09

As noted above, most people will probably go from iMovie '09 → iMovie 6. But you may very well want to go the other direction. Maybe you want to begin in iMovie 6, and then finish up in iMovie '09, because:

- **You want to send the finished movie to YouTube.** Only iMovie '09 has that feature built right in.

- **You want to use the newest video effects.** With video stabilization, green screen, picture-in-picture, travel maps, and cutaways, iMovie '09 is clearly the superior tool for these functions.

Figure 11-4:
Your partially finished iMovie '09 movie is now safely ensconced in iMovie 6. It's represented by a single icon on the Clips shelf. Drag it down to the Timeline and start editing.

- **You want to use iMovie '09's titles.** The newer version offers better-looking text over video, not to mention far greater typographical control. (For example, only iMovie '09 lets you create different fonts, sizes, and colors *within* a single title.)

Actually, the process of transferring an iMovie 6 project to its successor is almost the same as going the other way. Here's what you do:

1. **When your iMovie 6 project is ready to export, choose Share → QuickTime.**

   The Share dialog box appears.

2. **From the pop-up menu, choose Expert Settings. Click Share.**

   You arrive at the dialog box shown in Figure 11-3 (bottom).

3. **Follow steps 2 through 5 on page 258.**

   Creating the transfer movie is exactly the same, no matter which direction you go.

4. **Open iMovie '09. Choose File → Import Movies.**

The Open dialog box appears (Figure 11-5).

5. **Locate and open your Transfer Movie.**

The former iMovie 6 movie is now safely ensconced in iMovie '09, in the Event you specified. You can add it to a project and begin your final surgery on it.

TIP There's no reason you can't go back and forth between the two iMovies, repeating the process as necessary. You're not losing any video quality with each trip.

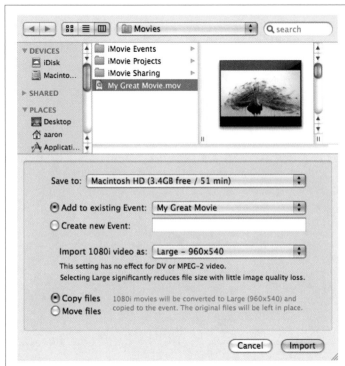

Figure 11-5:
Before you find and open your Transfer Movie, specify whether you want it to become part of an existing Event or a new one. (See page 30 and page 37 for details on this process.)

Part Two:
Finding Your Audience

2

Exporting to iPod, iPhone, Apple TV, or Front Row

Apple, as you may have noticed, is really into the electronic presentation of video. The company thinks that the traditional destinations for your home movies—like sending your movie to a DVD or recording it back to tape—are ancient history. What Apple *really* wants you to do with your finished masterpiece is to post it on the Web (see Chapter 13) or transfer it to another Apple machine, like an iPod, iPhone, Apple TV, or Front Row (to play on your Mac from across the room).

That's what this chapter is all about: sending your finished masterpiece to another fine piece of Apple merchandise.

Exporting the Movie to iTunes

As it turns out, the steps for exporting a movie to Apple's four video-playing machines (iPod, iPhone, AppleTV, and Front Row) are nearly identical. All of them involve exporting the movie to iTunes, which is the loading dock for iPods, iPhones, Apple TVs, and even Front Row. The only difference is the size of the movie you're creating.

So, for the sake of saving the Brazilian rainforest, the instructions appear here only once, with the necessary variations written out along the way:

1. **When your project is ready for prime time, choose Share → iTunes.**

   The "Publish your project to iTunes" dialog box appears (Figure 12-1). You've probably never seen a dialog box quite like this one.

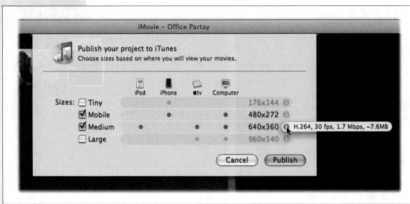

Figure 12-1:
This unusual-looking dialog box is just Apple's way of offering you some ready-made compression settings for typical playback gadgets. Point to the ❶ button to see some techier details.

In essence, iMovie is offering you various screen sizes for exporting your finished movie. The faint gray dots indicate which sizes are appropriate for which kinds of gadgets.

For example, the iPhone's screen is 480 by 360 pixels, which matches the dimensions of the Mobile option here. A standard-definition TV set has 640 by 480 pixels, which is why that's an option for the Apple TV. That's also why iPods prefer 640 by 480 videos: It's just in case you connect them to a TV for playback. (The iPhone has both a screen-size recommendation and a Tiny option—176 by 144—which is for those iPhone-wielding fans who attempt to watch your videos over a cellular connection.)

2. **Turn on the checkboxes that correspond to the sizes you want to export.**

You can actually turn on *more than one* of these checkboxes. If you do that, you'll wind up with *several* copies of this video.

> **TIP**   If you point to the ❶ button without clicking, a tooltip appears. As shown in Figure 12-1, it tells you more about the exported movie file you're about to create. For example, you'll see the file format (H.264); the number of frames per second (fps); the Internet speed required to watch the video from the Web (in megabits per second)—for comparison, a typical cable-modem connection is 2 megabits per second); and the file size (in megabytes).

3. **Click Publish.**

Now the time-consuming exporting and compression process begins. Feel free to switch into other programs—check your email or surf the Web, for example—while iMovie crunches away in the background. A progress bar lets you know how much farther iMovie has to go.

When it's all over, iTunes opens by itself. If you click the Movies folder, you'll see the new exported movies nestled there (Figure 12-2). They're named after the project and the size you exported. For example, you might see "Birthday Party–Mobile" and "Birthday Party–Medium."

Figure 12-2:
Here, tucked in among your other movies, are the exported ones from iMovie. To watch one, double-click it; it starts playing in the lower-left corner of the screen. Click that area, once, to make the movie play bigger, in a window of its own.

From iTunes to iPod, iPhone, Etc.

Once your movies are in iTunes, getting them onto your iPod, iPhone, Apple TV, or copy of Front Row works just like it always does:

- **iPod, iPhone.** Connect the iPod or iPhone to your Mac. Its icon shows up in the column at the left side of iTunes. Click the Movies tab and select the movies you want copied over to your i-gadget when they sync (Figure 12-3).

- **Apple TV.** Same deal here. The Apple TV's name and icon show up in the left-side column of iTunes. Click it, and then click the Movies tab and turn on the movies you want synced to the Apple TV, so you can enjoy your iMovie productions on the big screen.

- **Front Row.** Front Row, of course, is the built-in movie/music/DVD player that's built into every current Mac model (except the Mac Pro). It's designed to be operated and enjoyed from a couch across the room—all the fonts and menus are presented in huge, razor-sharp text—which is why all Front Row computers come with a tiny white remote control.

TIP   If you lose the remote, you can also open Front Row by pressing ⌘-Esc or, on some models, F1.

Figure 12-3:
When iTunes notices that you have an iPod, iPhone, or Apple TV, the corresponding icon appears in the Source list (left). Click the gadget's name to make the tabs appear (main window), where you can specify what music, movies, and other stuff you want to copy to your i-gadget at the next sync. On the Movies tab, you'll find all of your iMovie '09 exports.

The catalog of movies and music presented by Front Row is simply whatever you've got in iTunes. All you have to do to see your videos, therefore, is to use the remote to choose Videos. Your exported iMovie masterworks appear right there, ready to watch (Figure 12-4).

Figure 12-4:
Here's the Front Row listing of your videos. Lo and behold, here are all the movies you've exported from iMovie, ready to enjoy!

Exporting to YouTube and the Web

If you ask Apple, the DVD has had its day in the sun. The format is over 10 years old. *Nobody* puts movies on DVD anymore. Plastic shiny discs that have to be—ugh—*mailed?* That's such an old-fashioned, clumsy, *physical* way to share video.

The real action is on the Internet, that billion-seat megaplex where unknown independent filmmakers get noticed, and where it doesn't cost you a penny to distribute your work to a vast, worldwide audience.

It's all about YouTube, baby. One hundred million videos watched per day. It costs nothing to sign up and post your videos there.

Or put your videos up on your MobileMe account. It costs $100 per year, but man do videos look fantastic on your MobileMe gallery. They're available at multiple frame sizes to accommodate visitors with Internet connections of different speeds. Your fans can even skim your iMovie '09 movies using your mouse pointer, just like you can on your Mac.

Or what the heck: Post videos on your own Web site.

This chapter covers all three ways of making your opus viewable on the Web.

Method 1: iMovie to YouTube

By far the easiest way to post your movies on the Internet is to use iMovie '09's YouTube command.

YouTube, of course, is the insanely popular video-sharing Web site, filled to the brim with hundreds of millions of funny home videos, TV excerpts, amateur short films, memorable bloopers—and now your iMovie projects. Once you've posted your iMovie there, other people can find it by Web address, by searching for your name, by searching for videos by description, and so on.

You can't post to YouTube from iMovie, however, unless you have a YouTube account. To get one (it's free), point your Web browser to *www.youtube.com/signup* and fill in the blanks. After you do that, YouTube sends an email to the address you specified. (Not always immediately, however. The path to YouTubeness is not always instant.) The email, when it finally arrives, contains a link that says "Confirm your email address". What it really means is, "Click me to confirm that you're a real person with a real email account and not one of those annoying software robots that tries to set up thousands of bogus YouTube accounts in hopes of spreading spam."

Posting to YouTube (First Time)

Suppose your movie is now ready for the masses. Here's what you do:

1. **Choose Share → YouTube.**

   A *sheet* (dialog box attached to the window) appears. Since you're a YouTube virgin, it probably looks something like Figure 13-1, bottom—empty.

2. **If your YouTube account name doesn't already appear in the pop-up menu, click Add.**

   A strikingly plain window prompts you for your YouTube account name. Enter it and click Done.

3. **Enter your password.**

   Don't worry—iMovie won't use your YouTube password to post the embarrassing footage you forgot to delete. If you can't trust iMovie, who can you trust?

4. **Fill in the name, description, and tags (keywords) for your movie (see Figure 13-2).**

   The name and description will appear right beside the movie on YouTube.

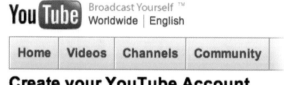

You Tube Broadcast Yourself ™
Worldwide | English

| Home | Videos | Channels | Community |

Create your YouTube Account

Figure 13-1:
Top: The first stop on the YouTube Express is
signing up for a free YouTube account.

Bottom: Account in hand, you can give iMovie
the information it needs to launch you to
YouTube stardom.

Join the largest worldwide video-sharing community!
Sign up now to get full access with your YouTube
account:
- Comment, rate, and make video responses to your
  favorite videos
- Upload and share your videos with millions of other
  users
- Save your favorite videos to watch and share later
- Enter your videos into contests for fame and prizes

You Tube™ Publish your project to YouTube

Account: ilifer08@gmail.com   (Add...) (Remove)
Password: ••••••••
Category: People & Blogs
Title: Scrolling Image with Credits
Description:

Tags: iMovie, tricks

	iPhone	átv	Computer	YouTube	
Size to publish: ○ Mobile	•		•	•	480x272
○ Medium		•	•	•	640x360
○ Large		•	•	•	960x540
● HD			•	•	1280x720

☑ Make this movie personal

(Cancel)   (Next)

5. **Specify what size you want the movie to be.**

   YouTube can play movies in any of the four sizes listed here: Mobile, Medium,
   Large, or HD (assuming your source video is of high enough resolution). For
   details on this table-like dialog box, see page 266; for now, it's enough to note
   that YouTube can play back all four of these sizes. Be aware that going all HD
   can be fraught with peril (see the box on page 272). Whatever you do, if you
   think your audience uses dial-up modems, choose the Mobile option.

You Tube™ Publish your project to YouTube

Account: [▲▼] (Add...) (Remove)

Password: [   ]

Category: [People & Blogs   ▲▼]

Title: [June in Michigan   ]

Description: [   ]

Tags: [   ]

	iPhone	▲tv	Computer	YouTube	
Size to publish: ○ Mobile	●		●	●	480x272 ⓘ
○ Medium		●	●	●	640x360 ⓘ
○ Large		●	●	● /	960x540 ⓘ
● HD			●	●	1280x720 ⓘ

☐ Make this movie personal

(Cancel) (Next)

Figure 13-2:
While the description lets you tell people about the movie you're uploading, the Tags are keywords to ensure that your video comes up when other YouTubers search for such flag words.

POWER USERS' CLINIC

HD YouTube Videos

For years, YouTube earned a reputation as an all-you-can-eat buffet of grainy, pixellated webcam rants. But it's fighting back. YouTube has now opened its doors to the elite snobs of Internet video by offering videos in high definition (720p HD).

"Hey!" you say, "I'm editing in HD! Let's make the most of this YouTube thingy." Before you dive in, here are some good things to know about how it really works.

First, the upload and conversion process takes longer than it does for lower-res movies. Not only do you have to wait for iMovie to convert your project, but after the huge file gets uploaded to YouTube, their computers have to do their own round of file-crunching. In other words, don't expect your hi-def YouTube video to be available within minutes of uploading it.

Once your video is viewable on YouTube, some of your loved ones may have a choppy ride when they try to watch it. If they have an older computer or a slow Internet connection, it simply won't play smoothly for them. Luckily, they can turn off the HD option by clicking the tiny HD button just underneath your video.

If you don't mind these niggling issues, then go all the way. HD YouTube videos are worth it.

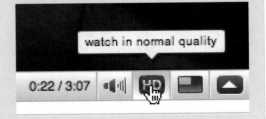

6. **Turn on "Make this movie personal", if you like.**

Most YouTube movies are available to the entire universe of people on the Internet. If you'd rather control who gets to see your epic, though, turn on this checkbox. Now, *nobody* will be able to see it unless you specifically invite them by sending them its Web address.

7. **Click Next.**

A dialog box appears reminding you that it's naughty to upload TV shows, movies, or anything else that you don't have the copyright for.

8. **Click Publish.**

iMovie springs into action, compressing and uploading your video. This part can take a while. Feel free to check your email while iMovie crunches away.

When the upload is finally complete, you see the message shown in Figure 13-3.

Figure 13-3:
Newly posted YouTube videos aren't available to the masses immediately.

9. **Tell a friend, view the movie, or just return to iMovie.**

If you click "Tell a Friend", your email program opens. Your Mac thoughtfully opens a new, outgoing message, types "My Great iMovie!" in the Subject line, and fills in the body with a message that alerts your fans to the presence—and the Web address—of your new video.

NOTE   The "Tell a Friend" feature isn't perfect. If you use Apple's own Mail program, the outgoing message includes the correct clickable address for your movie (such as *www.youtube.com/ watch?v=tdcark_siiU*). But if you use another program, like Microsoft Entourage, the address includes only *www.youtube.com/watch*, which doesn't take your fans *directly* to the movie. This seems to be a bug.

Posting to YouTube (After the First Time)

After you've done all that account setting-up, the posting-to-YouTube process is much simpler. Once the finished project is open on your screen, choose Share → Publish. The dialog box shown in Figure 13-2 appears. Then follow the preceding instructions from step 4.

TIP　If you upload a movie that's *exactly* the same length as one that you uploaded earlier, YouTube may reject the new video, claiming that it's a duplicate. The solution is to humor it. Make the new video a fraction of a second longer or shorter.

After the Movie is Up

Once you've successfully posted a video on YouTube, you won't forget it, thanks to the new icons and labels that identify it in the Projects list (Figure 13-4).

Published online

Figure 13-4:
After you've published a project to YouTube, iTunes, or MobileMe, the Projects list reminds you—and lets you know which of iMovie's four standard export sizes you used. If you see the yellow exclamation point, beware! Your version of the project no longer matches what you shared on YouTube/iTunes/MobileMe!

Quality indicators

Published online but out of date

At this point, you have several movie-management options:

- **Tell another friend about the movie.** Click the project's name and then click the "Tell a friend" link that appears above the storyboard.

- **Watch the YouTube video yourself.** Click the project's name and then click the "Visit" link above the storyboard.

- **Edit the movie and republish it.** As soon as you start making changes to the published project, all hell breaks loose. A yellow exclamation-point icon appears at the top of the storyboard, along with the notation "out of date." And just in case you didn't get the point, a warning box appears, too.

Click OK to dismiss the warning box. Finish making your changes, and then choose Share → YouTube again. Repeat the publishing process starting from step 4 on page 274.

NOTE   Actually, this process doesn't *update* or even *replace* the original version of the video; it just uploads another copy of it.

You'll have to delete the original manually—and you can't even use iMovie's "Remove from YouTube" command to do that. You have to go to YouTube, sign into your account, and delete the old.

• **Delete the movie from YouTube.** Once you feel that a movie has outlived its usefulness (or become embarrassing), you can remove it from YouTube. Just click the project's name in iMovie and then choose Share → "Remove from YouTube".

UP TO SPEED

Getting a MobileMe Account

MobileMe, Apple's subscription online service, provides everything you need to put a collection of your movies online. A MobileMe membership will set you back $100 per year.

Mac OS X makes it easy to sign up for an account, and a two-month trial account is free. If you don't already have an account, start by choosing → System Preferences.

Click the MobileMe icon, and then click Sign Up. Your Web browser opens up to the MobileMe sign-up screen; simply follow the steps.

When you return to System Preferences, you'll see that the Mac has filled in your account name and password automatically. You're now ready to use your MobileMe account—and to post iMovie masterworks to it.

Method 2: iMovie to MobileMe

YouTube certainly is the people's video-sharing service. It's got the most videos and the most eyeballs watching them, and it offers buttons that let your audience leave fan mail (or hate mail) in the comments and rate your work on a five-star scale.

YouTube does not, however, have the best quality. The page containing your movie is cluttered and ugly. And unless you post a high-definition file to YouTube (page 272), your videos look grainy and small.

If you publish your masterwork to a MobileMe account, though, it's a whole different world. The presentation is classy and glamorous—in high definition, even—and the movie itself is nice and big (see Figure 13-5).

MobileMe is Apple's $100-per-year suite of Internet services and conveniences: synchronizing of calendars and Web bookmarks among the different Macs in your life, a backup program, the ability to check your email online, and iWeb publishing, which lets you generate your own Web pages.

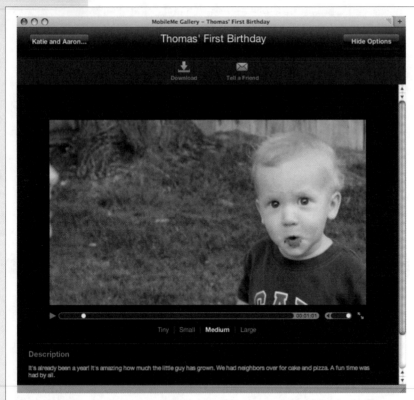

Figure 13-5:
Movies you post to MobileMe look quite a bit better than they do on YouTube. The background is dark and classy, the scroll bar and volume controls are easy to figure out, and the top, left button takes you back to the full "table of contents" for the movies and iPhoto slideshows on your site.

Here's how you get your movie into your MobileMe gallery:

1. **With your project on the screen before you, choose Share → MobileMe Gallery.**

   The dialog box shown in Figure 13-6 appears.

2. **Fill in the title and a description for your movie. Then choose what frame size you want for your movie: Mobile, Medium, or whatever.**

   Medium is a great size if your viewers have high-speed Internet connections (like cable modems or DSL). If they're using dial-up or slow DSL, choose Mobile instead.

   TIP   You can choose *more* than one size, if you like. See page 277 for details on these size options. (Incidentally, iMovie keeps track of which sizes of each project you've exported to your MobileMe gallery. If you see some of the Size checkboxes dimmed, it's because you've *already* posted versions of this project in those sizes.)

3. **Turn on the "Allow movie to be downloaded" checkbox, if you like.**

   Do you want to let people watch your movie *online only*—to stream it, in other words? If so, leave this checkbox turned off.

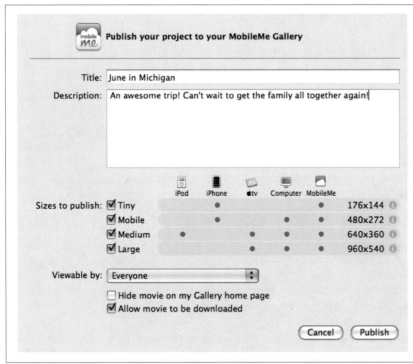

Figure 13-6:
*If you've ever published a
video to YouTube, this
dialog box should look
distinctly familiar. Here
you can specify a title,
description, and frame
size for your Web movie.*

Or do you want to permit them to download the movie as a file to their hard drives? That means they can play the movie even when they're not online. It also means they could edit your movie, incorporate it into their own presentations, and so on, if they were so inclined. If that's OK with you, turn on this checkbox.

4. **Hide the video from the unwashed masses by turning on "Hide Movie on my Gallery home page", if you like.**

   If you do that, then nobody will see the movie's icon on your MobileMe gallery home page. The only way they'll be able to watch your movie is through a personal invitation from you—one that includes the movie's Web address. So turn on this checkbox for movies that you don't want the whole world to see.

5. **Click Publish.**

   iMovie begins the time-consuming process of compressing and uploading the movie. When it's finished, you see a message much like the one in Figure 13-3 (page 273).

6. **Click "Tell a Friend", View, or OK.**

   The first button opens a new, outgoing email message, ready to address and send to your adoring public. The second takes *you* to the MobileMe Gallery to enjoy the online version of your flick. And clicking OK just takes you back to iMovie.

After the Movie Is Up

Once you've successfully hung a new movie in your MobileMe Gallery, the project takes on new icons and labels in iMovie (Figure 13-4, page 274).

As with YouTube, you can now manage the online movie in several ways:

- **Tell another friend about the movie.** Click the project's name and then click "Tell a friend" above the storyboard.

- **Watch the video yourself.** Click the project's name and then click Visit above the storyboard.

- **Edit the movie and republish it.** Once you edit the project, iMovie makes it very clear that the online version no longer matches the master version by displaying a yellow exclamation-point icon, the words "out of date," and a warning dialog box. Click OK to dismiss the warning box. Finish making your changes, and then choose Share → "Re-publish to MobileMe Gallery". Then repeat from step 2 of the previous instructions.

    NOTE When you republish to MobileMe, iMovie actually does *replace* the original published movie. You don't wind up with two versions, as you do with YouTube.

- **Delete the movie from your Web gallery.** To take down a movie—perhaps because of rampant picketing from special-interest groups who declare your film to be offensive, despite never having seen it—click the project's name in iMovie and then choose Share → "Remove from MobileMe Gallery".

Custom Web Pages: Three Roads

What's amazing about the MobileMe Web Gallery is that it's so perfectly tailored for presenting movies. The black screen, the high-tech scroll bar, the absence of text…it's just awesome. Unless, of course, you *want* to control the background, the look, and the text on the Web page. Why can't you embed a movie into a *normal* Web page, just like any ordinary person?

Actually, you can embed your iMovie movies onto your own custom Web pages in any of three different ways:

- **The iWeb way.** Use iWeb, which is one of the other iLife '09 programs. It's a Web-design program that requires zero hand-coding, so you don't need to know HTML (the language of the Web). You just pick a design template, type new text, slap in some pictures or movies, and you're done. iMovie can hand off a movie to iWeb with only a couple of mouse clicks; from there, you can incorporate them into the Web pages that you design.

    TIP Once you've designed a Web site in iWeb, you can post it on your MobileMe account (if you're paid up) *or* post it on the Web using space provided by, for example, your Internet provider. In other words, you don't *have* to post it to a MobileMe page.

- **The iDisk way.** Copy an exported QuickTime movie to the Movies folder of your iDisk (an Internet-based "virtual hard drive" that comes with a MobileMe account). Then use the HomePage features at Apple's Web site (instead of the layout tools in iWeb) to set up your pages. (HomePage is another template-based Web-page creation program that came before iWeb.)

- **The freehand way.** Suppose you're a savvy, Webmastery kind of person, and you design your own Web pages and post them on the Web without any help from sissy templates like iWeb and MobileMe HomePage. In that case, you can embed *any* movie into *any* of your Web pages—without paying Apple *any* money every year.

UP TO SPEED

Meet the Media Browser

The *Media Browser* is a common, central multimedia library for your Mac that's designed to facilitate sharing photos, music, and movies between Apple programs. You can open the Media Browser in programs like Keynote, Pages, Numbers, iDVD, GarageBand, iWeb, and iMovie. (The Media Browser looks slightly different in every iApp; Figure 13-8 shows what it looks like in iWeb.)

And here's what you'll see there: music from iTunes (complete with your playlists) and GarageBand; photos from iPhoto (complete with your albums) and Photo-Booth; and movies from iMovie, iPhoto, iTunes, and the Movies folder in your Home folder.

The Media Browser is especially important to iMovie because it provides by far the easiest way for you to hand off your videos to use in iWeb, Keynote, or any other program that speaks Media Browser-ese.

In fact, iMovie even uses the Media Browser when you upload videos to YouTube or your MobileMe gallery. If you watch the progress bars closely, you'll see that these are actually two-step procedures. First, iMovie creates a compressed QuickTime version of your movie and puts it *in the Media Browser;* then it uploads that movie to the Web. The movie you uploaded, however, *remains* in the Media Browser. That's how iMovie always seems to know which size versions of each project you've sent to the Web (Figure 13-4)—because they're still sitting right there on your hard drive!

The rest of this chapter covers all three of these methods of creating your own Web pages with movies on them.

Method 3: iMovie to iWeb

This isn't a book about iWeb, of course, but here's enough information to get your movie onto a Web page of your own design—and hang the whole thing on the Internet for the masses to see:

1. **With the finished iMovie project open, choose Share → Media Browser.**

   The dialog box shown in Figure 13-7 appears (see page 280 for a description of its options).

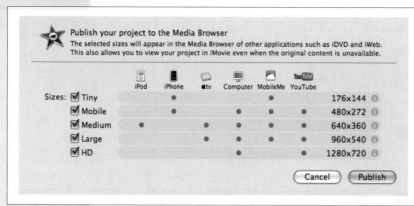

Figure 13-7:
*The Media Browser
(page 279) is your one-
stop shopping center for
all the music, photos, and
movies on your
computer. You're about
to load it up with even
more movies to share
with your other Apple
programs.*

2. **Choose the size(s) you want for the movie on your Web page.**

   You can choose multiple sizes to send to the Media Browser, if you like, although, of course, you're using up more hard drive space. (Word to the wise: In general, choose Tiny or Mobile. Use Medium only if all of your fans use high-speed Internet connections.)

3. **Click Publish.**

   iMovie cranks away, compressing your project down to an exported QuickTime movie file in the size you specified.

   NOTE   iMovie keeps track of which sizes of each project you've exported to the Media Browser. If you see some of the Size checkboxes dimmed, it's because the Media Browser *already* has versions of this project in those sizes.

4. **Open iWeb (Figure 13-8).**

5. **Open the Web page you want to edit, or choose File → New Page to create a new one. Click the Media button at the bottom of the screen (or choose View → Show Media Browser).**

   Clicking the Media button opens—what else?—the Media Browser.

6. **Find the movie you exported in step 3 and drag it wherever you want it on the page.**

   If you drag it on top of one of the sample photos, it snaps nicely into alignment. Finish editing your page as usual in iWeb.

7. **Edit the page title, subtitle, and description text.**

   Don't be concerned by the presence of all the Latin ("Lorem ipsum dolor amet…"); that's just placeholder text. Simply drag your cursor through it and type new stuff to replace it.

Figure 13-8:
Welcome to iWeb, a what-you-see-is-what-your-Web-site-will-look-like editing world for Web sites. The left column lists the Web pages you've made so far; the links at the top connect to them. The small Inspector palette (here labeled QuickTime) lets you tweak your movie's characteristics.

8. **Edit the design of the page, if you like.**

   Choose View → Show Inspector. The Inspector window's eighth tab, labeled QuickTime, is a palette of movie-frame options. (First, click the movie itself.) You can control its start- and endpoints, choose the poster frame (the part of the clip that shows when it *isn't* playing), and whether or not the clip autostarts, loops, and shows its playback controls.

9. **In the lower-left corner of iWeb, click Publish Site. In the confirmation box, click OK.**

   This is the big moment: iWeb connects to the MobileMe Web site and transfers the video and its page to the server. This magic requires, of course, that you already have a MobileMe account (page 275). It can also take a *very* long time. When the upload is complete, a dialog box appears containing three buttons: Announce (email the site's address to your friends), Visit Site Now, and OK.

   Congratulations—you've just published your own Web site with a movie in it.

   TIP You don't need a MobileMe account to use iWeb. If you maintain your own Web site, for example, click your site's name in the left column of the iWeb window and you see a list of options for that Web site. Click the "Publish to" menu and choose either FTP Server or Local Folder.

   If you know your Web server's FTP (file-transfer protocol) settings—usually an address and a password—you can enter that information directly into iWeb, which makes publishing your iWeb site a piece of cake. If you upload files to your Web server some other way, choose Local Folder. You wind up with a folder of correctly linked HTML documents and folders on your hard drive. All you have to do is manually upload them to your Web site.

What You Get When You're Done

When you see what you've created with iWeb, you'll be impressed: It's a professional-looking, stylishly titled Web page with your movie plugged right in. Clicking the ▶ button under your movie starts playback.

> **NOTE** In the Web addresses for your MobileMe Web sites, capitalization counts. If your friends type one of these addresses into a Web browser with incorrect capitalization, they may get only a "missing page" message. It might work better to send your friends a much shorter, easier-to-remember address. You can convert long URLs into shorter ones using a free URL-redirection service. At *www.tinyurl.com*, for example, you can turn that long address into something as short as *http://tinyurl.com/bus4*.

Editing or Deleting the Web page

To update your movie, launch iWeb and make your changes, and then click the Publish button again at the bottom of the screen. iWeb sets about updating the movie page online.

To delete a page, click its name in iWeb's left-side panel (the Site Organizer) and press the Delete key. Then click Publish at the bottom of the window to tell iWeb, "OK, make the online version of my site match what's in iWeb." Deleting a movie page like this also deletes all the online movie files, which frees up space on your iDisk.

Method 4: HomePage

Although using iWeb is incredibly simple, it entails a lot of sitting and waiting for the program to compute and upload things. HTML aficionados also complain that iWeb's behind-the-scenes HTML code can be a tad unorthodox.

Fortunately, there's yet another way to go about creating, editing, and managing your video galleries online: Visit your MobileMe Web site and use HomePage. The advantage here is that you can make changes to your movie pages even when you're far from home, using any Web-connected computer.

> **NOTE** Even though you paid for a MobileMe account, everything related to HomePage is still branded with .Mac (the old name for MobileMe). That's because Apple hasn't done anything with HomePage for *years*—but that doesn't mean *you* can't do something with it.

To get started with HomePage, first you have to export the video from iMovie as a QuickTime movie with modest dimensions and frame rate, as described in Chapter 14 (page 292). Once you've done that, copy the movies you want to publish to the Movies folder of your iDisk, as shown in Figure 13-9.

Figure 13-9:
To summon your iDisk icon to the screen, choose its name from the Go menu in the Finder (top left). The icon appears on your desktop, bearing your member name (top right). Double-click it—and wait—to see its contents (bottom). Then copy the movies you want to post online into the Movies folder.

Once your movie is in the iDisk's Movies folder, you're ready to create your Web pages. Go to *http://homepage.mac.com*, sign in, and then click one of the "Create a page" tabs on the HomePage screen to view the styles of pages you can create. Some of your formatting options are shown in Figure 13-10. The iMovie tab offers special movie-showcase layouts in a far wider range of styles than iWeb offers. But you're free to use your movies on the other Web page designs here, too, like baby announcements, writing samples, invitations, and so on.

Click the miniature image of the design you want. HomePage asks which movie in your Movies folder you want to place on your new Web page, as shown in Figure 13-10. Select a movie and then click Choose. After a few moments, your new video page appears with the movie already inserted.

To finish the project, edit the chunks of dummy text on the page, as shown in Figure 13-11. (Try to avoid misspellings and typos unless you want an audience of 400 million to think you slept through fourth-grade English.) Finally, click Preview to see how the Web page will look. When everything is just the way you want it, click Publish. The page goes live, as indicated by a confirmation dialog box.

Figure 13-10:
The HomePage home page offers a gallery of predesigned Web pages. The iMovie category includes special designs intended exclusively for QuickTime movie playback, but you're welcome to choose a design from any other category; just stick a movie anywhere Apple left a space for a photo. Your movie occupies only a small rectangle in the center of your visitors' screens; the rest is graphic fluff to fill up the window.

TIP   You can create as many Web pages as your iDisk will hold. When you return to the main HomePage screen, a list of your existing Web pages appears, complete with Add Site, Add Page, Delete, and Edit buttons.

Corporations and professional Web designers may sniff at the simplicity of the result, but it takes *them* a lot longer than 2 minutes to do their thing.

Editing Your Web page

To make changes to your Web site using the HomePage tools, log back into *homepage.mac.com*. You're back at Figure 13-10. At the top left of the page is the list of Web pages you've created so far. Click the name of the movie you want to edit, and then click the small Edit button beneath it. You're ready to proceed as shown in Figure 13-11.

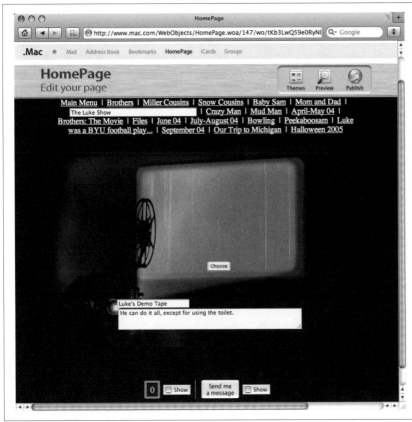

Figure 13-11:
Here's where you edit your movie page before unleashing it on the Web—for example, adding or editing a title and a description. To choose a different movie, click the tiny Choose button beneath the movie scroll bar. When everything looks good, click Publish. You've just updated your Web page.

Behind the Screens

Behind the scenes, iMovie builds your movie Web site by placing new Web page (HTML) documents in the Sites folder of your iDisk (Figure 13-9). You can make changes to your Web page by editing these documents.

Method 5: Posting a Movie on Your Site

Maybe you prefer the control and freedom of putting movies on your *own* Web page, designed the way you like it, without any hand-holding from Apple's templates or having to sign up for a MobileMe account.

If you already have a Web site, you can export a QuickTime version of your flick (see Chapter 14) and upload it to your Web site, no matter what the Web-hosting service. (Most Internet accounts, including those provided by AOL, Earthlink, or your cable-modem or DSL company, come with free space for Web pages uploaded in this way.)

This is the most labor-intensive route, but it offers much more flexibility if you know how to work with HTML to create more sophisticated pages. It's also the route you should take if you hope to incorporate the resulting movie into an existing Web site (that is, one where the movies aren't the only attraction).

This isn't really a book about Web design. But to get you started, a free PDF appendix to this chapter, called "Movies on Custom Web Sites," awaits you on this book's "Missing CD" page at *www.missingmanuals.com*. It provides the HTML code you need to post a movie on your Web page, make it pop up in a window or play embedded, looking into QuickTime Streaming Server, and other advanced topics.

From iMovie to QuickTime

For the best and most cinematic viewing experience, play your finished iMovie productions on TV, from a DVD, a tape, or an Apple TV, or at high resolution on a big computer screen. That way, your public gets to see the full-sized picture that your camcorder captured. (iMovie '09 can't play your movie on a tape or export the finished project to a tape for archiving and viewing—but iMovie 6 can. See Chapter 11 for details.)

When you want to distribute your movies electronically, you can convert them into QuickTime files instead. Both Mac and Windows machines can play these files right on the screen with little more than a double-click. Your distribution options for QuickTime files are far greater than for videocassette or DVD, too. You can email a QuickTime file to somebody or post it on the Web for all the world to see (Chapter 13). You can put bigger QuickTime files onto a disk, like a recordable CD, DVD, external hard drive, or an iPod, to transport them. You can export only the *audio* portion of your movie—or only the video portion.

This chapter covers all of these techniques, step by step.

Understanding QuickTime

A computer displays video by flashing many still images in rapid succession. But if you've ever worked with graphics, you know that color graphics files are data hogs. A full-screen photograph file might occupy 5 or 10 MB of space on your hard drive and take several seconds to open up.

Most computers today are fast enough to open and flash 30 full-screen, photographic-quality pictures per second. Problem is, movies of that size and quality consume hundreds of megabytes of disk space, and take many hours to download from the Web or by email—a guaranteed way to annoy citizens of the Internet and doom your moviemaking career to obscurity.

That's why most QuickTime movies *aren't* full-screen, photographic-quality films. In fact, most QuickTime movies are much "smaller"—in three different dimensions:

- **The window is much smaller.** It's rare to see a QuickTime movie that, when played back, fills the computer screen. Instead, most QuickTime movies today play in a much smaller window (Figure 14-1), therefore requiring far less data and resulting in far smaller files.

Figure 14-1:
Here's the same movie in two playback sizes. High-definition movies are, at a minimum, 1280 pixels wide and 720 pixels tall (1280 × 720). Cut each dimension in half (640 × 360), and the resulting video is one-quarter the size of the original. That makes a big difference to the size of the files on your hard drive (and to Internet playback). Using the same video compression settings, this 28-second clip weighs in at 32 MB in high definition, and only 7 MB in the smaller size.

- **The frame rate is lower.** Instead of showing 30 frames per second, many QuickTime movies have far lower frame rates; even 15 frames per second produces smooth motion. On the Web, especially during live QuickTime broadcasts, still lower frame rates are common, like two or five frames per second. This kind of movie is noticeably jerky, but sends so little data that people using telephone-line modems can watch live events in this format.

- **The video is *compressed*.** This is the big one—the technical aspect of QuickTime movies that gives you the most control over the resulting quality of your movie. In short, when iMovie uses QuickTime to compress your video, it discards information that describes each frame. True, the picture deteriorates as a consequence, but the resulting QuickTime movie file is a tiny fraction of its original size. The following section describes this compression business in much greater detail.

The bottom line is that by combining these three techniques, iMovie can turn a 10-gigabyte digital movie into a *3-megabyte* file that's small enough to email or post on your Web page. The resulting movie won't play as smoothly, fill as much of the screen, or look as good as the original footage. But your viewers won't care. They'll be delighted to be able to watch your movie at all, and grateful that the file didn't take hours to download. (And besides, anyone already familiar with Quick-Time movies knows what to expect from them.)

NOTE The newer the QuickTime version your Mac has, the better and faster the movie-exporting process is. Mac OS X's Software Update feature is supposed to alert you every time a new version becomes available (if you have it turned on in System Preferences).

A Crash Course in Video Compression

The following discussion explores some technical underpinnings of QuickTime technology. It may take you a few minutes to complete this behind-the-scenes tour of how a computer stores video. But without understanding the basics, iMovie's QuickTime-exporting options will seem utterly impenetrable.

Spatial compression

Suppose you overhear a fellow Mac fan telling her husband, "Would you mind running to the grocery store? We need an eight-ounce box of Cajun Style Rice-A-Roni, and an eight-ounce box of Cajun Style Rice-A-Roni, and also an eight-ounce box of Cajun Style Rice-A-Roni."

You'd probably assume that she's enjoyed a little too much of that new-computer smell. Why didn't she just tell him to pick up three boxes of it?

When it comes to storing video on a hard drive, your Macintosh faces the same issue. When storing a picture file, it has to "write down" the precise color of *each pixel* of each frame. It could, of course, store the information like this:

- *Top row, pixel 1:* Beige

- *Top row, pixel 2:* Beige

- *Top row, pixel 3:* Beige

…and so on. Clearly, this much information would take a lot of space and a lot of time to reproduce.

Fortunately, when Apple engineers were designing QuickTime in the 1980s, it occurred to them that the individual dots in solid-colored areas of the picture don't need to be described individually. That top row of pixels could be represented much more efficiently, and take up a lot less disk space, if the Mac were simply to write down:

- *Top row:* 60 consecutive pixels of beige

This simplified example shows the power of *compression software*, whose job it is to make graphics files smaller by recording their pixel colors more efficiently. This kind of compression explains why a JPEG file always takes up far less space on your hard drive (and less time to download by email) than, for example, the Photoshop document that created it; the JPEG file has been compressed.

This form of file-size reduction is called *spatial* or *intraframe* compression. iMovie analyzes the picture on each individual frame and reduces the amount of information needed to describe it.

Temporal compression

But there's another way to reduce the size of a QuickTime file. Not only is there a lot of redundant color information from pixel to pixel in a single frame, but also from *frame to frame*.

Suppose, for example, that you've captured some footage of a man sitting behind a desk, talking about roofing materials. Picture the first pixel of the back wall in that piece of footage. Chances are good that this pixel's color remains absolutely consistent, frame after frame, for several seconds at least, especially if the footage was shot using a tripod. Same thing with the rug, the color of the desk, the fern in the pot beside it, and so on. These elements of the picture don't change at all from one frame to the next.

Here again, if it were your job to record what's on each frame, you could choose the slow and laborious method:

- *Frame 1:* The upper-left pixel is beige.

- *Frame 2:* The upper-left pixel is still beige.

- *Frame 3:* The upper-left pixel is *still* beige.

…and so on. This time, however, a clever QuickTime movie would record the details of only the *first frame*. "The upper-left pixel on the first frame is beige," it might begin. In filmmaker terminology, that first, completely memorized image is called the *key frame*.

Thereafter, rather than memorizing the status of every pixel on the second frame, the third frame, and so on, the Mac might just say, "On the next 60 frames, pixel #1 is exactly the same as on the first one." That more efficient description just made the resulting QuickTime file a *lot* smaller, as shown in Figure 14-2. (The subsequent, shorthand-recorded frames are often called *delta frames* by the geeks.)

This kind of shorthand is called *temporal* or *interframe* compression, because it refers to the way pixels change over time, from one frame to the next.

Figure 14-2:
When iMovie saves a QuickTime movie, it doesn't bother writing down the description of every pixel on every frame. If a lot of areas remain identical from frame to frame, the QuickTime movie doesn't remember anything more than, "Same as the previous frame." In this example, the faded portions of the picture are the areas that the QuickTime movie data doesn't describe—because they're the same as the first (key) frame. (At last you understand why, using a tripod for your footage doesn't just give your movies a more professional look. By ensuring that most of the picture stays exactly the same from frame to frame, a tripod-shot video helps to produce smaller QuickTime files.)

About Codecs

When you save your QuickTime movie, you'll be asked which of several schemes you want to use for compressing your footage. To use the technical terminology, it asks you to choose a *codec* from a long list. That term is short for compressor/decompressor, the software module that translates the pixel-by-pixel description of your footage into the more compact QuickTime format, and then *un*translates it during playback.

Each QuickTime codec works differently. Some provide spatial compression, some temporal, some both. Some are ideal for animations, and others for live action. Some work well on slower computers, others on faster ones. Some try to maintain excellent picture quality, but produce very large QuickTime files on the disk, and others make the opposite tradeoff. Later in this chapter, you'll read about each of these codecs and when to use them.

In the meantime, all of this background information should help explain a few phenomena pertaining to converting DV movies into QuickTime files:

- **Saving a QuickTime movie takes a long time.** It's nothing like saving, say, a word-processing document. Comparing every pixel on every frame with every pixel on the next frame involves massive amounts of number crunching, which takes time. (Some codecs take longer than others, however.)

- **QuickTime movies don't look as good as the original video.** Now you know why: In the act of shrinking your movie down to a file size that's reasonable for emailing, copying to a CD-ROM, and so on, a codec's job is to *throw away* some of the data that makes a movie look vivid and clear.

- **QuickTime is an exercise in compromise.** By choosing the appropriate codec and changing its settings appropriately, you can create a QuickTime movie with excellent picture and sound. Unfortunately, it will consume a lot of disk space. If you want a small file on the hard drive *and* excellent picture and sound, you can make the QuickTime movie play in a smaller window—320×240 pixels, for example, instead of 640×480 or something larger—or at a slower frame rate. The guide in this chapter, some experimentation, and the nature of the movie you're making all contribute to helping you make a codec decision.

The Export Pop-up Menu

After you've finished editing your iMovie production, the first step in exporting it as a QuickTime movie is to choose Share → "Export using QuickTime".

The "Save exported file as" dialog box appears (Figure 14-3). Here, you'll eventually type a name and choose a folder location for the file you're about to save. But for now, resist the temptation.

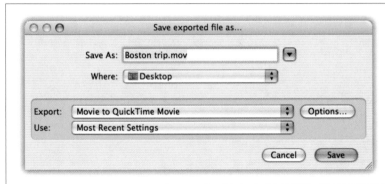

Figure 14-3:
*This is the first dialog box of
many that you'll encounter as
you crawl down Alice's rabbit
hole of QuickTime compression
options.*

The real power lies in the buttons and pop-up menus elsewhere in this little box. For starters, the Export pop-up menu (visible in Figure 14-3) gives you a wealth of conversion options. This is your opportunity to save your film as:

- **An AVI file to give to your Windows PC-using friends.** Choose Movie to AVI.

- **A huge folder full of still images, one per frame of your movie.** Choose "Movie to Image Sequence". Click Options to specify the file format—like JPEG or Photoshop—and how many stills per second you want.

- **A soundtrack.** Here's a great opportunity to convert the audio tracks of your movie into standalone sound files. Choose "Sound to AIFF", "Sound to Wave", or whatever format you want.

  You'll find this feature very handy every now and then. For example, certain troubleshooting situations, usually involving an out-of-place noise, call for exporting and reimporting your finished soundtrack—in essence, temporarily splitting it apart from the video. (You can even edit the soundtrack file in GarageBand or another program along the way, if you're so inclined. That's one way to get rid of the occasional pop or crackle.)

- **A movie that's formatted for the iPod, iPhone, or Apple TV.** Of course, there are easier ways to go about these tasks; see Chapter 12.

But most of the time, you'll ignore this Export pop-up menu. Usually, you'll want to leave it set to "Movie to QuickTime Movie", and then click the Options button to make some settings changes.

The Options button opens a very important dialog box: the Movie Settings box (Figure 14-4). Here's where you can export your finished product with *exactly* the size-smoothness-speed compromise you want.

You'll notice that this box has three buttons for video: Settings, Filter, and Size. Below that, you get one Settings button for Sound; at the bottom of the box, you get options for *Internet streaming*. All of these settings are covered in the next few pages.

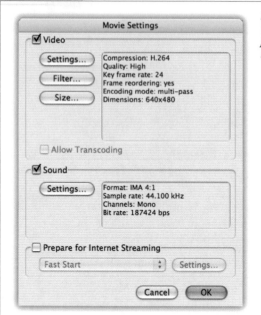

Figure 14-4:
When you click Options, you get the Movie Settings box. It's just a summary screen for the dialog boxes that hide behind it: Settings, Filter, Size, and so on.

The Settings Button

The Settings button for video takes you to the powerful Standard Video Compression Settings dialog box (Figure 14-5), the heart of the entire Options software suite. Here's what the controls do:

Compression Type pop-up menu

The Compression Type pop-up menu at the top lets you choose one of several dozen codecs—or None, which means that iMovie won't compress your project at all. Each codec compresses your footage using a different scheme that entails different compromises. See page 289 for details. For now, note that for live video that will be played on modern computers, the H.264 codec almost always produces the highest quality at reasonably small file sizes.

Frames per second

The number you specify in the Frame Rate box makes an enormous difference in the smoothness of the QuickTime movie's playback. As always, however, it's a tradeoff—the higher the number, the larger the QuickTime file, and the more difficult it is to email, store, or transfer. You can type any number between 1 and 60 in the Frame Rate box, or choose from the pop-up menu to the right of the box.

Here's what you can expect from these settings:

- **8, 10.** These movies are very compact, and make good candidates for transmitting over the Internet. They also look very jerky.

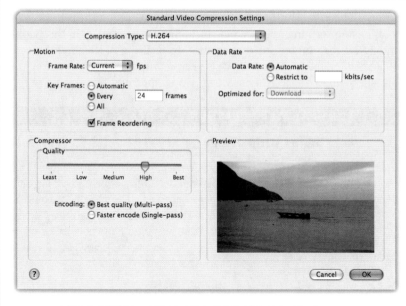

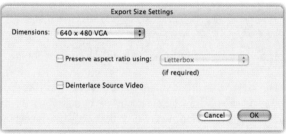

Figure 14-5:
Top: This dialog box gives you point-by-point control over the look, size, and quality of the QuickTime movie you're exporting. Not all of these controls are available for all codecs. Furthermore, only some of the codecs have an Options button in the middle of the dialog box.

Bottom: Here's where you can specify the dimensions of the movie you're saving, in pixels. (This box appears when you click the Size button shown in Figure 14-4.)

- **12, 15.** These are the most common frame rates for today's QuickTime movies on the Internet. By playing only half as many frames as you'd see on a TV show, the QuickTime movie saves a lot of data, making itself smaller on the disk and more likely to succeed when played over slower connections. And yet this many frames per second tricks the eye into perceiving satisfying, smooth motion. Most people can sense that they aren't seeing quite the motion quality they'd see on TV, but don't miss the other 15 frames each second.

- **24, 25.** An actual Hollywood movie plays at 24 frames per second, and the European television signal (PAL) plays at 25. These settings, in other words, are provided for situations where you want excellent motion quality, without going all the way to the extreme of 29.97 frames per second of the American TV standard (NTSC). You save a little bit of disk space, while still showing as many frames as people are accustomed to seeing in motion pictures.

• **29.97.** If you're wondering how this oddball number got into the pop-up menu, you're not alone. As it turns out, every source that refers to television broadcasts as having 30 frames per second (including other chapters in this book) is rounding off the number for convenience. In fact, a true television broadcast plays at *29.97* frames per second. iMovie can reproduce that rate for you, if it's important to do so. In fact, this is iMovie's top frame rate.

RARELY ASKED QUESTION

30 fps Drop-Frame

OK, I'll bite. Why on earth did the USA, which is supposed to be so technically advanced, settle on a TV standard that plays at such an oddball frame rate? Why is it 29.97? Why wasn't it rounded off to 30?

The 29.97 frame rate, known in the TV business as 30 fps drop-frame, dates back to the dawn of color TV. As they prepared to launch color TV broadcasts in January 1954, network engineers wanted to make sure that the expensive black-and-white TV sets of the day could receive the color shows, too. (Talk about backward-compatible software!)

Trouble was, when they tried to broadcast a color signal at the then-standard 30 frames per second, the extra color information wound up distorting the audio signal. Eventually, they hit upon a discovery: If they slowed down the frame rate just a hair, the distortion disappeared. The video, meanwhile, looked just as good at 29.97 frames per second as it did at 30.

A standard was born.

• **30.** This is the proper setting for full-quality high-definition footage.

> **NOTE**   If you're not working with hi-def video, then ignore 30 in the Frame Rate pop-up menu; it's for suckers. *Standard*-definition video, at least in North America, is itself 29.97 frames per second. So asking iMovie to save a QuickTime movie with an even *higher* rate is like thinking you'll be wealthier if you exchange your dollar bills for quarters. If you *do* try choosing 30 from the Frame Rate pop-up menu, when you click OK, you'll be scolded, told you're out of line, and then returned to the dialog box to make another choice.

As described under "Quality slider" in the previous section, you don't have to export your movie in its entirety just to see the effects of different frame-rate settings. Create a dummy project that contains only a few seconds of movie, and try exporting it at each frame rate. Then play back the short QuickTime movies. You'll get a self-taught course in the effects of different frames-per-second settings.

Key frame every _ frames

You read about *key frames* earlier in this chapter—they're the full frames that get memorized in your QuickTime movie, so that the QuickTime file can store less data for subsequent frames. (See Figure 14-2, page 291.)

In most cases, one key frame per second is about right. In movies that will be played back from beginning to end and never rewound or scrolled, it's safe to increase the number in this box.

FREQUENTLY ASKED QUESTION

Oddly Shaped Movies

I'm doing a project where I need my movie to be perfectly square, not in a 4:3 width-to-height ratio. But every time I try to specify these dimensions in the QuickTime Settings dialog box, I get a distorted, squished iMovie movie. What can I do?

What you're really asking is how to crop your movie.

iMovie '09, of course, is capable of cropping your video—but only in the standard 4:3 or 16:9 aspect ratios (see page 166).

Unfortunately, neither iMovie nor QuickTime Player Pro (Chapter 15) have a simple method of cropping the picture in any other aspect ratio.

There is software that can do so, however: AutoDesk Cleaner (*www.autodesk.com*), the $475 professional QuickTime-compression software. As shown here, it lets you draw a dotted-line rectangle that indicates how you'd like to crop the picture.

Apple's professional video editing programs, Final Cut Pro and Final Cut Express, can freely crop video, too.

If you're using iMovie for professional purposes, a program like one of those is a worthwhile investment. Think of it as a much more powerful and flexible version of the Standard Video Compression Settings dialog box (Figure 14-5). Its sole purpose is to compress movies, using much more efficient and intelligent software than that built into iMovie.

And if you have more expertise than cash, the freeware program ffmpegX can crop video, too. You have to do it by typing in coordinates (rather than adjusting a visual cropping frame), but it works. (You can download ffmpegX from this book's "Missing CD" page at *www.missingmanuals.com*.)

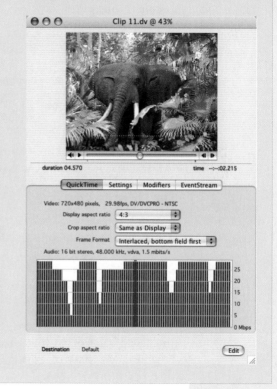

Quality slider

This slider gives another tradeoff between the size of the resulting QuickTime file and the quality of its picture. In general, the proposed value (usually Medium or High) gives the best balance between file size and picture quality. But on important projects, by all means experiment. Export a representative sample of your movie several times, moving the slider each time, so that you can compare the results.

Limit data rate

Each delivery mechanism—a CD-ROM, a cable modem, a 56 K modem, and so on—delivers information at a different rate. If you want to ensure that no frame-skipping or jerkiness happens when somebody plays your movie, in the Data Rate section of the dialog box, turn the checkbox next to "Restrict to" on, and then type a number into the box.

The precise number you type depends on your goals for the movie you're exporting. In other words, it depends on what kind of gadget will be playing the movie data.

Here are some guidelines:

If the movie will be played by:	Use this maximum data rate:
56 K modem	5 K/second
T1 or cable modem	20 K/second
CD-ROM	100 K/second
Hard drive	250 K/second

iMovie automatically adjusts the picture quality as necessary, on a moment-by-moment basis, so that the QuickTime movie never exceeds this rate.

The Filter Button

As noted in Chapter 6, iMovie '09 doesn't have all of the special effects that were present in iMovie 6; it's missing the flashy ones like Lens Flare and Rain. But unbeknownst to nine out of 10 iMovie fans, you still have access to an enormous range of visual effects, which you can apply to your movie on its way *out* of iMovie. Simply click the Filter button in the Movie Settings dialog box (shown in Figure 14-4) when you export a QuickTime movie.

The dialog box shown in Figure 14-6 appears. By opening the various flippy triangles, you'll find a lot of favorite effects that were in the old iMovie (color balance, brightness and contrast, lens flare, fake old-film grain)—and a few that weren't (blur or sharpen, emboss).

The list of effects appears in the scrolling list at top left; a preview of the result appears at lower left. Use the controls on the right side of the dialog box to affect the intensity and other settings of each effect.

As you work, remember that whatever filter you apply here applies to the *entire movie* you're about to export. You might be inclined to pooh-pooh this whole feature, in that case. Really, when would you ever want to apply the same degree of blur to an entire movie?

But with a little forethought, you can still apply an effect to just one clip. The trick is to create a new iMovie project containing *only that clip*. Export it using the Apple Intermediate Codec (page 43) to make sure that you retain all your digital-video size and quality—and apply the filter you want in the process. Save this exported chunk somewhere easy to find—on your desktop, for example.

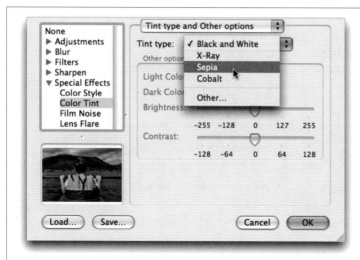

Figure 14-6:
The Filter dialog box has special effects that let you adjust the color, brightness, or contrast of the footage; sharpen or blur it; add a phony lens flare; or even add fake film noise like scratches and dust. Using both the Load and Save buttons, you can even save an effects configuration you've created onto your hard drive, so you'll be able to apply exactly the same settings to another clip at another time. (Unfortunately, you can apply only one effect at a time.)

When it's all over, you can reimport your exported, processed clip into the original iMovie project.

> **WARNING**   iMovie preserves your Options settings from export to export, even if weeks or months elapse in between. That's an especially treacherous feature when it comes to these filters. Next time you sit through a 45-minute export you may find that the resulting movie is all embossed and color-shifted because those are the settings you used last time. The only way to escape this nightmare is to reopen the Filter dialog box, and then choose None.

The Size Button

And now, back to your tour of the Movie Settings dialog box shown in Figure 14-4.

The Size button on the Movie Settings dialog box summons the dialog box shown at the bottom of Figure 14-5, where—after clicking "Use custom size"—you can specify the dimensions for the playback window of your QuickTime movie. Of course, the larger the window you specify, the longer the movie will take to save, the slower it will be transmitted over the Internet, and the larger the resulting file will be.

Keeping the dimensions you specify here in a width-to-height aspect ratio of 4:3 (for standard video) or 16:9 (for high-def video) is important. The QuickTime software plays back most smoothly if your movie retains these relative proportions. Furthermore, if the width and height you specify *aren't* in one of those ratios, iMovie has to squish the picture accordingly, which may lend a funhouse-mirror distortion effect to your film.

Most QuickTime movies play in one of several standard sizes, like 320×240 or 640×480—both examples of the 4:3 aspect ratio. Still, there are dozens of other possible sizes that maintain the correct proportions.

Audio Settings

In the Movie Settings dialog box shown in Figure 14-4 is a *second* button called Settings, which lets you specify how—and by how much—your soundtrack is compressed in the exported QuickTime movie (Figure 14-7).

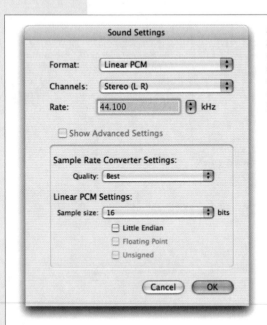

Figure 14-7:
It probably goes without saying that the better the audio quality you specify, the larger your QuickTime movie will be. In any case, this is the dialog box where you make such decisions. Audio isn't nearly as data-greedy as video, so compressing it isn't quite as urgent an issue (unless you want your movie to play over the Internet).

Format

When most people think of codecs—those who've even *heard* of codecs, that is—they think of *video* compression. But iMovie gives you a choice of audio codecs, too. The Format pop-up menu lets you specify which one you want to use.

Many of them aren't, in fact, appropriate for movie soundtracks. Remember that these codecs are provided by QuickTime, not by iMovie, and that QuickTime is designed to be an all-purpose multimedia format. It's supposed to be just as good at creating pictureless sound files as it is at creating movies. It's also supposed to recognize every format that ever trudged through the music industry—including plenty that nobody uses anymore. The ones you might conceivably care about are these:

- **AAC.** If you choose this audio codec, you'll save your soundtrack in AAC format—the same one used for songs you buy from the iTunes music store. The sound quality is superb, although it depends on the settings you choose when you click Options. (For example, choose 128 Kbits/second from the Bit Rate pop-up menu to match the quality of iTunes songs.) The file size, meanwhile, is only a fraction of the original. It's a welcome and useful choice for movies not intended to be played over the Internet.

- **AMR Narrowband.** This item stands for Adaptive Multi-Rate, and is intended for movies in the 3GPP format (a standard developed for cell phones). Use it if you have a 3GPP-compatible phone. For other phones, use the Qualcomm PureVoice codec (described below), click Options, and then turn on the Half Rate option.

- **Apple Lossless.** This item is a truly *lossless* audio compression option. Lossless means that although this codec cuts the audio track's file size in half, it doesn't lose *any* of the sound quality in the process. The resulting files are too big for the Web or emailing, but Apple Lossless is great when you're saving a movie for best-quality playback from a hard drive.

- **IMA 4:1.** This codec was one of the first QuickTime movie audio compressors. It provides excellent audio quality—you *can't* change it to a sample size less than 16-bit—and plays back equally well on Windows and Macintosh. It's great for movies that will be played on a hard drive or CD, or over a fast Internet connection.

- **QDesign Music 2.** This is an aging sound codec that's still useful for online or emailed movies. It maintains terrific audio quality, but compresses the sound a great deal, producing files small enough to deliver over dial-up modems. Apple's favorite example: One minute of music from an audio CD requires 11 MB of disk space, but after compression by this codec, it consumes only 150 KB and sounds almost as good.

Rate, Size

A computer captures and plays back sound by capturing thousands of individual slices, or snapshots, of sound per second. As though describing somebody at a wine tasting, computer nerds call this process *sampling* the sound.

The two controls here let you specify *how many samples* you want the Mac to take per second (the sampling Rate) and *how much data* it's allowed to use to describe each sample (the sampling Size).

Even if that technical explanation means nothing to you, the principle is easy enough to absorb: The higher the Rate and Size settings (see Figure 14-7), the better the quality of the audio and the larger the size of the resulting QuickTime file. Here are a few examples of the kind of file-size increases you can expect for each of several popular rate and size settings. (Note that the information here is *per channel*. If you're going for stereo, double the kilobyte ratings shown here.)

- **11 kHz, 8 bits.** Sounds like you're hearing the audio track over a bad telephone connection. Tinny. Use it only for speech. 662 KB per minute.

- **11 kHz, 16 bits.** Sounds a lot better. Roughly the sound quality you get from the built-in Mac speaker. 1.3 MB per minute.

- **22 kHz, 16 bits.** Starting to sound very good. Suitable for playing on a computer equipped with external speakers. 2.6 MB per minute.

• **44.1 kHz, 16 bits**. This is the real thing, the ultimate audio experience. CD-quality audio. Suitable for listening to with headphones. The ultimate storage and transmission headache, too—this much data requires 5.3 MB per minute, mono. But of course, you'd never go this far without also including the stereo experience, so make that 10.6 MB per minute in stereo.

Use: Mono/Stereo

These radio buttons let you specify whether or not your movie's soundtrack is in stereo.

Exporting your QuickTime movie with a stereo format is often a waste of data. Many computers, including Power Macs, Mac Pros, and Mac Minis, don't *have* stereo speakers.

Furthermore, even though most camcorders include a stereo microphone, there's virtually no separation between the right and left channels, thanks to the fact that the microphone is mounted directly onto the tiny camcorder. Nor does iMovie let you edit the right and left audio channels independently. Even if people are listening to your movie with stereo speakers, they'll hear essentially the same thing out of each.

Therefore, consider using the Mono setting when you're trying to minimize the amount of data required to play back the soundtrack.

The Video Codecs: A Catalog

When you decide to export your iMovie production as a QuickTime movie, you can exert a great deal of control over how the Mac produces the resulting movie file by clicking Options in the dialog box shown in Figure 14-3 (page 293), and then clicking Settings (Figure 14-4, page 294). You get access to a long list of codecs. Few of these codecs are very useful for everyday use. Many of them are intended for:

• **Saving still frames (not movies)**. Examples: BMP, PNG, Photo-JPEG, JPEG 2000, TGA, TIFF, Planar RGB.

• **Keeping around for old times' sake, despite having been technologically surpassed**. Examples: Cinepak, Component Video, Sorenson.

• **Professional cameras and high-end production firms**. Examples: Apple Pixlet Video, Apple ProRes, MPEG IMX, HDCAM.

Most of the time, the compressor called H.264 will make you and your audience the happiest.

> **NOTE** The list of codecs in your dialog boxes may not match what you see here. Your codecs reflect the version of QuickTime that you have, which may be older or newer than version 7.6, described here.

Here are some of the codecs that *aren't* totally useless:

- **Animation.** This codec is significant because, at its Best quality setting, it maintains *all* of the original picture quality, while still managing to convert files so that they're smaller than files with no compression at all. (As the name implies, this codec was originally designed to process video composed of large blocks of solid colors—that is, cartoons.) The resulting file is huge when compared with the other codecs described here, but not as huge as it would be if you chose None in this pop-up menu.

- **Apple Intermediate Codec.** You can read all about this clever, sneaky codec on page 43. It's how Apple makes it possible for iMovie to handle high-definition video and AVCHD video at standard-video speeds: by first *converting* it into this intermediate format for use on the Mac. Your primary interest in this codec is for transferring videos back and forth between iMovie versions.

- **DV/DVCPRO-NTSC.** Suppose you've just completed a masterful movie, and the thought of compressing it to a much smaller, image-degraded QuickTime movie breaks your heart. You can use this codec to turn your finished, effect-enhanced, fully edited iMovie production into a new, raw DV clip, exactly like the DV clips that iMovie captures when it imports from a tape camcorder.

  You might do so if, for example, you wanted to send a full-quality DV clip to somebody electronically, or as an alternative to the Apple Intermediate Codec for moving video between editing programs. (*DV*, of course, means digital video; NTSC is the format used in the Western Hemisphere and Japan. DVCPRO50 is a high-end variation used in professional TV cameras.)

- **DV-PAL, DVCPRO-PAL.** These options are here so that you can export your iMovie masterpiece in the European video format (PAL), while retaining full size and frame rate. (DVCPRO and DVCPRO50 are slight variants of the DV format, intended for use with expensive professional broadcast TV video gear.) Unfortunately, the quality of the video suffers when you make this kind of conversion, especially in action scenes.

- **H.264.** This is it—Apple's favorite. It's also the format of satellite TV, high-definition DVD, iPod and iPhone video, .Mac Web gallery video, newer YouTube videos, and other quality-dependent video uses. Technically speaking, it's a flavor of *MPEG-4*, described later. It looks spectacular, compresses relatively well, and it scales beautifully from cellphone screens all the way up to high-definition TVs. It's not, however, the fastest codec on earth. If the client is standing beside you, tapping his foot, the MPEG-4 Video codec takes less time to export.

- **Photo - JPEG.** This codec (also called Motion JPEG) doesn't perform any temporal (frame-to-frame) compression. Each movie frame is saved as an individual, full-sized color picture. The disadvantage is, of course, that the resulting files are extremely large. In other words, Motion JPEG is occasionally useful when editing video, but never for distributing it.

So what good is it? Motion JPEG is the format used by many professional DV-editing machines (like those from Avid, Accom, and Discreet). Because there's no key-frame business going on, editors can make cuts at any frame. (Doing so isn't always possible in a file created by a codec that stores only the *difference* between one frame and the next. A particular frame might contain data that describes only new information.)

NOTE   Motion JPEG is *not* the same thing as MPEG, which is the format used to store movies on the DVD discs you can rent from Blockbuster. Despite the similarity of names, the differences are enormous. For example, MPEG uses temporal compression and requires special software to create it.

- **MPEG-4 Video**. MPEG-4 is an older version of the H.264 codec described above. (By the way, AAC, the audio format of the iTunes music store, is an audio version of MPEG-4.) It compresses your movie much more quickly, although the files aren't as small and the quality isn't as good as H.264.

- **None**. If quality is everything to you, and disk space and Internetability are nothing, you can use this option, which (like the DV codecs) doesn't compress the video at all. The resulting QuickTime file may contain so much data that your computer can't even play it back smoothly. You can, however, put it in a cryogenic tank in anticipation of the day when superfast computers come your way.

Saving a QuickTime Movie

All right—having read all of that theory of QuickTime and compression, you're ready to do the actual exporting.

1. **Choose Share → "Export using QuickTime".**

   The "Save exported file as" dialog box appears (Figure 14-3).

2. **Type a name for your movie.**

   Unless, of course, you want to name your movie whatever the current project is called, as iMovie suggests.

   Don't remove the letters *.mov* from the end of the file's name, especially if it might be played on Windows computers. That suffix is a requirement for machines that aren't savvy enough to know a movie file when they see one.

3. **Navigate to the folder where you want to store the resulting QuickTime file.**

   You can simply press ⌘-D if you want your QuickTime Movie saved onto the desktop, where it'll be easy to find.

4. **Make sure the Export pop-up menu says "Movie to QuickTime Movie". Click Options, and then click Settings at the top of the next dialog box.**

The dialog box shown in Figure 14-5 (top) appears.

5. **Choose your compression options, and then click OK.**

You return to the "Save exported file as" dialog box.

6. **Click Save.**

Now the time-consuming compression process begins. Compression can take a long time to complete—from a minute or two to an hour or more, depending on the settings you selected, the length of your movie, and the speed of your Mac.

Feel free to switch into other programs—check your email or surf the Web, for example—while iMovie crunches away in the background.

A progress bar lets you know how much farther iMovie has to go.

When the exporting is complete, the progress bar disappears. Switch to the Finder, where you'll find a new QuickTime movie icon (Figure 14-8). Double-click it to see the results.

TIP You can click Stop during the export process, but you'll wind up with no exported movie at all.

Figure 14-8:
When you double-click the resulting QuickTime movie on your hard drive (left), it opens into your copy of QuickTime Player, the movie-playing program described in Chapter 15. Press the space bar or click the play arrow to start the movie playback (right).

Exporting High-Definition for the Web

High-definition video on the Web is coming of age. And not the learning-how-to-walk coming of age, either—the real deal, the can-I-borrow-the-car coming of age. Major online video-sharing sites like YouTube and Vimeo offer an HD option, so getting HD movies *out* of iMovie has become pretty important.

HD on the Web is generally in the format called 720p. It's a video image created when your TV paints 720 lines down the screen, really fast. (It's not quite as sharp as *1080p*, for obvious reasons, but it's still really great-looking.)

In computer terms, 720p video has dimensions of 1280 × 720 pixels or greater. (Don't attempt to convert *standard-*definition footage, like that from a DV tape, into hi-def format. The results will look terrible.)

Weirdly, iMovie doesn't have a simple, HD-quality export option. Fortunately, QuickTime does.

To export a hi-def video suitable for uploading to You-Tube, Vimeo, or some other HD video-sharing site, export your movie as a QuickTime file, as described on these pages. Use the following settings:

- **Size: 1280 × 720.** These dimensions are the small-est a video can be and still qualify as HD. Any smaller, and sites like YouTube, for example, won't label or play it as a hi-def video.

- **Deinterlaced.** When you choose the size for your movie, you can also turn on Deinterlace Source Video. (It deinterlaces video that would otherwise be displayed by rapidly alternating two inter-leaved sets of horizontal scan lines—created, for example, by a so-called 1080i hi-def camcorder.)

- **Compression Type: H.264.** This compression scheme looks fantastic, and online video Web sites accept it.

- **Frame Rate: original (but no greater than 30 frames per second).** The frame rate controls the smoothness of the video; it tells QuickTime how many images per second to flash by when the movie plays. If you somehow ended up with a frame rate slower than 30 frames per second in your iMovie project, don't bother trying to make the frame rate *higher*. It won't make the video look any better, and may make it look a lot worse.

- **Audio: AAC (256 kbps or higher).** AAC is a great audio codec (compression format). The major video sharing sites think so, too.

QuickTime Player

If iMovie is the program on your hard drive that's the master of *DV* and *HD* files, its sibling software, the corresponding master of traditional *QuickTime* movies, is QuickTime Player, a small, free program that comes with every Macintosh. (It's in the Applications folder.) It does three things very well: show pictures, play movies, and play sounds (Figure 15-1).

If you're willing to pay $30, you can upgrade your copy of QuickTime Player to the Pro version. Doing so grants you a long list of additional features, most notably the ability to *edit* your QuickTime movies, not just watch them.

There are two reasons QuickTime Player is worth knowing about. First, if you turn your iMovie projects into QuickTime movies (Chapter 14), QuickTime Player is the program you'll probably be using to play them on your screen. Second, the Pro version acts as an accessory toolkit for iMovie, offering you the chance to perform several tricky editing maneuvers you couldn't perform with iMovie alone.

This chapter covers both versions of the program, using QuickTime 7.6 for illustration purposes.

QuickTime Player (Free Version)

The free version of QuickTime Player is designed exclusively to *play* movies and sounds. You can open a movie file by double-clicking it, by dragging it onto the QuickTime Player icon, or by opening QuickTime Player and then choosing File → Open. As shown in Figure 15-1, a number of controls help you govern the movie's playback:

- **Audio level meters.** This tiny graph dances to indicate the relative strength of various frequencies in the soundtrack, like the VU meters on a stereo. If you don't see any dancing going on, then you've opened a movie that doesn't have a soundtrack.

- **Resize handle.** Drag diagonally to make the window bigger or smaller.

  TIP   When you drag the resize handle, QuickTime Player strives to maintain the same *aspect ratio* (relative dimensions) as the original movie, so that you don't accidentally squish it. If you want to squish it, however (perhaps for the special effect of seeing your loved ones as they would look with different sets of horizontal and vertical genes), press Shift as you drag.

  If you press Option while dragging, meanwhile, you'll discover that the movie frame grows or shrinks in sudden jumping factors of two—twice as big, four times as big, and so on. On slower Macs, keeping a movie at an even multiple of its original size ensures smoother playback.

- **Scroll bar.** Drag the diamond (or, in the Pro version, the black triangle) to jump to a different spot in the movie.

  TIP   You can also press the right and left arrow keys to step through the movie one frame at a time. If you press *Option*-right or -left arrow, you jump to the beginning or end of the movie. In the Pro version, Option-arrow also jumps to the beginning or ending of a selected stretch of the movie.

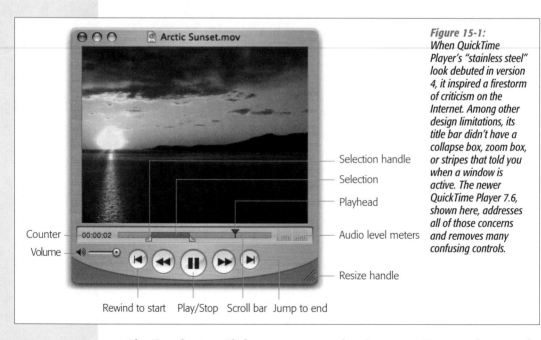

Figure 15-1:
When QuickTime Player's "stainless steel" look debuted in version 4, it inspired a firestorm of criticism on the Internet. Among other design limitations, its title bar didn't have a collapse box, zoom box, or stripes that told you when a window is active. The newer QuickTime Player 7.6, shown here, addresses all of those concerns and removes many confusing controls.

- **Play/Stop button.** Click once to start, and again to stop. You can also press the space bar, Return key, or ⌘-right arrow for this purpose. (Or avoid the buttons altogether and double-click the movie itself to start or stop playback.)

TIP   You can make any movie play automatically when opened, so that you avoid clicking the Play button. To do so, choose QuickTime Player → Preferences → Player Preferences, and turn on "Automatically play movies when opened."

• **Selection handles.** These tiny black triangles appear only in the $30 Pro version. You use them to select, or highlight, stretches of footage.

• **Volume.** If you like, you can make the soundtrack louder or softer by dragging this slider with your mouse or clicking in its "track." You may find it easier, however, to press the up or down arrow keys.

TIP   To mute the sound, click the little speaker icon, or press Option-down arrow. Press Option-up arrow to make the volume slider jump to full-blast position.

• **Counter.** In hours:minutes:seconds format, this display shows how far your diamond cursor has moved into the movie.

If you have QuickTime Pro, the counter reveals the position of the selection handle you've most recently clicked (if any).

FREQUENTLY ASKED QUESTION

QuickTime Player vs. QuickTime Player Pro

What's with all of these dimmed menu commands that say PRO beside their names?

That's Apple's subtle way of saying, "Just *look* at all you'd get if you upgraded your free player to the Pro version! All of these features await you!"

If you're convinced, then for $30, Apple will sell you a password that turns your copy of QuickTime Player into QuickTime Player Pro. (To obtain this password, call 888-295-0648, or click the Upgrade Now button to go online to *www.apple.com/quicktime/buy*.)

To record your password, choose QuickTime Player → Registration. Your password gets stored in your Home-folder → Library → Preferences folder, in a file called QuickTime Preferences. (Remember that when you upgrade to a new Mac.)

Once you've upgraded, you gain several immediate benefits—not the least of which is the permanent disappearance of the "upgrade now" advertisement. Now QuickTime Player is QuickTime Player Pro, and it's capable of editing your movies, as described later in this chapter.

It can also import many more sound and graphics formats, and—via the File → Export command—convert sounds, movies, and graphics into other formats.

Oh—and all of those dimmed commands come back to life and lose the little PRO logos.

Undo	⌘Z
Redo	⇧⌘Z
PRO Cut	⌘X
Copy	⌘C
PRO Paste	⌘V
PRO Delete	
PRO Select All	⌘A
PRO Select None	⌘B
PRO Trim to Selection	
PRO Add to Movie	⌥⌘V
PRO Add to Selection & Scale	⌥⇧⌘V
Find	▶
Special Characters...	⌥⌘T

- **Rewind, Fast-Forward.** By clicking one of these buttons and keeping the mouse button pressed, you get to speed through your movie backward or forward, complete with sound. This is a terrific way to navigate your movie quickly, regardless of whether you're using QuickTime Player or QuickTime Player Pro.

- **Jump to Start, Jump to End.** These buttons do exactly what they say: scroll to the beginning or end of your movie. In the Pro version, they can also jump to the beginning and ending of the selected portion of the movie (if any). All of this, in other words, is exactly the same as pressing the Option-left arrow or -right arrow keys.

> **TIP** Try minimizing a QuickTime Player window while a movie is playing. It shrinks to the Dock—and *keeps on playing*. Do this enough times, and you'll know what it's like to be Steve Jobs on stage.

Hidden Controls

Don't miss the Window → Show A/V Controls command. As shown in Figure 15-2, this is where you can fine-tune the video and audio you're experiencing.

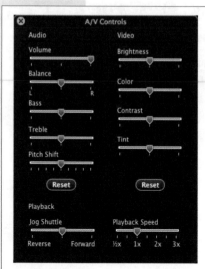

Figure 15-2:
Here's where you can adjust a QuickTime movie as though it's a TV set. Boost the brightness, turn up the treble, correct the color, and so on. Oddly enough, the two Playback sliders at the bottom aren't settings at all. Rather, they're real-time controls. Dragging the Jog Shuttle handle, for example, actually triggers forward or reverse playback at high speed, and dragging the Playback Speed handle makes playback proceed at the indicated multiple of real time. (Be careful, though. This one is also a setting. If you leave the slider at 3X and close the window, your movie will always play back at 3X and you probably won't know why.)

Fancy Playback Tricks

Nobody knows for sure what Apple was thinking when it created some of these additional features—exactly how often do you want your movie to play backward?—but here they are. Some of these features are available only in the unlocked Pro version of QuickTime Player, as indicated below:

- **Change the screen size.** Using the View menu commands, such as Double Size and Full Screen, you can enlarge or reduce the actual "movie screen" window.

Making the window larger also makes the movie coarser, because QuickTime Player simply doubles the size of every dot that was present in the original. Still, when you want to show a movie to a group of people more than a few feet away from the screen, these larger sizes are perfectly effective.

- **Play more than one movie.** You can open several movies at once and then run them simultaneously. (Of course, the more movies you try to play at once, the jerkier the playback gets.)

As a sanity preserver, QuickTime Player plays only one soundtrack—that of the movie you most currently clicked. If you really want to hear the cacophony of all the soundtracks being played simultaneously, choose QuickTime Player → Preferences, and turn off "Play sound in front most player only". (The related checkbox here, "Play sound when application is in background", controls what happens when you switch out of QuickTime Player and into another program.)

TIP   If you have QuickTime Player Pro, you can use the View → Play All Movies command to begin playback of all open movies at the same instant. It's a handy way to compare the quality of two or more copies of the same exported movie, each prepared with a different codec.

- **Play the movie backward.** You can play the movie backward—but not always smoothly—by pressing ⌘-left arrow, or by Shift-double-clicking the movie itself. (You must keep the Shift button pressed to make the backward playback continue.) There's no better way to listen for secret subliminal messages.

- **Loop the movie.** When you choose View → Loop and then click Play, the movie plays endlessly from beginning to end, repeating until you make it stop. (Loop Back and Forth makes it loop backward again, from end to beginning.)

- **Play Selection Only (Pro only).** View → Play Selection Only, of course, plays only what you've highlighted on the scrubber bar.

- **Play All Frames (Pro only).** If you try to play a very large movie that incorporates a high frame rate (many frames per second) on a slow Mac, QuickTime Player skips individual frames of the movie. In other words, it sacrifices smooth motion in order to maintain synchronization with the soundtrack.

But if you choose View → Play All Frames and then play the movie, QuickTime Player says, "OK, forget the soundtrack—I'll show you every single frame of the movie, even if it isn't at full speed." You get no sound at all, but you do get to see each frame of the movie.

QuickTime Player Pro

If you've spent the $30 to upgrade to the Pro version of QuickTime Player, you've unlocked a number of additional features. Some of these are playback tricks described in the previous section; others are especially useful for iMovie work. Read on.

Presenting Your Movies

After going to the trouble of editing down your footage (as described in Part 1) and exporting it as a QuickTime movie (as described in Chapter 14), what you may want to do most of all is to *show* the movie to other people. Even the non-Pro version of QuickTime Player can play movies, of course, but the Pro version offers a much better showcase for your work: the View → Present Movie command.

"Presenting" your movie is the best possible way to view a QuickTime movie on your screen. When you use this command (Figure 15-3), QuickTime Player blacks out the screen, automatically magnifies your monitor image (by choosing a lower resolution) so that the movie fills more of the screen, and devotes all the Mac's power to playing the movie smoothly. (To interrupt the movie, press ⌘-period.)

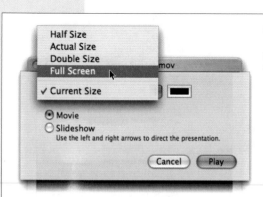

Figure 15-3:
The Present Movie command makes the movie fill your screen (although enlargement makes the movie grainier and coarser, which is why Apple gives you a choice here).

Editing Movies

The most powerful feature you gain in the Pro version is its ability to *edit* QuickTime movies. You can rearrange scenes, eliminate others, and save the result as a new movie with its own name.

All of this is perfectly possible within iMovie itself, of course, but sometimes you'll want to edit one of the QuickTime movies you've already exported from iMovie— to make it shorter for emailing, for example.

> **TIP** QuickTime Player can open all of iMovie's favorite formats (page 43). In fact, you can find all of the clips that iMovie knows about—every last shred of video in your Event browser—tucked away in your iMovie Events folder (see page 53), ready for double-clicking to examine in Quick-Time Player. This trick may come in handy if you want to edit a clip you've already imported, using some feature that's available only in QuickTime Player but not in iMovie.

Selecting footage

Before you can cut, copy, or paste footage, QuickTime Player needs to provide a way for you to specify *what* footage you want to manipulate. Its solution: the two tiny L-shaped handles beneath the horizontal scroll bar, visible in Figure 15-4.

These are the "in" and "out" points, exactly like the crop handles in iMovie. By dragging these handles, you're supposed to enclose the scene you want to cut or copy.

> **TIP** You can gain more precise control over the selection procedure by clicking one of the L-shaped handles and then pressing the right or left arrow key, exactly as when using the scrubber bar under iMovie's Monitor window. Doing so expands or contracts the selected chunk of footage by one frame at a time.
>
> You may also prefer to select a piece of footage by Shift-clicking the Play button. As long as you hold down the Shift key, you continue to select footage. When you release the Shift key, you stop the playback, and the selected passage appears in gray on the scroll bar.

Figure 15-4:
QuickTime Player Pro has a little-known subtitling feature, complete with freedom of type style. Copy some formatted text from a word processor; highlight a slice of footage in QuickTime Player; and choose Edit → "Add to Movie". The copied text appears as a subtitle on a black band, beneath the picture, as shown here.

Once you've highlighted a passage of footage, you can proceed as follows:

- Jump to the beginning or end of the selected footage by pressing Option-right or -left arrow key. (This doesn't work if one of the handles is highlighted.)

- Deselect the footage by dragging the two L-shaped handles together again.

- Play only the selected passage by choosing View → Play Selection Only. (The other Movie menu commands, such as Loop, apply only to the selection at this point.)

- Drag the movie picture out of the Player window and onto the desktop, where it becomes a *movie clipping* that you can double-click to view.

- Cut, copy, or clear the highlighted material using the commands in the Edit menu.

TIP   If you paste some copied text directly into QuickTime Player Pro, you get a 2-second title (such as an opening credit) at the current frame, professionally displayed as white type against a black background (Figure 15-4). QuickTime Player automatically uses the font, size, and style of the text that was in the text clipping. You can paste a graphic image, too; again, you get a 2-second "slide" of that still image.

If you find it easier, you can also drag a text or picture *clipping file* directly from the desktop into the QuickTime Player window; once again, you get a 2-second insert. To make the text or picture appear longer than 2 seconds, drag or paste it several times in a row.

In either case, you specify the fonts, sizes, and styles of your low-budget titling feature by format-ting the text that way *before* you copy it from your word processor. (This feature requires a word processor that preserves such formatting on the Clipboard. Most modern text processors, includ-ing Stickies, TextEdit, and Word, and most email programs, are all examples.)

Pasting footage

After cutting or copying footage, you can move it elsewhere in the movie. Specify where you want the pasted material to go by first clicking or dragging in the horizontal scroll bar, so that the black Playhead marks the spot; then choose Edit → Paste. The selection triangles (and their accompanying gray scroll bar section) show you where the new footage has appeared. (That makes it easy for you to promptly choose Edit → Cut, for example, if you change your mind.)

There are several variations of the Paste command at your disposal, too. They work like this:

- The Edit → "Trim to Selection" command is like the "Trim to Selection" com-mand in iMovie, in that it eliminates the outer parts of the movie—the pieces that *aren't* selected. All that remains is the part you first selected.

- The Edit → "Add to Movie" command adds whatever's on the Clipboard so that it plays *simultaneously* with the selected footage—a feature that's especially use-ful when you're adding a *different kind* of material to the movie. (See Figure 15-4.)

- If you highlight some footage and then choose Edit → "Add to Selection & Scale", whatever you're pasting gets stretched or compressed in time so that it fits the high-lighted region, speeding up or slowing down both audio and video. The effect can be powerful, comical, or just weird. (Can you say, "Alvin and the Chipmunks"?)

TIP   You can edit sounds exactly as you edit movies, using precisely the same commands and shortcuts. Use the File → Open command in QuickTime Player Pro to locate a sound file you want to open. It opens exactly like a QuickTime movie, except with only a scroll bar—no picture.

Exporting Edited Movies

After you've finished working on a sound or movie, you can send it back out into the world in any of several ways.

The Save As command

If you choose Edit → Save As, you're offered only two options, both of which can be confusing:

- **Save as a reference movie.** You'll almost never want to use this setting, which produces a very tiny file that contains no footage at all. Instead, it's something like an alias of the movie you edited. It works only as long as the original, unedited movie remains on your hard drive. If you try to email the newly saved file, your unhappy recipient won't see anything at all.

- **Save as a self-contained movie.** This option produces a new QuickTime movie—the one you've just finished editing. Although it consumes more disk space, it has none of the drawbacks of a "reference movie" file.

The Export command

Usually, your primary interest in using QuickTime Pro will be to export its edited clip, either for use in iMovie or to use in other programs (PowerPoint, Web pages, and so on).

When you find yourself in that situation, choose File → Export. The resulting dialog box should look familiar: It's the Save As dialog box that appears when you save an iMovie project as a QuickTime movie. This is your opportunity to specify the size, frame rate, color depth, special effects, and many other aspects of the movie you're about to spin off.

This is also where you can convert the QuickTime movie into some other format: AVI (Windows movie) format, Image Sequence (which produces a very large collection of individual graphics files, one per frame), and so on—or convert only the soundtrack to AIFF, System 7, or WAV (Windows) formats, for example.

How to Use QuickTime Player with iMovie

But as an iMovie fan, what you'll probably want to do the most is open your iMovie clips in QuickTime Player Pro, make changes to them, and then save them for further use in iMovie.

In that case, you'll probably adopt a routine like this:

1. **In iMovie, Control-click (or right-click) the clip you want to edit. From the shortcut menu, choose "Reveal in Finder".**

   You switch to the desktop, where the movie file's icon is highlighted and waiting in whatever window it calls home.

2. **Option-drag the movie icon to your desktop to make a copy of it. Double-click the copy.**

   The movie clip opens before you in QuickTime Player. Edit it as described in this chapter. (The following pages walk you through some rather spectacular special-effect edits.)

When you're finished editing, go on:

3. **Choose File → Save.**

You now have an edited version of the clip on your desktop.

4. **Switch back to iMovie. Choose File → Import Movies, then navigate to the desktop and open the edited movie.**

   After you indicate which Event you want it to join, the edited video becomes a new iMovie clip, which you can use to replace the original in your project, if you like. After the import, you can delete the one you saved to the desktop in step 2.

So why did you edit a copy, and not just save changes to the original clip?

Because if you edited one of iMovie's clips behind its back, iMovie wouldn't be able to update the tiny filmstrip movie that it uses to represent your video while you're editing. (It creates that filmstrip movie only when you import video the official way.)

And if the clip and its filmstrip don't match, you can't export the results—they're locked in iMovie forever.

Advanced QuickTime Pro: Track Tricks

As far as QuickTime Player is concerned, a piece of footage is nothing more than parallel *tracks* of information: audio and video. Most movies have only two tracks—one video and one audio—but there's nothing to stop you from piling on multiple audio tracks, overlapping video tracks, and even specialized layers like a text track or an animation track.

The key to understanding the multiple simultaneous tracks in a QuickTime movie is the Movie Properties dialog box (Figure 15-5). It opens when you choose Window → Show Movie Properties (⌘-J).

Here's some of the fun you can have at this point:

• **Turn off tracks.** Turn off the Enabled checkbox for any track you want to hide/ mute. This fascinating command highlights an intriguing feature of QuickTime Player Pro—its ability to embed more than one audio or video track into a single movie. If you really wanted to, you could create a movie with six different soundtracks, all playing simultaneously.

   Or maybe you've created two different versions of a movie—one with throbbing, insistent background music, and one with New Age noodling. Using this option, you can quickly and easily try watching your movie first with one soundtrack, and then with the other.

• **Extract Tracks.** Click a track name and click the Extract button (top left). "Extract" actually means *copy and separate* into a new Player window. (If you double-click a soundtrack, it appears as nothing but a scroll bar with no picture.)

At this point, you can copy some or all of the extracted track, in readiness to paste it into another movie.

• **Delete Tracks.** As the name implies, this button removes the selected track from the movie. For example, after experimenting to see which of several soundtracks you prefer (as described above), you'll want to delete the rejected versions before you save the final movie.

Now that you know the general workflow, here are a few recipes that illustrate how iMovie + QuickTime Player Pro = Fun and Creativity.

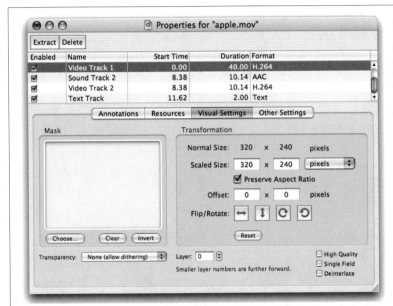

Figure 15-5:
The Movie Properties dialog box shows you all the parallel streams that go by when you play a movie: the various video, sound, and even text tracks. The Visual Settings tab is particularly useful for iMovie fans, because it lets you do things you can't do in iMovie (like flip a movie 90 degrees).

Flip a Clip

So you're making a gag movie of your buddy at work. You have a shot of him leaving the starting line in a potato-sack race at the office retreat. You want to splice in some old footage of Olympic track star Carl Lewis breaking through the tape, making it look like that's your buddy at the finish line. Only one problem: Your buddy is running from left to right in the shot, and Carl Lewis, in his shot, is running from right to left. How will you ever make that look right?

By fixing it first:

1. **Open the clip in QuickTime Player Pro.**

   See the steps on the previous two pages.

2. **Choose Window → Show Movie Properties (⌘-J).**

   The Properties dialog box appears (Figure 15-5).

3. **Click Video Track, and then click Visual Settings.**

You can now apply all kinds of freaky changes to this video track. The simple Rotate commands are available in iMovie itself—but not the *Flip* commands.

4. **Click the first Flip button (the first arrow button visible in Figure 15-5).**

As you watch, your entire video picture flips, mirror image.

5. **Save the edited movie. Switch back into iMovie and import the QuickTime file as described on page 44.**

Suddenly, you're a master at comedy.

The Video Wall

QuickTime Player isn't fussy. It's perfectly happy to accept two, three, four, or more videos, all pasted into the same clip. You can move, scale, and shrink them independently, creating a video-wall effect like the one shown in Figure 15-6.

To create this effect, just repeat the preceding steps, over and over again. The trick, of course, is keeping track of which videos are on top, so that you can control the overlapping.

Actually, it's not terribly difficult if you have good concentration and an assistant with a notebook; see Figure 15-6.

Figure 15-6:
Each time you paste another layer of video, it becomes a new track, listed independently in the Properties palette. (You might want to rename each track to help you keep them straight. Do that by double-clicking a track's name.)

To specify the front-to-back layering of your videos, choose a layer's name, and then click Visual Settings. Use the Layer control, circled here, to move this video track closer to the front of the stack. (Lower-numbered tracks cover up higher-numbered ones.)

Part Three:
iDVD '09

3

iDVD Basics

iDVD—the program, the legend—turns iMovie movies and iPhoto slideshows into Hollywood-style DVDs that people can watch on TV sets. iDVD lets you design DVDs' main menu screens, add playback controls, and otherwise dress up iMovie movies, resulting in dynamic, interactive DVDs that look amazingly professional. iDVD handles the technology; you control the style.

Not only are there lots of pro-style features and effects, but you can even burn widescreen DVDs—that is, ones with wide, rectangular, cinematic proportions that fit today's plasma and LCD digital TV screens.

The software requirement is iDVD. The hardware requirement is a DVD recorder, inside, or connected to, your Mac.

Why iDVD?

Don't look now, but Apple thinks that the era of the DVD has passed. iDVD '09, according to Steve Jobs, is "for people who still want to make DVDs." (His subtext: "Those losers!") The real action, he believes, is on the Internet.

But don't tell that to the 120 million U.S. families who don't have high-speed Internet access—or any Internet access at all—and therefore can't see online video. These people aren't on YouTube. They can't see your .Mac gallery. They almost certainly have DVD players, though. And producing your movies on DVD offers a wealth of benefits: They're small, light, and easy to mail. DVDs can last a long time—a century, if you believe the manufacturers—if you stick to brand-name blanks like Verbatim and Imation, and keep the burned discs in a cool, dry place.

Getting iDVD '09

If you own iMovie '09, you also have iDVD '09, because they both come on the same iLife DVD from Apple.

NOTE iDVD wasn't updated *at all* in the '09 version of the iLife suite. No new themes. No new features. It's precisely the same software that came with iLife '08.

You don't have to worry about iDVD's system requirements; if you can run iMovie, you can also run iDVD. But here again, faster computers work a lot better than slow ones. Even though the iDVD in iLife '09 has the same version number as the one that appears in iLife '08, Apple says it requires Mac OS X 10.5.6 or later.

What You're In For

In the following chapters, you can read about integrating movies, still pictures, and sound in very flexible ways; overriding Apple's design templates; and unlocking iDVD's darkest secrets. But what most people do at first is usually much simpler: They create the movie in iMovie, and then hand it off to iDVD for burning. Or they burn a DVD directly from the camcorder, using the OneStep DVD feature.

This chapter guides you through both of those rituals. Most of what you're about to read, though, covers the iMovie-to-iDVD sequence, which entails six broad steps:

1. **Prepare your audio, video, and pictures.**

   In addition to movies, iDVD can incorporate audio and graphics files into your shows. iDVD doesn't, however, give you any way to *create or edit* these files. You have to prepare them in other programs first.

2. **Insert chapter markers.**

   In a commercial Hollywood DVD, you can jump around the movie without rewinding or fast-forwarding, thanks to the movie's *scene menu* or *chapter menu*. It's basically a screen of bookmarks for certain scenes in the movie. (Although this chapter is about iDVD, you actually add your chapter markers in iMovie; see page 326.)

3. **Export the finished iMovie video.**

   iMovie '09 has a "Share to iDVD" function that makes sticking your home movie onto DVD very convenient.

4. **Design the menu screen.**

   In iDVD terms, a *menu* doesn't mean the kind that drops down from the top of the screen. Instead, a DVD menu is a menu *screen*, usually containing buttons that you click with the remote control. One button, called Play, starts playing the movie. Another, called Scene Selection, might take you to a second menu screen full of individual "chapter" buttons, so your audience doesn't have to start watching from the beginning if they don't want to.

DVD menu design is at the heart of iDVD. The program lets you specify where and how each button appears on the screen, and also lets you customize the overall look with backgrounds and titles.

5. **Add the movies to the DVD.**

Remember those videos you exported in step 3? Now that you've got a handsomely designed menu screen ready and waiting, you can drop them into place.

6. **Burn your DVD.**

To create a DVD, iDVD compresses your movie into the universal DVD file format, called *MPEG-2*, and then copies the results to a blank recordable DVD disc. This process, called *burning*, lets you produce a DVD that plays back either in a computer or in most set-top DVD players.

This chapter covers the details of these six steps.

Phase 1: Prepare Your Video

For the most professional results, prepare your video in iMovie (or another video editing program) before importing it into iDVD. Here are a couple of key issues to keep in mind.

Overscanning and You

Millions of TV viewers every day are blissfully unaware that they're missing the big picture. In TV's early days, the little cathode-ray guns inside the TV worked by painting one line of the TV picture, then turning around and heading back the opposite direction. To make sure that the screen was painted edge to edge, these early TVs were programmed to overshoot the edges of the screen—to use the technical term, to *overscan* the screen.

TV technology is much better now, but even modern standard-definition tube TVs exhibit overscanning. The amount varies, but you may be missing as much as 10 percent of the picture beyond the left and right edges (and often the top and bottom, too).

TV producers are careful to keep the action and titles in the part of the frame that's least likely to be lost in the overscan. If you plan to edit your film, the TV-safe area is suddenly your concern, too. The overscanning effect means that when you show your iMovie productions on a TV, you'll lose anything that's very close to the edges of the frame. In particular, broadcasters refer to two danger margins of a video image: the *title-safe area* and the *action-safe area* (see Figure 16-1).

NOTE   Flat-panel TV sets like plasmas and LCDs don't have picture tubes, and therefore don't overscan.

COMPLAINT DEPARTMENT

What About HDTVs?

It's pretty amazing that a cheapo program like iMovie lets you edit and play high-definition video. Ahead of the curve, baby!

Well, sort of. Once you're finished, where are you going to play the finished hi-def movie? You can send it to the Web, or you can view it on your Mac—but weirdly enough, Apple doesn't have any suggestions for getting your hi-def movies onto your hi-def *television*. (Sure, you can burn a DVD, but DVDs aren't hi-def.)

It isn't that Apple's ignoring HDTVs. The problem is that its answer—the Apple TV—is, in Steve Jobs's words, "a hobby." Not many people have an Apple TV, and most people may never get one as long as the Apple TV remains an Apple hobby. (That said, if you *do* have an Apple TV, it can play 720-pixel high-def video files from your Mac, so it's at least an option.)

So without an Apple TV, how *do* you get your hi-def home movies onto your HDTV? There are dozens of answers, none great. Here's a brief rundown of the most prominent methods.

- **Connect your computer to your HDTV**. With the right cable and the right connections, you may be able to treat your HDTV as an external monitor for your Mac. Usually, you'll connect the DVI port on the Mac to the VGA jack on the TV, so you'll need (what else?) a DVI-to-VGA cable. (Some HDTVs have DVI ports instead of VGA, which means that a plain old DVI cable fits the bill.) Amazon.com has cables galore, so you shouldn't have trouble finding one.

Of course, the problems with this approach are that (a) your computer and TV might not be in the same room, and (b) you have to run back to the Mac to control the movie playback. Laptop owners win this round.

- **Use your Xbox 360/PS3/Tivo HD/[Insert Device Name Here].** Each of these living-room-connected machines is capable of playing back videos. But copying your videos onto their hard drives isn't a simple process. Let Google be your friend in hunting down the step-by-steps. Almost certainly, you'll spend a lot of time exporting your movies via QuickTime, so get to know Chapter 14 well.

- **Burn a Blu-ray Movie.** The screamingly obvious solution, of course, is, "Burn your movie to a Blu-ray DVD, and then play that on your TV!" How ironic, then, that, at least at this writing, Macs don't come with Blu-ray burning drives. And even if they did, you can't use iDVD '09 to burn them. You'd have to buy another company's Blu-ray burner and another company's software—like Toast, for example.

The whole thing, alas, is complicated and expensive. Steve Jobs wasn't kidding when he called Blu-ray a "bag of hurt."

The title-safe area

When a TV chops off parts of your title, making it difficult or impossible to read, your audience can't help but notice (see Figure 16-1). In some old versions of iMovie, you had to be careful when preparing onscreen credits and titles: If you chose the largest font size, they could wind up getting lopped off at the outer limits of the screen. In iMovie '09, however, you don't have to worry: The program doesn't let a title expand into the outer 10 percent on either side.

Title-safe boundary   Action-safe boundary

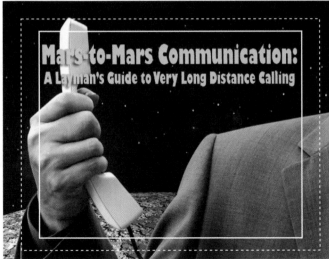

Figure 16-1:

Top: Avoid placing key visual action outside the action-safe area of your video. Objects that appear outside the title-safe area may be cropped; objects outside the action-safe area almost certainly will be cropped by North American picture-tube TV sets.

Bottom: Although you should keep all key visual elements within the title-safe area, you can let non-vital portions of those elements (like the knuckles and cord in this example) stray into the action-safe area.

The action-safe area

Professional broadcasters also refer to the *action-safe* area of the screen. It's not quite as broad a margin as the title-safe area, because your audience can usually figure out what's going on even if the action is slightly clipped at the outer edges of the screen. Still, it's vital that your action remains mostly within the central portion of the screen.

Imagine, for example, a science-fiction video. A mysterious enemy teleports your hero and his sidekick to a moon of Jupiter. The sidekick throws something to the hero—something that can save the day. In Figure 16-1 at top, for example, what's in the hero's hand may be obvious to you, but most TV viewers would have a hard time guessing what it is because it's outside of the action-safe area.

In Figure 16-1 at bottom, the sidekick's hand and the phone he throws appear completely within the action-safe area. Even if the TV winds up chopping off the outer edges of the picture, the visual story is preserved, and your hero can safely call home.

> **NOTE**   Readers and their lawyers will please forgive the science of this example, in that (a) there's no such thing as teleportation; (b) there's no air to breathe on the moons of Jupiter, let alone to talk with; (c) the hero and his colleague would die almost instantly from catastrophic depressurization; and (d) even assuming the hero could make the call out, the speed of light ensures that it would take hours for his message to reach earth. When writing computer books, authors are limited to the royalty-free art collections they have on hand. The art used here appears courtesy of Ulead's Royalty-Free Media collection.

You can keep your action within the action-safe area in one of two ways:

- **Frame correctly to begin with.** Keeping important visual features and motion away from the edges of your video as you record it is by far the easiest solution.

- **Resize the footage.** You can resize your video and center it within the frame using iMovie's Crop tool (see page 166). This approach, however, may degrade your video quality.

Phase 2: Insert Chapter Markers

If you've ever rented or bought a movie on DVD, you're already familiar with *chapters*, better known as scenes (Figure 16-2).

DVD chapters let viewers skip to predefined starting points within a movie, or pick up where they last left off watching, either by using the scene menu or by pressing the Next Chapter or Previous Chapter buttons on the remote control.

As part of its effort to de-emphasize the DVD, Apple took the chapter-marker feature out of iMovie '08—but when the uproar was deafening, restored it in iMovie '09, better than ever.

Actually, there are *four* ways to go about it. In spite of iMovie '09's chapter-marking prowess, all four options have their place:

- **Use iMovie '09.** Hands down the easiest and most convenient. This will probably be your chapter marker of choice 99 percent of the time.

Figure 16-2:
*Most DVDs have
something called a scene
menu, like this one (from
the movie Ronin), which
lets viewers jump directly
to their favorite scenes in
the movie. Your DVD
scene menus probably
won't be quite this
elaborate, but you get
the idea.*

- **Export the movie to iMovie 6.** If you ended up with your movie in iMovie 6 (the reasons and method are covered on page 256), you can head straight from there to iDVD. The older iMovie has a really great chapter-adding feature.

- **Export the movie to GarageBand.** GarageBand has convenient chapter-adding features, too—*and* a Send to iDVD command just like iMovie's. If you use GarageBand to edit your audio tracks anyway (page 222), it might make sense to add your chapters at that point.

- **Use iDVD's automatic chapter-marker feature.** iDVD can add markers to a movie *for* you—but it places them at even intervals, like every 4 minutes. You don't have the freedom to place the markers where you want them—at logical scene breaks, for example.

The first method is described on the following pages. The other three are covered in this chapter's free downloadable appendix, "More Chapter Markers." It's available on this book's "Missing CD" at *www.missingmanuals.com.*

> **NOTE**   Any DVD markers you create also appear on an Apple TV or anything else that works with QuickTime files: iTunes, iPods, iPhones, Front Row, QuickTime Player, DVD Player, and most DVD players.

Markers in iMovie '09

Chapter markers in iMovie '09 work something like sticky notes in a book. You grab one, stick it where you want it, and then type a name for it. It's about as easy as it gets.

Before you begin, turn on the Advanced Tools, a process covered on page 80.

Then, if you examine the upper-left corner of the project window closely, you'll find two little stowaways:

- **Comment markers.** The tiny brown speech bubble represents *comment markers*. The idea here is to let you annotate your movie. It can remind you of further work you want to do ("Maybe add a different song here"), identify someone in the video (in a way that won't actually appear during playback), and so on.

- **Chapter markers.** The tiny orange bubble with a white arrow inside represents *chapter markers*—the ones that survive the transition to a DVD.

Both kinds of markers can be very handy when you're working on longer projects, because a pop-up menu lets you jump directly to the marked moments without having to hunt and scroll.

To add a marker, drag your mouse from one of these marker "trays" directly to the appropriate spot in your project. Once you release the mouse, a small rectangular marker appears at that spot in the filmstrip, numbered sequentially (Figure 16-3).

Figure 16-3:
To insert a chapter marker, just drag one from the "tray" above the Project window onto the appropriate spot in your project. Rename it by double-clicking the text so it becomes editable, and then type whatever you want. You can select any of your markers using the handy marker menu that sits next to your marker tray.

> **TIP**   Double-click one of these markers to rename it; you're not stuck with numbers. Type "Day 3: Disney," for example, or "Mom Takes a Spill." Whatever chapter names you choose will show up in your DVD menus.

If your project is long, and the chapter markers are plentiful, they become an efficient navigational tool. There's a tiny pop-up menu above the project-area scroll bar. Click the ▼ to reveal a list of all your markers, both comments and chapters. Choose one to jump to that spot (and highlight the chosen marker).

TIP   You can also insert chapter markers without dragging. Control-click (or right-click) any spot in a filmstrip and, from the shortcut menu, choose Add Chapter Marker. This method inserts chapter markers at the Playhead, which is incredibly handy if you're skimming your project and find the precise spot for the next marker.

Chapter-marker pointers

A few things to note about chapter markers:

- **When you move, copy, or erase clips, chapter markers go along for the ride.** iMovie associates chapters with individual clips.

- **There's a "secret" unlisted chapter.** iMovie and iDVD always create one more chapter than you see on the iDVD Chapters list. This extra chapter corresponds to the very beginning of your movie (00:00:00), and starts out with the label "Start". (You don't see it until you arrive in iDVD.)

  TIP   To get rid of the secret "Start" chapter, create your own chapter marker at the very beginning of your project.

- **Your finished iDVD screens can fit up to 12 buttons per screen.** That's "up to," because the actual number depends on the *theme* you pick.

Phase 3: Export from iMovie '09

If you skipped the chapter marking fun in Phase 2, sending your masterpiece to iDVD is just one menu click away: choose Share → iDVD. iMovie takes the time to encode your movie into a format iDVD recognizes. Once the encoding is done, iDVD opens, creates a new project, and then plugs your movie into the DVD menu.

NOTE   Behind the scenes, what format do you guess Apple uses for the encoding step that comes pre-iDVD? None other than Apple Intermediate Codec, the same format used for encoding AVCHD footage for editing (page 7) and the same one used for preparing a clip to go fast, slow, or in reverse (page 141).

Export the Movie as a File

Sharing to iDVD via the menu command has one potentially annoying outcome: it always inserts your movie into a new project. Not a big deal if you're starting from scratch, but if you want more than one iMovie on a single DVD, the "Share to iDVD" command only works once.

Happily, this isn't the only way to insert a movie into iDVD. You can also incorporate additional movies into an *existing* DVD—but only if you've first exported them as QuickTime files.

Follow the instructions on page 258, which guide you through creating a Quick-Time movie file in the Apple Intermediate format.

TIP   Save the file into your Movies folder. That way, iDVD will have easy access to it, as described later in this chapter.

POWER USERS' CLINIC

Exporting from Final Cut

If you're reading this book, then you're probably using iMovie to edit your movies. But it's conceivable that you're using one of Apple's two more powerful programs, Final Cut Express or Final Cut Pro. And there's no reason you can't turn those movies into DVDs using iDVD, too.

In Final Cut, click the sequence (movie) you want to export, and then choose File → Export → QuickTime Movie. In the Save dialog box that appears, choose Chapter Markers from the Markers pop-up menu (if, of course, you've actually added these markers). Turn off "Make movie self-contained."

From the Setting pop-up menu, choose NTSC DV (the North American video standard) or PAL (Europe). Navigate to your Movies folder, and then click Save. Final Cut creates a tiny QuickTime file on your hard drive—a reference movie, it's called—which is much smaller and faster to create than a full, self-contained QuickTime movie. As long as you don't delete the original movie files used in your Final Cut project, iDVD knows exactly what to do.

Finally, go to iDVD and add the movie to your menu screen as described in Chapter 17.

Phase 4: Design the Menu Screen

Once your movies are safely exported from iMovie, and you've added chapter markers if you want them, open up iDVD itself.

The opening screen gives you four options (Figure 16-4, top):

- **Create a New Project.** In this program, "project" refers to a DVD that you're designing. It's not a "project" as iMovie refers to it.

- **Open an Existing Project.** Just burning a DVD doesn't mean the end of your project. You can open it up again later to burn another copy of that DVD, or make changes, and *then* burn it.

- **Magic iDVD.** This feature, too, avoids any iMovie involvement. But this time, Magic iDVD creates a DVD using a bunch of pictures, movies, and music files as its raw material. See page 347.

- **OneStep DVD** is a one-click method of dumping a videotape onto a DVD, right from the camcorder, bypassing iMovie altogether. See page 345.

To create a new DVD for the first time, click Create a New Project. You now have three choices to make (Figure 16-4, bottom):

- **Name the project.** What you type here won't appear on the DVD; it's just a file name for organizational purposes on your Mac.

- **Choose where to save it.** iDVD suggests your Documents folder, but you can choose anywhere you like.

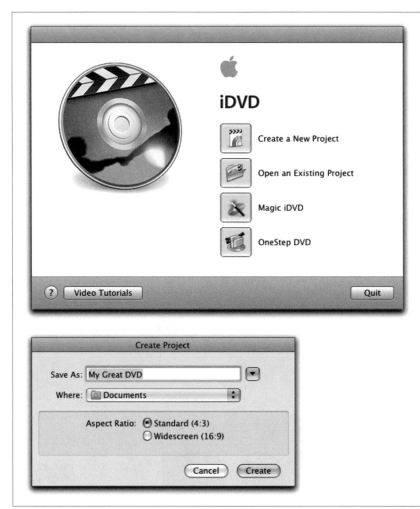

Figure 16-4:
Top: You have four options. Or you can ignore this dialog box and choose commands from the File menu, like Open Recent.

Bottom: Choose a name, location, and aspect ratio for the movie.

• **Choose an aspect ratio.** This is actually a pretty big decision: iDVD is asking what shape TV you'll be playing the DVD on.

If you choose Standard (4:3), then the DVD will perfectly fit standard, traditional, squarish TV screens. But when played on widescreen sets, you'll get black vertical bars on either side of the picture.

If you choose Widescreen (16:9), then the opposite will happen. The DVD will look fantastic on, and completely fill, high-def TV screens and other widescreen sets—but will have *horizontal* letterbox bars when played on an older, standard set.

TIP   You can always change your mind about the aspect ratio later by choosing Project → "Switch to Standard (4:3)" or "Switch to Widescreen (16:9)".

Once you've made your choices, click Create.

> **NOTE** If you've arrived here from iMovie '09, iMovie 6, or GarageBand, you may not see the options shown in Figure 16-4. Instead, you might see a predesigned menu screen like the one shown in Figure 16-5. If you added chapter markers, for example, you'll find two buttons: Play (meaning "Play the movie from the beginning") and Scene Selection. On the finished DVD, this button takes your audience to a second screen, which is filled with individual buttons for the chapters you created. In fact, this second screen may well have arrows that lead to *third and fourth* screens, since iDVD menus vary in the number of buttons that fit per screen.

All about Themes

The design of the DVD menu screen that's now before you is called a *theme:* a unified design scheme that governs how the menus look and behave, complete with attractive backgrounds, coordinated typography, and background music (Figure 16-5).

> **TIP** If the Apple logo appears in the lower-right corner of your iDVD Project, you can intervene. Choose iDVD → Preferences and turn off "Show Apple logo watermark".

iDVD '09 has over 150 of these themes. Each theme family contains a main-menu screen, a chapter navigation screen, and an extras screen for bonus DVD features you can build with iDVD.

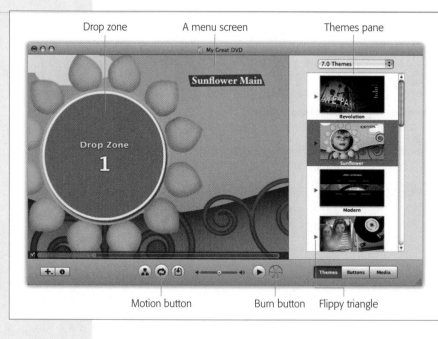

Drop zone   A menu screen   Themes pane

Motion button   Burn button   Flippy triangle

Figure 16-5:
In iDVD, you add, edit, and manipulate the buttons, pictures, movies, and titles that make up the menus for your DVD. The "drawer" at the right side is a permanent fixture, always open and always on the right. It's the portion identified here as the Themes pane.

It takes a lot of individual design decisions to make a theme. For example:

- **Background image or video**. Whatever art appears in the background, whether still images or video clips, is part of the theme. The movement of the desert in the Anime Pop theme is one example of video in action.

    NOTE   Many themes are animated with a repetitive looping; many have music, too. The Motion button (⇆) turns the looping motion and the music on and off while you're working on a DVD. (It doesn't affect the finished DVD, however.)

- **Button type**. The buttons in an iDVD project can be either little graphics or text phrases that your audience will click with the remote control.

- **Button look**. The look of your buttons can vary. Text buttons may have simple backgrounds; graphic buttons may have borders.

- **Button positions**. Each menu can accommodate up to 12 buttons, depending on the theme you've chosen. Themes are preset to place their buttons in certain favored positions.

- **Drop zones**. *Drop zones* are areas into which you can drag a favorite video clip (sometimes more than one) that plays continuously as a background for the main menu screen. If you've ever seen a commercial Hollywood DVD movie, you've seen this effect. One key scene from the movie plays over and over, looping until you choose one of the buttons on the menu screen—or go quietly insane. *Dynamic* drop zones can even move across the screen, passing in front of each other, providing amazing visual effects.

- **Text boxes**. Text boxes let you freely add text blocks to your menu screens. You could use one, for example, to provide instructions to your viewers, copyright notices, or details about what they're about to see.

- **Font selections**. Themes also specify the color, font size, and typeface for menu titles and buttons.

Figure 16-6 shows two very different looks for the same project. The difference lies only in the chosen theme.

Choosing a Theme

iDVD '09 starts up with a very cool-looking, high-tech, black-on-black theme called Revolution Chapters (Figure 16-6, bottom), but goodness knows, you're not stuck with that one. A wide range of canned themes awaits your inspection.

To see them, make sure that the Themes button is selected (lower-right corner of iDVD). Then choose a theme *set* from the pop-up menu at the top of the Themes palette. iDVD has four built-in sets, each named for the version of iDVD that first included them: 7.0 Themes, 6.0 Themes, 5.0 Themes, and Old Themes (from iDVD 3 and 4).

Figure 16-6:
iDVD Themes can create strikingly different menu screens for similar projects.

Top: The Forever theme (shown in the traditional 4:3, squarish shape here) displays gracefully sliding photos (or videos) in the drop zones as they float from right to left; a string quartet plays.

Bottom: The Revolution Chapters theme (shown in its widescreen, 16:9 shape) has a stunning, high-tech look. Its features two counter-rotating cylinders, one bearing your project's name and the other displaying what you've put into the drop zones.

Within most themes, you can click the flippy triangle (Figure 16-5) to reveal *variations* of that theme—a complementary menu design for the scene-selection screen, for your DVD extras page, and so on. If you've bought additional themes online, this pop-up menu may offer other choices. In any case, you can use this pop-up menu to switch between them, or just choose All to see all installed themes in a single scrolling list. Scroll through the list of themes, clicking each one to see what it looks like in the main work area, or just rely on the little thumbnail icons to get a sense of the theme's overall flavor.

NOTE All of the themes in the 6.0 and 7.0 collections appear, at first, to be suitable only for widescreen DVDs. If you're making a standard 4:3 DVD, then every time you click one of these themes, the Change Project Aspect Ratio warning box appears, asking if you really intended to *change* the project to 16:9. It gets annoying fast. (Yes, you could turn on "Do not ask me again," but then it changes to widescreen every time *without* asking you.)

So for best results in looking over the themes, do so in widescreen mode, just to avoid being interrupted by that warning. You can always switch to the 4:3 version of a theme later by choosing Project → "Switch to Standard (4:3)".

If your DVD menu system consists of only a single screen—the main menu you've been looking at the whole time—it takes on your chosen theme instantly. A movie that has chapter markers in it, however, has at least one additional menu screen: your scene-selection screen. In that case, when you click a theme thumbnail, iDVD asks if you want to apply the theme family to the entire project, so that the main menu and the Scene Selection menus match; almost always, this is what you want. Figure 16-7 shows how.

TIP You can also apply a theme to all the menus later by choosing Advanced → "Apply Theme to Project". Or you can apply a theme only to the *submenus*—not the main screen—by choosing Advanced → "Apply Theme to Submenus".

Figure 16-7:
As a rule, always use a single theme family for your entire project. When this message appears, turn on "Do not ask me again," and then click OK. Doing this ensures that every screen in your project looks consistent. Good idea, good design.

When you're happy with the way the new theme looks, you're ready to proceed with your iDVD design work. Fortunately, you don't have to commit to the theme right now; you can change to a different theme at any time until you actually burn the DVD.

TIP You can buy additional themes, or download free samples, from other companies (like *http://iDVDThemePAK.com*). Install them by creating a folder called Favorites in your Library folder (the Library folder in the main hard drive window, not in your Home folder), and then putting them inside.

The Inevitable Paragraphs about Aspect Ratio

As you probably know, there are two popular *aspect ratios*—screen shapes—for television these days: standard 4:3 and widescreen (see page 56). iDVD '09 can create DVDs in either format; see Figure 16-8. You're asked to choose which format you want when you first create a project, and you can switch to the other format at any time, using the Project menu.

Now, it turns out that all of the iDVD 6.0 and 7.0 themes have been cleverly designed to look great on *both* standard and widescreen TV sets. Figure 16-8 explains all. So if the menu screens will always look good, regardless of TV shape, why not just choose widescreen format for *every* DVD you make?

Figure 16-8:
Each of the "widescreenable" themes comes in two versions: a standard 4:3 version (top) and a widescreen version (bottom). The question is: What happens if you create a widescreen DVD, and then play it on a 4:3 standard television? If you'd like to find out, choose View → Show Standard Crop Area. iDVD responds by dimming the outer right and left edges of the picture, showing you which portions won't appear on a 4:3 traditional television. What you'll discover is that Apple has cleverly designed the widescreen themes so that all the important stuff—drop zones, buttons, titles, and so on—are close enough to the center that they won't be chopped off on a standard TV. In fact, in most cases, there's very little difference between the 4:3 version of a theme (top) and the not-chopped-off portion of a widescreen theme (bottom). The bottom line: Choosing widescreen format for a DVD generally means that the menus will play beautifully on both standard and widescreen TV sets. But the video on the DVD is another matter.

Because the *video* on your DVD isn't so accommodating! If it's been shot in wide-screen, and it's played back on a standard set, you'll probably wind up with letter-box bars above and below. And if it's been shot in standard 4:3 format, then playing it on a widescreen set will result in black bars on the sides. The bottom line: Choose the aspect ratio for your DVD according to the aspect ratio of the video that's on it.

Drop Zones: The Basics

Drop zones let you use video, slideshows, or stills as the backgrounds of your menu screens. They're purely decorative, designed to entertain your audience as they study their choices on the menu. (You install these videos or pictures by *dropping* them into the designated *zones* in the menu design—hence the name.) Not every theme has drop zones, but most of the iDVD 5, 6, and 7 themes do. As if you couldn't guess, the words "Drop Zone" (Figure 16-9) indicate where the drop zones are.

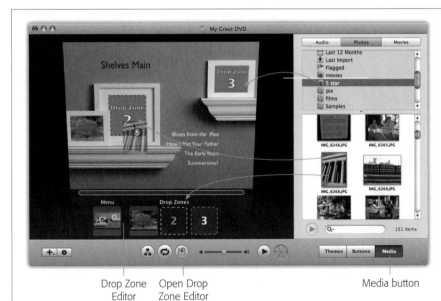

Drop Zone   Open Drop   Media button
Editor   Zone Editor

Figure 16-9:
Double-click any drop zone, or click the Drop Zone Editor button, to bring up the interactive Drop Zone editor shown here. Note that drop zones aren't always perfect rectangles or squares, so your video or photo may get clipped around the edges. You can fill drop zones with individual photos, bunches of photos (for a slideshow effect), or movies.

TIP If you don't see the telltale phrase "Drop Zone" followed by a number, choose iDVD → Preferences. Click the General icon, and then turn on "Show drop zone labels." (Turning off this checkbox only hides the words "Drop Zone," not the drop zones themselves.)

Note that not all drop zones may be onscreen at once; the drop zones in several themes take their time in parading onto the screen, or rotating through it. To see all the drop zones in your chosen theme, click the Show Drop Zones button below the screen. As shown in Figure 16-9, you're now shown thumbnail placeholders for all of the drop zones in this theme's animation.

Filling drop zones

iDVD gives you four ways to fill these empty gray spaces with videos and pictures:

- **Drag directly into the full-size rectangle.** This technique is shown in the top example in Figure 16-9. Most of the time, you'll be dragging videos or pictures from the Media Browser. (Click the Media button at the lower-right corner of iDVD, and then click either Photos or Movies at the top.)

- **Drag into the Drop Zone editor.** To open the new Drop Zone editor, click Editor as shown in Figure 16-9. Thumbnails appear beneath the menu screen with dotted lines, all present and accounted for, so that you don't have to wait for them to cycle into view in the main display window.

   TIP   The drop zone wells are also navigational bookmarks; if you click one, the monitor window displays that moment in the menu animation.

- **Let iDVD fill the zones.** Choose Project → Autofill Drop Zones. iDVD loads photos or movies—of its choosing—into the drop zones of the theme automatically.

- **Choose a picture or movie from the hard drive.** Control-click (or right-click) a drop zone; from the shortcut menu, choose Import. Find and open a movie, slideshow, picture, or folder full of pictures. iDVD uses that material to fill the drop zone.

Drop zones: the details

No matter which view of the drop zones you're using, here's how things work:

- **Hiding the drop zones.** Drop-zone animation can be stunning, but filling the zones can take time and tweaking. When you're in a hurry, or when you actually prefer the theme design *without* those zones, you can remove the drop-zone elements from the theme entirely. Choose View → Inspector (or press ⌘-I), and then turn off "Show drop zones and related graphics".

- **Adding to a drop zone.** Drag any video, photo album, image, or collection of images right into a drop zone outline to install it there. You can drag icons out of the Finder, or directly out of the Media pane.

   NOTE   Albums in drop zones can display 99 images at most. What you'll get is a mini-slideshow, right there within the drop zone. (More on dragging out of the Photos pane in Chapter 19.)

- **Replacing items in a drop zone.** Just drag something new into the drop zone.

- **Removing items from a drop zone.** To empty out the drop zone, drag away from the spot, just as you'd drag something off the Mac OS X Dock or the Sidebar. You get a cute little puff of smoke to indicate the movie or picture's disappearance.

- **Turning on motion.** If you've installed video into a drop zone and it doesn't seem to be playing, click the Motion button (⟳) at the bottom of the iDVD window, or press ⌘-J.

  Turning off Motion also turns off any background audio track and brings motion menus and motion buttons to a standstill.

  NOTE The status of the Motion button has no effect on the final DVD, which always shows the animations and plays the music.

- **Editing a drop-zone slideshow or movie.** If you've created a movie or slideshow drop zone, you have some additional editing powers available to you—like deciding what order the photos appear in the slideshow, or which part of the movie loops within the zone. (See page 376 for more on Drop Zone editing.)

Redesigning the Theme

You can change every tiny aspect of your theme—if you have the time and patience. If you're so inclined, turn to Chapter 18 for a full discussion of theme creation.

Phase 5: Add Your Movies

See page 351 for details on the many ways to install movies and pictures into the guts of your DVD.

Phase 6: Burning Your DVD

You're almost ready to burn the DVD. Before you go using up a blank disc, however, test it to make sure that it works on the virtual DVD player known as the Macintosh.

Previewing Your Project

iDVD's Play button (▶) lets you test your DVD to avoid unpleasant surprises. It enters Preview mode, which simulates how your DVD works on a standalone set-top DVD player. You even get a simulated remote control to help you navigate through your DVD's menus, movies, and so on, as shown in Figure 16-10. To return to iDVD's edit mode, click Exit or Stop (■).

> **TIP** Instead of using the arrow buttons on the remote to highlight and click screen buttons, just use your mouse. You'll find it's not only less clumsy, but also a decent indication of how your DVD will play back on computers that can play DVDs.

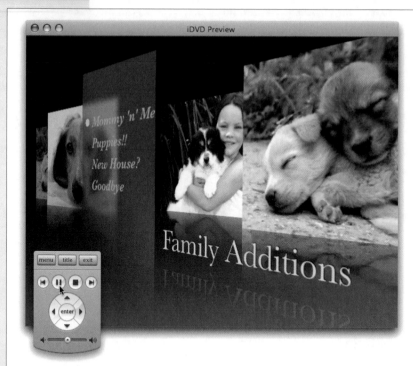

Figure 16-10:
To "click" your onscreen buttons, use the arrows on the remote to highlight the one you want, and then click the Enter button in the middle of the remote. Click the ◄ or ► buttons to skip back or forward by one chapter, or hold them down to rewind or fast-forward.

Checking for Errors

A DVD is a complex beast. Behind the scenes, there's all kinds of programming and linking going on—and any number of things could result in a DVD that doesn't work right after it's burned.

Before you proceed, click the DVD Map icon identified in Figure 17-5 (page 357). On the map, red stop-sign icons or yellow exclamation-point triangles appear on any screen of your DVD where problems await. For example:

- You created a slideshow, but forgot to add slides to it.

- You created a new menu screen, but didn't add anything to it.

- You haven't filled in all the drop zones.

Work through these alerts, resolving the problems one by one.

Maximum DVD Playback Time

When a DVD-burning program goes to work, it faces an important decision. Given that a blank single-layer DVD contains a limited amount of space (4.7 GB or so), how much picture-quality data can it afford to devote to each frame of video?

GEM IN THE ROUGH

Secrets of the Theme Scrubber

iDVD's scrubber bar (the thin white scroll bar beneath the menu screen) lets you preview the animation for a certain theme. You can let it play automatically (click the Motion ⇄ button) or you can drag the scroll handle to zip through it, watching how the theme changes over time. Or press the arrow keys to step one frame at a time.

Many themes, including the one shown here, include a "play once" introduction—a preliminary animation that plays before your menu buttons even appear. It's represented in iDVD by a crosshatched area of the scrubber bar, to the left of the main section (which represents the looping portion of your menu animation). Some themes also have a crosshatched area at the end, a "play-out" portion that helps link back to the beginning of the loop.

At times, you might want to turn off that introductory animation—for example, when you're designing secondary menu screens (like the Scene Selection screen). If you turn off the checkbox to the left of the scrubber, you hide the crosshatched section of the scrubber bar. You also eliminate the introductory portion, both as it plays in iDVD and on the final, burned DVD. Now, only the main, looping portion of the menu-screen animation plays. (You can always restore the intro by turning the checkbox back on again.) Similarly, the checkbox at the right end of the scrubber hides the play-out animation.

Speaking of scrubber-bar secrets: If you turn off the Motion (⇄) button at the bottom of the iDVD screen, you bring the menu's animation to a halt. (This step doesn't affect the motion in the finished DVD.) Once Motion is turned off, you can drag the scrubber. Oh, and you can choose View → Hide Motion Playhead to tuck the scrubber bar out of sight and View → Show Motion Playhead to bring it back.

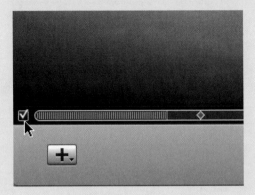

iDVD offers three approaches. (You make your choice for the *current* project by choosing Project → Project Info, or for *future* projects by choosing iDVD → Preferences, and then clicking the Projects button.) As Figure 16-11 shows, your options are:

- **Best Performance.** Your video will look fantastic, and your Mac can burn the disc relatively quickly. On the downside, the DVD you burn this way can contain a maximum of 60 minutes of video for standard DVDs. (You get about 120 minutes for dual-layer DVDs; see page 344.)

  The Best Performance option thinks like this: "Since I don't have to fit very much video on this disc, then hey—I can devote the maximum amount of data to each frame of video, for great quality. But it's a fixed amount. Not having to calculate how much data to allot to each frame will save me time and make the burning process go quickly."

NOTE Part of what makes this method burn your disc so fast is that it does a lot of advance work in the background *while* you're designing your DVD. That's good because it saves you time, but bad because, on slower Macs, it can make iDVD feel sluggish. If your Mac bogs down, choose Advanced → "Encode in Background" to turn off that feature.

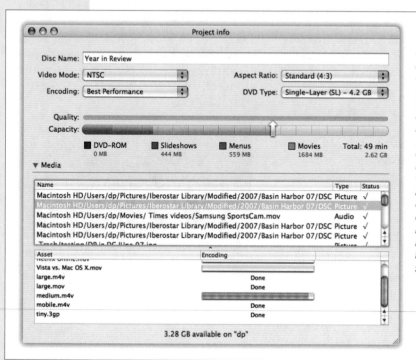

Figure 16-11:
This panel shows all the details of your DVD: how much material is on the disc, which aspect ratio, what kind of DVD (single- or dual-layer), and so on. Note: As the white arrow moves from green (excellent) into yellow, orange, and then red on the Quality graph, the video quality goes down. If you change the encoding setting for a one-hour video from Best Performance to Professional, you'll see that the Pro option gives superior results.

Before you burn a disc, confirm that a checkmark appears next to each *asset* (that is, each picture, movie, soundtrack, or what have you).

- **High Quality.** This option lets a standard DVD hold up to 120 minutes of video (or, on double-layer blanks, nearly four hours' worth). The tradeoff: It takes a lot longer to burn your DVD, since iDVD performs a deep analysis before burning.

  This option makes iDVD think, "I'm going to use every micron of space on this blank DVD. I'm going to analyze the amount of video, and divide it into the amount of space available on the DVD. The amount of data used to describe an individual frame of video will vary from project to project, and it will take me a lot longer to burn the DVD because I'm going to have to do so much analysis. Also, I can't get started with that analysis until after the whole DVD is done; Background Encoding, described on page 345, isn't available with this setting. But at least my human will get two hours of great-looking video per disc."

The High Quality setting uses the same trick that movie studios use on their Hollywood DVDs: *variable bit-rate (VBR) encoding.* Professional DVD companies use advanced software to analyze each piece of the movie, using more or less data to describe each frame, depending on how much action is visible. The disc conserves data for when the video needs it the most. The trouble is, the analysis required by VBR encoding takes a very longtime. That's why High Quality takes longer to burn a disc than Best Performance.

- **Professional Quality.** This advanced encoding method, new in iDVD '09, is what you should use for the really important stuff. It takes twice as long as High Quality to burn a DVD, because it takes *two* passes through your material, one frame at a time. It's *double* variable bit-rate encoding. The result is better, richer color and, especially, sharper-looking photo slideshows. The Professional method can fit two hours of video onto a single-layer blank DVD—and produces truly amazing-looking discs.

One Last Techie Look

Part of iDVD's job is to *encode* (convert) your movies, music, and pictures into the MPEG-2 format required by standard DVDs. It's actually a big, hairy job, one that Apple and iDVD try to hide from you, for fear of freaking you out.

Nonetheless, if you inspect what's going on with your encoding before burning the disc, you'll be a better person for it.

To do so, open the Project Info Window (choose Project → Project Info, or press Shift-⌘-I). The dialog box that appears shows how close you are to filling up the DVD with your movies, menus, and other elements. Figure 16-11 has the details.

> **TIP** If you click the tiny storage-space readout at the right-end of the graph ("4 GB," for example), it cycles among different displays: how many minutes' worth of material your DVD will have, and how many separate tracks (individual playable bits) you've set up.

Shopping for Blank DVDs

iDVD can burn most kinds of blank DVDs. As you shop, pay close attention to what you're buying:

- **DVD-R.** These are single-sided blanks that you can record only once—permanently. Of all these formats, DVD-R is the least expensive and the one that will play on the most DVD players. (Capacity: 4.2 GB, or 2 hours of video.)

- **DVD+R.** At one point, this competing format caused no end of grief to people whose Macs could burn only DVD-R—and weren't paying attention to the + sign when they bought blanks. Today, all Macs can burn DVD+R just as easily as DVD-R, and all but the most ancient DVD players can play both types.

- **DVD-RW or DVD+RW (Rewritable)**. Same idea, except that you can erase these and use them again. (When you insert a DVD-RW that you've used before, iDVD automatically offers to erase it.) Some older DVD players can't play these, though.

- **DVD+R DL (Double Layer)**. This kind of blank holds 7.7 GB—close to four hours of video. All current Mac models can record onto these blanks, and all current DVD players can play them after they've been burned.

Older Macs may not be able to record onto double-layer discs, however.

TIP   To find out if your Mac can burn double-layer discs, choose Project → Project Info. If the DVD Type pop-up menu offers a choice of Double-Layer (DL), then you're one of the lucky ones.

The Burn

When you've finished editing your disc and testing it thoroughly, it's time to proceed with your burn. This is the moment you've been waiting for.

1. **Choose File → Save Project (⌘-S).**

   This might be a good opportunity to confirm that your hard drive has some free space, too. It needs *twice* the amount of free space that your project itself takes up. Use the Project Info graph (Figure 16-11) as your guide.

2. **Click the Burn button twice.**

   See Figure 16-12.

Figure 16-12:
The first click on the gray, closed Burn button "opens" it, revealing a throbbing yellow-and-black button. The second click begins the encoding and burning process, which can take hours.

3. **Insert a blank DVD when your Mac asks for it.**

   Be sure you're using the correct kind of disc for your DVD burner. For example, don't attempt to burn 1× or 2× blanks at 4× speed.

4. **Wait.**

   It can take iDVD a *very* long time to process all of your audio, video, and photos, encoding them into the proper format for a DVD. Your wait time depends on how complex your project is, how fast your Mac is, and which encoding setting you've chosen. The bottom line is that this period is usually measured in hours, not minutes.

For best results, make sure that no background programs are busy—downloading e-mail, playing iTunes music—while you're capturing directly to DVD. A busy computer may introduce video glitches (like dropped frames) into the video capture.

Eventually, though, a freshly burned DVD pops out of your drive.

NOTE After your new DVD pops out, a message says, "Your disc has been created. If you want to create another DVD, insert another disc now." Sure enough, if you want to spin out multiple copies of your project, you can insert another blank DVD now, so that iDVD can record it without having to repeat all that time-consuming encoding. Otherwise, click Done.

OneStep DVDs, Magic iDVDs

If you've read this far, you now know that even a simple iMovie-to-iDVD transfer can involve quite a bit of effort and learning. That's why Apple came up with not one, but two, different ways to shorten the distance between your camcorder and a finished DVD:

• **OneStep DVD.** This is a one-click method of dumping a video tape on to a DVD. You just plug in a camera and record directly to a DVD, bypassing iMovie altogether. The result is exactly like the cassette, with the same footage in the same order as you shot it on your camcorder.

In effect, One Step DVD turns a *tape* camcorder into one of those DVD camcorders. It's a handy way to offload footage from a bunch of tapes, either because blank DVDs are cheaper than tapes, or because tapes have a more limited shelf life.

• **Magic iDVD.** Here again, the idea is to automate a lot of the gruntwork involved in designing a DVD. But this time, instead of using raw material straight from your camcorder, Magic iDVD knits together existing files on your hard drive. You choose a bunch of pictures, movies, and music files, and boom—iDVD produces the disc for you.

The result doesn't have to be a finished product. You wind up with an iDVD project that you *could* burn right away, but that you're also welcome to edit and fine-tune.

Here's a walk-through of both features.

OneStep DVD

As noted above, OneStep DVD is designed to convert the tape in your camcorder into an identical DVD in your Mac. It's very simple, and very limited. For example:

• iDVD can record only from a prerecorded MiniDV tape in a camcorder or a movie file on your hard drive. It can't record from the TV, a cable box, an analog-digital converter box, or your digital camcorder's video pass-through feature. It also can't record from a *hi-def* tape camcorder or any tapeless camcorder.

• You can't edit the video or choose which parts to include.

• You can't customize your project in any way. The resulting DVD won't have a theme, a menu screen, or buttons. Instead, it will be an autoplay DVD—a disc that begins playing automatically when inserted into a DVD player.

> **NOTE** Like iMovie, OneStep DVD doesn't play well with 12-bit audio, which is the standard audio-recording setting for most new digital camcorders. Record your video using the 16-bit setting (which you change in the camcorder's menus); otherwise, your audio and video may drift apart on the DVD.

Here's how you use OneStep to copy a tape onto a DVD:

1. **Insert a recorded DV tape into your camcorder, and connect the camcorder to your Mac using a FireWire cable. Turn on the camcorder and set it to VCR or Play mode.**

   Chapter 1 (page 26) has details.

2. **In iDVD, choose File → OneStep DVD.**

   If your Mac's DVD drive has a slide-out tray, it now opens automatically.

   > **TIP** If, instead, you choose File → OneStep DVD from Movie, you can choose a finished Quick-Time movie from your hard drive. iDVD turns it into a DVD that will play automatically and instantly, in "kiosk mode," when inserted into a DVD player.

3. **Insert a blank recordable DVD.**

   Close the DVD tray, if necessary.

4. **Wait.**

   iDVD takes over your camera, automatically directing it to rewind, play back, and then stop (Figure 16-13).

   > **TIP** You don't have to let iDVD rewind your tape to the beginning. You can specify where you want the transfer to begin, just by cueing up the tape in the camcorder before you begin the steps above. Then, the instant iDVD begins rewinding the tape, press Play on the camcorder right away. You've convinced OneStep that the tape has just been rewound completely. iDVD starts the capture at that point.

   Ordinarily, iDVD imports video until the end of the tape, or until it sees 10 seconds of blank tape, whichever comes first. But you can override this setup, too. Whenever you feel that you've transferred enough of the tape, press the Stop button on your camcorder to end the capture process. OneStep moves right ahead to the compression and burning stages.

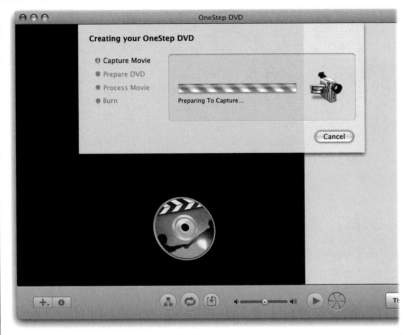

Figure 16-13:
The OneStep DVD process automates capturing, preparing, processing and burning a DVD from the contents of your camera's tape. OneStep doesn't actually begin recording the disc until after its video-encoding phase, which can take minutes or hours after the video-capturing process is complete. You can click the Cancel button at any time during this processing (encoding) stage to quit without burning. No harm done.

After the capture process is complete, iDVD takes the normal amount of time to compress your video and burn it to disc, so schedule the whole thing for a time (a *long* time) when you won't need your Mac. Go get coffee, found a new religion, or do something else that will occupy you as the tectonic plates move on inexorably and California continues its long, slow slide into Alaska.

Magic iDVDs

The magic of Magic iDVD all happens in a single dialog box, shown in Figure 16-14. It's a fun, easy way to put together a project for iDVD, or even to skip the whole editing thing and put together an instant DVD. You choose the movies and photos you want to include, choose the theme (menu design) you prefer, and then click Create Project to produce a new, ready-to-edit (or ready-to-burn) iDVD project.

Magic iDVD isn't *completely* on autopilot, however. You have to exhibit just a tiny bit of effort:

• **Name your DVD.** Edit the text box to the right of DVD Title.

• **Choose a theme.** All of the menu-screen templates (themes) are listed in a horizontal scrolling list; the pop-up menu above groups them by iDVD version (7.0, 6.0, and so on). (See page 333 for details on themes.)

Figure 16-14:
Using Magic iDVD is just like going shopping. "I'll take these movies, that slideshow, those audio clips, that theme…and wrap them up to go, please." Select the media you want to use, and then drop them into the wells on the lower left of the window. Click Create Project to start a new project using all your selections, or click Burn to create an instant DVD.

- **Add movies.** Click Movies (top right), and then drag the icons of the videos you've selected into the movie wells. (You can also switch to the Finder, and then drag them into the wells right from the desktop.) If you drop several movies at once, iDVD reassigns them to their own individual wells.

- **Add slideshows** Click Photos (top right), and then drag pictures into a Photos cell. What you're creating here is a slideshow, so don't drag *individual* photos. Either drag albums from your iPhoto list, or select *batches* of photos that you drag en masse into a well. To add music to this new slideshow, click the Audio button to view your iTunes master list. Now you can drag either an individual song or a complete playlist onto any well where you've already installed some pictures. A ◄)) icon appears superimposed on that cell.

- **Remove stuff if necessary.** If you change your mind about something, you can remove a movie or slideshow by dragging its icon out of a well (or by selecting a well, and then pressing the Delete key). And what about audio? The only way to remove audio from a slideshow is to remove the slideshow itself. You can, however, change the audio by dropping a new music track on top of an occupied slideshow well.

- **Preview your DVD.** Click the ▶ button to see what iDVD has built for you using the raw ingredients you fed to it (Figure 16-15).

Figure 16-15:
A Magic iDVD has only two buttons on its main menu: Movies and Slideshows. It autofills all drop zones with selections it makes from the movies and pictures you've included.

- **Create a new iDVD Project—or burn, baby, burn.** If it all seems close enough to something you can use, click Create Project. iDVD builds a standard iDVD project containing all the elements and choices you've set up in the Magic iDVD window. You're free to edit, rearrange, delete, or otherwise tweak the elements; you've still saved a lot of time. Or if the preview makes you think that what iDVD has done is just perfect—or good enough—click the Burn button twice. iDVD asks you for a blank DVD. The rest is just a matter of waiting.

DVD Menus, Slideshows, and the Map

Chapter 16 shows you how easy it is to convert a single iMovie project into a genuine DVD. But iDVD is capable of far more. You can use it, for example, to make a DVD that contains *six* of your greatest iMovie masterpieces all on one disc. Or you can create a *slideshow* DVD, which happens to be one of the world's greatest methods for displaying digital photos. (You can even incorporate movies *into* a slideshow.) And you'll never know joy like that of designing your own navigational menu system, complete with menus within menus.

This chapter shows you how, by doing a few more things manually, you can gain far more power and freedom.

Adding Movies

When you get right down to it, all iDVD really does is add window dressing—menus, buttons, and so on—to movies, music, and photos created in *other* programs. Take movies, for example. As Chapter 16 makes clear, you can transfer an iMovie project into iDVD via the Media Browser. But that's just the beginning of the ways you can add movies to your iDVD projects. You can also:

• Use the File → Import command.

• Drag movies into the iDVD window from the desktop.

• Choose movies from the Media Browser.

The following pages take you through these additional methods.

The Import Command

iDVD's File → Import command lets you install video, audio, pictures, and background movies onto whatever menu screen you're editing; see Figure 17-1.

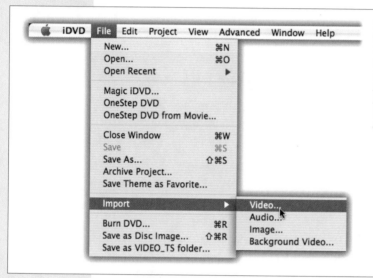

Figure 17-1:
When you choose File → Import → Video, the Open File dialog box appears, so that you can navigate to a movie and select it. (You can't select more than one movie to import at a time.) When you click Open, iDVD loads the movie and adds it to the current menu screen.

The Finder

Another great way to install a movie into an iDVD menu screen is to drag it there, either right off the desktop or from an open folder window. Figure 17-2 tells all.

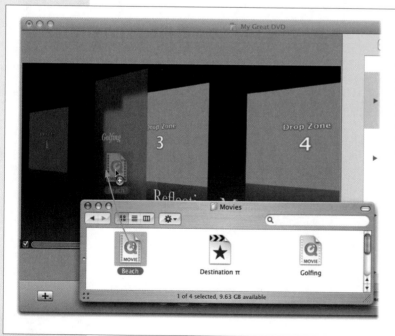

Figure 17-2:
Here's a quick way to install a movie into one of your menu screens: In the Finder, position the window that contains the movie so that you can see it and the iDVD menu screen at the same time. Then just drag the movie onto the displayed menu and drop it there.

The Media Browser

Dragging files in from the Finder is great, but it assumes that you know where your movies are. Fortunately, if you're a little fuzzy on where you've stored all your movie files, iDVD can help. Click the Media button, and then click the Movies button at the top (see Figure 17-3).

> **TIP** The Media Browser shows the movies in your Movies folder. But you can also tell iDVD to list the movies it finds in *other* folders on your Mac. Choose iDVD → Preferences, click the Movies tab, click Add, and then navigate to, and select, the additional folder you want it to monitor for movies. Repeat for additional movie folders.

Figure 17-3:
At the top of the Media Browser, you see all of the movies in all of the logical places on your Mac: your iMovie projects, movie files in your Movies folder, camera movies from iPhoto, and non-commercial videos from iTunes. Expand the flippy triangle of one of these categories to see what's in it. Drag the movie you want into the menu screen to make it part of your DVD-in-waiting.

Submenus ("Folders")

Depending on the theme you've chosen, iDVD may impose a limit of six or 12 buttons on a menu screen. Fortunately, that doesn't mean you're limited to 12 movies per DVD. You can accommodate more movies by creating *submenus*—additional menu screens that branch off from the main menu. You can even make *sub*-submenus (Figure 17-4).

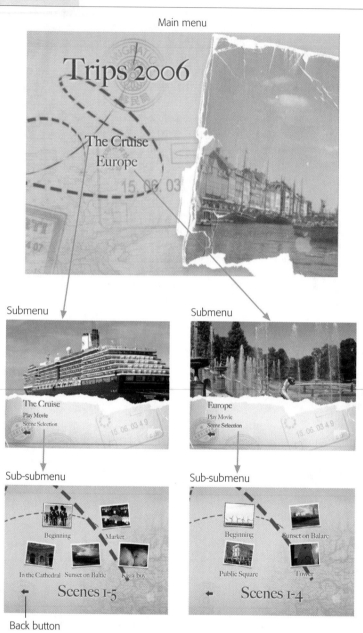

Main menu

Submenu

Submenu

Sub-submenu

Sub-submenu

Back button

Figure 17-4:
An iDVD menu screen can't hold more than six or 12 buttons. If you try to place any more, you'll have to branch off into submenu screens, or even sub-submenu screens. This DVD has two movies, each of which has chapters within. When your audience clicks a movie's name (with the remote control), they go to a submenu screen with a Play button (to play the whole movie) and a Scene Selection button (to open yet another menu screen, this one showing your chapter markers so that the audience can choose a point to begin playback). These submenus create extra room for navigation through your project. As your projects grow more complex, you must use folders (submenus) to add enough space to showcase all your pictures and movies.

You may have seen this effect already, in fact, if you've tried to create an iMovie DVD containing more than a handful of chapter markers.

You can also create this effect manually. Whenever you choose Add Submenu from the + pop-up menu at the lower-left corner of the screen, iDVD adds a submenu button to the current menu screen. In some themes, especially those that began life in previous versions of iDVD, this button looks like an actual folder; in most, it's simply a new text button. Behind the scenes, though, this button represents a second menu screen, a blank canvas with room for yet another six or twelve buttons.

WORKAROUND WORKSHOP

Temporary Buttons

When you try to add more buttons to a menu screen than iDVD can handle, the program gracefully announces that you've added too many buttons. If you click OK, iDVD eliminates the new button you tried to add. If you click Temporarily Allow—often a more convenient choice—iDVD permits you to add those extra buttons to your menus for now, so that you have the convenience of (for example) cutting and pasting them to other menu screens.

But with great power comes great responsibility. iDVD wants you to understand that you can't actually burn a DVD with too many buttons on a menu screen. If you forget to dispose of the extra buttons before clicking the Burn button, another warning message appears, and your burning efforts come to a grinding halt. Avoid over-buttoned menus by creating generous and well-thought-out submenus.

Navigating Submenus

Navigating iDVD folders while building your project is pretty easy, once you master these tips:

- **Open by double-clicking.** Double-click any folder or submenu button to "open" it—that is, to bring up the menu screen it represents.

- **Return by clicking the arrow.** Each submenu screen contains a Back arrow. Click it to return to the parent menu.

- **Names may not match.** A folder/submenu button's label doesn't have to have any relationship to the title that appears on the corresponding screen. You can edit the text individually in both places.

- **Themes don't have to match.** Each menu screen can have its own theme. If you change a screen's theme and want to apply it to the entire project, choose Advanced → "Apply Theme to Project". Want to apply a theme to just the submenus below the currently displayed menu? Choose Advanced → "Apply Theme to Submenus" instead.

- **Mind your minutes.** The more folders and more themes you add to your project, the closer you come to iDVD's video menu limit of 15 minutes. Reaching that limit isn't such a remote possibility, either; 1-minute video loops on seven menu screens take up nearly all your available space, even if you use the same background video on every menu.

NOTE   When you try to add a new menu that takes up too much space, you'll see a message
that says, "Total menu duration exceeds 15 minutes". Click Cancel to eliminate the new menu you
tried to add. Click Ignore to add the menu despite the warning, with the understanding that you'll
have to solve the space issue manually before you burn the DVD. Or click Fix to make iDVD
shorten the menu's loop so that it fits within the remaining video menu space on your disc.

The DVD Map–and Autoplay

As you can see, menus and submenus can build up with alarming rapidity. At
times your projects may grow out of control; pretty soon, you feel like Hansel and
Gretel with not enough bread crumbs.

iDVD's Map pretty much eliminates these navigation problems. It's a living, interactive diagram whose icons represent your DVD's menus, videos, and slideshows
and reveal how they're connected. As your menu and button layouts grow more
complex, you can use the map screen to help you keep track of your menu structure.

To view the map, click the Map button at the bottom of the main iDVD window;
it's identified in Figure 17-5. The element you were working on appears with
colored highlighting (Figure 17-5). When you're finished working with the Map,
click the Map button again, or click Return.

NOTE   Each menu tile includes a flippy triangle. Click it to expand or collapse that limb of the
menu tree, for ease in managing complex projects.

Editing in the Map

The Map is interactive; you can actually design and edit your DVD on this single
screen. For example:

- Delete a bunch of menu screens or other elements all at once. Select them by
  Shift-clicking them individually (Shift-click a second time if you select an icon
  by mistake), and then press the Delete key.

- Similarly, you can quickly apply new themes to the menu screens of your DVD
  without ever leaving the Map. Select the relevant menu icons, and then click the
  new theme on the Themes pane.

  You can even add new menu screens and slideshows on the Map screen. Start
  by highlighting a menu screen's icon in the Map. When you choose Project →
  Add Submenu or Project → Add Slideshow, you'll see that it now links to a secondary screen. At that point, you can specify *which* movies or *which* photos you
  want on those new screens by clicking Media, then either Photos or Movies, and
  then dragging your selections onto the newly created Map tile.

- iDVD lets you apply change characteristics of multiple menu screens simultaneously using the Map. Just Shift-click to choose the menu icons you want,
  choose View → Show Inspector (⌘-I) to open the Inspector palette, and then
  make any changes you like. You're affecting all of those menu screens at once.

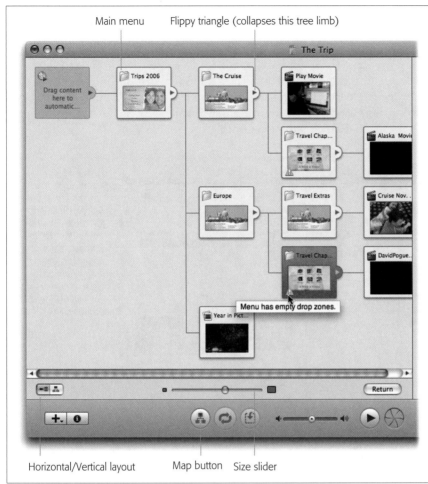

Figure 17-5:
You can view the map either as a horizontal tree or a vertical one. Use the size slider to adjust the icons' size. Option-drag the background to scroll the whole window diagonally—a much faster method than adjusting the scroll bars individually. Open a menu or slideshow for editing by double-clicking its icon. Watch out for yellow exclamation points, which indicate problems you should fix before burning.

Horizontal/Vertical layout   Map button   Size slider

- Watch out for the yellow triangle exclamation points. When you see one, point to it with your cursor (Figure 17-5). You'll see that iDVD has identified some problem with that menu screen—it contains no buttons at all, for example, or it's got drop zones that you haven't filled.

Autoplay

The Autoplay tile is the key to a *great* iDVD feature: It lets you create DVDs that start playing instantly when inserted into a DVD player. No menus, no remote control—just instant gratification.

Hollywood DVDs use this Autoplay behavior to display video *before* the menu screen appears. You know—a bright red FBI warning, previews of coming attractions, or maybe just a quick snippet of the movie on the DVD. You can do that, or you can use the Autoplay feature to create a DVD that *never* gets to the menu screen—a DVD consisting *only* of Autoplay material. That is, you insert the DVD, and the whole thing plays automatically.

You could design a project this way for the benefit of, for example, technophobic DVD novices whose pupils dilate merely contemplating using a remote control. Or you could design your DVD that way for use in a kiosk, or just to avoid having to muck around with menu designs.

The key to this feature is the Autoplay tile, the very first one in Map view (at the top or the left, depending on the view you've chosen); see Figure 17-6. Whatever you drag onto it will play automatically when the DVD is inserted, before your viewers even touch their remote controls.

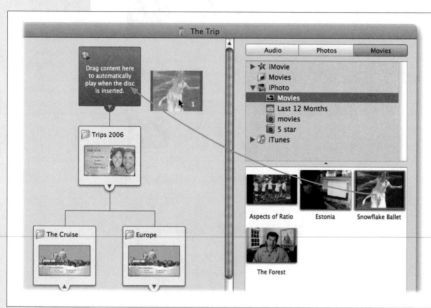

Figure 17-6:
If you decide to add or replace your Autoplay material, just drag new stuff right onto it. Or, to eliminate the Autoplay segment, drag it right off the tile. It disappears in a tiny puff of Mac OS X cartoon smoke.

These are the kinds of things you can put on the Autoplay tile:

- **A video clip.** Click the Media button, and then click Movies at the top of the pane. Drag the movie you want directly onto the Autoplay tile to install it there.

- **A still image.** Click the Media button, but this time click Photos at the top. Now iDVD shows your complete iPhoto collection, including all of your albums. To use one of these images as a startup screen for your DVD project, just drag it onto the Autoplay tile. (You can add audio to it, too, just as you'd add audio to a slideshow—by dragging in an audio file from the Audio section of the Media pane.)

TIP   If you tinker with the graphics tools in a program like Photoshop or AppleWorks, you could come up with a decent replica of the standard FBI warning that appears as the Autoplay of a commercial DVD. You could precisely duplicate the wording and typographical look—or you could take the opportunity to do a hilarious spoof of the usual warning.

- **A slideshow.** Once you've got the Photos list open as described above, you can also drag an entire iPhoto album onto the project icon. Alternatively, you can click and ⌘-click just the photos you want, and then drag them en masse onto the Autoplay icon. In fact, you can even drag photos—as a group or in a folder—right out of the Finder and onto this icon.

To control how long your still image remains on the screen, or how quickly your Autoplay slideshow plays, double-click the Autoplay tile. You arrive at the Autoplay slideshow editor, a screen just like the one shown on page 363, where you can adjust the timing, the transitions, and even the audio that plays behind the picture(s).

Note that unless you also turn on looping, described next, the DVD will eventually have to show *something* after playing the Autoplay material. For that reason, it's a good idea to designate a basic main-menu screen anyway—something to appear after the Autoplay cycle is complete.

Looping

If you highlight the button for a movie, slideshow, or Autoplay tile—either in Map view or on a menu screen—and then choose Advanced → Loop Movie (or Loop Slideshow), you unleash another raft of possibilities. You can make a DVD that repeats the highlighted material (a slideshow or movie) over and over again and, in fact, *never* gets back to the menu screen.

That would be a great way to create a DVD containing a self-running, self-repeating slideshow of digital photos to play on a TV at a party or wedding reception. You could also use it to create a self-looping kiosk display at a trade show.

In any case, the DVD will loop endlessly—or at least until it occurs to someone in your audience to press the Menu or Title button on the remote, which displays your main menu. At this point, the Menu button redisplays the previous menu screen; the Title button causes a return to the main menu.

DVD Slideshows

The DVD may be the world's best delivery mechanism for digital photos. Your friends sit there on the couch. They click the remote control to walk through your photos (or, if you choose, they let the slideshow advance automatically). Instead of passing around a tiny pile of fragile 4×6 prints, your audience gets to watch the photos at TV-screen size, looking sensational—accompanied by a musical soundtrack of your choice.

In iDVD '09, in fact, you can incorporate *movies* into your slideshows. Sure, this feature may seem to violate the very definition of a slideshow, but whatever—the ability to mix stills and videos adds a lot to the visual record of your life.

If you've installed movies into an iDVD menu screen, installing photos will seem like a piece of cake. Once again, you can do so using several different methods, each with its own advantages:

- **iPhoto albums.** Click Media, then click Photos. iDVD presents your entire iPhoto picture collection, complete with the albums you've used to organize them.

  The great thing about this system is that iPhoto albums contain well-defined image progressions. That is, you presumably dragged the photos into an emotionally satisfying sequence. That's exactly how iDVD presents the pictures—as they appear in the album, from the first image to the last.

- **Folder drag-and-drop.** If the pictures you want to add aren't in iPhoto, you can also drag a folder full of them right off the desktop (or from a Finder folder) and onto an iDVD menu screen. iDVD creates a slideshow from the images, all right, but puts them into an unpredictable sequence.

- **Slideshow Editor.** iDVD features a special window called the Slideshow Editor, in which you can add individual photos to the slideshow and drag them into any order you like. This approach takes a little work, but it gives you the freedom to import images from many different sources without having to organize them beforehand.

NOTE A DVD slideshow (*any* DVD, not just those produced by iDVD) can contain at most 99 slides, and one DVD can contain at most 99 slideshows. The designers of the DVD format obviously recognized that there's a limit to the patience of home slideshow audiences.

iPhoto Albums

You can use either of two approaches to create iDVD slideshows from your iPhoto album collection. One way begins in iPhoto; the other begins in iDVD.

Starting in iPhoto

As part of the much-heralded integration of iPhoto, iTunes, iMovie, and iDVD, iPhoto offers a menu choice that exports albums and slideshows to iDVD. In the iPhoto Source list, click the album or slideshow you want to export, choose Share → "Send to iDVD", and then wait as iPhoto transfers the data.

TIP If you do a lot of this, you can add a "Send to iDVD" button to your iPhoto toolbar (at the bottom of the window). Just choose View → "Show in Toolbar" → "Send to iDVD".

Now, although the steps are the same for the iPhoto entities called *albums* and *slideshows*, the results in iDVD are different.

- If you export an iPhoto *slideshow* (a set of photos to which you've applied music, panning and zooming effects, specific crossfade styles, and even individual, per-slide timings), iDVD treats the result as a movie. Your audience will see a frozen slideshow when they press the Enter or Play buttons on their remote.

They'll see the pictures in the sequence, and with the timings, *you* specified; they'll have no control over the show. You can work with this movie as you would any other movie you've imported.

- If you export an *album* (a "folder" full of photos, assembled and arranged by you), iDVD treats the result as a *slideshow*—a collection of pictures that your DVD audience can peruse, one at a time, using the arrow buttons on their remote controls. The rest of this discussion applies to these DVD slideshows.

In iDVD, an album slideshow is represented by a like-named submenu button. Double-click it to view the list of pictures inside, change their sequence, and make other adjustments, as described on page 363.

> **NOTE** If, while in iPhoto, you make changes to your album—by adding photos or rearranging them, for example—click iPhoto's iDVD button again. Instead of adding a second copy to your DVD project, iDVD is smart enough to update the existing slideshow. This way, you can update your albums as often as you like without any adverse affects on your iDVD project. Note, however, that you *don't* enjoy this luxury when you use the Photos pane within iDVD. Dragging an album out of the Photos pane onto a menu a second time gives you a second copy.

Starting in iDVD

If you haven't already been working in iPhoto, there's an even easier way to turn iPhoto albums into living slideshows. Just click the Media button, then the Photos button, and voilà: You're presented with the tiny thumbnails of every digital photo in your collection. You even get to see the list of albums, exactly as they appear in iPhoto (Figure 17-7). From here, you can drag either albums or arbitrary groups of selected thumbnails onto a menu screen to become a slideshow.

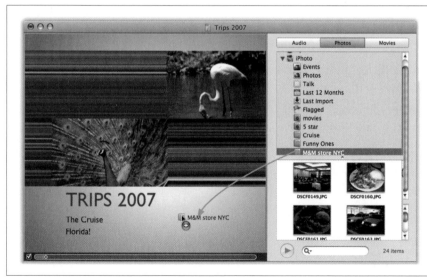

Figure 17-7:
To add a new slideshow, drag an album (from the Photos pane)—or even a batch of selected photos—onto your iDVD workspace. You can also select several and drag them en masse. (The usual multiple-selection tricks apply: ⌘-click several albums or photos in turn to select all of them, for example.)

Drag Folders from the Finder

Suppose you don't keep all your pictures in iPhoto. (Hey, it could happen.)

In that case, you may prefer to drag a folder of photos out of the Finder and onto an iDVD menu screen. (Make sure that the folder contains nothing but pictures and movies. If it contains any other kind of document, or even other folders, iDVD may complain that it can't handle the "Unsupported File Type: Unknown Format.")

The folder shows up on the menu screen as a new slideshow button. You're ready to edit your slideshow, as described below.

Add a Slideshow, Worry About the Pictures Later

If all of your photographic masterpieces aren't already together in iPhoto or even in a Finder folder, you can also bring them into iDVD individually.

To do that, start by creating a new slideshow folder: From the + pop-up menu (lower-left corner of iDVD), choose Add Slideshow (or choose Project → Slideshow, or press ⌘-L). iDVD creates a new, empty slideshow. Double-click it to enter the Slideshow Editor described next.

The Slideshow Editor

No matter how you got your slideshow folder button into iDVD, you still edit it the same way: by double-clicking it to open iDVD's Slideshow Editor. See Figure 17-8 for a quick tour.

Adding or omitting slides and movies

If you want to add new pictures to the slideshow, use the following techniques:

- **Drag from the Finder.** Drag an image, a selection of several images, a folder of images, or some movies directly into the slide list.

- **Click Media, then Photos or Movies.** Drag a picture, a set of several shots, an iPhoto album, or a movie into the slide list.

- **Import an image.** Choose File → Import → Image. Navigate to any picture file, select it, and then click Open.

  > **TIP** Before clicking Open, you can highlight several photos to bring them all in at once. If the ones you want appear consecutively in the list, click the first one, and then Shift-click the last one, to highlight all of them. If not, ⌘-click each photo file that you want to import. Either way, click Open to bring them all into iDVD simultaneously.

To remove a picture or a movie from the list, just click it and then press the Delete key. You can also remove a whole bunch of pictures or movies simultaneously by first Shift-clicking them or ⌘-clicking them, exactly as described in the previous Tip, before pressing Delete.

Figure 17-8:
The iDVD Slideshow Editor lets you build and customize your slideshows. Each slide appears in order, with its number and a thumbnail; you can move them around by dragging, delete the ones you don't want, or add new ones by dragging graphics from the desktop or the Media pane of the Customize drawer. The buttons in the lower-left corner switch between a list view and an icon view (shown here). Click Return to go back to iDVD's menu-editing mode.

Reordering slides and movies

To change the sequence of slides and movies, just drag them around. Once again, you can select multiple thumbnails at once (see the preceding Tip) and then drag them en masse.

Renaming slides or movies

Click the name below each thumbnail to open a name-editing box.

Slideshow Settings

iDVD offers some useful options when you click the Settings button at the bottom of the Slideshow Editor window:

- **Loop slideshow.** If you turn on the "Loop slideshow" checkbox, the slideshow repeats endlessly, or until your viewer presses the Menu or Title button on the DVD remote control.

- **Display navigation.** When you check this option, you'll see navigation arrows on the screen as your slideshow plays. Your viewers can click these buttons with their remote controls to move back and forth within your slideshow.

  Navigation gives your viewers a feeling of flexibility and control. On the other hand, they can always use the < and > buttons on their remote controls even if no arrows appear on the screen. (Furthermore, you may consider the majesty of your photography marred by the superimposed triangle buttons.)

- **Add image files to DVD-ROM.** When iDVD creates a slideshow, it scales all of your photos to 640×480 pixels. That's ideal for a standard television screen, which, in fact, can't display any resolution higher than that. But if you intend to distribute your DVD to somebody who's computer savvy, you may want to give them the original, full-resolution photos. They won't see these photos when they insert the disc into a DVD player. But when they insert your DVD into their *computers*, they'll see a folder filled with the original, highres photos, for purposes like printing, using as Desktop wallpaper, and so on. (In other words, you've created a dual-format disc that's both a DVD-video disc and a DVD-ROM.)

- **Show Titles and Comments.** You can add comments for each image in your slideshow—and then, at your discretion, have them appear onscreen during the slideshow.

When you click Settings, and then turn on "Show titles and comments", you're telling iDVD to display photo names and comments *both* in the Slideshow Editor *and* on the TV screen when the DVD plays. Now you can click the gray "Add comments" text below each slide title to add your custom text.

TIP This can be a great feature if you've named your pictures, say, "Martha gives Dad a kiss," but not so great a feature for pictures named "IMG_NK01219", "IMG_NK01222," and so on. If you want to use photo titles and comments, keep them succinct, meaningful, and easy-to-read.

- **Duck audio while playing movies.** In iDVD '09, you can now incorporate movies into your slideshow. You can nestle videos right in among your still photos; they begin playback automatically during the slideshow. But what happens if you've added some background music to your slideshow—and it drowns out the talking in the movies? Or, worse, what happens if the video has a music track of its own—and now you've got two clashing soundtracks?

NOTE This option is supposed to make your slideshow music automatically lower its volume whenever a movie plays, to avoid these clashes.

Slideshow Options

Other Slideshow Editor features include:

- **Slide Duration.** Using this pop-up list, you can specify how much time each slide spends on the screen: 1, 3, 5, 10 seconds, "Fit to Audio", or Manual. Manual, of course, means that your audience will have to press the Next button on the remote control to change pictures.

Fit to Audio appears in the pop-up menu only after you've added a song or playlist to your slideshow. In this case, iDVD determines the timing of your slides automatically—by dividing the length of the soundtrack by the number of slides in your show. In other words, if the song is 60 seconds long, and you've got 20 slides in the show, each slide will sit on the screen for 3 seconds.

TIP   "Fit to Audio" offers a nifty way to create a simple, no-fuss DVD "mix tape" that you can play on your home theater system. Drop a song into the Audio well (see the next page) but add only one photograph, which may be the album art for that song or a graphic showing the song's title. Make a series of "slideshows" this way. Once you burn the whole thing to a DVD, you can choose a song to start playing in its entirety with the album cover on the screen. (If you add an album-in-a-playlist instead of just one song, you can choose an album to play in the same way.)

- **Transition.** You can specify any of several graceful transition effects—Dissolve, Cube, and so on—to govern how one slide morphs into the next. You can try each of these styles for yourself by selecting one and then watching your slideshow. (Click ▶ to start the show; click it again to return to the editor.) Viewing just a few slides shows you how the transitions work on real images.

The transition you specify here affects all slides in the show; you can't set transitions on a slide-by-slide basis. Note, too, that transitions *add* to the time your slides spend on the screen. If you've chosen 3 seconds for the slide duration, each slide will actually hang around for nearly 5 seconds, when you consider the time it spends morphing.

Slideshow audio

Music has a profound impact on the effect of a photo slideshow. You can't appreciate how dramatic the difference is until you watch the same slideshow with and without music playing.

The easiest way to add music to a slideshow is to click Media, and then click the Audio button at the top of the pane. Conveniently enough, iDVD shows your entire iTunes music collection, complete with any playlists you've assembled, as well as any GarageBand pieces you've made (Figure 17-9).

When you find suitable musical accompaniment, drag its name out of the Garage-Band or iTunes list and onto the Audio well (also shown in Figure 17-9). You can even drag an entire playlist into the well; the DVD will play one song after another according to the playlist, so that the music won't die ignominiously in the middle of the slide show. You can also drag a sound file from any Finder window or the desktop—and directly onto this Audio well.

NOTE   When it's empty, the Audio well looks like a small speaker (◀)). When it's occupied, its icon identifies the kind of audio file you've installed; the little icon says, for example, AIFF, AU, or MP3. The icon used when you add a playlist rather than a single song varies, usually showing the first audio file type used in the playlist.

To try out a different piece of background music, drag a new song or audio file into the Audio well. And if you decide that you don't want music at all, drag the file icon directly out of the Audio well and onto any other part of the screen. An animated puff of smoke confirms your decision.

Figure 17-9:
The Music list includes your iTunes tunes, plus any music you've created using GarageBand. Such songs make great soundtracks, because you've tailored them to the mood and the length of the slideshow. (Your GarageBand pieces show up in iDVD only if you've opened GarageBand's Preferences, clicked the General tab, and turned on "Render an audio preview when saving." Oh, and one more thing: iDVD won't see your GarageBand pieces unless you keep them in your Home → Music → GarageBand folder.)

Leaving the Slideshow Editor

To return to iDVD's menu editor, click Return at the bottom.

Burning Your Slideshow

Once you've designed a slideshow DVD, previewing it and burning it onto a blank DVD works exactly as described beginning on page 344.

Since most people have never thrilled to the experience of viewing a digital-camera slideshow on their TV sets, a few notes are in order:

- Your viewers can use the remote control's Next and Previous buttons to move forward or backward through the presentation, no matter what timing you originally specified when you designed the show.

- They can also press the ❚❚ button to freeze a certain picture on the screen for greater study (or while they go to the bathroom). Both the slide advancing and music stop until they click the Pause or Play button, again.

- If the audio selection or playlist is shorter than the slideshow, the song starts over again.

- Your viewers can return to the main menu screen by clicking the Menu button on the remote.

- When the slideshow is over, the music stops and the main menu screen reappears.

Designing iDVD Themes

Some of Apple's iDVD themes offer great backgrounds but weak audio. Others provide terrific sounds but so-so text. Some create a nearly perfect package, while others seem broken beyond repair. Fortunately, in the end it doesn't matter, because iDVD lets you adapt themes to your taste and save them as new *Favorites*.

Favorites let you move beyond built-in themes and presets to create truly customized DVD menu systems. You can change fonts for titles, adjust the length of the looping background video, move buttons around and change their styles, switch the fonts and colors for button and menu titles, move text around the screen, substitute new background art or background patterns, replace or remove the audio loop that plays when the main menu is onscreen, and much more. Let this chapter be your guide.

> **NOTE** One thing you'll notice in this chapter, and in iDVD in general: Learning the ⌘-I keystroke is incredibly useful. That's the shortcut for the View → Show Inspector command. It opens a floating black panel, illustrated often in this chapter, filled with formatting options that are specific to whatever was selected: a button, a text block, or the menu screen itself. (You hide this panel the same way: with another ⌘-I.)

iDVD's Built-in Themes

iDVD's built-in themes vary in complexity. Some offer completely realized presentations. Others provide little more than colors and fonts, leaving it up to you to mold them. Either way, the built-in themes, both old and new, provide an excellent jumping-off point for your DVDs.

All five collections—7.0 Themes, 6.0 Themes, 5.0 Themes, Old Themes and Favorites—appear in the Themes pane. As you study the scrolling list, you'll notice that:

- **Favorites appear together.** When you choose Favorites from the pop-up menu at the top of the pane, all Favorites (themes that you've created) appear together in the same list. (This list is empty when you start out using iDVD.) Themes you've bought from other companies (like *www.idvdthemepak.com*) are listed separately in the pop-up menu.

- **You can view several sets at once.** To view just one Theme set, select its name from the Theme Set pop-up menu. To view all themes, choose All instead.

- **The ribbon means Favorite.** A gray prize ribbon appears in the lower-left corner of certain themes. This icon lets you know that the theme is a Favorite—a theme that you created yourself. You'll find out how to create Favorites later in this chapter.

Editing Buttons

When iDVD was first introduced, its flamboyant button thumbnails generated a lot of excitement. Each button could show a small video or photo, offering visual previews of the linked material.

Times have changed. These days, text buttons have quietly replaced the old button designs. In the 6.0 and 7.0 theme collections, *no* main-menu buttons display videos or pictures; all the buttons are simple text labels.

If you choose one of the older themes for that reason, you don't have to be content with the proposed button style. You can move your buttons around, change the labels on them, and so on.

Changing Button Names and Fonts

To change what a certain button is called, click the name once, pause, and then click a second time to open the editing box. As shown in Figure 18-1, you can both retype the name and change the type size and font.

Keep these points in mind when working with iDVD text:

- **Be succinct.** DVD screens are small, so there's not much room for long and involved text.

- **Be contained.** Don't let one text box overlap another.

- **Spell check.** Nothing speaks worse of your attention to detail than a lovingly crafted masterpiece called "For Mouther's Day."

> **TIP** If your buttons' text labels are crashing into each other, try making the text wrap into a narrow column, so that it's several lines long. Just press Return to start a new line.

Figure 18-1:
In iDVD, little font, size, and style menus appear right beneath any text box or button that you're trying to edit. You can use only one text style per text box, however.

Button Styles

When you sit there and hit the arrow buttons on your DVD player's remote, how does a commercial Hollywood DVD indicate which onscreen option you've selected? Well, that button sprouts some kind of highlighting. It lights up, or changes color, or gets underlined, or sprouts an indicator bullet. All of these options, and more, are now available in iDVD's new Buttons panel (Figure 18-2).

But wait, there's more. Just because a theme comes with text-only buttons doesn't mean you have to be content with that. The Buttons panel lets you turn them into picture or movie-preview buttons. Here's how to use the Buttons panel:

1. **Select the buttons you want to change.**

   Most of the time, you'll want to choose Edit → Select All Buttons (⌘-A), so that all the buttons on a menu screen will match. But you could, in theory, make different buttons highlight in different ways.

2. **Click Buttons (lower-right corner of the screen).**

   The Buttons panel appears, filled with button design options (Figure 18-2).

3. **Choose a button style from the pop-up menu at the top.**

   The first three (Text, Bullets, Shapes) all create text-only buttons, but they're somewhat inconsistent.

   For example, the options in the Text and Bullets categories affect only what happens when a button is highlighted by the remote control. That is, the button has *no* special graphic treatment when it's *not* selected; it's just words on the screen. When it's selected with the remote, the affected buttons indicate that they're highlighted either by displaying a fancy underline (Text styles) or a bullet shape next to their names (Bullet styles, shown at lower left in Figure 18-2).

   The Shapes panel, on the other hand, adds a colorful background to the chosen buttons even when they're *not* selected (lower right in Figure 18-2). You have no control over the visual presentation of a button when it's *highlighted*; that effect is built into the style. (It's usually a starburst that appears next to the button's name.)

If you choose any of the bottom four commands from the pop-up menu, you turn the buttons into picture- or movie-preview buttons. Figure 18-2 shows you how.

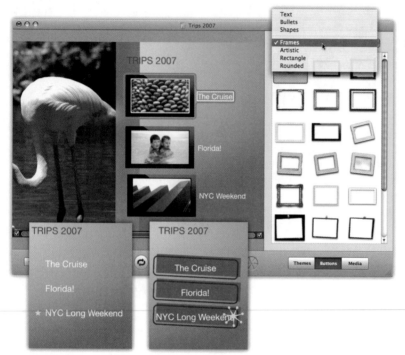

Figure 18-2:
Choose the button or buttons you want to change (top). Click Buttons (lower-right). To turn text buttons into picture or movie buttons, choose Frames, Artistic, Rectangle, or Rounded from the pop-up menu. Click the shape you want; the selected buttons sprout picture or movie previews. (To turn them back into text-only buttons, choose Text, Shapes, or Bullets from the pop-up menu.)

4. **Click the button style you want.**

   You've now changed the text or picture/movie style for the selected buttons, including what graphic they use to indicate that they're selected. But you haven't yet decided what *color* highlighting those selected buttons will have.

5. **Click an empty spot on the menu screen. Choose View → Show Inspector (⌘-I).**

   The floating Menu Info window opens.

6. **Click the Highlight button.**

   Now the Color Picker dialog box opens.

7. **Choose the color you want for the highlighting.**

   See page 190 for details on using the Color Picker. The point is that you're changing the color for the underline, bullet graphic, or starburst that appears when the selected button is highlighted.

8. Click the ▶ button to try out your new buttons.

iDVD's DVD-player simulation mode appears, complete with virtual remote control.

Justification, Drop Shadows, and Thumbnail Size

iDVD '09 sports a new floating palette that's dedicated exclusively to button editing. To open it, click a button and then choose Show → Inspector (or press ⌘-I.) As shown in Figure 18-3, this panel looks different depending whether you're editing text-only buttons or picture buttons.

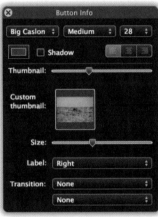

Figure 18-3:
Left: This version of the Button Info panel lets you control the button's name's font, size, color, style, shadow, and alignment within its box.

Right: For picture buttons, you get more controls. They cover the picture's size, looping point (or slideshow "poster frame"), and where its label appears relative to the picture: Right, Left, Above, Below, or Center.

Moving Buttons

Each theme comes with predetermined locations for your buttons. In fact, internally, each theme stores separate layout maps: one that specifies the button positions if you have *three* buttons, another for *four* buttons, and so on.

iDVD lets you move your buttons around just by dragging. In fact, a new iDVD '09 feature makes it easy to align them (see Figure 18-4).

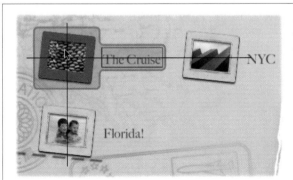

Figure 18-4:
As you drag buttons around, you'll know when you've got them lined up with each other. Horizontal or vertical guidelines appear, as shown here, and you feel a subtle snapping when the thing you're dragging is lined up with something else on the screen.

TIP   In general, buttons snap into alignment automatically. But if you really, truly want totally free rein to drop buttons anywhere (even though the result might be a little ugly), click the background of the menu, and then choose Show → Inspector (or press ⌘-I). In the Menu Info panel, click "Free positioning."

Removing Buttons

To remove a button from a menu screen, click it once, and then press the Delete key.

TIP   You can also click the first button, and then Shift-click another button, to highlight all of the buttons in between. Or ⌘-click individual buttons to highlight only those.

Of course, if you're removing a button in order to move it to a different menu screen, you can use the Cut and Paste commands in the Edit menu.

Editing Picture and Movie Buttons

In some themes—including all of the iDVD 6.0 and 7.0 main-menu screens—the buttons on your menu screen are just bits of text.

But in some of the older themes, and in the chapter screens of some newer ones, buttons are actually tiny pictures or tiny movie clips that preview the movie or slideshow that's in store. And you can turn any text-only buttons *into* picture or movie buttons easily enough, as shown in Figure 18-2 (page 370).

Here's how you control what appears on these preview buttons.

1. **Click the preview button once, pause, and then click a second time.**

   Don't just *double-click*; you'll actually open another menu screen or movie if you do that.

   Some controls appear above the button, as shown in Figure 18-5.

2. **Drag the slider to the spot you want.**

   The slider is a map of your entire movie or slideshow, from start to end. Pinpoint where you want the button's video playback to begin. Or, if it's a slideshow button, you're setting the *poster frame*: the one photo that appears on the button itself. Then again, if your button links to a movie, it doesn't have to have an animated preview. You can turn on the Still Image checkbox to choose a still poster frame from the movie, something that doesn't actually play.

   TIP   The picture on a button doesn't have to be a scene from the movie or slideshow. It can be any graphic you want. Click the button, choose View → Show Inspector, and then drag any graphics file right onto the "Custom thumbnail" image, either from the Finder or the Media panel. You'll see the button change instantly.

3. **Click anywhere on the background to deselect the button.**

   Turn on the Motion button ⇆ to see the video play in the button.

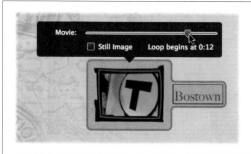

Figure 18-5:
Here's where you control where the video loop begins on a button preview. For buttons that link to movies, you get to pick the starting frame. For buttons that link to slideshows, you pick which photo appears on the button.

Editing Text

Although most people focus primarily on iDVD's drop zones, video buttons, and so on, text also plays a critical role. It's a dependable, instantly recognizable part of a DVD menu system.

The text that you can fiddle with falls into two categories (in addition to button labels, of course):

- **Menu titles** help viewers figure out where they are in the DVD menu system by providing clues to the current context: "Our Vacation," "Pictures (Week 1)," and "Scene Selection," for example. Title text usually appears at the top of the screen, although you can put it anywhere you like.

- **Text boxes** can appear anywhere on your screen. You can fill them with whatever explanatory text you think is appropriate: instructions, introductions, a description of the project, and so on.

> **TIP** In iDVD, as in life, brevity is the soul of captions.

Here is a boatload of techniques to help customize your text. Each method changes the selected text on only the *currently displayed* DVD menu screen.

- **Create a text box.** To add a text block, choose Project → Add Text (⌘-K). Double-click the placeholder text and type away.

- **Select the text box.** Click it once. Colored highlighting appears. Now you can drag the box to move it, press Delete to *re*move it, Shift-click another text box to highlight both at once, use the Copy command so you can paste them onto another menu screen, and so on.

- **Change the text.** To highlight a piece of text, double-click anywhere inside it. You'll note that iDVD automatically highlights the entire phrase, meaning that you can just begin to type, replacing the entire text blob, without first dragging across it. (Of course, if you want to edit only part of the existing text, drag with the mouse first.) Press Return or Enter when you're finished.

- **Choose a font, size, weight, color, and alignment.** Whenever you're editing the text, you can use the mini-formatting palette to change the typeface (Figure 18-6). For more options, use the Text Info palette (also shown in Figure 18-6).

Figure 18-6:
Two ways to format a text block.

Top: When you click to edit, you get this miniature pop-up panel of font options.

Bottom: If you hit ⌘-I, you get a more complete formatting panel, which now includes shadow, color, and justification options.

You're not allowed to mix and match fonts *within* a text box, but each *text block* (each button label, title, and text box) can have a different look.

- **Add (or remove) a drop shadow.** Use the Shadow checkbox in the Text Info palette to add a faint shadow behind and below the text that creates an easier-to-read, almost 3-D effect.

- **Position the title or text box.** You can drag titles and text boxes anywhere on the screen you like. Be careful not to park one where the *overscanning* effect of older TVs ("Phase 1: Prepare Your Video" on page 323) might chop off some of your letters. To avoid this problem, choose View → Show TV Safe Area before you drag, taking care to keep the text inside the superimposed guideline rectangle.

Editing Backgrounds

The menu-screen background provides a look and atmosphere that defines the entire screen. As a result, choosing a new background can add a unique twist to an existing theme.

Here's what you can use as a replacement for the Apple-supplied backgrounds.

A Still Photo

Yep, you can replace the one that came with the Apple theme. In some cases, this simple action makes the theme look *completely* different.

> **NOTE**   iDVD never distorts a photo that you install as a background. If it's not the right shape for your TV screen, you'll wind up with black letterbox bars to fill the gap. If you really care, you can prepare the photo in a program like Photoshop or Graphic Converter before installing it as a menu graphic. The dimensions for a *standard TV set* should be 720 × 540 pixels; for a *widescreen set*, use 854 × 480. (For the PAL system used in Europe, use 768 × 576 for standard, 1024 × 576 for widescreen.)

To bring this change about, drag the photo from the Media Browser (click Media, then Photos) or the Finder into any of these three spots:

- **Any empty spot on the menu.** Avoid the drop zones.

- **The Menu Info panel.** See Figure 18-7 for details on the Menu Info panel, also known as the Inspector panel.

Background well (drag a picture or movie here)

Figure 18-7:
Click a blank spot on the menu, and then press ⌘-I to open the Inspector window for the menu itself. You can now drag a new photo into the Background well shown here.

• **The Drop Zone editor.** You met this handy row of drop-zone wells in Chapter 17, but they harbor a little secret: Another version of the Background well lurks at the left side. See Figure 18-8.

A Group of Photos

You can also drag an album full of photos, or just a handful of random ones, onto any of the Background areas described above. They become a slideshow that plays while the menu is on the screen.

To make this work, drag the photos into the Drop Zone editor's Background well (Figure 18-8). You can't drag them into an empty spot on the menu, or into the Inspector panel.

Menu background

Figure 18-8:
To change the menu background, open the Drop Zone editor. The leftmost icon is a background-image "well." Drop a picture or movie here to install it as this menu screen's new, improved background. Drag the icon out of this well to reinstate the original background.

Background well:
Drag pictures, album, or movie

Click to open
Drop Zone editor

A Movie

Now, instead of a photo background, you can also create moving, animated, *video backgrounds*, just like the ones on many commercial Hollywood DVDs.

Here again, Apple wanted to make sure you'd find a way to install a movie background, so it gave you several places to aim for:

- **Any empty spot on the menu.** Avoid the drop zones. Drag a movie's icon directly onto the background—but as your cursor arrives, press the ⌘ key. A shortcut menu sprouts from your cursor, offering two choices: "Add movie" or "Replace background." Can you guess which one to click? (Hint: "Replace background.")

- **The Inspector panel.** See Figure 18-7 again.

- **The Drop Zone editor.** See Figure 18-8 again.

Once you've installed the movie, you can control how *much* of it loops on the menu screen. Click the menu background, press ⌘-I to open the Menu Info panel (shown in Figure 18-7), and then adjust the Loop Duration slider.

Some Notes

Before you delve into the exciting new career of background replacement, keep these points in mind:

- **Your video will loop.** Your background video file will play, then restart and play again as long as your audience leaves the menu on the TV screen. There's no way to make a video background play just once. Unless you take special care when creating your video, menu looping will create sudden, sharp, sometimes distracting transitions between the end and start of your video.

- **Video tends to move.** If you're not careful, video can hide or overwhelm your titles, buttons, and drop zones. "Audition" your videos and make sure they work with your menus before you burn. In particular, watch for moving objects and scenes that are too bright or too dark.

- **One menu only.** These techniques change only the currently displayed menu screen. To apply the change to *all* menu screens, choose Advanced → Apply Theme To Project.

    NOTE   The total durations for *all* videos on *all* your menus can't exceed 15 minutes. Weird, huh?

Menu Audio

Some of Apple's canned themes come with musical soundtracks, and some don't. If you'd like some music to play during, for example, the Shelves theme, you'll have to install it yourself.

You can also *replace* the music that comes with any of Apple's themes with a song you like better. In the case of musically challenged themes like Anime Pop, this ability is a true blessing, possibly saving lives and sanity. Installing a menu-screen soundtrack is a heck of a lot like installing a menu-screen background movie.

POWER USERS' CLINIC

Designing Video Loops in iMovie

Background videos don't have to jump between the end of one play-through and the beginning of the next. If you're willing to take a little time in iMovie, you can eliminate sudden visual changes that create unpleasant jumps. Consider these techniques:

Fade Out. Create a smooth fade-out at the end of the movie clip, and a smooth fade-in at the beginning, using the Fade Through Black transition style described in Chapter 5.

Use Cross Dissolve. If you prefer, you can design your movie so that the end cross-dissolves into the beginning each time it loops.

Use the Split Clip command in iMovie to break off the final 4:02 (four seconds, two frames) of your movie. Now drag this clip to the front of your movie, and add a 4-second cross dissolve between this clip and the original start of your movie; finally, export your work.

You can choose a different length for the crossfade; just make sure that the moved ending clip lasts at least two frames longer than the desired transition time. This method works particularly well on stock footage, such as windswept grass, fish in an aquarium, and so forth.

You may discover a couple of drawbacks to this method. First, the start and end audio and video will overlap, and you may not like the results. Second, the background video will, unfortunately, start with the crossfade. There's no way yet to make it start playing from an un-crossfaded spot, unless you do some clever cutting and pasting in iMovie. iDVD '10, perhaps? (Probably not.)

What to Drag

You can drag an audio file or QuickTime movie, either from the Finder or from the Music pane in iDVD (click Media in the lower-right, and then Audio at the top). For example, you can drag a song—or even a whole playlist—out of your iTunes list.

> **NOTE** That's not a typo; you can drag QuickTime movies, too. iDVD harvests only the soundtrack and ignores the video.

Where to Drag

Once again, you can drag audio into any of three spots:

- **The existing background.** That is, drag an audio file or movie directly into an empty spot on the menu, as shown in Figure 18-9. (Avoid the drop zones.)
- **The Menu Info panel.** Click an empty spot on the menu screen, and then press ⌘-I to open the Menu Info panel. At center (see Figure 18-7) is an "audio well," where you can drag an audio or movie file in or out.

- **The Drop Zone editor**. See Figure 18-8. You can drag an audio file onto the same spot where you'd drop a background *movie*.

Figure 18-9:
If you've got a decent music collection already in iTunes, adding background music is easy. Keep in mind that some of the most satisfying and appropriate soundtracks of all are the ones that you create yourself, using GarageBand. Any finished compositions that you've exported from GarageBand show up in this iTunes list, too. (In fact, even the soundtracks included with iDVD were made in GarageBand! Apple's a company that eats its own dog food, as the saying goes.)

Incidentally, iDVD doesn't do much to help when your background video and background audio aren't the same length. If the music is too short, it repeats until the video is finished playing, cutting off the music if necessary to start in sync with the video track. If the music is too long, the video repeats until the music ends, cutting off the video mid-repeat. Use the Duration slider in the Menu Info panel (Figure 18-7) to set the loop time, which applies to both sound and video.

Or, if you're really a perfectionist, you could always use GarageBand to match the soundtrack length to the video. Create a nice fade-out at the end of the audio, and a fade-in at the beginning, so that the looping won't be quite so jarring.

> **TIP** Remember, this technique affects the background music of only the currently displayed menu screen. To apply the change to *all* menu screens, wrap up by choosing Advanced → Apply Theme To Project. And make sure you don't exceed your total menu-length budget (15 minutes).

Replacing Menu Audio

To replace a custom audio file with another, repeat the steps you used to install the music to begin with. iDVD replaces the current track with the new one.

Removing Menu Audio

To remove audio, drag it out of the Audio well, either the one in the Menu Info panel or the one in the Drop Zone editor. Puff! When the audio well is empty, it shows a speaker icon (◀»).

If you want to remove *all* audio from your menu screen, you may have to drag twice: Your first drag removes custom sounds, and the second removes the theme sound, if one exists.

Adjusting Menu Audio Volume

You can control your menu screen's audio volume using the slider in the Menu Info panel (Figure 18-7). Don't forget to check your audio before burning; this slider affects the final DVD.

Saving Favorites

After applying all the techniques described so far in this chapter, you may end up creating masterpieces of adapted iDVD themes. Fortunately, iDVD allows you to save and reuse these modified themes after you adjust them to your liking. Here's how to go about it:

1. Choose File → "Save Theme as Favorite".

   The Save sheet (dialog box) appears at the top of the window.

POWER USERS' CLINIC

Secrets of the Theme Files

Whenever you save a new Favorite theme, iDVD does a fair amount of administrative work. Behind the scenes, it creates a new theme file on your hard drive. If you decided to share your theme with other account holders, this file appears in the Library → iDVD → Favorites folder. If not, it winds up in your Home → Library → iDVD → Favorites folder. Unlike regular themes, whose names end with the suffix .theme, Favorites use a .favorite file name extension.

Why is this important to know? Because it tells you how to remove a saved Favorite: Just drag the .favorite file out

of the secret folder and into the Trash. The next time you open iDVD, that favorite no longer appears in the Themes pane pop-up menu.

It's also worth noting that when you create a Favorite, iDVD copies all relevant materials, including background audio and video, to the newly created theme. (Don't believe it? To view these materials, navigate to the saved .favorite file. Control-click or right-click its icon; from the shortcut menu, choose Show Package Contents. Then open the Contents → Resources folder.)

---

2. **Type the name for your new theme. Turn on "Shared for all users", if you like.**

   If you're the only person who uses your Mac, never mind. But if you share a Mac with other students, co-workers, or family members, each of whom has a Mac OS X *account*, the "Shared for all users" option makes your new theme available to other people who use the machine. (Otherwise, your masterpiece appears in the list only when *you* use iDVD.)

   When you save a Favorite, you no longer need to keep the original theme on which it was based, as far as iDVD is concerned. Feel free to discard, rename, or move the original theme files from their original locations on your hard drive.

   (The box below offers the details.)

3. **Turn off "Replace existing" if you want to create a new entry in the theme list.**

   If you turn *on* "Replace existing", iDVD treats your adapted theme as a replacement for the one you based it on.

4. **Click OK.**

   iDVD saves your theme as a new Favorite. You'll be able to apply it to other DVDs in the future by choosing its name from the Themes pane. (Choose Favorites from the pop-up menu to see its listing.)

Advanced iDVD

Although iDVD appears simple, straightforward, and direct, there's more power lurking inside than you might expect. You can see, change, and control things you never knew you could—if you're willing to try new and unusual approaches. Some of these approaches require add-on software programs. Others demand nerves of steel and a willingness to dive into hidden iDVD files.

In this advanced chapter, you'll discover how some of these sideways (and back-ward and upside-down) methods can expand your iDVD repertoire.

iDVD: The DVD-ROM Maker

iDVD's ability to add data files to the DVD-ROM portion of your disc may be its least-known feature. When it creates a DVD-ROM, iDVD sets aside a portion of your DVD for normal computer files. This area of the disc won't show up on a DVD player—only on a computer.

With iDVD, you can store any variety of data on your DVD. Here are just a few ways you can use this feature to enhance your disc:

- **Store documents that relate to your DVD contents.** The DVD-ROM area provides a perfect place to store copies of documents that concern the material presented in the DVD. This might include the script used to film a movie, the different versions that eventually led to a final event invitation, extended family narratives, copies of email and other correspondence, and so on. Remember: TV sets aren't much good for displaying text, but a DVD-ROM and a com-puter can come to the rescue. Or store the full-resolution versions of the digital photos featured in your DVD slideshow (one of the most common uses for this feature).

- **Store Web pages.** Web pages are perfect additions to the DVD-ROM disc area. Create a Web site that relates to your DVD and add your source files to the disc. When it's distributed, your viewers can open these files with an ordinary Web browser. For example, a DVD with a training video can contain supplementary lessons in HTML (Web page) format.

- **Store email-quality versions of your video.** Use the DVD-ROM area of your disc to store small, compressed versions of your video, or "wallet-size" pictures from a slideshow, suitable for email. Now your audience can share your movie experience with other people.

Adding Files to DVD-ROM

iDVD's DVD-ROM file management couldn't be simpler. Just drag icons out of the Finder and into the DVD-ROM Contents list (Advanced → Edit DVD-ROM Contents), as shown in Figure 19-1.

Figure 19-1:
By using the Add Files button or by dragging, you can store documents, folders, programs, and other computer files on a DVD. Anyone who receives a copy of your disc can access these files on a computer. In other words, iDVD can burn DVDs that go beyond the realm of simple video.

Drag icons into this window from the Finder

Organizing DVD-ROM Contents

The DVD-ROM Contents pane lets you organize your files in several ways:

- **Add folders.** Click New Folder to add a folder to your list.

- **Remove things.** Either drag files or folders right out of the list, or select them and then press the Delete key. (Dragging out of the list gives you the cool puff-of-smoke animation.)

- **Move items into or out of folders.** You can drag icons into one of the little folder icons to file them there—or drag them out again to remove them.

- **Create subfolders.** Drag one folder into another to create subfolders.

- **Rename a folder.** Double-click the name of a folder to select and edit it. Press Return or Enter when you're finished typing.

• **List/hide folder contents.** You can click a folder's flippy triangle to expand it and see what's inside, exactly as in Finder list views.

Uncover Your DVD Project File

Behind the scenes, iDVD stores all the pieces of your project inside the .dvdproj "file" that you created when you first saved your work. However, the .dvdproj file isn't really a file, even though it looks like a single icon on your desktop. It's actually a *package*—a disguised Mac OS X folder—that contains many subfolders and files. To peek inside, follow these steps:

1. **Quit iDVD.**

   Never mess with your project files when iDVD is running.

2. **Control-click (or right-click) the project file. From the shortcut menu, choose Show Package Contents.**

   You've now opened that "file" into a folder window.

3. **Open the Contents → Resources folder.**

   You're in. Here are all the different files that make up your DVD. (See Figure 19-2 for an example.)

Figure 19-2:
Your .dvdproj file stores all the movies, sounds, graphics, and data associated with your iDVD project in a series of hidden subfolders and files. This column-view shot shows the progression of folders within folders.

So what is all this stuff?

• Your **ProjectData** file stores all the settings for your DVD project, in the form of a binary *property list*. It tells iDVD how to put together the menus, sound files, graphics, and other pieces that comprise your DVD.

NOTE If you're an inquiring soul, drag the ProjectData icon onto the icon of a binary XML editor, like Apple's (free) Property List Editor. Turns out ProjectData is just a humble XML file, and—as long as you're careful not to make or save any changes—you can pass an enlightening afternoon studying its contents to discover how it's structured.

- iDVD stores compressed video files—the ones that your audience will actually see on the DVD player—in the **MPEG** folder. If you really want to, you can play one of these files right on your Mac. To do so, copy it to the desktop, add an .m2v suffix to its file name, and watch it using a program that can play MPEG-2 files (like VLC, a free movie player from *http://www.videolan.org/vlc*).

- If you're using an older theme, one whose buttons are represented as little pictures or videos, then a **Thumbnails** folder stores the tiny QuickTime videos that play on the buttons. Double-click one of them to play it in QuickTime Player right on your Mac.

iDVD doesn't fill the remaining folders until it actually burns the DVD. At that point, iDVD uses these folders to store intermediate files as it works. For example:

- In the **Menu** folder, iDVD stores MPEG-2 (.m2v) files that represent the video loops used on your menu screens, complete with buttons, thumbnails, and so on.

- As you could probably guess, the **Slideshow** folder stores all the digital pictures and movies you've chosen for use in your slideshows, and the **Audio** folder contains all the sound files. (You could double-click one of the sound files to play it in QuickTime Player, if you really wanted to.)

- The **Overlay** folder holds *menu overlays* (videos that animate buttons when your viewers highlight them) and *motion overlays* (animations that play on top of drop zones—the Theater theme curtains or the Brush Strokes paint effect, for example).

AppleScripting iDVD

As any power user can tell you, AppleScript is one of the best features of the Mac operating system. It's a built-in, relatively easy programming language that lets you control your programs by writing little software recipes known as *scripts*—and lets your programs control each other by issuing invisible commands. (Not all programs respond to AppleScript commands, but, happily, iDVD does.)

As it turns out, you don't have to compose your own AppleScript programs to capitalize on iDVD's AppleScript-friendliness. Apple has created a series of useful scripts that you can download and install right now, for free, and use without having to type up a single line of code.

You'll find them on Apple's iDVD scripting page. Visit *www.apple.com/applescript/archive/idvd* to read about them and download them.

NOTE   Once you've downloaded and uncompressed these AppleScripts, you'll want to drag them into your Home → Library → Scripts folder, so you can trigger them by choosing their names from the Script menu. (If there isn't already a tiny black scroll icon on your menu bar—the Script menu—use the AppleScript Utility program to put it there.)

In any case, choosing an AppleScript's name from this menu is a very convenient and quick way to run it. In the following list, only the items identified as droplets or applications don't belong in your Script menu.

Here are some of the canned AppleScripts for iDVD:

- **iDVD Companion.** This is an actual application (not a script) that endows iDVD with the floating palette shown in Figure 19-3. This palette offers a number of useful controls that aren't available in iDVD alone, like one that snaps your menu buttons back into horizontal or vertical alignment (buttons that you've dragged freely, for example).

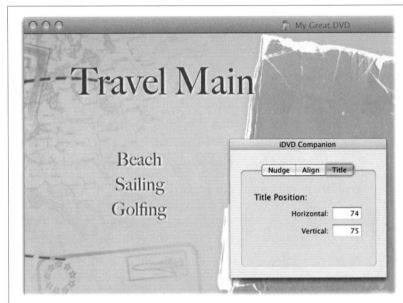

Figure 19-3:
iDVD Companion, a free program from Apple, isn't actually an AppleScript, but it uses AppleScript to add new features to iDVD—like the ability to align buttons that you've dragged by hand, or to specify the exact position of a text box on the screen.

iDVD Companion also offers a menu of all your menu screens, so that you can jump directly to any portion of your menu system; a list that lets you jump to any slideshow in a certain DVD project; a quick menu command that lets you turn the automatic button grid on or off; and more.

- **Create DVD From Folder.** This script is a *droplet*—a little application icon that does its work when you drag and drop something onto it. In this case, when you drag a folder of files onto this droplet, it opens iDVD and creates a new project automatically, based on the folder's contents and hierarchy. Complete instructions and examples come with the download.

- **Photoshop to iDVD.** This script automatically converts whatever document is currently open in Photoshop into a background image for the current menu screen in iDVD. It can be a real timesaver if you like to create your own DVD backgrounds.

- **iTunes to iDVD.** You know from Chapter 18 how to turn an iTunes song into the background music for a menu screen. But if you're already *in* iTunes, you can use this script to turn a selected track into the audio background for the current menu.

- **Sequential Movie.** This droplet creates a series of iDVD menu screens that guide your audience through a sequence of movies. It results in a well-structured and well-ordered movie sequence that's ideal for how-to projects (letting your viewers follow the steps in order), video treasure hunts (keeping your viewers from skipping ahead to clues before they're ready), educational videos (increasing the complexity of your instruction gradually as the lessons proceed), and so on.

NOTE   These scripts are getting pretty old. They still work, but they haven't been updated in ages. Some, like the "iTunes to DVD" script, aren't even useful anymore. (iDVD has its own window into your iTunes collection.)

Archiving Your Project

Ordinarily, iDVD doesn't store any videos, photos, or sounds in your iDVD project file. It remains a tiny, compact file that stores only *pointers* to those files elsewhere on your hard drive.

That's why, if you delete or move one of those media files, iDVD mildly freaks out.

In early versions of iDVD, you couldn't transfer a project from one Mac to another for this very reason. And that meant that you couldn't *design* a DVD on one Mac (one that lacked a DVD burner, for example), and then *burn* it on another. You also couldn't back up your project file, content that you'd included all of its pieces.

Fortunately, in more recent versions, Apple came up with a solution. The Archive Project command lets you completely "dereference" your project, so the project file *contains* every file that you've in corporated into your project:movies, photos, sounds, theme components, and DVD-ROM files. Your project file is now completely self-contained, ready for backup or transfer to another computer.

It's also now really, really huge.

Follow these steps to produce your archive:

1. **Save your project.**

   If you forget this step, iDVD reminds you.

2. **Choose File → Archive Project.**

   The Save As panel shown in Figure 19-4 appears.

Figure 19-4:
*The Archive Project's Save As panel lets you
specify whether you want to include themes and
encoded files in your archived project. You can
save quite a bit of disk space by leaving these
options unchecked. The Size indicator to the right
of "Include themes" tells you how much space
your project will occupy.*

3. **Turn checkboxes on or off, if you like.**

   "Include themes" copies your theme files into the project—something that's
   unnecessary if you're using standard Apple themes. This checkbox is important
   only if the themes you've used come from other companies, were designed by
   you, or are modified versions of Apple's originals. "Include encoded files" is the
   more important option, because it's very unlikely that all of your sounds, photos,
   and movies are also on the destination Mac.

   Turn the boxes on and off to see how much space you'll recover.

4. **Name the archive file, choose a folder location for it, and then click Save.**

   Wait as iDVD builds the new archive. This can take a few minutes, so be
   patient. You may be working with *very* large files.

Archived projects look like any other projects, in that they use the same .dvdproj
extension. But inside, they're very different. For proof, simply open it as a package
(Control-click its icon; from the shortcut menu, choose View Package Contents).
Inside its Contents → Resources folder, new folders called Assets and Themes store
the extra archived elements (Figure 19-5).

Figure 19-5:
*When archiving a project, iDVD
creates additional folders
within the new project bundle.
The Assets folder stores
original copies of your audio
and video files (in the "av"
subfolder), DVD-ROM content
(in "data") and images (in
"stills"). If you've chosen to
save themes, they show up in
the Themes folder.*

NOTE In order to turn your photos and videos into DVD material, iDVD must *encode* (convert) them into a format called MPEG. Depending on your Preferences settings, iDVD may constantly be working on this time-consuming task, or it may do the job only when you burn the DVD. Either way, an archived project also stores any MPEG files iDVD has created so far. They'll save you time when you burn the DVD, but they'll make the archive's file size balloon up like a blimp.

If you'd rather keep the file smaller, choose Advanced → Delete Encoded Assets before saving the archive. iDVD removes the encoded MPEG files—but you'll pay for this gesture in re-encoding time when you're ready to burn your discs.

Copying the Archive to a Different Mac

Suppose that you've designed a DVD using a Mac that lacks a DVD burner. Now, as Apple intended, you've used the Archive command to prepare it for transfer to a Mac that *does* have a burner.

Transfer the archive project using any convenient method: copy it across a network, transfer it using iChat, copy it onto an iPod, or whatever. (It's too big for email, of course, but you could instead post it on a Web site for downloading.) The project opens normally on the other machine, with all of its pieces intact, ready to touch up and burn.

Disk Images

Thanks to a handy iDVD feature, you can save your project as a computer file called a *disk image*.

You may have run into the disk-image (.dmg or .img) format before; it's a popular storage format for software you download. It's so popular because you get a single, self-contained file that *contains* many other files, arrayed inside exactly as though they're on a disk. When you open a disk-image file, in fact, it turns into a little hard-disk icon on your desktop, with all of its contents tucked inside.

NOTE Don't confuse a disk image with a project archive; they're two very different beasts. A disk image is a virtual disk, a bit-for-bit copy of the data that would appear on an actual, physical DVD—it just happens to be stored on a hard drive rather than a DVD.

Project archives, in contrast, contain all the source project material used by iDVD. The only thing that can read or "play back" a project archive is iDVD itself.

To turn an iDVD project into a disk image, save it. Then, choose File → "Save as Disc Image" (Shift-⌘-R). Choose a file name (for example, *Summer Fun.img*) and a location, and then click Save. Now wait as iDVD compresses your movie data and saves it to disk. All of this takes just as long as an actual DVD burning, so now's your chance to catch up on some magazine reading.

When it's all over, you'll find a new .img icon—a disk image—on your desktop. Disk images are amazingly high-octane, cool stuff for two reasons:

- **You don't have to burn a disc to watch your movies.** Mac OS X's DVD Player program can play back a disk image just as though it's a real DVD. You see all the menus, slideshows, and other iDVD features you've grown to love.

As shown in Figure 19-6, the trick is to open the Video_TS folder. Never heard of it? Well, it's an important folder on *every DVD ever made*—it's where all the video files reside—and there's one on your disk image, too.

Figure 19-6:
Apple's DVD Player utility (in your Applications folder) can play back disk images as well as physical DVDs. In the Finder, double-click the disk image to make the virtual DVD appear on your desktop. In DVD Player, choose File → Open DVD Media, as shown at top. In the dialog box that appears, choose the Video_TS folder you want to play. Navigate into the disk image, choose the Video_TS folder, and click Choose. Press the space bar to start playback.

TIP   This is a handy way to test a DVD before you use up a perfectly good blank. The tip doesn't work for dual-layer DVDs, though, because disk images don't indicate where the "break" is between dual layers.

• **You can burn a new copy whenever you want, without waiting.** You can use Roxio Toast (a beloved commercial burning program) or Mac OS X's own Disk Utility program to burn the disk image onto a real DVD—without having to wait for the excruciating multi-hour encoding process again. Figure 19-7 provides the amazingly simple instructions for this long-sought solution.

Figure 19-7:
Double-click your disk image in the Finder to make its virtual disk appear. Then open Disk Utility (in your Application → Utilities folder), click the virtual disk, and choose Images → Burn. Disk Utility prompts you to insert a blank DVD. Do so, and then click Burn.

Professional Duplicating

Maybe you've organized a school play, and you want to sell copies of the performance to parents as a fundraiser. Maybe you want to send out "new baby" videos to your family circle. Or maybe you've used iDVD to create a video brochure of your small business's products and services.

In each of these cases, burning the DVDs one at a time on your own Mac looks like a time-consuming, expensive hassle. Furthermore, home-burned DVDs involve a laser recording a pattern on an organic dye, which deteriorates over time. On commercial DVDs, the signal is stamped directly into the plastic.

Accordingly, when you want to make more than a handful of copies of your DVD, you might want to consider enlisting the aid of a *DVD service bureau*. (DVD service bureaus are middlemen between you and the large replication plants, which don't deal directly with the public.)

Technically, these companies offer two different services:

- **Duplication.** Duplicated discs are copies of your original DVD. Service bureaus use banks of DVD burners, five or 10 at a time, that churn out copy after copy on DVD-Rs (the same kinds of blanks as you used). You pay for materials and labor, usually by the hour. (Discs with less data burn more quickly, producing more discs per hour.) This is the way to go if you need fewer than 100 copies of your disc. (On the other hand, remember that some DVD players don't play DVD-R discs.)

- **Replication.** Replication is designed for huge numbers of copies, 200 and up. In this process, the company actually presses the DVDs just the way Hollywood movie studios do it—and the results play back in virtually every DVD player.

  Replicated discs are produced in factories. When replicated, the data from your master DVD-R is placed on a pressed 4.7 GB "DVD-5" disc—a standard DVD, not a DVD-R. You can also replicate to dual-layer discs. Just ask your salesman for details. Expect to pay about a dollar per disc for a run of 1,000 discs. Smaller runs will cost more per disc, larger runs less, but $1,000 is about the least you'll pay for a replication job.

  NOTE   DVD service bureaus often call themselves *replicators,* even though they offer both duplication and replication.

Prepare to Copy

All DVD service bureaus accept DVD-R masters, of the sort that iDVD burns. Nevertheless, keep these tips in mind:

- **Submit two.** Always submit two copies of your master. It costs you almost nothing in materials and time, and can save your project if one of the discs fails.

- **Use name brands.** Burn your masters on the best-quality discs available. Brand-name blanks, like Verbatim, Maxell or TDK, are less likely to lead to duplication problems. (One replicator complains that if you hold those cheapie 30-cent discs up to the light, you can see light pass right through them!)

- **Use DVD-Rs.** Despite the format wars in DVD standards (DVD-R vs. DVD+R), the -R standard is better for replication. Many factories, in fact, don't accept +R discs, which leads to manufacturing problems.

- **You don't need a DVD burner.** If your Mac doesn't have a DVD burner, most service bureaus can create the DVDs from a disk image (which you can create directly from iDVD). You'll pay a little extra for the conversion.

- **Collect your copyright documentation.** Every replicator will ask you to sign a copyright release stating that you have permission to use the material on your disc. (If you're not asked about this, run away screaming. It's a red flag that you're dealing with an unsavory replicator.)

As a rule, anything you've videotaped is yours. You own it. If you use music from a friend, then a simple signed and dated letter will do: "Casey is my friend and has the right to use my music." If you're using royalty-free material, make a note of it. And if you're using music you bought from the iTunes music store (or ripped from a commercial music CD), well, you may be on thin ice.

Choosing a Replicator

When choosing a service bureau or replicator, start by getting references—preferably on *recent* projects. Do your legwork and make the calls. You can also check with the Better Business Bureau to see if a service bureau has a history of customer complaints.

> **TIP** Choose a licensed replicator. Replicators and manufacturers must pay a small royalty on every DVD they produce, because DVDs are copyrighted technology. Some factories, even in the U.S., operate with questionable practices–some pay all their fees, some pay part of their fees, some don't pay fees at all. Reputable service bureaus don't work with gray-market replicators.

Take cost into account when picking a service bureau, but keep in mind that you often get what you pay for. It may be worth paying extra to find a technically savvy reseller that will ask the right questions, hold your hand as needed, and make sure that your project turns out right.

Working with Replicators

When submitting a work order, be *very* specific. Unless you specify Amray cases (the Blockbuster-style cases, with a little plastic hub that holds the center of the DVD) and cigarette-stripped shrink wrap (standard clear plastic wrapping, so named because you pull a strip to open it, just as on a pack of cigarettes), you may end up with DVDs shoved into CD jewel cases. Sit down with your salesperson and go through all the options, from packaging to turnaround time.

Complex packaging takes more time and costs more. Consider ordering your discs in bulk paper sleeves or "slimline" cases (the most basic DVD delivery cases), without printing on them, to save on costs and time. To save even more money, you may be able to set up a deal where you pay to replicate 1,000 discs but package only 200 of them.

Fulfillment

If you're interested in *selling* your DVD masterpieces, you may want to hire yet another company to package, mail, and collect payment for them. *Fulfillment* companies, many run by DVD service bureaus, build a basic Web site, take orders, and mail out your discs. All you have to do is provide your iDVD masters, sign the contracts, pay the setup bills—and start working on your Oscar acceptance speech.

Making DVDs Last

Your homemade DVDs (which are "burned" using dyes) probably won't last the 100 years expected of commercial DVDs (which are etched with lasers). But don't get too depressed by the occasional article about homemade DVDs "going bad" in a matter of months. Most cases of "DVD rot" come down to one of two things: problems created during manufacturing or poor handling by their owners.

There's not much you can do about manufacturing errors, apart from buying name-brand blank DVDs. As for handling, these tips should ensure that your recordable DVDs will last for years:

Store your discs in a cool, dry place. DVD-Rs are sensitive to both temperature and humidity. In an ideal world, DVDs would love to live in a cupboard that's 68 degrees Fahrenheit with 30 to 50 percent humidity. In the real world, room temperature is fine as long as temperature swings aren't a fact of life. Recordable DVDs hate large changes in humidity, too.

Keep your discs out of the light. Prolonged exposure to ultraviolet light degrades the organic dyes in the recordable layer, possibly making the data on your discs unreadable. Regular light may also hurt your discs, primarily through heat.

Don't flex your discs. With their laminated polycarbonate layers, recordable DVDs are very sensitive to bending or flexing. In fact, the quickest way to destroy your disc is to bend it. So don't. Store your discs in soft envelopes or in cases where you pinch a center hub to release the DVD. Don't store them in CD jewel boxes that have a snap-on hub.

Hold discs by the edges. Fingerprints, scratches, and dust on the disc surface interfere with a laser's ability to read data. DVDs are much more sensitive than CDs in this regard, because the data is crammed together so much more tightly.

Don't stick on labels. Adhesive labels throw off the disc's balance—and might even ruin your drive when the heat makes the glue melt. Instead, use a CD-safe marker to write on your DVD-Rs.

Part Four: Appendixes

4

iMovie '09, Menu by Menu

As you've certainly noticed by now, iMovie doesn't look like a standard Mac program. Part of its radical charm is that almost all of its functions are represented visually onscreen. There simply aren't many menu commands. But don't get complacent: You'll miss some great features if you don't venture much to the top of the screen.

Now documenting the iMovie menu commands is tricky because they're constantly changing. The command that says Select All Events one minute might say Select All another, and Select Entire Clip a minute after that. The wording is always driving at the same gist—delete things, select things, and so on—but changes according to the situation.

Here's a rundown of the commands in iMovie's menus:

iMovie Menu

In Mac OS X, the first menu after the menu is named for the program you're using—in this case, iMovie.

About iMovie

This command opens the "About" box containing the requisite Apple legal information. There's really only one good reason to open the About iMovie window: It's the easiest way to find out exactly which version of iMovie you have.

Preferences

Opens the Preferences window (Figure A-1). (*Keyboard shortcut:* ⌘-comma.) Here's a tour.

General Tab

- **Show Advanced Tools.** This may not be Apple's finest interface-design moment, but whatever: When you turn on this option, a motley assortment of additional features shows up in random iMovie places. On the central toolbar, the Keyword button appears. "Paint to select" editing becomes available (page 82). So does "Paint to reject" or "Paint to mark as Favorite" editing (page 100).

  This option reveals additional drag-and-drop menu options that show up when you drop one clip onto another. Specifically, they are Cutaways (page 94), Green Screen (page 143), Picture-in-Picture (page 148), and additional replace options (page 79).

  And in the Video Adjustments panel, individual sliders appear for Red, Green, and Blue color intensity (page 165).

- **Display Time as HH:MM:SS:Frames.** Ordinarily, iMovie shows you the lengths of clips and selections using seconds—for example, "8.5s," meaning 8.5 seconds.

  Experienced video editors, however, are used to looking at timecode displays, which take the form of minutes:seconds:frames—for example, "02:08:15." If you turn this checkbox on, then iMovie adds the frames to all time readouts. Instead of "8.5s," you'll see "8:15." (There are 30 frames per second in North American video.)

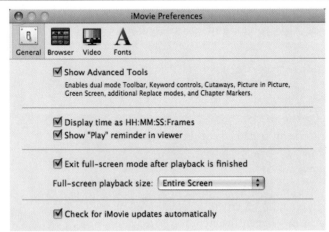

Figure A-1:
You can get to this box quickly by pressing ⌘-comma, which isn't so hard to learn considering it's also the keystroke that opens the Preferences box in iPhoto, iTunes, GarageBand, and most other Apple and Microsoft programs. What isn't typical, though, is the way Apple has split apart four sets of preferences. In this box, you'll find options that govern the entire iMovie program. In the Project Preferences box, there are options that you set independently for each movie-editing project.

• **Show "Play" reminder in viewer.** From the day you first tried iMovie, you might have noticed the message that appears in the Viewer window whenever you're pointing to a filmstrip: "Press the space bar or double-click to Play." Apple wanted to make really, really sure that you knew how to play your video.

Once you've got that technique under your belt, though, you might feel that this message is unnecessary. You can turn it off with this checkbox.

• **Exit fullscreen mode after playback is finished**. Pretty much what it says. If this option is turned on, then every time you finish playing back a movie in full-screen mode, you return to iMovie. If it's off, then you stay in full-screen mode for more playback experimentation.

• **Fullscreen playback size**. See page 84 for details on this option.

• **Check for iMovie updates automatically**. If this option is turned on, then iMovie sends out an electronic feeler each time it's open and you're online, checking to see if a new update is available. If so, you're invited to download and install it.

Browser Tab

• **Show date ranges in Event list**. If you turn this option on, then each Event in your Event list sprouts, in tiny lettering, a legend like "Oct 25, 2007–Nov 1, 2007," to let you know the time period covered by the video inside.

• **Use large font for project and Event lists.** You guessed it: This option enlarges the type size in these two lists.

• **Always show active clip badges.** Many of the changes you can make to a project clip (things like stabilization, color changes, or volume adjustments) will result in a tiny badge appearing on the top-left corner of the clip (for our examples, a hand, a sun, and a speaker icon, respectively). Unchecking this options makes those permanently invisible.

• **Clips in Event browser use project crop setting.** You can read about the aspect-ratio problem on page 56. And you can read about how you want your project to *handle* the aspect-ratio problem on page 57.

But the choice you make for handling mis-fitting footage in your *project* doesn't do anything in the *Event Browser*. That is, setting up letterbox bars for the project itself doesn't create letterbox bars as you peruse your source clips in the Event Browser—unless you turn on this option. Then the Event Browser displays your clips with the same Crop or Fit setting you've selected for the project.

• **Automatically stabilize clips that have been analyzed.** Once clips in the Event Browser have been analyzed (page 154), iMovie can automatically stabilize them as you add them to your project. Leave this unchecked, and iMovie won't stabilize project clips unless you tell it to via the Inspector.

- **Show Fine Tuning buttons**. The "buttons" referred to here are shown in Figure 3-13 (page 92). They appear when you point to a filmstrip without clicking. And when you click one of these little buttons, you get the orange vertical clip-cropping handles that let you lengthen or shorten a clip by up to 1 second.

  If the appearance of that little button confuses you or clutters your life, you can hide it by turning off this button. Even then, you can still make those orange clip-cropping handles appear when you want them—just by pressing the Option and ⌘ keys.

- **Double-click to: Edit/Play**. If you choose Edit, double-clicking a clip will bring the Inspector out of hiding, allowing you to make changes to the clip. If you select Play, double-clicking will work just like pressing the space bar; iMovie will start playing the clip from the playhead on.

- **Clicking in Event browser…** These three options let you control what happens when you click a filmstrip in the Event Browser. On a freshly installed copy of iMovie, you get a 4-second selection. But you can also opt to have one click select the entire clip or deselect everything (because you prefer to drag to make selections, not click).

Video Tab

- **Video Standard**. Depending on the video standard used in your part of the world (see page 18), you want to select the standard that will work on the TVs and DVD players where you live.

- **Import 1080i video as: Large/Full**. Page 32 offers a full description of this option, which pertains solely to video you import from high-definition camcorders.

Fonts Tab

This tab gets full treatment on page 183.

Shop for iMovie Products

This isn't so much a command as it is a marketing ploy. It opens your Web browser to a page on Apple's Web site that offers to sell you camcorders, plug-ins, blank DVDs, and other accessories.

Provide iMovie Feedback

This command takes you to a Web form on Apple's site where you can register complaints, make suggestions, or gush enthusiastically about iMovie. (Don't expect a return call from Steve Jobs, however.)

Register iMovie

This is a link to yet another Apple Web page. Registering iMovie simply means giving Apple your contact information so you can access Apple's online support documents, receive upgrade notices, get special offers, and so on. There's no penalty for not registering, by the way. Apple just wants to know more about who you are, so that it can offer you exciting new waves of junk mail.

Check For Updates

If iMovie isn't set to check for Apple patches and bug-fix updates automatically, you can make it check manually on your command, using this option.

Hide iMovie, Hide Others, Show All

These aren't iMovie's commands—they're Mac OS X's.

In any case, they determine which of the various programs running on your Mac are visible onscreen at any given moment. The Hide Others command is probably the most popular of these three. It zaps away the windows of all other programs—including the Finder—so that the iMovie window is the only one you see.

> **TIP**   If you know this golden Mac OS X trick, you may never need to use the Hide Others command: To switch into iMovie from another program, hold down the Option and ⌘ keys when clicking the iMovie icon in the Dock. Doing so simultaneously brings iMovie to the front and hides all other programs you have running, producing an uncluttered, distraction-free view of iMovie.

Quit iMovie

This command (*keyboard shortcut*: ⌘-Q) closes iMovie after offering you the chance to save any changes you've made to your project file. The next time you open iMovie by double-clicking its icon, the program reopens whatever project document you were working on.

File Menu

As in any Mac program, the File menu serves as the program's interface to the rest of the Macintosh world. It lets you import movies and video, manage Events, create or duplicate projects, or quit the program.

New Project

Creates a new project in the Projects list, ready for filling with video snippets from the Event Browser.

New Folder

Creates a simulated file folder in the Projects list, into which you can drag individual projects. It's a tool for managing long project lists as your editing skills grow.

Duplicate Project

Creates a duplicate of the project you're working on. This is a great trick for generating alternate versions—a shorter edit, a raunchier one, and so on.

The great thing about creating and duplicating projects, of course, is that you're not using up any more hard drive space. A project is, behind the scenes, just a tiny text file; it doesn't store any video. The instructions in that text file just refer to the video that's actually stored in your Events.

Project Properties

This command opens the all-important Project Properties dialog box (Figure A-2), which is a lot like Preferences except that the settings you make here apply only to one project—the one you're working on.

General Tab

- **Aspect Ratio.** This pop-up menu specifies the movie-frame proportions of your project, as described on page 56.

- **Theme.** This is where you choose a theme for your project, if any. Page 127 has a lot more information about themes.

- **Automatically add (pick a transition).** Here, you control whether or not iMovie puts in transition effects automatically between all clips in your project—and if so, which transition, and how long you want it to last. Details are on page 128. If you pick a theme, this menu turns into a plain ol' checkbox, and the theme titles and transitions are chosen for you.

Timing Tab

- **Transition Duration.** Drag this slider left or right to determine how long a newly added transition will take.

- **Theme Transition Duration.** This slider works the same as above, but affects the specially animated theme transitions iMovie uses with its themes (page 129).

- **Applies to all transitions.** If you opt for this choice, the duration slider affects all transitions, those already placed and those you have yet to place. (It means that you'll lose all custom duration adjustments you've already made to transitions in the project.)

- **Applies when added to project.** This one means "Leave the durations of the transitions I've already adjusted alone. But make all incoming transitions this long."

- **Title Fade Duration.** This slider controls how long the text of your titles takes to fade in and fade out during their appearances in your movie.

- **Photo Duration.** When you first drag a photo into your storyboard, it turns into a "still video" clip. This slider lets you specify how long those clips play when first placed into the storyboard. (You can always adjust their timing later, of course.)

- **Applies to all photos.** Just like with the equivalent setting for transitions, if you pick this option, the duration slider affects all photos, those already placed and those you have yet to place. (It means that you'll lose all custom duration adjustments you've already made to photos in the project.)

- **Applies when added to project.** This one means "Leave the durations of the *photos* I've already adjusted alone. But make all incoming photos this long."

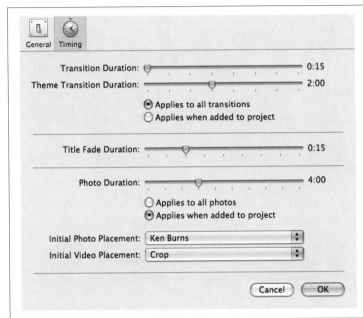

Figure A-2:
This is the preferences dialog box—for the project you're working on. Commit the corresponding keystroke to memory: ⌘-J.(It stands for proJect—get it?)

- **Initial Photo Placement.** This pop-up menu tells iMovie how to handle photos that don't exactly fit the aspect ratio of your movie project. It can either Crop them (enlarge to fill the frame), "Fit in Frame" (add letterbox bars), or Ken Burns (perform a slow zoom and pan).

- **Initial Video Placement.** Similarly, this pop-up menu controls what happens when you add mis-fitting video to a project. iMovie can either enlarge it to fit the frame (Crop) or add letterbox bars ("Fit in Frame").

Move to Trash

To delete most things in iMovie, like transitions, titles, or sound clips, you just click the item and then press the Delete key.

Things that represent more effort, however, like projects, Events, and imported video, require more effort to delete—and those steps always begin with this command, whose wording changes to reflect whatever is highlighted (for example, "Move Event to Trash" or "Move Entire Clip to Trash").

They wind up in the Macintosh Trash, as described on page 54, so that you can recover them if you change your mind.

Move to Rejected Clips Trash

This saves you a trip to the Rejected Clips view (page 108). Select this and any clips you have already rejected will go directly to the Macintosh trash without passing Go.

Space Saver

This command is another way to reclaim a lot of disk space. It rounds up all your unwanted or unused video and purges it from your hard drive; details are on page 109.

Consolidate Media

Collects media for a given project so that it all lives on a single drive. More on this on page 55.

Merge Events

iMovie generally splits imported video into Events—shots that were filmed on the same day. You may sometimes find it useful, however, to combine several Events into a single Event, like the three days' worth of video from a single weekend getaway.

To use this command, first highlight the Events that you want to merge. (Click one, and then ⌘-click each additional one.) Then choose this command. You'll be asked what you want to name the new, combined Event.

Split Event Before Selected Clip

Conversely, you may sometimes want to split an Event in two. That's the purpose of this command. Highlight a filmstrip within the Event, and then choose this command; iMovie creates a second Event containing the selected filmstrip and everything that followed it. If the first event was called Vacation, the second one is called Vacation 1.

Move Rejected Clips to Trash

You can read about this command on page 109. It moves all footage that you've marked as rejects into the Trash, for permanent removal from your hard drive.

Adjust Clip Date and Time...

You'll use this command to fix any event footage that just didn't happen when iMovie thinks it happened. To set iMovie straight on footage dates, follow the instructions on page 61.

Analyze for Stabilization

This menu item tells iMovie to examine a clip so it can be stabilized when added to a project. Page 154 has details, but don't plan on analyzing a lot of footage unless you have an extra month or two. (It takes a long time.)

Optimize Video Full/Large

Some cameras store video in formats that are very processor-intensive, notably the H.264 format. On even moderately speedy Macs, these clips look jittery during scrubbing, ruining one of iMovie's coolest features. To smooth things over, you can use this menu item to convert your clips to Apple Intermediate Codec (see page 43). The resulting files take up a lot more disk space than H.264, but they scrub much more smoothly. Use the Full option to preserve HD footage in full quality, or the Large option to use Apple's HD-lite. (Read more aboiut this choice on page 32.)

Import from Camera, Import Movies, Import Camera Archive, Import iMovie HD Project

Every video-editing project begins with one of these four commands, which bring in the raw materials for your project from either a camcorder, a movie file on the hard drive, a camcorder archive, or an older iMovie version. Chapter 1 describes all four methods in great detail.

Page Setup, Print Project

It might seem peculiar to find a Print command in a video editing program. But there are times when the Print command might be helpful:

- You're working on a long project that doesn't fit into the iMovie window. By making a printout, you can see the big picture.

- You might want to share a visual representation of your project, identifying particular transitions, clips, or titles for someone who isn't sitting there in front of your screen with you.

- Your Event Browser is overflowing with clips, and you're sorting through them, trying to decide which to trim or delete.

In all of these cases, you can print your Events or projects for a handy reference.

> **TIP** Use the Print Preview button to get an accurate view of your output before you commit it to ink and paper.

Note, however, that:

- The Print command prints whatever project or Event(s) you have selected, so be sure to select the proper ones in the left-side list before you begin. (Remember, you can select more than one project or Event by ⌘-clicking them.)

- The Print command respects the magnification levels you're using to view your clips. That is, the half-second zoom means a lot of frames on your printed page; the 30-second zoom means very few.

- iMovie attempts to fit everything on a single page. If it can't, it reduces the thumbnail sizes of the entire printout as much as necessary, all in an effort to fit the number of "preferred" pages you've specified (Figure A-3).

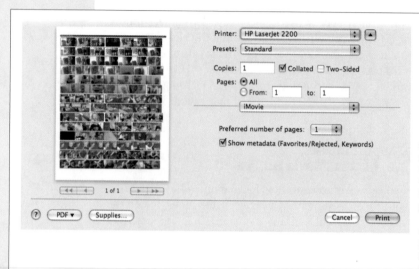

Figure A-3:
If you choose iMovie from the third pop-up menu, you discover that two handy options have been lurking. "Preferred number of pages" determines iMovie's target maximum for the printout, although if your project is too long to fit this number of pages even with tiny thumbnails, additional pages will come out. The "Show metadata" checkbox will include keyword, favorite, and reject markings in the printout.

- When you print Events, you get a divider on the printout that identifies each Event.

- If you choose, you can also include favorite, keyword, and reject markings in your printout (Figure A-3).

Edit Menu

The Edit menu contains all of the editing commands described in Chapter 2 and Chapter 3. In fact, along with the various drag-and-drop editing techniques described in this book, the commands in the Edit menu are the only tools you need to build your movies.

Undo

In iMovie, you can take back not only the last editing maneuver, not only the last 10, but an infinite number of steps, all the way back to the last time you opened iMovie. The ability to change your mind, or to recover from a particularly bad editing decision, is a considerable blessing.

The wording of this command changes to show you which editing step it's about to reverse. It might say Undo Merge Events, Undo Split, and so on. *Keyboard short-cut*: ⌘-Z.

Redo

We're only human, so it's entirely possible that sometimes you might want to undo your Undo.

For example, suppose that you've just used the Undo command a few times, retracing your steps back to a time when your movie was in better shape, and then decide that you've gone one step too far. That's when the Redo command is useful; it tells iMovie to undo your last Undo, so that you can step forward in time, redoing the steps that you just undid. (If you haven't yet used the Undo command, then Redo is dimmed.) *Keyboard shortcut*: Shift-⌘-Z.

Cut, Copy, Paste

You can use the Cut, Copy, and Paste commands just as you would in any other program: to move stuff around. You can cut, copy, and paste whatever you've selected: entire filmstrips or just chunks of them.

For example, you can cut a selection out of a clip and paste it into another spot, or you can copy a selection and paste it into another project.

Cut, Copy, Paste, and Clear (page 87) also work when you're editing text, such as the names of your clips or the text for your credits and other titles.

> **TIP** To get an interesting "instant replay" effect, try this trick: Copy a short bit of interesting video, such as your friend tripping over his shoelace and hitting the ground. Paste the snippet twice, so you wind up with three copies of the same short snippet all in a row. Now watch the playback and enjoy the fun!

Paste Adjustments

Once you've painstakingly edited the look of a clip (color correction, for example), a photo (a Ken Burns effect, for example), or some audio (boosting the volume, for example), you can rapidly enhance a bunch of other footage in the same way. Just copy the first clip, and then, after selecting the other clips, use the Paste Adjustments commands. You have a lot of options:

- **Video**: color changes
- **Audio**: volume changes
- **Crop**: crop, fit, or Ken Burns changes
- **Cutaway/Picture-in-Picture/Green Screen**: unique characteristics (such as fade and opacity) of these clips
- **Video Effect**: video effect changes
- **Stabilization**: stabilization and zoom changes
- **Speed**: timing changes
- **Map Style**: type of map changes

Delete, Delete Entire Clip (Reject, Reject Entire Clip)

More ways to get rid of stuff. If you've selected only a portion of a filmstrip, you can use the Delete command (or press the Delete key) to snip out just that segment. Or add the ⌘ key to get rid of the entire clip, even though only a piece is highlighted.

The command might also say Delete Selection, depending on what's highlighted.

In the Event Browser, these commands say Reject instead of Delete, but only because rejecting, in iMovie, is the first step toward deleting footage for good. The box on page 108 has the details.

Select All Events

This command is a chameleon. It always means "Select All," but the wording changes.

• If a portion of a clip is selected in the Event Browser, it says Select Entire Clip.

• If an Event is selected in the Events list, it says Select All Events.

• If a clip is highlighted in the storyboard, the command says Select All (meaning all filmstrips).

• If some text is highlighted in a text box, the command says Select All (meaning all text in this box)

Keyboard shortcut: ⌘-A.

Select None

Memorizing this command (or better yet, its keyboard equivalent, Shift-⌘-A) is an excellent idea. It deselects everything, including clips and pieces of clips. That's useful when, for example, you want to use one of the "clip-painting" techniques described on page 82, which require that nothing is highlighted.

Trim to Selection

Use this command to trim excess ends off a storyboard clip after you've isolated a portion of it using the triangular handles under the Scrubber bar. *Keyboard shortcut*: ⌘-B.

Trim Clip End

You can fine-tune a clip's length with these commands—or, more practically, with the keyboard equivalents, Option-left arrow or Option-right arrow. Each press makes the clip one frame shorter or longer. (You're changing either the beginning or the end of the clip, whichever is closest to your cursor.)

Split Clip

It's often convenient to chop a clip in half, or even into three pieces; this command does the trick. Make a selection in any storyboard filmstrip; iMovie splits the clip at the beginning of the yellow selection border. (If the border doesn't go all the way to the end of the clip, you'll wind up with *three* pieces.)

Join Clip

If, having split a clip as described above, you want to *rejoin* the pieces, place them consecutively in the storyboard, and then use this command. This won't join clips that were never part of one clip to begin with.

Detach Audio

This handy command takes the sound from the selected project clip and puts it in as a sound effect (page 206), still synced up with the clip. It also mutes the clip the audio was taken from.

Mute/Unmute Clip

This completely silences a clip or restores the volume setting if the clip was already muted. Saves you a trip to the Inspector, so learn the *keyboard shortcut*: Shift-⌘-M.

Reveal in Event Browser

This handy option lets you click a clip in the storyboard, and then jump to the corresponding raw source clip in the Event Browser. Seeing the original clip gives you a lot more information; for example, you can see how much of the clip you've used, whether or not you've used pieces of the clip elsewhere in the project (as indicated by the orange stripes), whether or not you applied any cropping or color correction to the master clip, and so on.

Arrange Music Tracks

This command refers to background music tracks, the sort of floating background audio that plays from the beginning of the project (page 203). If you've set up more than one of these tracks, this command opens a window (page 205) that lets you change their sequence.

Unpin Music Track

Again, page 203 has more details. But this command applies to background music tracks that you've dragged horizontally, thus pinning them to specific video frames. And it means "Un-pin this puppy, so that it floats freely against the left side of the project."

Add Beat Marker

Tells iMovie to use that marker as a reference point for the Snap to Beats feature, covered on page 207. This command only works when an audio track is open in the Clip Trimmer.

Spelling

You use Mac OS X's built-in spell checker only when creating iMovie titles (Chapter 8).

Special Characters

You're creating a subtitle for an interview with the CEO of "I've Got a ¥en™" Productions. But how the heck do you type the ¥ symbol—or the ™ symbol? Easy one. You choose this command and double-click the symbol you want from the palette arrayed before you. *Keyboard shortcut*: Shift-⌘-S.

View Menu

This menu is mostly about changing the way iMovie displays your video clips while you work.

- **Favorites Only, Favorites and Unmarked, All Clips, Rejected Only**. These commands hide or show filmstrips in your Event Browser, according to how you've branded them: as favorite clips, rejected clips, or neither (Chapter 4). If you're ever looking for a filmstrip that you're sure you once had, check this menu; they may just be hidden.

- **Group Events by Disk, Group Events By Month, Show Most Recent Events at Top, Show Separate Days in Events**. All of these options control the way your Events are listed at the left side of the window. Chapter 2 has details.

- **Play, Play Selection, Play from Beginning, Play Around Current Frame, Play Full Screen**. These are pretty much self-explanatory, no? For details, see page 84. And learn the keyboard shortcuts.

- **Snap to Ends**. Wow, talk about obscure. When you're dragging an audio stripe, photo stripe, or text stripe in the storyboard, would you like iMovie's assistance in lining it up with the exact beginning of the filmstrip? If so, turn on this option. You'll feel and see a little snap of your cursor as you drag the stripe close to the clip end.

- **Snap to Beats**. This causes certain editing behaviors in iMovie to respect beat markers you've added to an audio track. Read page 207 to get the process down pat.

- **Audio Skimming**. When you skim (see page 69), iMovie generally plays the audio simultaneously, which may sound fragmented and disturbing. Turn off this option if you'd rather skim in silence.

- **Playhead Info.** When you turn this option on, a balloon pops out of the Playhead when you move it, identifying the date and time that video was shot, and pinpointing your cursor's location from its beginning point.

Text Menu

This menu is useful only when you're editing titles for your movie. All of its commands affect your typography, and all of them are described in Chapter 8.

Share Menu

In theory, anyway, the whole point of video editing is to produce a finished flick that you want to show somebody. This menu offers you eight different ways to export the finished product:

- **iTunes** is the first step toward landing your movie on an iPod, iPhone, or Apple TV.

- **iDVD** burns your movie to DVDs, with custom menus and all.

- **Media Browser** is used for getting your movie into other Apple software like Keynote, GarageBand, or iWeb.

- **YouTube** is YouTube, the world's most popular free video-sharing Web site.

- **MobileMe Gallery** is the custom photo- and movie-sharing site available to MobileMe subscribers.

- **Export Movie.** Like Share → Media Browser, this command offers a dialog box that lists four canned screen sizes. But like Share → "Export using QuickTime" (described below), it offers you a chance to store the resulting file with a name and folder location of your choice.

- **Export using QuickTime** turns your movie into a video file on your hard drive. But unlike Export Movie, this command gives you full access to the dozens of QuickTime options that give you infinite control over frame size, frame rate, audio compression, video compression, and more.

- **Export Final Cut XML.** If you have one of Apple's more powerful video editing programs, like Final Cut Express or Final Cut Pro, you'll be grateful for this option. It turns your entire iMovie project into an XML file, an exported project file. Later, you can open up this exported file in Final Cut to complete the editing with a far more powerful suite of tools. See Figure A-4 for some caveats and limitations.

> **NOTE** The exported file doesn't actually contain any video. It's just a description of your project—your edits—and references to the original captured video files that sit in your iMovie '09 Events folders. Final Cut therefore works from the original, unmodified clips, preserving all of their quality.

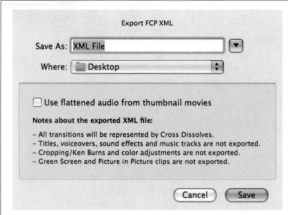

Figure A-4:
The exported project file doesn't completely reproduce your iMovie work. As noted here, there's quite a bit of stuff that doesn't make it through the transfer alive (music, titles, and so on). But that's OK; if you plan ahead, you'll never miss them. The whole point is to dress up the rough cut in Final Cut anyway.

Export FCP XML

Save As: XML File

Where: Desktop

☐ Use flattened audio from thumbnail movies

Notes about the exported XML file:

– All transitions will be represented by Cross Dissolves.
– Titles, voiceovers, sound effects and music tracks are not exported.
– Cropping/Ken Burns and color adjustments are not exported.
– Green Screen and Picture in Picture clips are not exported.

Cancel   Save

You'll also find Re-publish and Remove commands here, for use when your published masterpiece has been edited or has outlived its usefulness.

Chapters 12 through 15 cover all of these exports in detail.

Window Menu

This window is fairly standard in Mac OS X programs. The Minimize and Zoom commands are almost always present; they let you minimize iMovie (hide its window by collapsing into a Dock icon) or expand the window to fill your screen.

But iMovie's Window menu is quite a bit more detailed than the basics.

Precision Editor

This opens the Precision Editor tool described on page 96.

Clip Trimmer

This opens the Clip Trimmer tool described on page 90.

Clip Adjustments, Video Adjustments, Audio Adjustments

Each of these menu commands takes you to the Inspector and chooses the corresponding tab.

Cropping, Ken Burns, and Rotation

This just offers a menu command for all of the cropping tool stuff covered on page 238.

Show Projects Full-screen, Show Events Full-screen

Goes straight to the full-screen preview mode (page 84), previewing either your projects or your event footage.

Hide/Show Commands

Other commands here are "Hide/Show" commands for the various panels of iMovie: **Project Library, Event Library, Keyword Filter, Viewer, Music and Sound Effects, Photos, Titles, Transitions,** and **Maps and Backgrounds.** It's great to remember that these exist when you're trying to make room on your screen for editing.

Viewer

The **Viewer** command is a bit different. There's no way to hide the Viewer window—it would be a little tough trying to edit a video without being able to see it—but these three sub-commands let you change its size.

> **TIP** You can also make the Viewer almost any in-between size by dragging iMovie's central toolbar up or down.

Swap Event and Projects

Finally, this command flips the top and bottom halves of the editing screen, so that the storyboard is now on the bottom. The advantage is that there's no Viewer on the bottom, so you get an even more expansive workspace.

Viewer on Secondary Display

If you're lucky enought to have a second display hooked up to your Mac, you can use it to show the preview window, making a lot more room for your projects and events.

Help Menu

iMovie doesn't come with a manual—if it did, you wouldn't need this book. Instead, you're expected to learn its functions from the online help.

Search

This search box does two things when you type in text:

- If the text appears in a menu command, the command shows up in the resulting list. Pointing to the list item will even open up and highlight the corresponding menu command.

- If the text appears in the Help documentation, it will give a link to the corresponding help article, which opens in the Help window. (See next.)

iMovie Help

Choose this command to open the iMovie '09 Help window, where you'll see a list of iMovie help topics (Figure A-5).

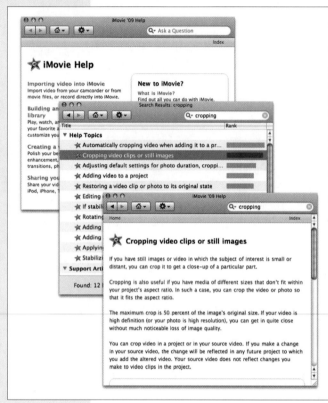

Figure A-5:
The Help Center's first screen offers big-ticket links like "What is iMovie?" and "Sharing Your Video Project." Most people, however, start by typing a phrase into the search box and then clicking Search (top). You get a list of Help pages that the Mac thinks might contain the information you want (middle). The Relevance graph indicates how confident the Help program is. (A longer bar means more occurrences of your search phrase relative to the text on that help page.) Double-click a topic to read the corresponding help page (bottom). Click the Back button at the top of the screen to return to the list of topics.

You can use this Help program in either of two ways:

- Keep clicking colored links, burrowing closer and closer to the help topic you want. You can backtrack by clicking the left arrow button at the top of the window, exactly as in a Web browser.

- Type a search phrase into the top window, such as *cropping,* and then click Search (or press Return), as shown in Figure A-5.

Either way, you'll probably find that the iMovie online help offers a helpful summary of the program's functions, but it's a little light on "what it's for" information, illustrations, tutorials, speed, and jokes.

Welcome to iMovie

Opens the Welcome screen that appeared the first time you ran iMovie.

Video Tutorials

Takes you to Apple's Web site, where a selection of handy video tutorials on iMovie basics awaits.

Keyboard Shortcuts

This is really just another link into the iMovie Help system, but a particularly valuable one. It takes you to a table showing about 50 keyboard shortcuts in iMovie. (They're among the listings in Appendix C of this book.)

Service and Support

Opens your Web browser and takes you online to Apple's iMovie help Web site. Which, by the way, is a pretty great resource for asking questions and getting answers.

Drag and Drop Menu

This is the menu that appears when you drag and drop footage onto underlying clips in your project (Figure A-6). The full list only appears if you've turned on the Advanced Tools in the iMovie preferences, which was covered in this appendix on page 400.

Figure A-6:
This unique menu only appears when you drop a clip from the Event Library onto another clip in your project. The long version of this menu only appears when you turn on Advanced Tools in the iMovie Preferences (page 400).

Replace

Entirely replaces the underlying clip with the footage you're adding, no matter how long either one is.

Replace from Start

Lengthens or shortens the added clip to match the length of the replaced clip, using the start of the Event selection and extending forward. So if the replaced clip is ten seconds long and the selection replacing it is only 5 seconds long, iMovie adds another 5 seconds to the *end* of the video chunk you're adding.

Replace from End

The same as "Replace from Start", but resizes the added event clip starting from the end of selection and extending backward. If a clip being replaced is ten seconds long, but the selection replacing it is only 5 seconds long, iMovie will add five seconds to the *beginning* of the selection.

Replace at Playhead

The same as the other "Replace from" options, but places the start of your selected footage at the project playhead (the exact point where you dropped in your chunk) and extends or shortens the footage at the beginning and end of your selection to fill the space left by the replaced clip.

Insert

Cuts the underlying clip at the playhead into two pieces, and plugs the added footage in between.

Audio Only

Adds just the audio track from the footage being dragged and dropped. The audio appears as a little blue banner running under your project clips.

Cutaway

Superimposes your added footage over the underlying clip, which continues to live underneath.

Picture in Picture

Places the added footage in a little box just like many TVs offer for watching two channels at once. This is covered in greater detail on page 148.

Green Screen

For footage shot with a green-screen background, superimposes everything *but* the green stuff onto the underlying footage, making it appear as if the green-screen subject is in the same place as the underlying footage. Also covered later on page 143.

Cancel

Hey, we all make mistakes.

Troubleshooting

Apple has come a long way since iMovie '08; in the '09 version, there are features new not just to iMovie, but new to consumer video editing, period. And you know what happens with brand-spanking-new features, right? Right: glitches.

Here's an impressive compendium of the problems that you may run into—and the world's best attempts at solving them.

Two Golden Rules

If there's any common wisdom at all about iMovie, here it is: a pair of golden rules that will stave off a huge number of problems down the road:

- **Use the latest version**. Each ".01" or ".1" upgrade zaps a whole host of bugs and glitches. These updates are free, so when your Software Update program advises you that one is available, jump at the chance to install it.

- **Set your camcorder to 16-bit audio**. The typical tape camcorder can record its audio track using either 12-bit or 16-bit audio. The factory setting is 12-bit, which gives people who aren't computer owners a chance to overlay a second audio track without erasing the original camera sound. Trouble is, 12-bit audio may slowly drift out of sync with the video when you burn the finished project to a DVD.

  Use your camera's menu system to switch to 16-bit audio. You, an iMovie aficionado, can easily overlay additional audio using your computer, so you give up nothing—except a lot of frustration. (Make this change *now*, before you record anything important.)

General iMovie Troubleshooting

Let's start general, shall we?

Weird Inconsistent Problems

When a program's preferences file becomes scrambled, all kinds of peculiar behavior can result. Buttons and functions don't work. Visual anomalies appear. Things just don't work right.

If iMovie starts having a bad hair day, suspect its preferences file. Quit the program, open your Home → Library → Preferences folder, and throw away the files called *com.apple.iMovie8.plist* and *com.apple.iApps.plist*.

The next time you run iMovie, it automatically builds a new preferences file. This file will have the original factory settings (for the options in, for example, the Preferences dialog box), but at least it will be healthy and whole.

> **NOTE** The same advice applies to iDVD. If the program begins flaking out on you, unexpectedly quitting or otherwise acting odd, open your Home → Library → Preferences folder and throw away the file called *com.apple.iDVD.plist*.

Keeping Your Hard Disk Happy

Remember the old expression "If Mama ain't happy, ain't nobody happy"? Well, if your hard disk isn't happy, iMovie won't be happy, either.

Here's a short list of maintenance suggestions. A little attention every week or so may help keep minor hard drive problems from becoming major problems:

- After installing or updating any software, use Disk Utility to repair permissions. (Disk Utility is in your Applications → Utilities folder. Click the First Aid tab, click your hard drive, and then click Repair Permissions.)

- Back up, back up, back up. Oh, and have a good backup? Use, for example, the Time Machine backup software built right into Mac OS X. It can back up your entire hard drive onto another hard drive, automatically, hourly, completely. Since hard drives are dirt cheap these days—a $60 drive would probably cover you—there's little reason not to set up this automatic backup system.

> **NOTE** Don't worry about arcane things like defragmenting your hard drive or manually running the background maintenance jobs. Modern Macs (with OS version 10.5 or later) do all this on their own.

Starting Up and Importing

Trouble getting going? Here's some advice.

iMovie Doesn't See the Tape Camcorder

Try these checks, in this order:

Make sure the camera is set to VCR or VTR or whatever the setting is called that plays back your tape. Check the FireWire cable connections. Turn the camcorder off and then on again. Quit iMovie, turn the camcorder on, and then reopen iMovie. Restart the Mac. Try a different FireWire cable.

Do you have a high-def tape camcorder (that uses the so-called HDV format)? If so, delve into the menus and make sure that the camcorder's output matches what you recorded.

See, these camcorders can record either standard-definition or high-definition video on the same tape. But when you connect the camcorder to a TV or a Mac, it has to know which format to transmit.

Usually, you get a choice of DV (which means standard definition, 4:3), HDV (high definition, widescreen, 16:9), and Auto. But Auto doesn't always work. If you're having problems, choose DV or HDV manually.

iMovie Doesn't See the Tapeless Camcorder

First, note that some camcorders refuse to enter PC connection mode unless they're plugged into a power outlet. They won't even consider entering PC mode when running on battery. (The camcorder's fear is that it will run out of battery power in the middle of the transfer, possibly corrupting and ruining some of your video scenes.)

Second, keep in mind that your Mac can't import video from AVCHD-format camcorders (see page 7) unless it has an Intel processor. Check your camcorder's box or manual—or just read the logos on its body—to find out if it's an AVCHD camcorder. Back on your computer, choose → About This Mac to see if you have an Intel Mac. (You'll actually see the word Intel on the resulting information screen. All Macs models developed since January 2006 have Intel processors.)

Finally, try plugging the USB cable into one of the USB jacks on the Mac itself, rather than into the USB jack on the Mac's keyboard. (The one on the keyboard is for low-powered gadgets only.)

If you've double-checked all three of these conditions, then quit iMovie and reopen it. Now, at long last, the Import screen should appear.

Video Looks Interlaced

You know the cool iMovie Preview window (page 35), where you get to see and even play the thumbnails for the video on tapeless camcorders before you actually import any video? Sometimes, that preview playback looks awful. It might be jerky or have nasty interlace lines, for example.

Rest assured that this is all just a problem with the preview. Once you actually import this footage, it looks fine.

No Sound from Tape Camcorder

If you're used to the old iMovie, you might wonder why you can't hear anything as you import footage from your tape camcorder. That's because iMovie no longer plays audio through the Mac when you're importing. If you want to hear the soundtrack as you import, leave the camcorder's screen open so that you hear the audio from the camcorder itself.

iMovie Crashes on Startup

If you can't even make it past the startup phase, start by deleting the preference files as described earlier (page 420).

Also consider rebuilding the iPhoto library; iMovie checks in with iPhoto every time you open it, and if there's something wrong with your iPhoto library, iMovie chokes. To rebuild the iPhoto library, quit iPhoto, and then reopen it while holding down the ⌘ and Option keys. In the resulting dialog box, you're offered several diagnostic options. Turn on all five, click Rebuild, and wait a very long time. When it's all over, iMovie should be much happier about doing business with the clean, fresh iPhoto library.

Can't Import from DVD Camcorder

See the note on page 40.

Dropouts in the Video

A *dropout* is a glitch in the picture. DV dropouts are always square or rectangular. They may be blotches of the wrong color or may be multicolored. They may appear every time you play a particular scene, or may appear at random. In severe circumstances, you may get lots of them, such as when you try to capture video to an old FireWire hard drive that's too slow. Such a configuration may also cause tearing of the video picture.

Fortunately, dropouts are fairly rare in digital video. If you get one, it's probably in one of these three circumstances:

- **You're using a very old cassette.** Remember that even DV cassettes don't last forever. You may begin to see dropouts after rerecording the tape 50 times or so.

- **You're playing back a cassette that was recorded in LP (long-play) mode.** If the cassette was recorded on a different camcorder, dropouts are especially likely.

- **It's time to clean the heads on your camcorder.** The electrical components that actually make contact with the tape can become dirty over time. Your local electronics store sells head-cleaning kits for just this purpose.

If you spot the glitch at the same moment on the tape every time you play it, then the problem is on the tape itself. If it's there during one playback but gone during the next, the problem more likely lies with the heads in your camcorder.

NOTE Different DV tape manufacturers use different lubricants on their tapes. As a result, mixing tapes from different manufacturers on the same camcorder can increase the likelihood of head clogs. It's a good idea, therefore, to stick with tapes from one manufacturer (Sony, Panasonic, or Maxell, for example) when possible.

Editing

Once you've learned the program's ins and outs, there's not much that can go wrong during editing.

Can't Drag Certain Photos into the Movie

If you open the Media Browser and try to drag an iPhoto photo into your movie but you get a "The file could not be imported" error message, it's probably a RAW file. (That's a high-end photo file format created by semiprofessional SLR cameras and intended for processing later on a computer.)

The solution: Return to iPhoto. Make a tiny change to the photo, like a small crop or brightness adjustment. When you exit editing mode, iMovie applies the change and, in the process, turns the RAW photo into a JPEG or TIFF-format photo, which iMovie can import.

Can't Use Audiobooks in Soundtrack

Yep, you can't use audiobooks as an iMovie soundtrack. They show up in the Media Browser, all right, but if you drag them into iMovie, nothing happens. Them's the breaks.

Filmstrips Don't Reflect Changes

It's true: If you crop a filmstrip or apply color adjustments to it, you'll see the changes on playback—but not on the filmstrip itself. iMovie always displays its original filmstrip, no matter what changes you make to it.

That can be a little upsetting when, for example, you've rotated a photo 90 degrees and you don't see the change in the filmstrip. But there's nothing you can do about it.

Thumbnails Are Blank or Corrupted

Sometimes the thumbnail files iMovie creates when it imports video (page 31) get corrupted during the import process. Sometimes, just skimming an event-with-corrupted-thumbnails even locks up your computer. To fix the problem:

1. Quit iMovie.

2. Open Home → Movies → iMovie Events → [Your Event Name].

3. Move the folder called iMovie Thumbnails to the Trash.

4. Restart iMovie.

iMovie notices the missing thumbnails and makes new ones. If the problem repeats itself, even with new thumbnails, you may need to trash the entire Event and import your footage again. Make sure you still have the footage before you trash the Event!

Exporting

When it's all over, certain roadblocks may stand in between you and your adoring fans.

"Compatible Version of iDVD Required"

If you get that message when you try to export a movie, you've probably renamed or moved one of the iLife programs.

Don't do that.

They're supposed to have their original names (iMovie, iPhoto, iDVD, iWeb, iTunes), and they're supposed to be in your Applications folder.

YouTube Turns You Down

If you export a movie to YouTube that has exactly the same duration as one you've already posted, YouTube may see the second movie as a duplicate and refuse to accept it—even if the two movie have different names.

The solution is simply to change the duration of the second movie, even if it's by only one frame.

Text Chopped Off on DVD

You create a movie in iMovie and add some good-looking titles and credits—yet when you send the movie to iDVD for burning, you discover that the text is getting chopped off by the TV.

Unfortunately, iMovie '09 doesn't seem to know about the TV-safe area that iDVD knows about (page 323). It's left to you to figure out how to avoid these margin areas of the screen. For example, keep your titles short and centered. And don't use subtitles at all, so they won't get chopped off at the bottom. Or just make your own title designs, as described on page 373.

Where to Get Help

You can get personal iMovie help by calling Apple's help line at (800) 500-7078 for 90 days after you bought the iLife DVD or a new Mac. (Technically, you can call within the first 90 days of *ownership*, but the clock really doesn't start until your first call.) After that, you can either buy an AppleCare contract for another year of tech-support calls ($170 to $350, depending on your Mac model), or pay $50 per individual call!

Beyond 90 days, however, consider consulting the Internet, which is filled with superb sources of fast, free technical help. Here are some of the best places to get your questions answered:

- **Apple's own iMovie discussion forum.** Here you can read user comments, ask questions of knowledgeable iMovie fanatics, or hang out and learn good stuff (the link appears on *www.apple.com/support/imovie*).

- **iMovie List.** There's a mailing list—several, actually—dedicated to iMovie and only iMovie. These lists are perfect places to ask questions without embarrassing yourself. Sign up by visiting *www.egroups.com* and searching for *imovie*.

- **Official iMovie help pages.** Apple doesn't freely admit to bugs and problems, but there's a surprising amount of good information in its official iMovie answer pages (*www.apple.com/support/imovie*).

- **Official iMovie tutorials.** Apple offers step-by-step instructions and movies at *www.apple.com/ilife/tutorials/#imovie*.

Master Keyboard Shortcut List

As you know, iMovie '09 was conceived with a single goal in mind: speed, baby, speed. And part of gaining speed is mastering keyboard shortcuts, so you don't waste time puttering around in the menus. So here it is, by popular, frustrated demand: The master list of every secret (or not so secret) keystroke in iMovie '09. Clip and post to your monitor (unless, of course, you got this book from the library).

> **NOTE** There are also a million shortcut menus—the contextual menus that appear when you Control-click (or right-click) almost anything on the screen. Most of the time, the commands you find there just duplicate what's in the menus. Learning the keyboard shortcut is still faster.

Panes, Panels, and Windows

Minimize iMovie	⌘-M
Show/Hide Music and Sound Effects	⌘-1
Show/Hide Photos pane	⌘-2
Show/Hide Titles pane	⌘-3
Show/Hide Transitions pane	⌘-4
Show Hide Maps and Backgrounds pane	⌘-5
Show/Hide Inspector	I
Show/Hide Inspector Video Adjustments tab	V
Show/Hide Inspector Audio Adjustments tab	A
Show/Hide Keywords window	K

Show/Hide Crop/Ken Burns/Rotation window	C
Show/Hide Voiceover window	O
Viewer size small/medium/large	⌘-8, ⌘-9, ⌘-0
iMovie Preferences window	⌘-, (comma key)
Project Properties	⌘-J

Event Browser and Storyboard

Scroll to top/bottom	Home/End
Scroll up/down	Page Up/Page Down
Show clip time/date	⌘-Y
Project Properties	⌘-J
iMovie Help	Shift-⌘-?
New Project	⌘-N
Delete project	⌘-Delete
Print Event browser or storyboard	⌘-P
View Favorite and Unmarked event footage	⌘-L

Playback

Play from cursor	space bar
Play the 2 seconds around cursor	[(left bracket key)
Play the 6 seconds around cursor	] (right bracket key)
Play selected footage	/
Play project (or Event) from start	\ (backslash)
Play projects full-screen	⌘-6
Play events full-screen	⌘-7
Play selection full screen	⌘-G
Exit full-screen mode	Esc
Lock Playhead	Hold down Control key

Editing

Import from camera	⌘-I
Export as file	⌘-E
Select All (or whole filmstrip)	⌘-A
Expand selection to playhead	Shift-A
Deselect All	Shift-⌘-A

Cut, Copy, Paste	⌘-X, ⌘-C, ⌘-V
Paste copied adjustments	Shift-⌘-V
Paste video adjustments only	Option-⌘-I
Paste audio adjustments only	Option-⌘-A
Paste crop/Ken Burns adjustments only	Option-⌘-R
Paste cutwaway, green screen, or picture-in-picture adjustments only	Option-⌘-U
Paste video effect adjustments only	Option-⌘-L
Paste stabilization adjustments only	Option-⌘-Z
Paste speed adjustments only	Option-⌘-S
Paste map style adjustments only	Option-⌘-M

Working with Clips

Add selection to storyboard	E
Mark selection as a Favorite	F
Mark selection as a Reject	R (or Delete, in Event browser only)
Unmark selection	U
Shift selection border	arrow keys (left, right)
Restore 1 hidden frame to clip	Option-right arrow (cursor near end of clip) or Option-left arrow (cursor near beginning)
Shorten clip by 1 frame	Option-left arrow (cursor near end of clip) or Option-right arrow (cursor near beginning)
Trim to Selection	⌘-B
Open Precision Editor	⌘-/
Open Clip Trimmer window	⌘-R
Apply numbered keyword	1, 2, 3, 4…
Remove all keywords from selection	0 (zero)
Undo	⌘-Z
Redo	Shift-⌘-Z
Split Clip	Shift-⌘-S

Music and Audio

Show/Hide Music and Sound Effects	⌘-1
Show/Hide Inspector Audio Adjustments tab	A
Show/Hide Voiceover window	O
Audio during skimming on/off	⌘-K
Mute/Unmute Clip	Shift-⌘-M
Turn on/off Snap to Beats	⌘-U

Editing Titles

Show/Hide Titles panel	⌘-3
Show/Hide Fonts panel	⌘-T
Bold	Shift-⌘-B
Italic	Shift-⌘-I
Underline	Shift-⌘-U
Outline style	Shift-⌘-O
Increase/decrease type size	⌘-plus sign, ⌘-minus sign
Left, center, right-justified text	⌘-{, ⌘-|, ⌘-}
Tighter/looser spacing (kerning)	Option-⌘-left arrow, Option-⌘-right arrow
Cut, Copy, Paste	⌘-X, ⌘-C, ⌘-V
Copy text formatting	Option-⌘-C
Paste text formatting	Option-⌘-V

Visual Cheat Sheet

iMovie, as you've probably gathered, is completely different from any program you've seen before—including previous versions of iMovie. It's filled with handy visual cues as to what's going on. But especially at first, learning all of those cues can become a full-time job.

iMovie is teeming with thin banners over and under your filmstrips (in green, blue, or purple); horizontal colored lines drawn right across them (in red, green, and orange); little white "badges" huddled in the corners of filmstrips; faint little corner badges that appear only when you *point* to a filmstrip; gigantic green or purple bubbles lying behind your entire project map; and on and on.

You practically need a cheat sheet to remember what they're all for—and on the next two pages, you'll find it.

Yellow banner:
Theme title

Brown banner:
Comment marker

Map clip
Animated travel
map

Crop badge
Double-click to
edit crop, Ken
Burns, or
rotation settings

Sun badge
Color adjustments
applied. Double-click
to edit

Interclip icons
Above: Theme transition
Below: Regular transition

Speaker badge
Volume adjusted.
Double-click
to edit

Gear bad
Click to m
adjustme

**PiP Effect
(blue border)**
Similar in appeareance
to Cutaways (gray
border) and Green
Screen effects (green
border)

Red stripe
Rejected footage

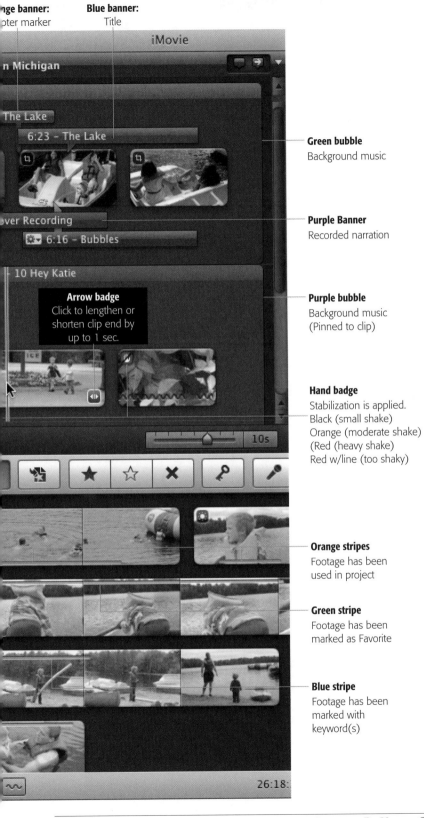

nge banner:
pter marker

Blue banner:
Title

iMovie

n Michigan

The Lake

6:23 – The Lake

Green bubble
Background music

ver Recording

6:16 – Bubbles

Purple Banner
Recorded narration

10 Hey Katie

Arrow badge
Click to lengthen or
shorten clip end by
up to 1 sec.

Purple bubble
Background music
(Pinned to clip)

Hand badge
Stabilization is applied.
Black (small shake)
Orange (moderate shake)
(Red (heavy shake)
Red w/line (too shaky)

10s

Orange stripes
Footage has been
used in project

Green stripe
Footage has been
marked as Favorite

Blue stripe
Footage has been
marked with
keyword(s)

26:18:

Index

Colophon

Rachel Monaghan and Adam Witwer provided quality control for *iMovie '09 & iDVD: The Missing Manual*.

The cover of this book is based on a series design originally created by David Freedman and modified by Mike Kohnke, Karen Montgomery, and Fitch (*www.fitch.com*). Back cover design, dog illustration, and color selection by Fitch.

David Futato designed the interior layout, based on a series design by Phil Simpson. This book was converted by Abby Fox to FrameMaker 5.5.6. The text font is Adobe Minion; the heading font is Adobe Formata Condensed; and the code font is LucasFont's TheSansMonoCondensed. The illustrations that appear in the book were produced by Robert Romano using Adobe Photoshop CS3.

Try the online edition free for 45 days

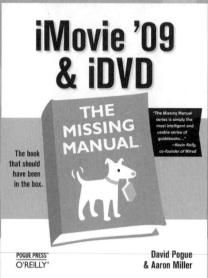

iMovie '09 & iDVD

THE MISSING MANUAL

The book that should have been in the box.

"The Missing Manual series is simply the most intelligent and usable series of guidebooks..."
—Kevin Kelly, co-founder of Wired

POGUE PRESS™
O'REILLY®

David Pogue & Aaron Miller

Get the information you need, when you need it, with Safari Books Online. Safari Books Online contains the complete version of the print book in your hands, as well as all of the other Missing Manuals.

Safari is designed for people who are in a hurry for information, so you can learn just what you need and put it to work right away. And with new content added as soon as it's published, you can be sure the information in Safari is the most current and relevant to the job at hand.

To try out Safari and the online edition of the above title FREE for 45 days, go to www.oreilly.com/go/safarienabled and enter the coupon code SGXFNCB.

To see the complete Safari Library visit:
safari.oreilly.com

Safari
Books Online